A Rising China and Security in East Asia

Identity construction and security discourse

Rex Li

Routledge
Taylor & Francis Group

LONDON AND NEW YORK

First published 2009
by Routledge
2 Park Square, Milton Park, Abingdon, Oxon OX14 4RN

Simultaneously published in the USA and Canada
by Routledge
270 Madison Ave, New York, NY 10016

Routledge is an imprint of the Taylor & Francis Group, an informa business

Typeset in Times New Roman by Pindar NZ, Auckland, New Zealand
Printed and bound in Great Britain by TJ International, Padstow, Cornwall

British Library Cataloguing in Publication Data
A catalogue record for this book is available from the British Library.

Library of Congress Cataloging-in-Publication Data
Li, Rex.
A rising China and security in east Asia: identity construction and security
discourse / Rex Li.
    p. cm.
    1. China—Foreign relations—East Asia. 2. East Asia—Foreign
relations—China. 3. China—Foreign relations—1976– 4. East Asia—
Politics and government. 5. East Asia—Foreign relations. 6. Elite (Social
sciences)—China—Attitudes. I. Title.
    DS518.15.L5 2008
    355'.03305—dc22   2008023450

ISBN10: 0-415-44940-5 (hbk)
ISBN10: 0-415-44941-3 (pbk)
ISBN10: 0-203-88694-1 (ebk)

ISBN13: 978-0-415-44940-3 (hbk)
ISBN13: 978-0-415-44941-0 (pbk)
ISBN13: 978-0-203-88694-6 (ebk)

For Shirley, Sonia and Sylvia

Contents

Illustrations

Maps

Figures

Preface

In a recent article published in *Newsweek*, Fareed Zakaria (2007/2008: 21–22), the editor of the US magazine, stated that the 'advent of China as a global power is no longer a forecast but a reality'. While his judgement may not be shared by everyone, few would dispute that China is rising rapidly, whether this is measured by its economic growth, military capability or political influence. Some view the ascendancy of China with great interest and enthusiasm. Others are troubled by the augmentation of Chinese power, fearing that it might bring about unpredictable repercussions in the East Asian region and the wider world.

Indeed, the management of the rise of China presents an enormous challenge for the international community. Zakaria (2007/2008: 21) argues that 2008 should be 'the year we craft a serious long-term China policy'. But a long-term policy towards China cannot be based entirely on the assessment of China's material power. Why do Chinese leaders and elites aspire to establish a great power status for their country? What path are they likely to take in achieving their national goals? How would they exercise their newfound power in the coming years? These are also important questions that the outside world should think about.

Like individuals, states have their distinctive identities, and their interests are often shaped by the identities they have enacted. The way states define and form their identities is also related to their perceptions of and interactions with other actors. Of all the countries in the world, the United States, Japan and Russia are arguably the most significant 'others' with whom China interacts intensely and regularly. A thorough understanding of Chinese security discourse of the three great powers in East Asia is crucial to the understanding of China's self-perception and aspirations, and thus the formulation of a sound China policy.

However, the outside world knows little about the security perceptions of China's policy elites and the internal debate among them. To be sure, there is some interesting and valuable work on China's perceptions of other great powers, but the linkage between this body of literature and the debate on China's rise remains insufficiently explored. Much of the current debate focuses on external perceptions of the consequences of growing Chinese power without taking into account China's self-identity and how this is related to its perceptions of other significant actors. In addition, despite the vibrancy and sophistication in the development of International Relations (IR) theories, few researchers have drawn on the rich theoretical insights of the discipline in their analysis of Chinese security perceptions.

This is the first book-length study that systematically utilizes various IR theories, including Realism, Liberalism, Constructivism and Postmodernism, to analyze Chinese perceptions of the East Asian powers' global and Asia-Pacific security strategy in the post-Cold War era. Based on a wide range of Chinese-language sources and Western academic literature, the study argues that the security discourse of Chinese policy analysts is closely linked to their conception of China's identity and their desire and endeavour to construct a great power identity for China. It also examines the debate among Chinese policy elites on how China should respond to the perceived challenge from the three major powers to its rise to a global status.

By offering an in-depth and theoretically grounded analysis of China's security discourse of the US, Japan and Russia in relation to the process of its identity formation, this volume seeks to contribute to the on-going academic and policy debate on the nature and implications of an ascendant China. In a sense, the book can be seen as an attempt to bridge the traditional divide between area studies and the IR discipline.

As such, this study should be of interest to scholars and researchers of Asian security and Chinese foreign policy, as well as international relations and security specialists. I have tried to write the book in an accessible style so that undergraduate and postgraduate students will find it useful in helping them gain a better understanding of China's international relations, and its security relations with other great powers in particular. Given the significance of the topic, it is hoped that professionals who are involved in foreign policy-making or dealing with China and Asia-Pacific security issues on a regular basis, such as government officials, diplomats and international journalists, will benefit from reading this book.

The research for this project began as part of a wider project on the Pacific Rim that was funded by the UK Economic and Social Research Council (ESRC). Further funding was provided by the Higher Education Funding Council for England at various stages of my research. The University, Faculty and School Research Committees of Liverpool John Moores University have also provided me with funding for research leave and other research expenses. I am grateful to these funding bodies and my own institution for their financial support, which has enabled me to develop the project.

At Liverpool John Moores University, I have had the pleasure of collaborating with Professor Ian Cook, Dr Nick White and other colleagues on an ESRC-funded project on the Pacific Rim. This has facilitated the development of many projects including the one on which this book is based. Dr Frank McDonough, who is a distinguished scholar of international history, has given me consistent encouragement and I have benefited considerably from his knowledge and expertise. During the early stages of this project, Professor David McEvoy provided invaluable financial assistance and I am very grateful for his help. I would also like to thank Phil Cubbin, who has kindly used his excellent cartographic skills to produce the maps for this book. Special thanks must go to Professor Chris

Frost, who has provided me with tremendous support and encouragement over the past few years. His appreciation of the value and significance of my research is gratefully acknowledged.

The research ideas and findings of this project have been presented in different forms at a variety of international conferences, seminars and track-II meetings. I have benefited greatly from the questions and comments from numerous scholars, officials and diplomats who attended these meetings. A number of friends and colleagues have kindly invited me to give presentations relating to my research at seminars and conferences they have organized. I would like to thank Professor Gerald Chan, Professor Hugo de Burgh, Professor Phil Deans, Dr Christopher Dent, Dr Christopher R. Hughes, Dr Tim Huxley, Professor Marika Vicziany and Dr Steve Tsang for their invitation, funding and hospitality.

I am also grateful to Professor Shaun Breslin, Professor Mary Buckley, Professor Gerald Chan, Professor Stephen Chan, Dr Christopher Dent, Professor Reinhard Drifte, Dr Tim Huxley, Professor Robert Singh, Dr Harumi Yoshino and Professor Suisheng Zhao for their encouragement and comments on my earlier work from which several chapters derive. I am particularly grateful to Professor Glenn Hook, Dr Robert Taylor and Dr Peter Ferdinand for reading a previous version of all the chapters. Their constructive comments have helped me enormously in improving the book. Thanks also go to the three anonymous reviewers for the publisher who have offered some thoughtful and valuable comments. Despite the helpful suggestions and comments from many colleagues and friends, I am solely responsible for any mistakes and misinterpretations in this book.

Moreover, I am indebted to many Chinese international relations scholars and think-tanks specialists with whom I have met during my research visits and at academic conferences and track-II meetings over the past decade and a half. The formal and informal discussions with this group of policy analysts on issues related to the project have certainly helped enhance my understanding of the complexity of Chinese security discourse.

Furthermore, I wish to thank Routledge's publisher Craig Fowlie who first suggested that I write a book on China's international relations. I would also like to thank Stephanie Rogers, the commissioning editor at Routledge, who has shown a great deal of interest in and commitment to this project since its inception. It is also a pleasure to have worked with Sonja van Leeuwen, the acting editor, and Leanne Hinves, editorial assistant, Stewart Pether, production editor, Camille Lowe, project manager at Pindar NZ, and Beth Gordon, copy editor. Their advice and patience are very much appreciated.

Last but not least, I owe a profound debt of gratitude to my wife Shirley and two daughters Sonia and Sylvia, who have been incredibly supportive throughout the research and writing process of this project. They endured so much when I was preoccupied with this work, both physically and mentally, and was away from home for research trips and other related activities. Their understanding and sustained support have given me immense strength, without which the project would not have been completed. With love this book is dedicated to them.

Abbreviations

ABM	Anti-Ballistic Missile Treaty
APEC	Asia Pacific Economic Cooperation
ARF	ASEAN Regional Forum
ASEAN	Association of Southeast Asian Nations
ASEM	Asia-Europe Meeting
CASS	Chinese Academy of Social Sciences
CIA	Central Intelligence Agency
CBM	Confidence-building measures
CCP	Chinese Communist Party
CICIR	China Institute of Contemporary International Relations
CIIS	China Institute of International Studies
CIS	Commonwealth of Independent States
CSCAP	Council for Security Cooperation in the Asia-Pacific
DPP	Democratic Progressive Party
DPRK	Democratic People's Republic of Korea
EAS	East Asia Summit
EU	European Union
FDI	Foreign Direct Investment
G7	Group of Seven
G8	Group of Eight
GATT	General Agreement on Tariffs and Trade
GDP	Gross Domestic Product
IAPS	Institute of Asia-Pacific Studies
IAS	Institute of American Studies
ICBM	Intercontinental-range ballistic missile
IISS	International Institute of Strategic Studies
IJS	Institute of Japanese Studies
IMF	International Monetary Fund
IR	International Relations
IRBM	Intermediate-range ballistic missile
IRCAEES	Institute of Russian, Central Asian and East European Studies
LDP	Liberal Democratic Party
LGNS	Leading Group on National Security

MFA	Ministry of Foreign Affairs
NAFTA	North American Free Trade Area
NATO	North Atlantic Treaty Organization
NMD	National Missile Defence
NPC	National People's Congress
NPT	Treaty on the Non-Proliferation of Nuclear Weapons
NSC	New security concept
NSS	National Security Strategy
ODA	Official Development Assistance
OSCE	Conference on Security and Cooperation in Europe
PLA	People's Liberation Army
PRC	People's Republic of China
RMB	Renminbi (Chinese currency)
SCO	Shanghai Cooperation Organization
SDF	Self-Defence Forces
SRBM	Short-range ballistic missile
TMD	Theatre Missile Defence
UK	United Kingdom
UN	United Nations
UNSC	United Nations Security Council
US	United States
USSR	Union of Soviet Socialist Republics
WMD	Weapons of mass destruction
WTO	World Trade Organization

Map 1 The Pacific Rim.

Map 2 China and East Asia.

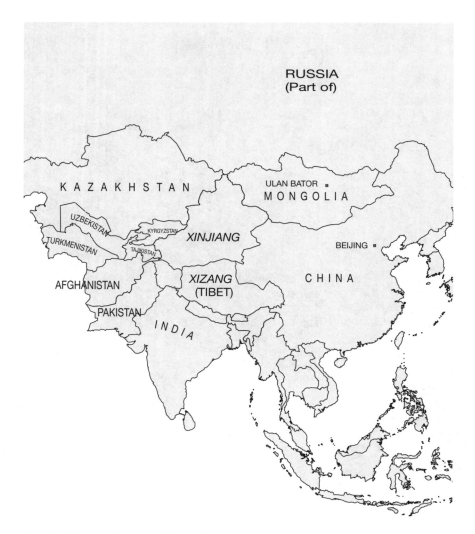

Map 3 China and Central and South Asia.

1 A rising China, international relations theories and Chinese security discourse of East Asian powers

The rise of China as a key player on the global stage is undoubtedly a significant phenomenon in international relations (Shambaugh 2005; Wang 2004). Much of the debate among Western scholars and analysts focuses on the questions of how Chinese leaders will use their growing power to pursue their national interest and how the world should respond to an increasingly powerful China. These are no doubt important questions, but they cannot be fully answered without taking into account Chinese security perceptions. How do Chinese leaders and policy elites view the structure of the post-Cold War international system? How do they perceive China's interests and its role in the changing security environment? How are these issues related to China's domestic political and economic agenda?

This book aims to analyze China's security perceptions, focusing in particular on its perceptions of the major powers[1] in East Asia – the United States, Japan and Russia – since 1989 (see Map 1). Ever since the establishment of the People's Republic of China (PRC), Chinese leaders have attached tremendous importance to great power politics in their security considerations and strategic calculations. In recent years, China has actively developed various types of 'strategic partnerships' with the major powers and actors around the world. There is no doubt that China has global aspirations but, for historical and geographical reasons, East Asia remains China's primary focus (see Map 2).

In terms of economic development and security concerns, East Asia is regarded by PRC leaders as the most important region. It is a region on which Chinese trade and economic activities depend substantially; it is a region where China has vital security interests as well as unresolved territorial disputes which may lead to military conflict in future. Not surprisingly, Chinese leaders have paid more attention to the intentions and strategies of the great powers in this region. After all, two of the East Asian powers – America and Russia – are also global powers, nuclear weapons states and permanent members of the United Nations Security Council. Japan, despite its somewhat limited security role, is widely known as an economic superpower with an expanding global profile.

For analytical clarity, East Asia is taken to encompass the countries in South East Asia and North East Asia (see Map 2). The book thus excludes systematic analyses of Chinese security perceptions of India, a major power in South Asia (see Map 3). This is not to suggest that India is not important and unworthy of consideration. On the contrary, India has immense economic potential and is a significant strategic player in the Asia-Pacific region. Indeed, it has gained greater prominence in Chinese strategic considerations in the past decade, especially since New Delhi's nuclear tests in 1998 and the events of September 11, 2001. Nevertheless, India is not a great power in East Asia, which is the geographical focus of this study. Moreover, India is not usually characterized by PRC elites and security analysts as a 'pole' or power centre in their conceptualization of a multipolar system. Inevitably, the discussion may cover issues relating to other countries within the Asia-Pacific, including Australia and South and Central Asian states (see Map 1 and Map 3).

The starting point for this study is 1989, which is a significant year when China had to face a series of unprecedented challenges both domestically and externally. Never had the PRC government had to deal with such an immense challenge to its authority as the Tiananmen democracy movement (Cheng 1990; Nathan and Link 2002). The crackdown of the student demonstrations in 1989 seriously undermined the legitimacy of the Chinese communist regime in the eyes of the international community leading to strong reactions and sanctions from the West.

Internationally, China became even more isolated following the downfall of the communist regimes in Eastern Europe towards the end of 1989. At the same time, the Cold War conflict between the United States and the former Soviet Union ended peacefully. The collapse of the bipolar system which had lasted for over forty years, together with the demise of communism in Eastern Europe and the political change in the Soviet Union under Gorbachev, brought huge uncertainties for China. The rapidly changing international landscape forced Chinese leaders to reassess their country's new security environment, especially the foreign policies of the major East Asian powers, and to respond to the challenge of a unipolar world.

The key argument of this book is that Chinese perceptions of the security strategy of the major powers in East Asia are extremely important in shaping China's foreign policy and its policy towards the region in particular. In addition, the book argues that Chinese security discourse on the three East Asian powers should be understood as part of a process of identity formation through which China seeks to construct and maintain a great power identity. As far as the level of analysis is concerned, the study focuses on the perceptions of PRC policy elites and international affairs analysts who are actively engaged in the articulation of Chinese security perceptions and have regularly published their work in specialist and policy-oriented journals.

There are five sections in this chapter. The first section highlights the significance of the research topic and provides the context within which the research problem emerges. The second critically reviews the current debate and the extant literature relevant to the concerns and arguments of the book. This is followed by a section on the research problem, including the aims and objectives of the study. The fourth section considers the chosen research methods and the related methodological issues with some discussion on the sources and data that are collected and used in this project. The final section explains the scope of the book and how it is organized.

Context of research

The re-emergence of China as a great power is arguably the single most important development in the post-Cold War world. The rapid economic growth of the PRC over the past decade, coupled with its high level of defence spending, has stimulated much interest and trepidation among policy-makers and analysts across the world. Although the continued augmentation of Chinese power is not predetermined, the profound effects of China's growing process cannot be underestimated.

Since the late 1970s, Chinese leaders have introduced a wide-ranging programme of economic modernization (Ash, Howe and Kueh 2003; Naughton 2006). In 2007, the Chinese economy grew 11.4 per cent in reaching 24,661.9 billion RMB. Indeed, between 1993 and 2007 the PRC enjoyed an average of 10 per cent GDP growth (see Fig. 1.1 and Fig. 1.2). It is now the world's fourth largest economy (Lardy 2006: 2). Meanwhile, China has gradually emerged as a major trading nation, and its economic and trade relations with most countries have broadened considerably. China has been actively involved in global economic activities and is fully integrated into the Asia-Pacific economy. The PRC is a member of all the major international and regional economic organizations, including the World Trade Organization (WTO), the World Bank, the International Monetary Fund (IMF), the Asian Development Bank, and the Asia Pacific Economic Cooperation (APEC) forum (Feeney 1994; Findlay 1995; Lanteigne 2005). Over 400 of the world's top 500 multinational corporations have now invested in the country (Shi 2002).

As a result, there has been a huge growth in China's foreign trade over the past two decades. From 1978 to 2007 China's exports grew from US$9.8 billion to US$1218 billion, and its imports grew from US$10.9 billion to US$955.8 billion (Lardy 1994: 30) (see Fig. 1.3). Between 1983 and 2007 actual Foreign Direct Investment (FDI) in China increased from US$916 million to US$74.8 billion (Lardy 1994: 63) (see Fig. 1.4). Indeed, China has become the third largest trading nation in the world (Lardy 2006: 2).

In addition, China has benefited from its involvement in a regional division of labour and economic cooperation in East Asia (Dent 2006, 2008; Rimmer 1995). It is integrated into a number of subregional economic groupings, or 'growth triangles', such as the Hong Kong-Guangdong-Shenzhen triangle and the Northeast China-Korea-Japan triangle. In addition, China is closely involved in the development of two subregional groupings: the Yellow Sea Economic Zone, including Liaoning and Shandong provinces, Japan and South Korea; and the Tumen River project that seeks to promote economic cooperation among China, Japan, North Korea, South Korea, Mongolia and Russia. Indeed, China has strong bilateral and multilateral economic relations with all its Asian neighbours. At the Association of South East Asian Nations (ASEAN) Plus Three summit in November 2002 at Phnom Penh, the former Chinese Premier, Zhu Rongji, and ASEAN leaders announced their decision to establish a China-ASEAN Free Trade

Area by 2010 which could become the world's third largest trading bloc (*Digital Chosunilbo* 2002; Cheng 2004).

Back in the 1990s, Western scholars had already predicted that China would overtake Japan as an economic superpower (Salameh 1995–96: 142) and that it might replace the United States as 'the number one economy in the world' (Kristof 1993: 59). To some observers, China will probably 'catch up with American total economic size … within a generation' (Garnaut 2005: 516).

Apart from its growing economic strength, there has been significant progress in China's military modernization (Blasko 2005; Shambaugh 2002a). According to the estimates of the International Institute for Strategic Studies (IISS), the PRC has increased its defence spending from US$11.3 billion in 1990 to US$122 billion in 2006 (IISS 2007; National Bureau of Asian Research 2008) (see Fig. 1.5). It has been purchasing a variety of weapons from Russia, Israel and other countries to upgrade its air and naval power. Beijing is reported to have spent an average of £650 million on Russian fighter jets and warships each year (*The Times* 2003). Over the past two decades, substantial improvement has been made in the People's Liberation Army (PLA) Navy's surface combatants, destroyers, frigates and submarine forces. Recent acquisitions from Russia include the well-known Sovremenny-class destroyers. In 2002 China ordered 8 Project 636 Kilo-class submarines from Russia (*The Times* 2003). The purchase of Russian aircraft such as Su-27 and Su-30 and the development of indigenous fighters (e.g. Jian-10 fighter-bomber) are further evidence of the PLA Air Force's modernization efforts.

Strategic forces are also a very important part of China's defence modernization. A sustained effort has been made to improve the range and accuracy of its missile force. In 1992 China had only eight intercontinental-range ballistic missiles (ICBM); today it has over forty of them. Similarly, the number of China's intermediate-range ballistic missiles increased from 60 in 1992 to more than 150 in 2007. In addition, Beijing now possesses over 900 short-range ballistic missiles (SRBM) (IISS 1992; US Department of Defense 2007). There are, of course, many weaknesses in China's military capabilities, but PRC leaders seem determined to press ahead with their defence modernization. They have introduced serious reforms in every aspect of their military forces, and if the reforms continue, in the next two decades the PLA may well become a very powerful army with a capability to project force beyond China's borders.

Many believe that the size, population and resources of China, combined with the enormous economic and military potential, make it almost inevitable that the country will achieve a great-power status. Others are, however, somewhat more sceptical about the prospects of a rising China. Indeed, following the collapse of the communist regimes in Eastern Europe and the former Soviet Union, there were speculations that China would follow the Soviet path of disintegration (see Ferdinand 1992 for a critical consideration of these speculations). Some researchers argued that Chinese provinces had gained much autonomy in economic decision-making since the 1980s as a result of a greater emphasis on the market economy and economic decentralization (Breslin 1996). They pointed out that regional au-thorities had become more assertive in promoting and protecting their interests, and that the central government had found it more difficult to co-ordinate the national economy. The rise of economic regionalism, according to Segal's (1994) analysis, might lead to political and military regionalism, and even the break-up of China.

Contrary to these predictions, the Chinese communist regime was able to survive and sustain its reform programme in the 1990s. However, the achievement of rapid economic growth in China is not without its costs. Critics have pointed to the numerous problems, such as regional disparities, income inequalities, widespread corruption, rising unemployment, labor unrest, rural discontent, environmental degradation and so on, which could seriously threaten the economic development of China (Cheng and Ngok 2004; Cook and Murray 2001; Minzner 2007; Murray and Cook 2002). More fundamentally, some scholars are questioning whether the PRC's economic growth can be sustained because of substantial institutional and structural constraints and weaknesses in its banking and financial system (Henderson 1999; Holz 2001).

Some writers argue that the accession of China to the WTO will present Chinese leaders with a formidable economic challenge. This, combined with other social and political problems, could trigger a major systemic crisis in the PRC. In his controversial book, *The Coming Collapse of China*, Gordon Chang (2002: xvi) predicts that China is 'in long term decline' and 'on the verge of collapse'. He contends that Beijing's WTO commitments would only hasten the demise of the communist regime. Some scholars agree with Chang's observations and analyses; others have challenged his prediction, arguing that it lacks a sophisticated methodology and/or convincing evidence (*Issues and Studies* 2002). Writing in 2006, Andrew Nathan (2006: 178) maintained that the Chinese Communist regime 'faces numerous problems but shows no sign of either collapsing or democratizing'.

Chang may have been viewed as an 'alarmist' but he is not alone in pointing out the gravity of the problems facing the Chinese leadership. Susan Shirk (2007), a well-respected China scholar and former Deputy Assistant Secretary of State in the Clinton administration, argues persuasively in her recent book *China: Fragile Superpower* that China's 'domestic threats' may seriously affect the PRC regime's security as well as its foreign relations.

Ten years ago, the late Gerald Segal (1999) published an article entitled 'Does China Matter?' in *Foreign Affairs*, contending that the middle kingdom was merely a second-rank 'middle power'. To Segal, the PRC's economic and military power had been over-exaggerated by outside observers and its political influence was minimal. Many commentators today may not share his view. In fact, most political leaders and analysts are working on the assumptions that China will continue to grow both economically and militarily and that it will become a great power in the not too distant future.

Indeed, over the past sixteen years there has been a heated debate in the West about the potential challenge of an increasingly strong and assertive China to both the Asia-Pacific region and to the world more generally (Christensen 2006; de Burgh 2005; Goldstein 1997/98; Goodman and Segal 1997; Li 2004b; Yee and Storey 2002). Western scholars and analysts have raised a whole range of questions relating to China's strategic intentions and future behaviour (Harris and Klintworth

1995; Zhao 2004a). What are the international repercussions of the rise of the 'sleeping giant'? Will a rich China contribute to regional and global prosperity, or will it threaten Western economic interests? Will a rising China be tempted to use military power to assert its territorial claims and achieve its national goals, or will it be constrained by the potent forces of global economic interdependence? Will a more open and reform-oriented China gradually move toward political liberalization and democratization, thus enhancing stability and security in the Asia-Pacific? Will a more prosperous and powerful China be a peaceful, responsible and constructive member of the international community that will respect and adhere to the rules of international organizations and regimes, or will it throw its weight around and challenge the norms of the international society?

While these questions are rigorously debated by Western scholars and analysts, Chinese leaders have launched a diplomatic offensive and actively engaged Asia economically, politically and, to a lesser extent, on security issues (Gill 2007; Medeiros and Fravel 2003). Relations between the PRC and its neighbouring countries have improved substantially since the early 1990s, and more significantly, China has made a conscious effort to present itself as a peaceful and constructive member of the international community (Shambaugh 2004/2005). For example, it has played a prominent role in tackling the 1997/98 Asian Financial Crisis, participated in international cooperation in fighting global terrorism after 9/11 and persuaded North Korea to return to the six-party talks. Some observers believe that China's soft power is rising steadily (Harris 2005: 491). Through trade, diplomatic and cultural activities, or what Kurlantzick (2007) calls 'charm offensive', Beijing is seeking to expand its influence in Asia and beyond.

The question is whether China's 'new diplomacy' represents a short-term tactic to strengthen its international power position or a long-term strategy of a 'peaceful rise' (Guo 2006; Koo and Smith 2005; Scott 2007; Sutter 2005a, 2005b). Western analysts are unsure whether China will become more demanding and assertive if Chinese economic and military power continues to grow. Specifically, how will China manage its complex and often difficult relations with other great powers? Will China be prepared to contest America's predominant position both in Asia and in the international system in the longer term? Will China compete with Japan, its historical rival, for regional hegemony, and if so, how will it do this? When and how will China use force against Taiwan to prevent the island's political leaders from gaining independence? Will China resort to military means to resolve its territorial disputes in the South China Sea, the Diaoyu/Senkaku islands and elsewhere in future?

Hitherto, the debate on China's security intentions seems to follow the theoretical logic of realism and liberalism, reflecting more of Western analysts' theoretical positions and expectations rather than Chinese security discourse. The literature focuses heavily on China's current strength and future potential, and whether PRC leaders will utilize their newfound power to push the Chinese agenda in Asia and seek regional hegemony. While China's motives and intentions are often taken into consideration in existing studies, relatively little scholarly enquiry has been conducted into the security perceptions of Chinese policy intellectuals. This book seeks to explore the perceptions of Chinese elites on the major powers in East Asia in relation to China's self-perception as an emerging power. Through a thorough analysis of Chinese security discourse, the study aims to dissect China's perceptions of other great powers in relation to its identity formation in the post-Cold War era, thus advancing the scholarly debate on the rise of China and its security implications.

The cognitive dimension of foreign policy is important in informing and shaping the decisions of political leaders. In an ideal world, one would wish to have access to high-level sources that may reveal the perceptions of foreign policy-makers on major international issues. This is, of course, very difficult, especially in a country like China where circulation of political information is closely monitored and tightly controlled by the government. However, a systematic and rigorous examination of the articulated perceptions of Chinese security experts will offer a conduit through which the security thinking of PRC leaders may be detected.

The increasing professionalization and institutionalization of China's foreign policy-making over the past three decades means that international relations scholars and security analysts are playing a more significant role in the policy-making process (Lampton 2001b; Zhao 2005). It is clear that the analysis of these specialists does attract the attention of Chinese decision-makers. In 1998, for example, the Foreign Affairs Leading Small Group specifically requested a list of 'important academics' in order to make a broader range of policy thinking available to the central leadership (Fewsmith and Rosen 2001: 153). Indeed, some leading scholars are regularly called upon to advise party and government officials on a variety of foreign and security policy issues.

Recent research indicates a growing influence of PRC scholars and think-tank specialists in various foreign and security policy areas, including Taiwan (Swaine 2001), arms control (Gill 2001) and international economic relations (Moore and Yang 2001). Their unique position in the Chinese polity and active participation in the discussion on current affairs in the news media make their views highly influential within and beyond the academic community and policy circles. According to Fewsmith and Rosen (2001: 153), this group of elites is best defined as 'public intellectuals' as they are seeking to shape public opinion as well as official policy. In this sense, their security discourse has a much wider intellectual and political significance, contributing directly to the process of identity construction in China.

Current debate and existing literature

This book looks at how Chinese elites perceive the major powers in East Asia within the wider context of the debate on China's rise. It therefore draws on the extant literature on the scholarly debate on the nature and repercussions of a rising China, as well as the perceptual dimension of Chinese foreign policy and China's security perceptions in particular. This literature offers various theoretical and analytical perspectives which inform the analysis of Chinese security discourse. In this section of the chapter, we review and critically evaluate current pertinent studies, showing what is lacking in the literature, what new research is needed and what contribution this study intends to make to knowledge in the field.

Theoretical perspectives on the rise of China

The literature on the debate over the nature, significance and consequences of the ascendancy of China is largely dominated by the realist and liberal schools of international relations. This debate has recently been joined by constructivist and postmodernist scholars who challenge certain suppositions of realists and liberals in the 'China threat' debate.

Realist interpretations: power and competition in an anarchic world

The realist view of international relations is based on the assumptions that the world is essentially anarchic and that there is no central authority governing the behaviour of individual states. To protect their national security and survival in such a self-help system, states must seek to acquire or maximize their power through economic and military means. It is therefore the structure of the international system that determines the behaviour of states within it (Morgenthau 1978; Waltz 1979).

The realist literature on the rise of China tends to focus on the relationship between structural change in the international system and great power emergence. For realist scholars, the emergence of China as a potential great power must be understood within the context of the end of bipolarity and the advent of a 'unipolar moment' following the disintegration of the Soviet Union. Soon after the revolutions in Eastern Europe in 1989, Charles Krauthammer (1990/91) argued in *Foreign Affairs* that the bipolar system would be replaced by one of unipolarity. This view is shared by other scholars who believe that the unipolar international system is here to stay (Mastanduno 1997; Wohlforth 1999; Krauthammer 2004). Writing in *The National Interest* twelve years later, Krauthammer (2002/03: 17) concluded that 'the unipolar moment has become the unipolar era'. Similarly, Stephen Brooks and William Wohlforth (2002: 21) maintain: 'If American primacy does not constitute unipolarity, then nothing ever will.'

In a widely-cited article published in *International Security*, Christopher Layne (1993) argues that in a world of unipolarity other powers will rise to challenge the predominant position of the United States. The emergence of great powers, according to Layne (1993: 9), is 'a structurally driven phenomenon'. States with successful economic expansion tend to become more ambitious and more capable of challenging the status quo, defending their increased overseas interests and commitments, and disrupting the dominance of the world major power (Gilpin 1981; Kennedy 1988). To realists, China falls within the type of rising powers described by Layne which may pose major problems for the US in a unipolar system (Christensen 2001). Layne (2006a, 2006b) believes that China's rise indicates the validity of his argument that unipolarity would cause the emergence of rival powers in the international system. But he argues that any attempts to prevent emerging powers from rising will be futile or counterproductive (Layne 1993:

45–46). This view is shared by Robert Ross (1999) who observes that geography and stable bipolarity between China and the US will contribute to regional peace and order.

Another structural change that encourages China to seek great-power status, according to realist analysis, is the changing balance of power in the Asia-Pacific region since the end of the Cold War. With the break-up of the Soviet Union and a perceived reduction of US military commitment to the region, many realist scholars predicted, a 'power vacuum' would emerge that would likely be filled by powerful regional players. Indeed, this was the focus of a number of studies in the early 1990s (Tow 1991; McGregor 1993; Malik 1993; Buzan and Segal 1994). While Japan and India were often referred to as potential candidates looking to fill the vacuum in the event of an American withdrawal from the Asia-Pacific, it was China that realists believed was the 'hegemon on the horizon' (Roy 1994, 1995). As Kenneth Waltz (1993: 66) argues, it would be 'a structural anomaly' for a country with a great power economy not to become a great power.

Realist scholars have also pointed out that eligible states will not become great powers unless their policy-makers make a 'unit-level decision' to respond to the structural factors driving them in that direction (Layne 1993: 9). But all the available evidence suggests, they argue, that the policy-makers in Beijing have chosen to take advantage of the structural change in the international system. In fact, ever since economic reform and the open door policy were introduced by Deng Xiaoping in 1978, Chinese leaders have been actively developing China's 'comprehensive national strength' (*zonghe guoli*) to position themselves to compete with other great powers politically, economically and militarily (see Chan 1999: 28–33 for an analysis of the Chinese conception of 'comprehensive national strength'). The end of bipolarity has therefore provided China with an excellent opportunity to elevate its status in the hierarchy of the international structure and to fulfil its great-power aspirations. Seen from the realist perspective, the rise of China is primarily a consequence of the fundamental change in the structure of the international system.

The analysis of realist scholars also reflects their theoretical perspectives on the nature of power in international relations. As Hans Morgenthau (1978: 29), the realist guru, puts it: 'International politics, like all politics, is a struggle for power. Whatever the ultimate aims ... power is always the immediate aim.' Realists tend to see power in terms of a zero-sum game where one actor's gain is another's loss (Mearsheimer 1990: 53). To many realist scholars, the growth of Chinese power would mean the relative decline of the power of other countries. They suggest that if and when China achieves its great-power status, it will throw its weight around and will not play by the rules of the international community. This line of argument is found in the work of Denny Roy (1993) and Gerald Segal (1995), among others, who warn that a rising China will present the international society with an immense challenge that will not be easy to manage. Specifically, an economically and militarily powerful China may pose a long-term threat to the stability and security of the Asia-Pacific region and the world in general (Menges 2005; Mosher 2000). In his book *The Tragedy of Great Power Politics*, John Mearsheimer (2001:

396–402) offers a particularly pessimistic prediction of the consequences of a powerful China for international security.

From a realist standpoint, a great power's behaviour is determined not so much by its intentions but by its capabilities. As a state's economy vastly expands, it will use its newfound power to extend its spheres of influence and defend its economic interests whenever and wherever these interests are challenged. As emphasized by realist scholars, this pattern of great power emergence has recurred many times in history: Britain, France, Germany, Japan, the former Soviet Union and the United States all went through similar paths (Huntington 1991: 2; Friedberg 1993/94: 16; Roy 1996a: 762). As an emerging power with a great civilization and a history of being humiliated by foreign countries, China will be likely to behave in the same way as other rising powers behaved in the past (Rachman 1995; Kristof 1993: 71–72; Waldron 1995: 18). Denny Roy (1994: 159–60; 2003: 74) argues that an economically and militarily powerful China would pursue a more aggressive foreign policy, and that it would be less likely to accommodate the other great powers in the Asia-Pacific region. This theme has been pursued further by Bernstein and Munro (1997a, 1997b) in their controversial publications predicting 'a coming conflict' between China and America. Other analysts also view China as a growing threat to the US (Gertz 2002; Timperlake and Triplett II 2002). To the proponents of 'civilizational realpolitik' like Samuel Huntington (1993; 1996a; 1996b), China represents one of the hostile non-Western civilizations that will challenge the security interests of the West in the post-Cold War era.

Clearly, realists are pessimistic about the international repercussions of great power emergence. According to power transition theory, a rising power will seek to challenge the status of the leading power in the international hierarchy, possibly resulting in war between them (Organski 1958; Organski and Kugler 1980). As the leading realist scholar Robert Gilpin (1981: 106–107) observes, a non-status quo power will attempt to change the international system by extending 'its territorial control, its political influence, and/or its domination of the international economy' until 'the marginal costs of further expansion are equal to or greater than the marginal benefits of expansion'. Following Gilpin, Roy (1994) and Buzan and Segal (1994) argue that China is a dissatisfied and non-status quo power seeking to 'right the wrongs' of its humiliating history and alter the existing rules of the international system that are thought to be created and dictated by the West. This view is, however, contested by some scholars who argue that China is in fact a status quo power, at least for the time being (Ross 1997; Johnston 2003). Indeed, the application of the power transition theory to the rise of China has been challenged by Zhu (2006) and Chan (2007), among others.

Realist authors are particularly critical of the liberal assumption that economic interdependence reduces the possibility of military conflict (Morgenthau 1978). States only pursue cooperation with each other, they argue, if it helps enhance their national interests or advance their status in the international system. International institutions are therefore incapable of mitigating 'anarchy's constraining effects on interstate cooperation' (Grieco 1995: 151; Mearsheimer 1994/95). Indeed, realist scholars assert that ASEAN states are important trading partners of China, yet their close economic relationships have not prevented the PRC from acting assertively in the South China Sea (Segal 1996). Economic interdependence, realists contend, can in fact increase the likelihood of armed confrontation among trading nations as they seek to gain or maintain their access to vital resources and materials essential to the pursuit of wealth and power in an anarchic world (Waltz 1979: 106). The links between China's activities in the South China Sea and its growing energy needs have been explored by scholars such as Chen (1994), Calder (1996), Garver (1992), Leifer (1995) and Salameh (1995–96). Their findings support the realist argument that the Chinese government is likely to be more assertive in defending existing oil supplies and finding new energy reserves in order to sustain its economic growth and achieve great-power status in the 21st century (see Lee 2005 for a thorough analysis of China's quest for 'oil security'). Given the tremendous importance of the South China Sea to China's national development, realists assert, Beijing will one day press its claim to the area even though it may involve military confrontation with ASEAN states. Consequently, various strategies of containment or constrainment of China have been advocated by Realist scholars (Krauthammer 1995; Rachman 1995; Roy 1993, 1994, Segal 1996).

Liberal interpretations: economic modernization, democratization and peace

Unlike the realists who tend to stress the importance of structural constraints to state actions, liberals believe that the behaviour of a state is determined largely by domestic factors such as culture, ideology and political structure. In the liberal view, a government that is democratically elected is less likely to go to war against the will of its own people, and a state that is more interested in economic development and trade is unlikely to invade its trading partners. Thus, democracy and economic interdependence help mitigate the effects of anarchy and promote peace and international cooperation (Doyle 1983; Fukuyama 1992; Russett 1993).

Liberals see China's gradual reemergence as an influential player in the international system as primarily a consequence of its successful economic reform and open door policy over the past two decades. A China that is committed to reform and trade should, in their view, be welcomed by the international community, for economic change will gradually transform the country into a more open and democratic one that will in turn be a stabilizing force in Asia-Pacific and global security. Scholars such as Conable and Lampton (1992/93), Funabashi, Oksenberg and Weiss (1994) and Lieberthal (1995) have focused their attention on the positive impact of economic reform on political change in China. As China becomes more prosperous, they argue, its emerging middle class will demand more political freedom and a greater degree of participation in the decision-making process.

Indeed, economic decentralization and increasing competition for economic benefits among different groups, organizations and regions have resulted in the rise of interest group politics in the PRC. Moreover, rapid technological change combined with growing economic and cultural interactions between China and the external world are said to have made it difficult for the regime to maintain tight social and political control (Gilboy and Heginbotham 2001). There now exist numerous semi-official and unofficial social organizations and publications, leading to a scholarly debate on the possible emergence of a civil society in China (White, Howell and Shang 1996; He 1997). Thus, economic development is seen as 'a vital part of and a crucial condition for the realization of democratization' (Chen 1993: 195).

Scholars have often referred to the experience of Taiwan, South Korea and other East Asian countries where economic modernization was followed by political liberalization and democratization (Conable and Lampton 1992/93: 146; Funabashi, Oksenberg and Weiss 1994: 65; Robinson 1994: 197). While the pre-Tiananmen democracy movement suffered a serious setback in 1989, the trend towards greater liberalization in China is believed to have accelerated as a result of further economic progress (Conable and Lampton 1992/93: 140–41; Zagoria 1993: 404). Competitive elections at the local level have now been introduced which allow Chinese villagers to choose their local officials (Shi 1999). Some liberal scholars are of the view that the limited democratic experiment will eventually result in more substantial reforms of institutions at higher levels and, over a longer term, a fundamental change in the political system (Overholt 1996: 71, 75–76; Pei 1998). Gilley (2004) predicts that democratization will ultimately take place in China when a pro-democracy faction emerges from the Chinese Communist leadership.

The assumption that a democratic China will be a peaceful China is based on the theory of democratic peace that is central to the liberal perspective on international relations (Doyle 1983, 1986; Fukuyama 1992; Rummel 1995; Russett 1993; Weart 1994). Liberals believe that democracies are restrained from fighting wars by constitutional mechanisms, as an unjustified war will not be supported by the people who have to bear the burdens of armed conflict. Moreover, democracies do not fight democracies, it is argued, because of their shared democratic ideals and moral values, greater transparency in communication, and more peaceful approaches to the resolution of conflict. Finally, within the 'pacific union' war can be prevented by trade interaction and economic interdependence among democratic nations (Sorensen 1992: 398–99).

Liberals are convinced that democratic regimes are more peaceful than other types of regimes. The proposition that democracies do not fight each other is so persuasive that even some realists subscribe to it (Krasner 1994: 17). Based on the democratic peace theory, therefore, liberals argue that a China that is moving towards political liberalization and democratization, albeit at a very slow pace, is less likely to use force to resolve territorial disputes with neighbouring countries and to use military means to pursue its great power ambition. While accepting the thesis that democracies do not fight democracies, some liberal scholars argue that the process of the transition from authoritarian to democratic systems can be rather destabilizing and may increase the possibility of war (Mansfield and Snyder 1995).

Indeed, the argument that the likelihood of war can be reduced by international trade and economic interdependence has long been advanced (Angell 1935; Cobden 1903; Rosecrance 1986) and continues to influence the thinking of many liberal scholars. They believe that a China that is increasingly linked to the world economy and has an interdependent relationship with its trading partners is less likely to take aggressive actions that will be detrimental to its own economic interests. Liberal authors such as Vincent Cable and Peter Ferdinand (1994) argue that growing economic linkages between the PRC and its neighbours would make military confrontation too costly to contemplate. Chinese leaders, says Michael Yahuda (1997: 22), have recognized that economic interdependence plays a vital part in sustaining China's economic growth, maintaining its social stability and legitimizing the rule of the Chinese Communist Party (CCP).

Christopher Findlay and Andrew Watson (1997) find that the level of China's trade interdependency has transformed the relationships between the PRC and the rest of the world. Similarly, Stuart Harris (1997: 151) argues that China's 'cognitive learning' in the areas of economic activity supports the liberal view that cooperation is possible, even among 'liberal' and 'non-liberal' societies. This analysis is shared by Samuel Kim (1994: 433) who argues that some 'global learning' is taking place in China. Based on their research on the impact of interdependence on China's foreign relations, both Robinson (1994) and Kim (1994) conclude that interdependence in one sphere does help facilitate interdependence in other spheres.

Given its multidimensional contacts with the outside world, liberals believe, China is becoming gradually involved in the global process of 'complex interdependence' (Keohane and Nye 1977) and is restrained by its participation in international institutions and regimes (Krasner 1983). Alastair Iain Johnston and Paul Evans (1999) and Guogang Wu (2007) have demonstrated in their work that China has become more active in participating in a range of multilateral security institutions, both at global and regional levels. To some liberal scholars, it is far more important to look at Chinese behaviour in coping with interdependence than the question of adaptation or learning (Moore and Yang 2001: 228). Indeed, Gerald Chan (2004a, 2004b, 2005) has researched China's compliance with international rules and norms in the areas of trade, environment protection, arms control and human rights.

Thus, the liberal response to the rise of China is not to contain it, but to try to integrate the nation into the international society (Gill 1999; Shambaugh 1996; Shinn, 1996; Vogel 1997). To scholars like Lampton (2007: 126), China's rise 'can mean only one thing: engagement'. From the liberal perspective, both China and its trading partners have common interests in maintaining stability and prosperity in the post-Cold War world (Bacani 2003), and they should seek to maximize their absolute gains through international cooperation (Stein 1982: 318). In this view, the realist preoccupation with relative gains would only perpetuate mutual suspicion about which state would gain more from cooperation and how it might use its enhanced capabilities to dominate other states (Waltz 1979: 105). Not surprisingly, the literature produced by liberal scholars regards the 'China threat' thesis as a reflection of realist fear of relative gains rather than a response to China's intentions and capabilities (Kristof 1993; Klintworth and Ball 1995; Klintworth 1996; Shambaugh 1997; Shambaugh 2004/2005).

However, the liberal (and indeed realist) analysis on China's rise has been criticized for being too state-centric. Shaun Breslin (2005: 735) believes that the debate on the potential challenge of a rising China tends to focus heavily on how the growth of the Chinese economy may threaten the economic position of other major powers such as Japan and the US. He acknowledges China's increasing importance in the world economy but argues that this does not necessarily equate with power. Drawing on the work of Robert Cox (1999) and Steven Gill (1995), Breslin (2005: 753) suggests that China's economic activities should be understood within the context of adjusting its domestic political economy to the 'requirements of mobile transnational capital'. He also points to the growing significance of the supra or transnational 'commodity driven production networks'. Chinese policy-makers are thus seriously constrained by what Anthony Payne and Andrew Gamble (1996: 15) call the 'structural power of internationally mobile capital' and the economic power of non-state actors. In his most recent study, Breslin (2007) has provided an in-depth and critical examination of China's role in the global economy in relation to both its domestic politics and economic globalization. He contends that Chinese economic power has been somewhat overstated by Western analysts including liberal scholars.

Realism, liberalism and the theory of trade expectations

Both realism and liberalism have offered valuable theoretical perspectives on the rise of China and its implications. As each of them has its strengths and weaknesses in explaining the nature of the China challenge, it may be fruitful to combine the insights of the two theories.

First, the re-emergence of China as a great power is generally interpreted by realists as a consequence of the structural change in the post-Cold War international system. However, the liberal view that domestic political and economic change plays a significant role in China's rise must also be taken into account. After all, Chinese leaders made a conscious 'unit-level decision' to achieve great-power status well before the late 1980s, although the changing international structure has provided a favourable environment for China to fulfil these ambitions.

Second, based on historical precedents, realists believe that great power emergence is destabilizing because rising powers tend to pursue expansionist policies to promote or protect their economic interests. This, it is argued, is determined by states' capabilities rather than their intentions. As a rising power, the PRC will follow the footsteps of its predecessors, which would antagonize other great powers and provoke armed combat in Asia. Such a deterministic view of the repercussions of China's rise is based on the assumption that history will repeat itself. But what happened in the past may or may not recur in future. This argument also ignores domestic constraints on foreign policy, such as decision-makers' perceptions and political structures. In this respect, the liberal theory of democratic peace seems more convincing. All the available evidence appears to suggest that economic modernization does lead to political liberalization, however slowly, and that democracy does not fight democracy. If China manages to sustain its economic growth, maintain its social cohesion and national unity, and become a fully democratic country, it will likely be a peaceful and cooperative member of the international community, but it will probably take several decades for China to reach this stage, if it ever does. In the foreseeable future, what would be the main factors shaping China's calculation of the utility of the use of force should there be major barriers to the achievement of its national goals?

Third, the realist apprehension of the potential threat of a prosperous and strong China is largely a reflection of a zero-sum conception of power that one actor's gain will be another's loss. While it is true that each state is seeking to enhance its capabilities in an essentially anarchic world, it does not follow that the growth of one country's strength necessarily means the decline of that of others. This realist interpretation of power is too static and pessimistic, as it reinforces existing suspicion and fear among states and precludes the possibility that all actors involved in international cooperation can have shared benefits. The liberal emphasis on absolute gains that encourages China and the outside world to work with each other appears to be more conducive to the furtherance of prosperity and security. However, would China take military action to resolve conflicts, even though it is economically interdependent with other countries? If so, under what conditions would China choose such an option?

Finally, realists and liberals disagree fundamentally on the adequacy of economic interdependence in managing the effects of an emerging China in the international system. Liberal scholars believe that growing economic and trade interactions between China and the outside world will aid Chinese leaders in appreciating the value of pursuing a peaceful foreign policy. Realists, however, contend that interdependence alone will not restrain the behaviour of a rising power. On the contrary, interdependence will increase the probability of conflict between the PRC and its neighbours as China becomes more dependent on external resources such as oil and grain imports. Given the volatility of Chinese foreign policy behaviours in the past few decades, there is no conclusive evidence to support either of the two arguments, but it does seem that economic interdependence can lead to peace or war, depending on the circumstances.

As Thomas Moore and Dixia Yang (2001: 229) point out, economic interdependence 'is not alone likely to transform either Chinese world-views or Chinese foreign policy'. Two crucial questions remain unanswered. Under what conditions will a strong but (inter)dependent China be a pacific China that is willing to resolve differences with other countries in a peaceful manner? And under what conditions will Chinese leaders take threatening and belligerent actions in pursuit of their national interests?

The answers to these questions, it has been argued, would depend on China's expectations of future trade (Li 1999b). This argument is based on Dale Copeland's (1996) theory of trade expectations which draws on both realist and liberal insights. Although realism and liberalism have made useful contributions to the theoretical debate on the causes of war, neither of them is adequate in our understanding of the dynamic relation between economic interdependence and war. This is demonstrated by their inability to provide satisfactory explanations for the outbreaks of the two World Wars (Copeland 1996: 6). Liberals argue that interdependent states are unlikely to go to war because of the benefits of trade. Yet the European powers did fight with each other during World War I, even though there had been a high level of trade among them before the war. Realists seem to be correct in predicting that a high degree of interdependence can lead to war due to the potential costs of economic vulnerability. However, Germany and Japan were much more dependent on outside resources in the 1920s than in the late 1930s when they initiated World War II. Realist theory therefore fails to prove the correlation between high dependence and war.

Realism and liberalism predicate their predictions of a state actor's decision to initiate war on 'a snapshot of the level of interdependence at a single point in time'. Copeland's theory, it is argued, offers a new variable (i.e. the expectations of future trade) that 'incorporates in the theoretical logic an actor's sense of the future trends and possibilities'. The theory thus shows 'the conditions under which high interdependence will lead to peace or war' (Copeland 1996: 17). Peace can be maintained, Copeland argues, for as long as trade levels are expected to be high into the foreseeable future. If, however, highly interdependent states expect serious restrictions on their future trade, they will not hesitate to initiate war to safeguard the economic wealth on which their long-term security depends (Copeland 1996: 7). Using historical evidence, Copeland analyzes Germany's decisions to fight World War I and World War II. In both cases, the findings reveal the same pattern of behaviour: German leaders decided to go to war because of negative expectations for future trade and high dependence on other countries (Copeland 1996: 19–20).

Following Copeland, Li (1999b) argues that whether a powerful China would pose a threat to regional and global security would depend largely on Chinese decision-makers' expectations for future trade. If Chinese leaders feel that current trade with the outside world would continue to expand and that it would help enhance the wealth and power of the Chinese nation, there would be little incentive for them to resort to the use of force to settle unresolved disputes. If, however, Chinese leaders are convinced that their trade prospects would deteriorate substantially in the near future undermining their ability to maintain the long-term prosperity and security of China, they would be likely to take the military option to avert vulnerability and decline. In other words, the PRC's future behaviour would be determined not only by the level of interdependence with its trading partners but by its expectations of the future trading environment.

While the theory of trade expectation does offer some interesting insights for the analysis of Asian security issues (Li 1999b, 2004a; Copeland 2003), one wonders whether the theory alone that draws entirely on realism and liberalism is sufficient in explicating and predicting China's foreign policy and strategic behaviour. The theory has rightly underscored the salience of the perceptual dimension of international relations, but it focuses heavily on political leaders' preoccupation with material interests. Little attention is paid to such ideational factors as ideas, values and identities which are arguably more important in shaping the decisions and actions of policy-makers. This brings us to other theoretical perspectives recently employed by scholars in the debate on China's ascendancy.

Constructivism: norms, identity and interests

A theory that has made a valuable contribution to the scholarly debate of the security implications of a rising China is constructivism. A relatively new approach to the study of international relations, constructivism is fast emerging as a mainstream International Relations (IR) theory. Unlike realism and liberalism, it places a strong emphasis on the ideational rather than the material aspects of international politics. In the constructivist view there is no objective knowledge and reality. Our understanding and perception of the world is historically and socially constructed. International relations should not be explained purely in terms of balance of power among state actors in an anarchic system. Instead, they are shaped by a cognitive process of socialization through which states acquire and define their identities and interests. As such, state behaviour can be constrained and indeed influenced by intersubjectively shared ideas and values, as well as institutions and norms. If 'anarchy is what states make of it' (Wendt 1992), it is possible to change institutions such as self-help and power politics via international interaction and social practice that aims to reduce conflict and promote global peace and security (Onuf 1989; Wendt 1999).

Leszek Buszynski (2004) is among the first scholars who seek to analyze Asia-Pacific security within a constructivist framework. Constructivists agree that the rise of China's power does present a considerable challenge to the world and to the Asia-Pacific region in particular. But they argue that the concern of a 'China threat' is not so much a result of the PRC's growing military capabilities, but the perceived Chinese behaviour that is interpreted as a threat to regional security or to the interests of other states. This point is made by Muthiah Alagappa (1998: 665–67) in his discussion of Japan's response to the rise of China. Alagappa asserts that Japan's perception of China illustrates the limit of the neorealist argument that state behaviour is determined by structural factors. If the realist assumption was to be correct, he observes, Tokyo would have taken measures to balance against China and seek to compete with Beijing globally. However, Japanese leaders have chosen to bandwagon with the United States while trying to engage China through dialogue and interaction via multilateral institutions in the region. What this shows is that ideational factors such as history, identity, actor interests and intersubjective understandings among states are just as important as, if not more than, material capabilities in shaping responses to the China challenge.

Similarly, David Kang (2007: 10) argues that the rapid growth in Chinese power 'has in the past three decades evoked little response from its neighbours' in terms of balancing behaviour. This is because East Asian responses to the rise of China are shaped by both 'interests' and 'identities', rather than by structural change alone. Kang (2007: 4) contends that East Asian states saw 'substantially more opportunity than danger' in China's re-emergence as a major power. China's rise to a great power status, according to Kang, is also viewed as a natural phenomenon given China's historical role as the dominant state in East Asia. Seen from this perspective, China's desire to maintain stable relationships with its neighbours is not inconsistent with its worldview when China occupied a central position in the region (see also Kang 2003; 2003/04). Kang's argument is, however, challenged by Amitav Acharya (2003/04) who contends that security in East Asia should be built on shared regional norms and institutions rather than a hierarchical order dominated by China.

Constructivists argue that social reality is determined by both material and ideational factors, but that reality is a product of 'social construction' and can change according to changing circumstances (Alagappa 1998: 665). This is why constructivist scholars tend to stress the positive features of the 'reality' that have sustained stability and prosperity across Asia since the late 1970s, including strategic pragmatism, commitments to economic growth and the trend towards democratization (Berger 2000: 425). They accept that the emergence of China as a pre-eminent power is a distinct possibility and may lead to a structural transformation in Asia with profound repercussions. But this is unlikely to happen for several decades. It is therefore important for other major powers in East Asia to create an international security environment within which existing security challenges can be managed while ensuring China does not feel threatened. Such a benign and stable environment will hopefully encourage China to develop in 'a benevolent direction' (Berger 2000: 428).

From a constructivist perspective, it is possible to socialize China into the liberal norms through regular participation in international institutions and regimes. A high level of interaction between the PRC and the outside world may gradually change China's strategic culture, norms of international behaviour and conceptions of its national identity. In the longer term, it is argued, increased participation will probably alter the ideas, beliefs and perceived interests that underpin Chinese behaviour (see Friedberg 2005: 34–36).

However, constructivists are not naïve in believing that perceptual transformation will take place overnight. They recognize the persistence of deep-seated mental constructs in political leaders and elites which may be resistant to pressure for change. Increased contact with other people can sometimes reinforce existing beliefs, identities and behaviour (Wendt 1992: 411). For example, the economic and cultural contact between China and Taiwan has expanded immensely in recent years but politically they are drifting further apart. The growth of Chinese power will indeed threaten regional stability if the PRC leaders resort to the use of force to resolve the Taiwan issue. But the China-Taiwan tension cannot be fully explained by the realist and liberal theories. At the heart of the problem, constructivists argue, is a clash of Chinese nationalism and an emerging Taiwanese nationalism (Hughes 1997). The nationalistic sentiment on both sides of the Taiwan Strait is so intense that neither is willing to compromise on the issue of sovereignty despite the recognition of the disastrous consequences of a cross-strait conflict for their increasingly interdependent economies (Alagappa 1998: 661; Berger 2003: 399–400).

Constructivists do not dismiss the relevance of material capabilities, but they believe that the debate on strategic intentions of an ascending China must take into account the ideational forces shaping regional relations. As Alagappa (1998: 661) puts it: 'Threat construction is a product of the interplay of capabilities and intentions ... the perception of intentions is strongly influenced by ideational factors.' The conflict of contending identities between the PRC and Taiwan seems to provide the most convincing evidence for the constructivist argument.

To push the theoretical debate further, Peter Hays Gries (2005a) draws on the insights of social psychology to consider the 'China threat' debate with special reference to US-China relations. He argues that group identification is a normal human behaviour and it does not inevitably lead to intergroup competition and identity conflict. His research indicates, however, that emotion does play a significant role in turning competition to conflict. Gries tries to bring individual agency in the debate on China's rise which is often dominated by discussion of structural factors. He concludes that 'the Chinese are neither innately pacifist nor hardwired for conflict', and that the way they 'construe the events of world politics' is shaped by 'history and culture' (Gries 2005a: 257).

Postmodernism: discursive constructions of self and other

In the past few years, scholars have begun to introduce postmodernist approaches and concepts into the academic debate on the rise of China. While postmodernism has had considerable influence on all social science disciplines for some time, it was not taken seriously by mainstream international relations theorists until the 1990s. Along with Feminist Theory, Critical Theory, Normative Theory and Historical Sociology, postmodernism belongs to a group of new theories called reflectivist theories which rigorously challenge many basic assumptions of neorealism and neoliberalism (Smith 1997: 165–90). In particular, postmodernists seek to subvert many of the ideas that form the foundations of IR theory and are especially critical of the rationalist claim that it is possible to develop universal explanations for international phenomena. They reject any form of meta-narratives, including Marxism and Critical Theory, which interpret history in terms of conflict among social classes.

Postmodernists share the views of constructivists that there is no objective reality as such and that the social reality is discursively constructed. They claim that we have no direct access to reality and our knowledge of the 'real' world is gained via particular discourses. To a postmodernist thinker like Jacques Derrida (2001), the social world is like a book which needs to be 'read' and the meaning of the 'text' only emerges through interpretations. Michel Foucault (1972) is particularly concerned about the power-knowledge relationship in that 'truth' cannot be separated from power relations. Those who are in dominant positions in society are often able to determine what should be regarded as truths. In this sense, discourses are practices and our knowledge of the social world is located within specific discursive contexts. To understand the reality, postmodernists contend, we must try to unpack the discourses that are accepted as 'truths'. Thus, to find out how meaning is constructed, we need to focus on deconstruction of the 'texts' that are supposed to convey truth. As there are many 'stories' in the world requiring different interpretations, international relations are best conceived as 'intertextual relations' (Der Derian and Shapiro 1989).

A significant contribution to the debate on China's rise from the postmodernist perspective has been made by Changxin Pan (2004: 306) who focuses specifically on the US literature on the 'China threat'. By deconstructing this body of literature, Pan questions many 'problematic assumptions' of American scholars. He argues that the assumption that there is a pre-existing and objective Chinese reality to be observed and analyzed is seriously flawed. China scholars, Pan contends, are not 'disinterested observers' who can stand back from the 'reality' and offer neutral and value-free analysis of a rising China and how it may impact on the rest of the world. On the contrary, they are part of the 'China threat' problem that they claim to describe. By examining the US-dominated Western literature, Pan seeks to demonstrate how the 'China threat' debate reflects America's self-imagination rather than an objective social reality. As such, it should be interpreted as a 'normative, meaning-giving practice' that is used to 'legitimize power politics in US-China relations' (Pan 2004: 306).

Drawing on the work of Campbell (1998), Walker (1993) and other postmodernist IR scholars, Pan asserts that the United States needs to create a threatening 'other' in order to construct a universalized 'self'. It is therefore inevitable that China is deprived of its 'subjectivity' and is 'objectified' for the sake of preserving the US self. This type of dichotomized construction of self/other, according to Pan, has existed throughout American history. For over 40 years, the Soviet Union was treated as a threatening other and the end of the Cold War means that the Soviet other needs to be replaced. Naturally, a rapidly growing China becomes the most suitable candidate in a unipolar world where US security and predominance must be maintained.

To Pan, the discursive construction of China as other is rooted in the positivist epistemology. It is not surprising that the 'China threat' literature falls comfortably within the realist and liberal perspectives. The debate on China's challenge should thus be viewed in terms of 'theory as practice' which will have profound political consequences. This representation of China, Pan believes, can lead to dangerous policy prescriptions, such as a containment policy, which may have destabilizing effects on regional security and US-China relations in particular.

Like Pan, William Callahan (2005) considers the 'China threat' debate from a postmodernist perspective. His analysis of Chinese discourse on the 'China threat theory' shows that China is also engaged in a discursive practice through which rejection of Western concern of a powerful China is turned into the generation of external threats from America, Japan, India and other countries. A careful reading of the Chinese texts on the 'China threat theory' thus reveals a practice of 'estrangement' (Der Derian 1987) with the aim of affirming China's national identity. By treating any criticisms of China as 'foreign' and even 'mad', PRC elites seek to construct an identity that is distinctively Chinese. This negative form of identity production can be interpreted as a way of asserting a positive image of a China that is rising peacefully as opposed to the menacing image manufactured by the 'China threat theory' in the West (Callahan 2005: 709–10). Seen from this angle, the postmodernist notion of a dichotomized construction of self and other is evident in Chinese writings.

Taken together, the two studies offer some fresh insights that are not found in the dominant realist/liberal literature. Like many constructivist studies, the postmodernist literature highlights the necessity of paying greater attention to ideational factors that underpin security/threat perception and strategic culture when assessing the nature and implications of China's emergence as a major power in the world.

The study of Chinese foreign policy and China's security perceptions

The realist/liberal debate on the rise of China reviewed in the previous section can be seen as a continuation of the debate among scholars over how best to understand Chinese foreign policy (Ash, Shambaugh and Takagi 2006: Part 3; Yu 1994). In particular, it reflects the long-standing and unresolved debate on the level of analysis problem raised by Waltz (1959) and Singer (1961).

The realists, especially neorealists, tend to regard external factors and the structure of the international system as the main determinants of a state's foreign policy (Waltz 1979). This theoretical perspective has informed the work of many China scholars who argue that system factors play the most significant role in shaping the PRC's external policy (Ng-Quinn 1983, 1984; Tow 1994). Of particular relevance to this study is the large body of literature on the strategic interactions between China, the United States and the former Soviet Union, and the impact of this 'strategic triangle' on Beijing's security perceptions and policy. China's relations with America and Russia, respectively, are the subject of numerous studies in the field (see, for example, Nelson 1989; Ross 1993; Segal 1982; Zagoria 1962).

Indeed, the PRC's relations with other countries are usually analyzed within the context of great power relations. Peter van Ness (1970) and Robert Ross (1988), for example, argue that China's policy towards Third World countries in the Cold War years was based largely on the assessment of each country's relationship with the two superpowers. The emphasis on the role of polarity and great power politics in determining China's foreign relations is thus consistent with the realist analysis of post-Cold War Chinese foreign policy and the rise of China as a major power in the international system.

In fact, China has long been treated as a unitary actor whose foreign policy is based on rational consideration of national interest and strategic calculations (Whiting 1960; Ross 1988). However, this model has been challenged by scholars who argue that Chinese foreign policy is shaped primarily by domestic factors (Bachman 1994; Levine 1994; Zhao 1992). A prominent approach adopted by China scholars in the 1970s was to examine PRC foreign policy through the analysis of factional politics. Using the techniques of 'Kremlinology', some scholars sought to identify the various factions within the CCP leadership and consider how their different ideological views and political affiliations had impacted on their policy perspectives on China's domestic development and foreign relations. Specifically, they identified two major foreign policy debates among the top Chinese elites in 1965–66 and 1973–76. The former debate centred around the national security implications of American escalation in Vietnam, and the latter on the nature of external threat confronting China and how China should respond to the challenge (Lieberthal 1977; Yahuda 1972; Zagoria 1968).

Another domestic source of Chinese foreign policy is ideology, which has been studied extensively. Research has been carried out on the links between China's foreign policy behaviour and Mao's revolutionary outlook, his views of the world, his interpretations of the Leninist theory of imperialism, his writings on contradictions and the communist 'united front' strategy (Gittings 1974; Schwartz 1968b; Tsou and Halperin 1965; Yahuda 1983).

Finally, some scholars, notably historians and Sinologists, argue that it is difficult to fully understand the mindset of Chinese foreign policy elites without a good knowledge of Chinese history and imperial China's view of the world, in which China occupies a central and superior position within a hierarchical system (Fairbank 1968, 1969; Fitzgerald 1964; Ginsberg 1968; Mancall 1984). This Sinocentric mentality is said to have influenced the thinking of present-day Chinese leaders in their interactions with other countries, particularly their Asian neighbours. Other scholars, however, contend that the legacy of imperial China has been exaggerated and that traditional Chinese worldview has basically broken down as a result of China's encounters with Western imperialism in the 19th century (Hunt 1984; Schwartz 1968a).

Nevertheless, some scholars are convinced that the foreign policy of China is inescapably shaped by its enduring cultural heritage. Chih-yu Shih (1990, 1993) argues that traditional Chinese culture and philosophical thinking such as Buddhism, Daoism and Confucianism have continued to influence Chinese foreign policy behaviour. What is interesting about his approach is its combination of Chinese culture with Western social psychological theories in analyzing Chinese diplomatic practice.

Whether they subscribe to the unitary actor model, domestic politics explanations or historical approaches, most China scholars recognize the complexity of foreign policy decision-making. In some ways, this mirrors the theoretical development within the IR discipline. Despite the significant influence of the realist model of foreign policy-making (Morgenthau 1978; Waltz 1979), many scholars argue that state action is the outcome of a complex process of interactions between domestic and external factors (Hoffman 1960; Rosenau 1967; Vasquez 1983). Among the major sources of domestic influence on foreign policy decisions are the perceptions of policy makers.

Indeed, the relevance of the belief systems of political leaders to their decisions has been treated extensively in the comparative foreign policy literature (Axelrod 1976; Little and Smith 1988). Drawing on cognitive psychology, this literature seeks to analyze how decision-makers' behaviour is shaped by their belief systems. Much of the research in the field builds on the pioneering work of Harold and Margaret Sprout (1956) who distinguished the 'psychological milieu' from the 'operational milieu' in studying international politics. The importance of cognitive factors in foreign policy decision-making has been stressed by Snyder, Bruck and Sapin (1962) and others as a challenge to the rational actor decision-making model. It is interesting to note that one of the classic studies of the role of perception in foreign policy and international relations is produced by Robert Jervis (1976), a prominent realist scholar.

Essentially, what this body of literature shows is that political leaders, like all human beings, tend to look for what psychologists call cognitive consistency in that they only recognize things they expect to see. Decision-makers also have a tendency to fit any external stimuli into their pre-existing image systems. This is known as dissonance reduction in psychology. Cognitive dissonance can, as demonstrated in Jervis's (1976) work, lead to misperception in the interactions among foreign policy-makers of different countries. This may result in misunderstanding of each others' intentions, thus causing tension and conflict.

It is clear that elite perceptions play a huge part in international relations. Prior to the 1980s, studies of Chinese perceptions focused primarily on the top leaders, especially Mao's perceptions of the world. Very little, if any, attention was paid to the views of the international relations specialists who advised the Chinese leaders. This was due mainly to the lack of information on the foreign policy-making process in China and the role of foreign policy advisers in particular. It was also because of serious lack of documentary sources and data on which Western scholars could base their research in this area. From the early 1980s onwards, scholars began to gain a better understanding of the complex process and structure in China's foreign policy decision-making. A. Doak Barnett's (1985) path-breaking work *The Making of Foreign Policy in China*, which drew on wide-ranging interviews with Chinese officials and policy elites, together with other studies by David Shambaugh (1987), Tai Ming Cheung (1987), Nina Halpern (1988), Carol Lee Hamrin and Suisheng Zhao (1995), opened up a whole new area for further research which had previously not been possible. The most significant contribution to this genre of literature is Lampton's (2001a) edited volume which examines the complex process of China's foreign and security policy-making in various areas.

As China gradually opened its door to the outside world, it was possible for Western academics to develop collaborative research with Chinese scholars. Indeed, Harish Kapur (1987) put together a collection of articles by PRC scholars presenting the Chinese perspective of the world. More significantly, a wide variety of primary sources and data became available to Western researchers. Some scholars seized this new research opportunity and produced excellent studies of the perceptions of Chinese international relations analysts and security experts. Among the most influential works in this genre of literature are Gilbert Rozman's (1987) *The Chinese Debate about Soviet Socialism*, Alan Whiting's (1989) *China Eyes Japan* and David Shambaugh's (1991) *Beautiful Imperialist: China Perceives America*. Drawing extensively on the newly available Chinese-language sources and personal interviews, these studies provided in-depth analyses of the images and perceptions of Chinese scholars and policy advisers on the Soviet Union, Japan and the United States.

Moving beyond the country-based analysis of Chinese elite perceptions, Gerald Chan (1999) produced the first comprehensive study of Chinese perspectives on international relations. This was a major contribution to the literature in terms of both the depth and breadth of its analysis of the perceptions of China's international relations specialists. The research was based on the author's extensive interviews with PRC scholars and a wide range of Chinese-language material. It offers a broader conceptual framework within which Chinese perceptions of individual countries or specific international issues can be explored. More significantly, the study introduced the state of international relations in China to the outside world at a time when serious efforts were being made to develop the discipline.

Despite the importance of these works, most of them were published almost two decades ago. Since then, there have been dramatic changes in both China and the international environment. As the power and influence of the PRC have increased substantially since the end of the Cold War, the need to have a better understanding of China's self-perception and its security perceptions has never been more pressing.

However, there are few systematic studies of China's security perceptions in relation to its search for a great power identity. As noted earlier, the debate on the rise of China would be rather meaningless without taking into account the motives and considerations of PRC leaders and foreign policy elites. One way of advancing the debate is to analyze the security discourse of Chinese international affairs experts on China's perceptions of other great powers and its own position in the international system. But let us first consider what has been published in the field over the past two decades.

Basically, there are three categories of studies on China's security perceptions in the post-Cold War era. First, some scholars have attempted to examine China's perceptions of its overall security environment, especially the areas surrounding the PRC. This literature includes studies on China's security thinking and strategy after the Cold War (Denoon and Frieman 1996; Glaser 1993; Hu 1993, 1995; Li 1995; Shambaugh 1992), Chinese perspectives on the end of bipolarity and the 'New World Order' (Armstrong 1994; Garrett and Glaser 1989; Kim 1991), China's perceptions of internal and external threat (Nathan and Ross 1997; Roy 1996b; Shambaugh 1994b; Zhao 2004b), Chinese position on multilateral security cooperation in the Asia-Pacific (Garrett and Glaser 1994) and China's realpolitik views of international politics (Christensen 1996). The authors of these publications are able to discern a 'new thinking' in China's security policy in response to the break-up of the Soviet Union and the end of the Cold War; the relationship between the Chinese domestic reform programme and its foreign policy agenda; the close links among PRC leaders' sense of vulnerability, concern of domestic instability and perceptions of external threat; and China's approaches to various global and regional security issues. Taken together, this set of studies has provided much valuable information on China's security perceptions. However, with the exception of Zhao's (2004b) work, they were all published before 1997 and it is time to update the literature.

Some scholars have argued that it is necessary to go beyond the traditional preoccupation of military security when considering China's security thinking. Russell Ong (2002, 2007) has examined China's post-Cold War security interests within a broader concept of security, paying particular attention to the economic and political dimensions of the Chinese security agenda. This is certainly a valid analytical framework for analyzing PRC security perceptions given Chinese leaders' emphasis on developing 'comprehensive national strength' of their country in recent years. While Ong's work offers some useful insights into Chinese perceptions on various security issues in the post-Cold War era, it relies heavily on PRC official publications and the state media for information.

In their co-edited book on Chinese views of the post-Cold War world, Yong Deng and Fei-Ling Wang (1999) also take a broader approach to Chinese security concerns, their coverage of issues ranges from China's self-image and Chinese conception of national interests and human rights to trade, multilateral diplomacy and nuclear non-proliferation. The authors of this study have consulted a much wider range of Chinese-language material and the research findings have been enriched substantially by their sources. While most of the issues considered in the book remain relevant, its analyses of Chinese perceptions need to be revisited in the light of the changing international situation since the end of the 1990s.

Indeed, Deng and Wang (2005: 14–15) have put together another volume which seeks to explore the motivations behind Chinese foreign policy in the early 21st century. Based on extensive research of Chinese and English sources, the authors of the book conclude that Beijing's foreign policy is driven by three main factors: regime security, economic development and quest for great power status. In order to achieve their goals, it is argued, PRC leaders have made strenuous efforts to promote their country's image as a responsible rising power that is ready to fulfil its international obligations. Although the study does not directly focus on China's perceptions of other great powers, many of the themes covered are pertinent to this book.

Another important work is Avery Goldstein's (2005) *Rising to the Challenge*, which attempts to trace the origins and evolution of China's grand strategy in the 1990s and considers its implications for international security. According to Goldstein, PRC leaders have settled on a 'transitional grand strategy' designed to minimize the possibility that the rise of China is perceived as a threat to other countries and that it must be curtailed. This strategy, if successfully implemented, would enable China to continue its modernization programme and achieve the status of a great power in the next few decades. Unlike many other studies on Chinese strategic thinking, Goldstein's research is theoretically informed and based on a wide range of primary and secondary sources. As the focus of the book is on the evolution of the PRC's grand strategy, only one chapter is devoted to Beijing's relations with the major powers in the world which also includes India, ASEAN and the European Union (EU). Consequently, Chinese security perceptions of the East Asian powers remain insufficiently explored.

Michael Swaine and Ashley Tellis's (2000) study of China's grand strategy reaches a conclusion similar to that of Goldstein. They argue that China has adopted a 'calculative strategy' which would allow it to acquire comprehensive national power in a less confrontational security environment. Swaine and Tellis examine Chinese security perceptions and strategies in both historical and contemporary contexts. Their work is analytically rigorous and empirically sound, although it is based almost entirely on secondary sources and some of their observations have become dated.

In contrast to this type of literature, some authors focus specifically on China's perceptions of the changing security environment from the military angle. Daewon

Ohn's (2000) study of the development of PRC's grand strategy from 1978 to 1998 shows that it is closely related to Chinese military modernization. David Shambaugh (1994a, 1999) has written on the PLA's threat perceptions in relation to its military doctrine and China's defence capability. Based on Chinese military sources and interviews with PLA personnel, Shambaugh argues that PRC military analysts' perceptions of China's security environment are rather ambivalent compared to civilian security specialists, and that they have considerable concern over a range of latent threats to the PRC's national security. As such, the military writers are believed to be more inclined to recommend a tougher policy in response to external challenge to what they perceive as core national interests such as territorial claims.

The most comprehensive study of Chinese elites' security discourse from a military perspective is undoubtedly Michael Pillsbury's (2000) *China Debates the Future Security Environment*. In this important work, Pillsbury has utilized a variety of Chinese-language material to reconstruct the internal debates among PRC's security specialists on China's geopolitical position and military power vis-à-vis other major powers. While the book offers many illuminating insights into Chinese strategic thinking on a whole range of security and defence issues, a predominantly military focus is reflected in both the questions addressed and sources consulted. It is necessary to uncover Chinese perceptions of other major powers from a broader perspective, taking into account political, diplomatic, economic and other dimensions of their power and capabilities. Moreover, the text is organized in such a way that the Chinese views are presented mainly as quotations with minimum analytical and interpretive comments. In terms of sources, the publications used are confined to the period of 1994 to 1999. Clearly, there is a need to broaden the scope of coverage as well as the range of sources in assessing China's changing perceptions of the great powers over the past 18 years.

The second category of literature on Chinese security perceptions is country-based. Not surprisingly, Chinese perceptions of the United States have attracted most academic attention. In a book-length study, Jianwei Wang (2000) has combined international relations theories with social psychological approaches to analyze Sino-American mutual images. His findings reveal serious differences and cognitive deficiencies between the two countries, which may lead to instabilities and uncertainties in future US-China relations. While this study is rigorous in terms of conceptual framework, research design and data collection, its treatment of Chinese security perceptions is very limited. In addition, the fieldwork for the project was conducted from 1990 to 1992, which has inevitably rendered the work outdated. The role of images and perceptions in US-China relations is also examined by a multidisciplinary group of scholars led by Hongshan Li and Zhaohui Hong (1998). As this study covers many areas over a very long period of time – from the 19th to the 20th century, it is not directly relevant to our understanding of Chinese perceptions of US global position and security strategy in the post-Cold War era.

Drawing extensively on primary sources and interviews with PRC officials and analysts, researchers such as Jianwei Wang and Zhimin Li (1992), Rex Li (1999a;

2000), Phillip Saunders (2000), Yong Deng (2001), Samantha Blum (2003) and Rosalie Chen (2003) have written on China's changing perceptions of America and US global and regional strategy. Again, the research in this literature was largely completed before 2000. The studies by Blum (2003) and Chen (2003) have given some consideration of the impact of 9/11 on China's perceptions but their use of primary sources is far from adequate. Moreover, Biwu Zhang (2005) has published an interesting paper on Chinese perceptions of US power and capability. More recent work on China's security perceptions includes articles by Peter Hays Gries (2005b) and Rosemary Foot (2006) looking at how PRC scholars and policy elites respond to America's unipolar position in the globe. However, few Chinese-language sources are cited in these otherwise perceptive and sophisticated studies. In addition, Denny Roy (2002, 2003) and Mohan Malik (2002) have offered some useful analyses of China's reactions to the US-led war on terrorism. Finally, based on a range of primary and secondary sources, Rex Li (2003a, 2006), Jing-dong Yuan (2005) and Peter van Ness (2006) have examined Chinese perceptions of and responses to 9/11, the Bush Doctrine and the Iraq war.

Chinese security perceptions of Japan are another area that has come under close scrutiny by Western academics. Joseph Cheng (1996) has analyzed the mutual perceptions of China and Japan in the first half of the 1990s, while Thomas Christensen (1996, 1999), Rex Li (1999c) and Jian Yang (2001) have probed Chinese views of Tokyo's Asia-Pacific security strategy and its alleged moves towards remilitarization. Other studies have examined how Chinese security elites perceive the significance and implications of the strengthening of the US-Japan security alliance (Garrett and Glaser 1997a; Christensen 1999; Yu 1999). Chinese apprehensions of Japan's growing political clout and military development have also been considered in Robert Taylor's (1996) work on Sino-Japanese economic and political relations and Reinhard Drifte's (2003) study of Japan's post-1989 security relations with China. These studies have invariably used the newly emerging Chinese-language sources in their examination of PRC elites' security perceptions of Japan, but again the focus of their analysis is largely confined to the pre-9/11 period.

A major contribution to our understanding of China-Japan relations is Ming Wan's (2006) book on the political, military, economic and societal dimensions of the interactions between the two countries. Another important work is Caroline Rose's (2005) study of Sino-Japanese reconciliation which has offered some valuable insights into Chinese perceptions of Japan. The controversies surrounding the intellectual debate on China's 'new thinking' on Japan in 2003 and the societal reactions to it have been examined by Peter Hays Gries (2005c). More recently, the concept of 'othering' has been deployed by Shogo Suzuki (2007) and Rex Li (2008) in their analyses of China's perceptions of Japan in relation to its national identity formation.

Although the role of Russia in China's assessment of its changing security environment and weapon acquisitions is considered in various publications reviewed above (see, for example, Glaser 1993; Hu 1995; Shambaugh 1992, 1994; Roy 1996b; Pillsbury 2000), no single study has been devoted exclusively to Chinese security perceptions of Russia. To be sure, studies of post-Cold War Sino-Russian relations usually take into account Chinese views of Russia's external policy (Anderson 1997; Dittmer 1994, 2004; Garnett, 2001). A significant contribution in this area is Sherman Garnett's (2000) edited book on Russia-China Relations which contains several chapters on China's perceptions of Moscow and its Asia policy. Of particular importance is the chapter contributed by Rozman (2000) who provides a clear review of Russian and Chinese assessments of each other, including their national strength, their role in the emerging world order and bilateral relations. In an article published in the US journal *Orbis*, Li Jingjie (2000), Director of the Institute of East European, Russian and Central Asian Studies at the Chinese Academy of Social Sciences (CASS), has presented a Chinese perspective on Sino-Russian strategic partnership. The US factor in Sino-Russian strategic relations has also been explored in Chenghong Li's (2007) work.

In addition, Bin Yu (2005, 2007) has written extensively on Sino-Russian interactions, offering some astute observations on Chinese perceptions of Russia's foreign and security policy. Recent developments in bilateral relations between Russia and China and their responses to the challenge of globalization have been explored in two well-researched articles by Peter Ferdinand (2007a, 2007b). Nevertheless, there is a glaring lack of systematic analysis of Chinese discourse of Russia's changing position in the international system and its security strategy. This is in sharp contrast to the small but growing body of literature on Russian perceptions of China (Lo 2004; Lukin 2002a, 2002b; Wilson 2004).

Other areas in Chinese security perceptions that have been monitored by Western scholars include the Korean Peninsula (Garrett and Glaser 1995, 1997b) and nuclear arms control (Garrett and Glaser 1995/96; Hu 1999).

The third category of literature on Chinese security perceptions has been contributed by a cohort of PRC scholars who have either pursued graduate studies at American universities or worked at Western research institutions and international affairs think-tanks as visiting scholars. Many of them are now occupying senior positions in Chinese academia and/or playing an advisory role in the Chinese foreign policy-making process. Naturally, they are familiar with the scholarly and policy debates within the PRC on China's perceptions of and relations with the external world. At the same time, they are in regular contact with their Western colleagues and have been able to publish their research in English in Western academic journals. As such, their work opens up a new window through which Chinese perceptions of a range of major security issues can be accessed by outside observers.

A prominent Chinese scholar in this field is Chen Qimao who has written on Taiwan and Sino-American relations (1987), Beijing's view of the post-Cold War international environment (1993) and China-Taiwan relations (1996, 2004). Wang Jisi, Dean of the School of International Studies at Peking University and one of China's top international relations and America specialists, has published on various topics including international relations theory and Chinese foreign policy (1994), the global and regional role of the United States (1997), China's Asia strategy (2004) and Chinese perceptions of US-China relations (2005). America's global position and strategy are also the subject of a study by Jin Canrong (2001), a scholar at CASS's Institute of American Studies.

Another Chinese scholar whose work is well known to Western researchers is Jia Qingguo of Peking University. He has written on the linkage between Chinese domestic politics and US-China relations (1996), Chinese perceptions of America's China policy (2001) and Beijing's policy towards the US since the end of the Cold War (2005). Wu Xinbo, a professor at Shanghai's Fudan University, has published extensively on China's security practice (1998), Sino-Japanese security relations (2000), Chinese foreign policy behaviour (2001), US-China relations (2004) and the US-Japan alliance (2005). Xia Liping (2001) of Shanghai Institute of International Studies has also written on the debate on China as a responsible power. More recently, Yang Bojiang (2006) of the China Institute of Contemporary International Relations has published an article on Sino-Japanese relations in the post-Koizumi era.

Other PRC authors such as Xu Xin (1993), Wu Baiyi (2001), Ji Guoxing (1996, 1998), Yang Jiemian (2001, 2002) and Anne Wu (2005) have published their work in the West on Chinese security perceptions, the evolution of China's security concept, energy security co-operation in the Asia-Pacific, the South China Sea dispute, great power relations, the Taiwan issue, China and the North Korean nuclear crisis and other topics. A publication that deserves special attention is Zhang Yunling and Tang Shiping's (2005) comprehensive discussion of China's grand and regional strategies.

The above review indicates a growing interest in China's security perceptions among Western scholars but it also reveals some serious gaps and deficiencies in the existing literature. First, many of the works in the field are rather narrowly focused and they tend to analyze Chinese images or views of a particular country or issue during a specific period of time. The United States and Japan have received extensive treatment in the literature but there is scant coverage of China's view of Russia. Detailed case studies are undoubtedly useful but Chinese perceptions of the three major East Asian powers need to be examined within a broader context of Beijing's overall assessment of its strategic environment.

Second, while some scholars have tapped into the variety of newly available Chinese-language materials emerging from China, others still rely primarily on official sources and the state media for their information. Many potentially useful documentary sources have not been fully and systematically exploited by researchers.

Third, some studies are based on confidential interviews with PRC officials, military analysts and security experts. Although this is an extremely valuable source of information for research on the foreign policy of an authoritarian country like China, the use of non-attributable sources does present certain methodological problems. As the data cannot be independently verified and the research cannot be replicated by others using the same data, the reliability of the projects concerned may be questioned.

Fourth, as mentioned previously, an increasing number of PRC scholars have published their work in the West which has no doubt enriched external knowledge of Chinese perspectives on international relations. However, one has to be aware of the constraints on the scholars who communicate their views to Western audiences on what may be considered politically sensitive issues in the PRC. In addition, these scholars may be well-informed of the current debate in China but their views may not represent a sufficiently wide spectrum of opinions within the Chinese academic and policy communities.

Fifth, much of the research in the literature was conducted prior to 2001 and it has inexorably been overtaken by events since then.

Finally, a conspicuous weakness in the existing literature on China's security perceptions is its lack of theoretical rigour. Most of the current studies are rather descriptive and policy-oriented. Although scholars may have made some theoretical points in their discussion, there is little in-depth theoretical analysis of Chinese views. Given the richness and diversity of the international relations literature (Chan, Mandaville and Bleiker 2001; Jackson and Sorensen 2003; Smith, Booth and Zalewski 1996), one would expect a more rigorous application of international relations theories to the examination of Chinese perceptions.

Most scholars believe that there is a strong realist tendency in Chinese elites' perceptions of international relations (see, for example, Glaser 1993; Christensen 1996). This is because China's conception of national interest is believed to be realist in orientation, albeit with some Chinese characteristics (Deng 1998). The assumption may well be correct, but little sustained effort has been made to investigate the extent to which Chinese perceptions of various countries and actors are influenced by realism. Do China's history and strategic culture play any part in shaping its realist outlook (Johnston 1995)? Have liberal ideas had much impact on Chinese security perceptions after almost thirty years' opening up to the outside world? In any case, realism is not a monolithic school of thought and it has developed into a number of variants over the years, including 'defensive' and 'offensive' realism. Of interest is that some questions have recently been raised over the nature and extent of the real disagreements between realists and neoliberals on issues of conflict and cooperation (Jervis 1999). Added to this dynamic debate is the theoretical contribution that constructivism has made to the field, not to mention the growing prominence of reflectivist theories such as postmodernism and Critical Theory.

However, very little of the latest theoretical advances in the discipline of international relations is reflected in the literature on China's perceptions of its international security environment and of other great powers in particular. In view of the inadequacies in the existing studies, there is an urgent need to carry out a systematic study to help us reach a more thorough and theoretically grounded understanding of China's security perceptions.

Research problem, objectives and aims of the study

The literature review in the previous section provides the intellectual, theoretical and policy context for the proposed study. It establishes the argument that a thorough understanding of Chinese security discourse is essential in assessing the nature of China's rise and the implications for global and regional security. The review also demonstrates that the existing literature on Chinese security perceptions is inadequate in that the views of PRC policy elites on the East Asian powers – the United States, Japan and Russia – have not been sufficiently explored in relation to China's self-identity and its role in the international system. In addition, the rich Chinese language sources and research materials emerging from the PRC in the past two decades have not been extensively utilized to analyze Chinese security discourse. Finally, much of the work on Chinese perception lacks theoretical depth and sophistication.

It is therefore time to conduct a systematic and in-depth analysis of China's perceptions of the major powers in East Asia within the context of the evolving international security environment in the post-Cold War era. But the way Chinese elites view other East Asian powers must not be separated from how they perceive their country's identity in terms of its past experience, present development and future direction.

What is national identity? National identity is usually considered as a form of collective identity in the sense that the identity of a group of people is defined and shaped by its internal cohesion and external relationship with other groups of people. Anthony Smith (1991: 143, 17) believes that national identity is 'perhaps the most fundamental and inclusive' collective identity which provides 'a powerful means of defining and locating individual self in the world through the prism of the collective personality and its distinctive culture'. There are different forms of collective identity. Some collective entities are considered as naturally evolving groups consisting of members with shared emotion or interests, while others may be created for particular purposes and functions. Even realists who are skeptical of the possibility and desirability of forming collective identities at the interstate level accept the idea of collective identity among individuals within a state in order to establish a corporate identity. Wendt (1999: 229–30) calls this 'a split personality' in realism.

Philosophers have long been immersed in the contemplation of the human condition and the meaning of individual identity with reference to such concepts as 'being', 'existence' and 'otherness' (Heidegger 2002; Sartre 2003). Identity is a major theme in the discipline of psychology. Research has been conducted on various stages of human development and the inner processes of individuals in their identity formation (Erikson 1994, 1998). Moreover, a social identity theory has been formulated by social psychologists (Abrams and Hogg 1990). Identity has also attracted the attention of sociologists who have researched the dynamics and tension between individuals and society (Durkheim 1997; Weigert, Teitge and Teitge 1986). Of particular relevance to the conceptualization of identity is the perspective of symbolic interactionism, which postulates that the interaction among human beings is based on their interpretation of the meaning of each others' actions. The creation of meaning and interpretation of such meaning through human encounters is important to the construction of the self. In other words, meanings are seen as 'social products' and 'creations that are formed in and through the defining activities of people as they interact' (Blumer 1986: 5).

The study of identity thus helps elucidate how individuals identify themselves in relation to the presence, perception and action of others. In this sense, the identity of the self is intimately linked to its perception of and interaction with the other. The construction of identity and difference is believed to be driven by biopsychological needs. Without the existence of the other, whether in a positive or negative sense, it is difficult to develop an identity that gives the self a significant meaning.

The scholarly insights into personal identity can be usefully applied to the analysis of national identity and international relations (Neumann 1992; Krause and Renwick 1996). Nonetheless, a country is not a person, and the composition, organization and activity of a nation-state are enormously complicated. Nation refers to a group of people who share a common language, culture and tradition. State, on the other hand, is an artificial construct that exists to define territorial boundaries and political authority. Some nations do not exist as independent sovereign states, while most states in today's world consist of different nations. National boundaries can be drawn and redrawn by force or through negotiations. 'In a state-centric world', as Samuel Kim (2004: 41) points out, 'the substantive content of national identity is the state, which defines itself as what it is as well as what it does'. This is not to say that the ethnic, cultural and historical elements are irrelevant in identity formation but national identity does not emerge naturally. Rather, it has to be nurtured and forged through socialization, education and sometimes inculcation. Often the enactment of national identity is related to nationalist movements and the process of nation-building.

Some scholars have prioritized the role of state in their conceptualization of national identity (Pye 1971; Verba 1971). However, the emphasis on state boundaries in shaping a country's identity has been questioned by Dittmer and Kim (1993: 6–13) who argue that national identity does not exist in 'boundaries without contents'. In their view, it is necessary to investigate why a specific group of people identify themselves with their country and government and what it is that they identify with. National identity, according to their 'synthetic theory', 'should be understood … as an ongoing process or journey rather than a fixed set of boundaries, a relationship rather than a free-standing entity or attribute' (Dittmer and Kim 1993: 11, 13). Thus, one has to appreciate both the dissimilarity and fusion of nation and state in conceptualizing national identity.

Why does national identity matter in foreign policy and international relations? National identity matters because it 'provides a cognitive framework for shaping its [a state's] interests, preferences, worldview and consequent foreign policy actions' (Kim 2004: 41). The actor has to know who it is (identity) before it knows what it wants (interests). Alexander Wendt (1999: 231) is correct in saying that '[W]ithout interests identities have no motivational forces, without identities interests have no direction'. If the identity theory formulated by sociologists and social psychologists offers any guides (Stryker 2002), a state (the self) forms its identity in relation to how it evaluates the perception of other states (the other) and their actions.[2]

Just as each individual plays a role in society, the state assumes specific roles in international society (Holsti 1970; Walker 1987). Wendt (1999: 225) argues that the state is 'a "group Self" capable of group cognition'. The state's roles can be based on a conscious choice on its part or enacted in response to the external environment, or a combination of both. The roles may vary over different periods of time and under different circumstances but they are an integral part of the process of identity construction. 'National role conceptions' are thus important to states in conducting their foreign policy (Holsti 1970). As Dittmer and Kim (1993: 15) put it: 'National roles ... perform the functions of mobilizing, testing, and validating an identity through interactions with other players in the same arena.' To define the role it plays on the international stage, a state needs to identify external reference groups (i.e. other states or non-state actors) that are considered significant in assisting it to measure its performance and/or achieve its objectives. These reference groups can be positive or negative, depending on their utility in forging an identity that the state wishes to possess.

However, national identity formation cannot be accomplished if it relies purely on the roles that states play in the international arena. There must be something more profound and unique to the nation that can be identified by the people of a particular country. This may have been developed over a very long period of time and its intrinsic values are shared by the people. National identity, as William Bloom (1993: 52) observes, 'describes that condition in which a mass of people have made the same identification with national symbols – have internalized the symbols of the nation – so that they may act as one psychological group when there is a threat to, or the possibility of enhancement of, these symbols of national identity'. Dittmer and Kim (1993: 17–19) refer to the 'national symbol system' in China as *guocui* (the national essence). It consists of a set of myths, rituals, beliefs and symbols as well as other cultural norms and historical memory. It is of course not unusual for the state to produce, amend or remove certain elements of the symbol system to forge a specific national identity. This is why Benedict Anderson (2006) considers the construction of nationhood as a way of creating an 'imagined community'.

The national identity of China has undergone various phases of change since 1949 when the PRC was established. The Chinese state has been playing an instrumental role in constructing an identity that reflects its domestic priorities and external interests. China's identity changed from a socialist state in the 1950s to a third world state in the 1960s, then to a reforming and modernizing socialist state from the late 1970s to the late 1980s (van Ness 1993: 199–203). Much of China's *guocui* was attacked and undermined from the 1950s to the 1970s. For example, traditional Chinese culture and philosophy were criticized, societal and family relationships were transformed, and history was rewritten to mirror the political agenda of the Maoist leadership. Only from 1978, when China began to introduce its economic reform and open door policy, some efforts were made to recover and rebuild the 'national essence' of China.

As mentioned at the beginning of this chapter, China faced a major crisis in 1989 following the student demonstrations in Tiananmen Square and subsequent political turmoil in Beijing and many other cities. The Chinese government had to deal with the biggest ever challenge to its legitimacy. In addition to the domestic crisis, PRC leaders witnessed the rapid collapse of communism in Eastern Europe. After the break-up of the Soviet Union, the US emerged as the world dominant power and China was left as one of the few remaining communist countries. The Gulf War of 1990–91 further consolidated America's leading position in the international system. It is not an exaggeration to say that China encountered an immense identity crisis which, if not handled carefully, could seriously jeopardize its reform programme and lead to political instability with far-reaching consequences. The CCP leaders were acutely aware that *neiluan* (internal disorder) could lead to *waihuan* (external catastrophe), as the fate of the Qing Dynasty had painfully demonstrated.

Given the volatile domestic situation and uncertain external environment, it was no longer viable for the PRC government to rely on its previous national identity as a reforming and modernizing socialist state to sustain the domestic consensus on China's future development and maintain its international position in a unipolar world. With the demise of the communist ideology, Chinese leaders had to establish a national identity that could be identified with by their people. They also wanted to forge an identity that would help motivate the Chinese population to support government policy. National identity, in the view of Kim and Dittmer (1993: 240), 'becomes fully activated when faced with a threat or an opportunity in its environment'.

To Chinese leaders and policy elites, the PRC needed to develop a new identity that would aid them in maintaining domestic cohesion and national unity, as well as projecting China as a coherent and distinct actor to the outside world. As communism had lost much of its appeal, nationalism seemed to be the most attractive tool for building a Chinese national identity. However, evoking nationalistic sentiment was a risky business, as mass nationalism could develop into an unruly political force. Nationalist emotion, once stimulated, might not be easily managed by the government. Certainly, PRC leaders did not want to see the sort of nationalism that would be xenophobic in nature, given China's dependence on the Western market and investment for its economic development. PRC leaders had to carefully craft a new identity for China that drew on Chinese people's nationalist feelings yet would not pose a threat to the regime and its policy. Thus, the enactment of a great power (*daguo*) identity seemed to be the most sensible option, as it was consistent with the nationalist reform agenda initiated by Deng Xiaoping in 1978.

I agree with Gilbert Rozman's (1999: 385) assessment that 'the notion of China as a great power ... has gained a clear-cut victory' compared with other contenders in China's quest for national identity in the 1990s. Chih-yu Shih (2005: 755) is also right in observing that greater emphasis was placed by the Chinese leadership on Beijing's relations with other great powers following the CCP's Fifteenth Party Congress in 1997. However, China's great power discourse began well before the mid-1990s, albeit implicitly and often obscured by socialist jargon.

In many ways, forging a great power identity is not a new endeavour in China because the aspirations of building a rich and powerful nation are deeply rooted in the Chinese psyche. To many Chinese elites, the quest for a great power status is a continuation of a lengthy process of modernization (*xiandaihua*) and national salvation (*jiu guo*) that has lasted for over a hundred years. Chinese nationalism emerged as a response to the challenge and threat of foreign powers in the 19th century. Prior to that era the concept of the 'Middle Kingdom' (*Zhongguo*) was largely a cultural one. For thousands of years, China as a political entity was established on the basis of dynasty and culture rather than the nation-state. It was the pre-eminent empire in Asia, and its cultural and political influence extended to most parts of the region. Indeed, the Asian order was essentially a Sino-centric order with China occupying a central role in a hierarchical system (Fitzgerald 1964; Fairbank 1968).

During the 19th century, the very foundation of 'cultural China' was shaken by the technology and military might of Japan and Western powers. As the Chinese empire began to crumble and the Qing Dynasty was incapable of preventing the invasion of China by foreign powers, Chinese elites and intellectuals started to search for ways to save their country. This included the 'Self-strengthening Movement' (1861–95) led by Li Hongzhang, Zeng Guofan and Zhang Zhidong; the 'Hundred Days' Reforms' of 1898 led by Kang Youwei and Liang Qichao; and the 1911 revolution led by Dr Sun Yat-sen that overthrew the Qing Dynasty (Spence 1990: part II). In his research on the late Qing and the early Republican era, Michael Hunt (1993) has demonstrated a clear link between Chinese intellectuals' preoccupation with the creation of a 'strong state' and their construction of an identity for China.

Despite their different strategies, all the reformers and revolutionaries during this period of time tended to follow the Confucian reformer Zhang Zhidong's formulation: Chinese learning for the essence, Western learning for practical use (*Zhongxue weiti, Xixue wei yong*). In other words, Western knowledge, science, technology, ideas and practices were treated as the means to achieve the aim of 'self-strengthening', thus preserving the essence of Chinese civilization. The idea of *ti-yong* was carried forward by Mao and other Chinese communists who sought to apply Marxism-Leninism, which was essentially a Western product, to defeat Western imperialism.[3] They saw Marxist-Leninist ideology as the best guide to ending China's poverty, backwardness and humiliation. In this sense, the communist revolution in China was, in essence, a nationalist revolution.

Indeed, ever since the founding of the PRC, the primary goals of Chinese leaders have been to end the division of China; to defend China's national sovereignty and territorial integrity; and to build an economically, politically and militarily powerful nation. Only a 'prosperous and strong' (*fuqiang*) China, they are convinced, can deter foreign aggression and intervention and regain what they perceive as their country's rightful place in the world. Clearly, Chinese elites were determined to change their negative self-images through self-assertion in order to regain their collective self-esteem (Kaplowitz 1990; Wendt 1999: 236–37).

What Deng Xiaoping sought to do when he returned to power in 1977 after being purged by the radicals was to continue his predecessors' nationalist cause by putting economic reform on top of the political agenda. He decided to shift the CCP's work from 'class struggle' to the 'four modernizations' – the modernization of agriculture, industry, national defence, and science and technology (Goodman

1994; Han Shanbi 1988). As Christopher Hughes (2006) has persuasively argued, nationalism was incorporated by the CCP leadership into the Chinese communist ideology in the 1980s to justify and facilitate the policy of 'reform and opening'. If Chinese nationalism was not noticeable by outside observers prior to the 1989 Tiananmen crackdown, it became highly visible in the 1990s (Li 1997). Chinese intellectuals and academics were actively engaged in an intellectual discourse that explicitly advocated nationalism (Zhao 1997).

Meanwhile, the Chinese government launched a campaign of patriotic (*aiguo*) education in 1991, promoting Chinese history, culture and tradition while stressing the importance of national pride, national unity and territorial integrity. The aim of the campaign was to convince Chinese citizens that the CCP was the true guardian of China's 'national interest' and 'national essence'. This attempt to develop a positive self-identity in order to boost the people's self-esteem can be seen as part of the process of identity construction in an anarchic international system (Mercer 1995: 241). Indeed, Wendt (1999: 236–37) regards 'collective self-esteem' as a significant national interest in addition to physical survival, autonomy, and economic well-being that have been identified by Alexander George and Robert Keohane (1980) as the key national interests. He believes that self-esteem is 'a basic human need of individuals' and is 'one of the things that individuals seek in group membership' (Wendt 1999: 236).

By emphasizing the intention of Western powers to foster a 'peaceful evolution' (*heping yanbian*) in post-Tiananmen China, the PRC government was trying to produce a 'discourse of danger' to underscore the threat emanating from the 'other' to the 'self'. The process of 'othering' can be very effective in asserting the national identity of a state, especially in times of crisis (Campbell 1998). This partly explains why nationalistic sentiments at the societal level have grown tremendously in the past 16 years, with the publication of many popular 'say no' books[4] and nationalistic literature as well as a surge of demonstrations against Japan and the United States. This phenomenon may be described as 'assertive nationalism' which sees 'a negative out-group referent that challenges the in-group's interests and possibly its identity' (Whiting 1995: 295).

Yongnian Zheng (1999) argues that the growth of Chinese nationalism in the 1990s should be interpreted as a response to the changes in China's external environment and its search for a new identity and a 'voice' in the existing inter-national system. However, there is no doubt that the CCP has been exploiting Chinese nationalism to sustain economic growth and preserve social and political stability, thus legitimizing its monopoly of power in China. In his penetrating studies on Chinese nationalism, Suisheng Zhao (2004c, 2005–06) has analyzed various forms of nationalism emerging in China since the early 1990s and has argued that the Beijing government is practising a 'pragmatic nationalism'. This kind of state-sponsored and regulated nationalism arguably provides the political foundation for China to build a great power identity in a period of unprecedented social and economic transformation.

As discussed previously, the state plays an important role in defining and cultivating the national identity of a country. And the PRC government has been playing such a part actively and proactively. Obviously, China does not construct its identity in a geopolitical vacuum. The relationship between China's economic success and its international status was vividly described by Deng Xiaoping (1983: 204) in 1983: 'The role we play in international affairs is determined by the extent of our economic growth. If our country becomes more developed and prosperous, we will be in a position to play a greater role in international affairs.' It is clear that China defines its identity as a great power within an international context and in relation to other great powers in particular.

This conception of national identity is closely related to China's historical legacy. Most Chinese elites are proud of their civilization and historical pre-eminence but also shamed by the 'century of national humiliation' (*bainian guochi*) (Callahan 2004). China faced a traumatic identity crisis during the Qing Dynasty in the 19th century precisely because of the challenge from Japanese and Western powers. Indeed, Chinese modern history has largely been overshadowed by its fluctuating relations with other great powers, whether as a victim, ally, rival or enemy. Throughout the Cold War years, China's foreign policy was seriously constrained by its strategic relations with the two superpowers. In this sense, Chinese discourse of the role of other great powers can be seen as part of its process of identity construction.

As Gilbert Rozman (1999: 384) observes: 'A great power's identity focuses on the country's past, present, and future in international relations, concentrating on its capacity to project power in comparison to other countries with their own ambitions.' China's perceptions of other great powers thus reflect its self-perception. Seen from this angle, the national goals, security intentions, global strategy and regional policy of other great powers are all connected to China's identity formation in that they may assist or hinder its pursuit of a great power status. This form of Chinese identity can be regarded as 'a product of images of the other great powers and the balance among them' (Rozman 1999: 384).

What do PRC leaders and policy elites mean when they refer to China's great power status? Their vision of a 'great power' (*daguo*) in the Chinese context is more accurately described as one of a 'strong power' (*qiangguo*). What this means is that China should possess what they call 'comprehensive national strength' (*zonghe guoli*). In other words, China must have economic and military power comparable to that of other major powers in the world. In addition, it should have significant political influence on global and regional affairs. This great power status should, however, be underpinned by China's ability to command widespread international respect. How others perceive China is taken seriously by Chinese elites in their search for a great power identity. This is consistent with the theoretical perspective of symbolic interactionism on the relationship between self and other in identity construction (Stryker 2002). Recognition is of tremendous importance to the creation of a state's positive self-image, thus enhancing its collective self-esteem (Honneth 1996; Wendt 1999: 236–37). A common perception held by Chinese elites is that the strength of China's great power status should also derive from the profundity, sophistication and 'greatness' of its culture and civilization. The increasing emphasis on the cultural substance of foreign policy in Chinese official and intellectual discourses is in some ways not dissimilar to the notion of 'soft power' (Nye 1990, 2004). Indeed, there has been extensive discussion and debate among Chinese scholars and analysts on the meaning and significance of soft power and its relevance in China's conceptualization and exercise of power.

The hypothesis of this study is that China's perceptions of the major powers in East Asia are closely linked to its desire and endeavour to construct a great power identity. As such, Chinese analysts and scholars view the power, capabilities and security strategies of these countries primarily in terms of their implications for China's pursuit of a great power status in the 21st century. This reflects their perception of the international system which is thought to be dominated mainly by the great powers and shaped by their policies, behaviours and interactions. Drawing on identity theory, the study also argues that Chinese discourse of how other East Asian powers perceive their relations with the PRC and the implications of a rising China contributes significantly to China's identity formation. As Wendt (1999: 327) puts it: '[A]ctors come to see themselves as a reflection of how they think Others see or "appraise" them, in the "mirror" of Others' representations of the Self.'

This study seeks to uncover Chinese security perceptions but it is more accurate and appropriate to consider the investigation as an analysis of discourse. Discourse conveys a much more profound meaning, as it refers not only to the articulation of ideas but a reflection of deliberation and contention. Michel Foucault (1972) considers discourses as part of broader social processes that are closely related to power relations in society. To Foucault, discourses are constantly exploited by different groups of people to fortify, challenge or subvert existing power-knowledge relations.

In this sense, the perceptions of PRC scholars and analysts should be seen as part of the *dialogue* and *debate* in Chinese policy circles on how China should view its own position in relation to other major actors in international society. Indeed, the Chinese perceptions examined in the study reflect contending narratives and interpretations of the 'reality' within officially sanctioned boundaries. Moreover, Chinese policy intellectuals' competing readings of international and security affairs are aimed at influencing official thinking and public opinion on foreign policy issues. Equally significant are Chinese scholars' conscious attempts to produce a distinctive discourse to counteract what they regard as the discourses manufactured and disseminated by Western countries to misrepresent China. All this is directly or indirectly related to the process of China's identity construction.

As to the objectives of this study, it focuses on the following research questions. First, it seeks to establish the content of China's perceptions of the national goals and security strategy of the United States, Japan and Russia since 1989. More specifically, this study examines how Chinese policy elites and security analysts perceive the three East Asian powers' global strategy and Asia-Pacific strategy in particular. The focus of the book is on the analysis of the articulated perceptions of PRC analysts that represent mainstream Chinese thinking on major security issues. However, one has to remember that it has become increasingly difficult to identify the views of analysts that fully reflect the thinking of the central leadership.

This is because scholars and security specialists have been allowed to engage in a more open discussion and even debate on various foreign policy issues in the past decade. This study will therefore take into account any debate among Chinese analysts that can be detected. In addition, the study seeks to investigate if there are any significant changes in China's perceptions of the East Asian powers during the period of time under consideration. If so, what were the main reasons behind such changes? And to what extent were they a result of significant developments in the international environment?

Second, this study attempts to explicate why Chinese analysts perceive other great powers in the way they do. Specifically, how and to what extent PRC analysts' security perceptions are linked to their conception of Chinese national identity? In what ways do these perceptions reflect a conscious/unconscious effort of enacting China's great power identity? To what extent do PRC analysts perceive the aspirations and security strategy of other East Asian powers as a threat to their great power aspirations?

Third, this book seeks to explore how PRC elites and analysts consider the impact of other East Asian powers' national goals and strategies on China. That is, how do the security strategies of these countries affect China's security environment? How should China respond to perceived external challenges or threats to Chinese interests? Does China see any opportunities arising from the policies of other East Asian powers, and how should China take advantage of the perceived opportunities? And lastly, how should China ensure that its aim of attaining a great power status will not be undermined by the security strategies of other major powers? Related to this is the important question of what path China should take in fulfilling its great power aspirations?

To analyze the complexity of Chinese security discourse, this book draws on various paradigms including realism, liberalism, constructivism and postmodernism. It rejects the claim that 'social reality' can be elucidated by one single theoretical perspective, as this parsimonious approach may lead the researchers to ignore certain important aspects of the phenomena they observe. In particular, the study challenges the widespread assumption that Chinese security perceptions can be explained by realism alone. To be sure, the realist emphasis on materialist interests should not be ignored but, as the book shows, institutional and ideational factors are also important in shaping the perceptions of political elites. Indeed, the case for analytical eclecticism has been advocated by a number of scholars of Asian security in recent years (Alagappa 1998: 61; Berger 2000: 411; Katzenstein and Okawara 2001/02; Kim 2004: 51).

Through an empirical and theoretical analysis of China's security discourse on the major powers in East Asia, this book hopes to make a significant contribution to the literature on the perceptual dimension of Chinese foreign policy. In particular, it intends to enhance our knowledge of China's perceptions of and responses to the changing international security environment in the post-Cold War era. More importantly, the study seeks to demonstrate the intricate relationship between Chinese security discourse and the process of national identity formation in China. While it is notoriously difficult to establish a direct link between perceptions and particular policies, a sophisticated understanding of PRC policy elites' security perceptions would hopefully help to make sense of China's current behaviour and possibly predict its future intentions. In this sense, the book seeks to achieve a broader aim of advancing the academic and policy debate on the security implications of the rise of China.

Research methods and methodology

There is no doubt that it has become much easier to obtain primary sources and data on most research topics on China in the past two decades. But scholars of contemporary China, especially Chinese foreign and security policy, still face considerable challenge in identifying and collecting materials that are directly related to their projects. The problem today is not just whether one can have access to the relevant sources but how to handle the proliferation of various types of data emerging from China. Before we embark on our research, a number of methodological issues need to be addressed. As this is essentially a study of perceptions, we must be absolutely clear about whose perceptions we are dealing with when referring to 'China'. More importantly, the main sources of information upon which our work is based have to be selected carefully and appropriately in order to obtain the most relevant data to test the hypothesis of this book.

Another question that needs to be considered is how authoritative or representative the selected sources are in reflecting mainstream Chinese thinking or the perceptions of PRC leaders and policy-makers. That is, to what extent do the articulated perceptions presented in the study mirror official Chinese security thinking on the major powers in East Asia? To what extent do they reflect the thoughts and opinions of the international relations experts and security analysts within the intellectual and academic community and policy circles in the PRC?

Ideally, one would like to be able to interview the political leaders and government officials who are responsible for foreign policy making in China but few Western scholars have been granted such high-level access to official thinking. This leaves us with two other channels through which information on Chinese security perceptions may be obtained, that is, documentary research and interviews with people who are close to the policy-making institutions.

This study is based primarily on documentary research with extensive use of primary sources in the Chinese language. It has adopted a qualitative approach to the collection and analysis of the data, which is considered as more appropriate for the project. Quantitative research is rooted in the positivist tradition which presupposes the existence of an objective world and the possibility of discovering 'truth' through 'scientific' enquiry (Hughes and Sharrock 1997). A quantitative content analysis of the relevant Chinese sources may well reveal the number of times a particular word or phrase has appeared in a publication and the number of times articles on certain themes have been published in specific journals. While quantitative data may generate some interesting information relating to the topic, it would not yield any significant results in terms of uncovering the factors or forces that shape Chinese security discourse.

To find out why certain themes are prominent and why certain countries and security issues are perceived by Chinese policy elites in particular ways, we need to interpret the meaning and significance of the contents of the publications under consideration. This type of qualitative research is underpinned by the philosophical thinking of interpretivism which is better equipped for 'culturally derived and historically situated interpretations of the social life-world' (Crotty 1998: 67). Perception is essentially about imagery, emotion and sentiment, aspects that are not quantifiable and easily measured. It has to be dissected within specific cultural, historical and political contexts through qualitative analysis.

Most of the publications consulted are published materials, although they are produced mainly for domestic audiences. To a large extent the data can be verified and the research may be replicated by others, thus enhancing the reliability of the research. However, it could be argued that a research project that relies entirely on one single method is not sufficiently valid (Flick 1998). This potential methodological problem may be rectified through triangulation, which allows a combination of research methods in order to improve the validity and reliability of the project (Denzin 1989). Specifically, the data collected from documentary research may be compared with information obtained through interviews. However, very few, if any, Chinese scholars would agree to give interviews to foreign researchers with the knowledge that the views they express would be attributed to them. This is understandable given the nature of the political environment in the PRC and the sensitivity of the topics concerned. Inevitably, interviews with PRC foreign policy analysts would have to be carried out in an informal and off-the-record basis. If these specialists are close to the government, their views can be extremely significant and invaluable to the researcher.

Therefore, in addition to documentary research, information that has been gathered through private conversations and public discussions with Chinese scholars and think-tanks specialists will be used for this research. Over the past decade and a half, I have had many opportunities to meet with a broad range of PRC international relations analysts in China and the United Kingdom through research trips, exchange visits, academic conferences and track-II meetings. They include scholars from various Chinese universities and research institutions including China Institute of International Studies, China Institute of Contemporary International Relations, the CASS Institute of American Studies, Institute of Japanese Studies, Institute of Russian, Central Asian and East European Studies, Institute of Asia-Pacific Studies, Institute of World Economy and Politics, and Institute of Political Science. I have met with some of these analysts more than once and in some cases several times both in China and the UK. For obvious reasons, their names are not listed here and their views and arguments will not be quoted directly unless they have appeared in open-source journals or books in the public domain. The formal and informal discussion with these scholars has enabled me to gain a much better understanding of the rapidly changing environment in China and Chinese perceptions on a wide range of security issues in particular. Some scholars have kindly provided me with valuable research material, others have assisted me in gathering information that I would not have otherwise been able to discover.

Let us now turn to the documentary sources that have been collected and consulted for this study. During the past 20 years, numerous scholarly and policy-oriented journals have been published in the PRC but very few of them have any real impact on the making of Chinese foreign policy. The articles in most open-source journals either repeat or elaborate the official position on international affairs or provide a theoretical justification for PRC policies on specific issues. This is not to say that Chinese scholars have no interests in scholarly debates and academic enquiries. But they are constrained by their political environment and do not wish to take personal risks by expressing independent opinions on sensitive issues. However, it should be pointed out that Chinese scholars and policy analysts have been able to present their own views and engage in limited debates in certain journals and forums since the mid-1990s. As Bonnie Glaser and Evan Medeiros (2007: 307) observe, 'there is a greater tolerance for a multiplicity of competing views on foreign policy topics and occasionally a willingness to re-evaluate government policy based on expert criticism and/or recommendations'.

The selection of journals for consideration in this study is based largely on the institutional affiliation of Chinese specialists. Specifically, the study will review the writings of Chinese analysts and security experts whose views are likely to attract the attention of Chinese leaders and senior government officials. In other words, only the journals published by the research institutes that are considered to have substantial input into China's foreign policy and/or significant impact on the security debates in the PRC will be examined systematically. Indeed, the growing significance of China's research institutes in its foreign policy-making process is recognized by many Western scholars (Glaser and Saunders 2002; Lu 1997: 130–36; Shambaugh 1991: 5–14).

The most important journal considered by this study is *Guoji wenti yanjiu* (Journal of International Studies), which is published by the China Institute of International Studies (CIIS), the think-tank of the Ministry of Foreign Affairs (MFA). The CIIS is headed typically by former senior Chinese diplomats such as Ambassadors Yang Chengxu and Song Minjiang. CIIS is now the full counterpart to the Royal Institute of International Affairs (UK) and other international affairs research institutes attached to foreign ministries in other countries. While most projects are generated by the institute's research sections themselves, some are commissioned by the MFA. Their studies are normally classified and consulted by MFA officials and Chinese leaders only. Many CIIS researchers are recruited from Chinese universities who have PhD degree and/or research experience abroad (Shambaugh 2002b: 584). The merger of CIIS and the State Council's former Centre for International Studies in 1998 means that the quality of the institute has been further strengthened. Because of CIIS's official link, articles published in the Journal of International Studies enjoy a semi-official status and are taken seriously by foreign diplomats and observers. Indeed, CIIS staff are regularly invited to present their views on specific issues and the outcomes of the meetings will be sent to high-ranking officials in the MFA and other relevant departments. MFA officials also attend conferences organized by CIIS researchers where views are exchanged on key international or regional issues. The MFA is generally regarded by the top leadership as the most professional and reliable information provider, especially in the past 10 years. 'The MFA's policy recommendations and opinions', as one scholar puts it, 'in a majority of cases prevail over those of other bureaucratic institutions in the battles for the hearts and minds of the central leadership' (Lu 1997: 117).

Another journal examined in this article is *Xiandai guoji guanxi* (Contemporary International Relations), a publication of the China Institute of Contemporary International Relations (CICIR), which has a research staff of over 400. From 1965, when CICIR was founded, to 1982, the institute was under the Central Committee of the CCP. From 1982 to 1999 the CICIR was transferred to the State Council but under the authority of the Ministry of State Security. In 1999 it was transferred back to the Foreign Affairs Office under the Central Committee. Some scholars believe that the bureaucratic influence of CICIR has declined since the mid-1990s (Shambaugh 2002b: 582–83), while others argue that the institute's research has little influence on MFA officials (Lu 1997: 133–34). Given its close connections with the party leadership, the CICIR has always been the main intelligence research organization in China and its impact on the central leadership should not be underestimated. Indeed, the CICIR has the specific responsibility of producing brief intelligence reports on major international events for Chinese leaders on a daily basis. As the intelligence reports prepared by the institute are for the consumption of senior party and government officials, they are normally restricted to internal circulation. However, some CICIR studies are published in Contemporary International Relations. Thus, the articles that appear in the journal are of particular relevance to this study.

The third major journal consulted is *Meiguo yanjiu* (American Studies) which is published by the Institute of American Studies (IAS) at CASS. Historically, the IAS has a close connection with senior Chinese leaders such as Zhou Enlai. Its former directors Li Shenzhi, Zi Zhongyun and Wang Jisi are all recognized experts on various aspects of American studies. Wang Jisi, for example, is now the Director of International Strategic Studies at the CCP's Central Party School and Dean of the School of International Studies at Peking University. Over the years, the institute has produced some very high quality research and thus enjoyed a good reputation among scholars as well as Chinese leaders and officials. Prominent members of the IAS have often been consulted by the Chinese government on issues relating to American foreign policy and Sino-US relations. They have also contributed articles to American Studies and leading journals on international affairs.

The fourth major journal consulted is *Riben xuekan* (Journal of Japanese Studies), which is published by the Institute of Japanese Studies (IJS) at CASS. Established in 1981 the IJS is probably the largest centre of Japanese studies in China, and has employed some of the most perceptive analysts on Japan's foreign relations and security strategy in the country. In addition, the institute is in regular contacts with scholars and research institutions in Japan, and has organized numerous high-profile international conferences on Japan's economy, society, politics and foreign policy. Indeed, the expertise of senior researchers on Japanese foreign policy and China-Japan relations is well known and the quality of their research is recognized by government officials. Their publications have appeared in the Journal of Japanese Studies and other prominent foreign affairs journals.

The last major journal examined is *Eluosi Zhongya Dongou Yanjiu* (Journal of Russian, Central Asian and East European Studies), which is published by the Institute of Russian, Central Asian and East European Studies (IRCAEES) at CASS. IRCAEES is the largest and most influential Chinese institute on the domestic politics and foreign relations of Russia, East European and Central Asian countries. It has long-standing interest and expertise in the study of the former Soviet Union and Eastern Europe. Following the collapse of communism in the region, the institute quickly adapted to the new international environment, refocusing and expanding its research to include Central Asia. IRCAEES employs some of the best researchers on Russian and East European affairs in China. It has extensive exchange programmes with scholars in Russia and Eastern Europe as well as the United States and EU countries. Some of the institute's staff such as Li Jingjie are well known by Western scholars and have published their work in the West. Not surprisingly, senior members of IRCAEES have regularly participated in track-II activities and are consulted by government officials. As such, articles published in the Journal of Russian, Central Asian and East European Studies are particularly useful for this study.

In addition to the five main publications, articles written by established experts on international security, East Asian affairs and the foreign policies of America, Japan and Russia in other respected journals have been taken into account. They include *Yatai yanjiu* (Asia-Pacific Studies), *Dangdai Yatai* (Contemporary Asia-Pacific), *Taipingyang xuebao* (Pacific Journal), *Taiwan yanjiu* (Taiwan Studies), *Taiwan yanjiu jikan* (Taiwan Research Quarterly), *Shijie jingji yu zhengzhi* (World Economy and Politics), *Zhanlue yu guanli* (Strategy and Management), *Guoji guanxi xueyuan xuebao* (Journal of the Institute of International Relations), *Waiguo wenti yanjiu* (Research on Foreign Issues), *Ouzhou* (Europe), *Ouzhou yanjiu* (European Studies), *Dongbeiya luntan* (Northeast Asia Forum), *Guoji guancha* (International Observation), *Heping yu fazhan* (Peace and Development), *Guoji jingji pinglun* (International Economic Review) and other publications. Moreover, some edited volumes and monographs which have had a considerable impact on the policy debates in China or on the discourse of Chinese international relations specialists have also been cited.

Taken together, the perceptions articulated by Chinese analysts in the above-mentioned publications can be said to reflect mainstream Chinese security thinking on the major powers in East Asia.[5] The value of the materials under consideration lies in their authors' unique positions in China's foreign policy-making process. Most of them are respected scholars and analysts of international and security affairs. Owing to their expertise, specialists in the China Institute of International Studies, the China Institute of Contemporary International Relations, the Institute of American Studies, the Institute of Japanese Studies, the Institute of Russian, Central Asian and East European Studies, and other research institutions and universities are frequently called upon to advise foreign policy-makers in Beijing, whilst their writings are consulted by senior party and state officials.

Among the numerous Chinese scholars and analysts cited in this study are Lu Zhongwei, Fu Mengzi, Liu Guiling, Zhang Wenmu, Yang Mingjie, Yang Wenjing and Sun Ru of the China Institute of Contemporary International Relations, Ma Zhengang, Ruan Zhongze, Song Yimin, Su Ge, Yuan Jian, Wang Haihan, Zhang Dalin, Lu Guozhong and Su Hao of the China Institute of International Studies, Wang Yizhou of the Institute of World Economy and Politics, Zi Zhongyun, Niu Jun and Tao Wenzhou of the Institute of American Studies, Feng Zhaokui, He Fang, Jin Xide, Liu Shilong, Ding Yingshun and Zhang Jinshan of the Institute of Japanese Studies, Zhang Yunling and Tang Shiping of the Institute of Asia-Pacific Studies, Li Jingjie, Xu Kui, Xu Zhixin and Li Yonghui of the Institute of Russian, Central Asian and East European Studies.

Other specialists whose articles have appeared in the journals consulted for this study include Liu Jianfei, Men Honghua and Li Zhongjie of the Central Party School, Yan Xuetong, Liu Jiangyong, Chu Shulong, Xue Li and Qiao Mu of Qinghua University, Wang Jisi, Jia Qingguo, Yuan Ming, Zhu Feng, Ye Zicheng, Liu Jinzhi, Ning Sao and Liang Gencheng of Peking University, Li Jingzhi, Pang Zhongying and Shi Yinhong of Renmin University, Wu Xinbo, Pan Zhongqi and Wang Gonglong at Fudan University, Xia Liping, Yang Jiemian, Wu Jinan, Zhang Tiejun and Jiang Xiyuan of the Shanghai Institute of International Studies, and Wang Hongfang, Zhu Zinchang and Shi Xiaojie of the Nanjing Institute of International Relations.

Some observers believe that the role of Chinese scholars and policy analysts in China's foreign policy-making process has been somewhat exaggerated (Yu 1994: 252–56). This view is challenged by others who argue that the policy influence of China's research institutes has increased over the years (David Shambaugh 2002b). Even those who are sceptical of the influence of research institutes on China's foreign policy decisions agree that 'individual scholars from these institutes with well established reputations for their expertise in some specific fields of study may have a greater impact on foreign policy decision-makers depending on their individual access to the leadership' (Lu 1997: 135).

Since the late 1990s, the avenues through which Chinese scholars and think-tank specialists may exert their influence on foreign policy-making have expanded considerably (Glaser and Medeiros 2007; Wang Yizhou 2007). For example, a Centre for the Study of Sino-US Relations (ZhongMei Guanxi Yanjiu Zhongxin) was established in December 2006. This new research centre is led by the CIIS which has brought together over 40 renowned scholars and experts from a range of universities and think-tanks in Beijing and Shanghai. The five senior advisors of the centre are all former ambassadors and diplomats who have worked in the US and Canada.

Indeed, the growing interest in the study of international relations has led to a rapid development of the international relations discipline in China (Breslin 2007: Ch. 1; Chan 1999; Li Wei 2007; Wang Yizhou 2004, 2006; Zi Zhongyun 1998). Many Chinese scholars are familiar with the concepts and arguments of their Western colleagues and frequently visit foreign universities and research institutes. It is not uncommon to see Chinese academics citing the latest Western publications in their work. Some journals, such as *Shijie jingji yu zhengzhi* and *Ouzhou yanjiu*, regularly publish theoretical articles that take into account theoretical debates in the IR community in America and Europe.

In the past decade, major universities have produced a large number of graduates with advanced degrees who are subsequently recruited into various think-tanks. At the same time, some prominent university professors have played an active role in offering advice to Chinese policy-makers. Their regular participation in policy-oriented seminars, preparation for commissioned reports for government departments and other activities have increased their profile and influence on the making of China's foreign policy. In addition, these professors frequently lecture at other universities and institutions and contribute to public discussion on major international issues via their commentary on television and in newspapers. Their views are therefore significant in shaping the direction of policy debates and possibly public opinion on major security issues in China.

Organization of the book

The book is organized around seven chapters. This chapter is followed by two chapters on China's security discourse of the United States, focusing on the George Bush Snr and Bill Clinton presidencies and the George W. Bush administration, respectively. The fourth chapter analyzes China's perceptions of Japan's global and regional security strategies. In the fifth chapter, it looks at the views of China's security specialists on Russia. This is followed by a detailed analysis of China's response to the security challenge of the three East Asian powers in relation to its efforts to construct a great power identity. The concluding chapter summarizes the key findings of this study, highlights its contributions to the existing literature and knowledge, and considers how this study will contribute to the on-going academic and policy debate on the nature and implications of an ascendant China.

2 Hegemonic aspirations in a unipolar world

US security strategy under the George Bush Snr and Bill Clinton presidencies

Of all the major powers in East Asia, the United States is the most powerful country and its security strategy is seen to have the greatest impact on China. As such, the security perceptions of Chinese scholars and analysts on the US deserve special attention. Chapters two and three are devoted to the analysis of Chinese security perceptions of America, with this chapter focusing specifically on the presidencies of George Bush Snr and Bill Clinton. The chapter begins by looking at how China perceives Bush's strategic thinking with particular reference to the end of the Cold War and the collapse of the bipolar international system. It then moves on to analyze Chinese views of Clinton's global strategy and how Chinese scholars see the strategic significance of Europe and the Asia-Pacific, respectively, in American security policy. The security issues in East Asia that concern Chinese elites the most are US-Japan security alliance and US-Taiwan relations. The views of Chinese elites on these two issues in relation to the challenge of a rising China are thus examined in detail. Finally, Chinese security discourse of the US is analyzed from various perspectives of International Relations theories, including realism, liberalism, constructivism and postmodernism.

The end of bipolarity and Bush's 'new world order'

With the termination of the Cold War in 1989, the bipolar structure (*liangji geju*) came to an end. This forced all the major powers to reconsider their positions in the international system. In China's view, the old international structure had disintegrated but a new one was yet to take shape. During this transitional period, there would be turbulences and uncertainties throughout the world. Unlike the two changes in the world structure during the 20th century, it would take a fairly long time for a new multipolar structure (*duoji geju*) to evolve (Chen Qimao 1990; Zhou Jirong 1991; Zhao Guilin 1991; Du Gong 1992; Xie Yixian 1993: 232–37). The reason for this was that the previous changes were basically determined by the great powers through a series of international conferences and various treaties following their victories in the two World Wars. For the defeated countries, there was no choice but to accept their positions within the new systems created by the winning powers. Thus, the processes of the structural changes were relatively brief and straightforward. The post-Cold War international structure, Chinese analysts believe, would be shaped by the strategic choice of the major powers as well as the dynamics of their domestic development, which could be a lengthy process. But they argue that no one single state is capable of dominating the international system and that the world is moving towards multipolarity (*duojihua*).[1]

Reluctant to accept the multipolar trend in world politics, the Chinese argue that American leaders made a strategic decision to shape the structure of the post-Cold War international system. Specifically, Washington was determined to establish a US-dominated unipolar world structure (*danji shijie geju*) in the late 1980s and early 1990s. Two major developments in world politics in the immediate post-Cold War era are believed to have had a significant impact on American strategic thinking. The first was the revolution in Eastern Europe in 1989 which was followed by the break-up of the Soviet Union two years later (Song Yimin 1992; Ye Ruan 1992: 300–01; Pan Shiying 1993: 35–36). To the Americans, the collapse of the regimes in the communist bloc represented a Western triumph in the ideological struggle between capitalism and communism which had lasted for over 40 years. It demonstrated the bankruptcy of the communist system and the strength of capitalist values. In this sense, the US claimed that it had won the Cold War. As Russia was no longer in a position to engage in a global rivalry with the United States, America became the sole superpower in the international system. George Bush Snr, the former US President, was quoted to have said: 'We were the leader of the West, we have now become the leader of the world' (Li Dongyan 1996: 55).

The second event that encouraged Washington to build a unipolar world structure was the swift American victory in the Gulf War in 1991 (Xue Mouhong 1992; Ye Ruan 1992: 301–02; Pan Shiying 1993: 35–36; Li Dongyan 1996: 55, 60–61). The Gulf crisis provided the US with an excellent opportunity to prove its military superiority and its capability of leading the world. Although the United Nations (UN) military operation was financed principally by Japan, Germany, Saudi Arabia, Kuwait and other countries, Chinese analysts point out, the Americans believed that the rapid defeat of Saddam Hussein indicated unambiguously that the US was the only country which had the political, economic and military strength to lead the entire world. Without American leadership, the UN would not have taken such a decisive action to end the Iraqi occupation of Kuwait. Indeed, it was the Gulf War that helped elevate America's status and reputation in the international community.[2] This in turn enhanced President Bush's confidence in putting forward his idea of building a 'new world order' (*shijie xinzhixu*), which laid the foundation of US global strategy (*quanqiu zhanlue*) in the post-Cold War era (Pan Tongwen 1992; Yin Chunling 1992: 282–85; Mao Desong 1993: 428–31).

In the eyes of the Chinese, the United States has had the hegemonic ambition (*baquan yexin*) of dominating the world ever since the end of World War II. But it was unable to fulfil its aspirations due to the enormous challenge from the Soviet Union. The collapse of bipolarity has strengthened America's volition to play a leading role in world politics. Taking advantage of the historically unique situation, the Bush administration advocated a world order that was said to reflect American values and serve American interests. Behind the rhetoric of the 'new world order', the US merely sought to advance its national interests. According to Chinese analysts, there were several key elements in America's global strategy during the Bush presidency. First, the US actively promoted Western/American values like 'freedom', 'private ownership', 'market economy', 'parliamentary democracy' and 'multi-party politics' as universal values throughout the world. Second, America was portrayed as the best qualified leader of the free world, which could not be replaced by any other countries. Third, to provide effective leadership, the US would need the support and co-operation of its friends and allies who would be expected to share Washington's global duties and responsibilities. In the meantime, America attempted to obtain the support of other great powers, such as Russia and China, in dealing with international issues. Fourth, the UN and other international organizations were utilized to legitimize American actions. Finally, American leaders would take any necessary measures to prevent regional conflict from threatening global peace and stability which might disrupt the US-sponsored 'new world order' (Ye Ruan 1992: 302–06; Mao Desong 1993: 429–30).

To realize its ambition of dominating the post-Cold War world, Chinese scholars and analysts note, the Bush administration assisted the former Soviet Union and East European countries in establishing Western capitalist political systems and reforming their command economies. It also tried to influence the internal development of the remaining communist countries via both overt and covert means. In addition, to fortify its leadership position within the Western alliance, America strove to establish a strategic partnership with West European countries, and with Germany in particular. The essence of the US strategy of 'new Atlanticism' (*xin Daxiyangzhuyi*), it is argued, was to play a leading role in European affairs (Wang Houkang and Jin Yingzhong 1992: Ch. 11). For example, the US supported the reunification of Germany after the collapse of the Berlin Wall and ensured that the reunified Germany remained in the North Atlantic Treaty Organization (NATO). In Asia, America promised to develop a 'partnership of global leadership' (*quanqiu lingdao huoban*) with Japan, which attracted enthusiastic responses from Japanese politicians. This move, Chinese analysts say, was designed to entice Japanese support for continued American presence in the region on the one hand, and to restrain Tokyo's ambition which might be detrimental to US interests on the other. In North, Central and South Americas, the aim of the US was to establish a free trade area (*ziyou maoyiqu*) and thus enhance America's competitiveness in its economic rivalry with Europe and Japan (Wang Jisi 1992: 9; Feng Tejun 1993: 326–29; Wang Fengwu and Xing Aifen 1993: 133–37; Ren Zhengde and Wu Jianxin 1993: 380–81; Li Dongyan 1996: 56–62). Indeed, American leaders were said to be concerned about growing Japanese and European challenges to US economic pre-eminence (Zhou Jirong 1991: 6; Ha Mei 1991: 13).

The Chinese argue that while the Bush administration realized that it was impossible to continue to be the 'world police' (*shijie jingcha*), it wished to play the role of a 'world judge' (*shijie faguan*) and a 'balancer' (*pinghengzhe*) between various forces in regional politics. In Europe, America saw Germany as a major ally, but it did not support the rise of Germany as an independent force in Europe due to the apprehensions of other European countries. Similarly, Washington sought to maintain a balance in Asia between Japan and other Asian states who were suspicious of a possible resurgence of Japanese militarism. In the Middle East, America continued to play the role of a mediator between Israel and Arab countries due to the importance of the region to US economic and strategic interests (Wang Jisi 1992: 9; Yao Wang *et al.* 1992: 9–10; Wang Yide 1993: 130).

Another important dimension of US global strategy under President Bush, according to Chinese scholars and analysts, was to exploit the UN and other international organizations in seeking legal justifications and political support for American policies and actions. Through various international mechanisms, Washington attempted to lay down the 'rules of the game' in the spheres of political, economic, military and scientific competition. The Chinese argue that the rules and regulations advocated by Washington in these multilateral forums tended to be favourable to the United States. For example, in the Uruguay Round of the General Agreement on Tariffs and Trade (GATT) negotiations, America urged the removal of trade restrictions over agricultural products and the protection of intellectual property. At the Group of Seven (G7) and APEC meetings, America was strongly opposed to the creation of regional trading blocs that would exclude or discriminate against outsiders. America also used its power in the IMF and World Bank to insist on the introduction of Western-styled economic reform as a pre-condition for loans and economic assistance to developing nations, aimed at undermining their command economies and state-owned enterprises. The main objective behind all these proposals, according to the Chinese, was to promote Western democracy through liberal free trade and the market economy, as global 'economic liberalization' (*jingji ziyouhua*) and 'political democratization' (*zhengzhi minzhuhua*) were regarded by the Bush administration as the best way of eliminating potential threats to American security and enhancing US global interests (Ha Mei 1991: 14; Wang Jisi 1992: 9; Wang Yide 1993: 130).

US global strategy under the Clinton administration

Despite the election of Bill Clinton as the new president of the United States in 1992, Chinese analysts believe that America's desire to build a unipolar world structure remained unchanged. Although President Clinton rarely referred to the 'new world order', he stressed on many occasions the importance of the US continuing to play a leadership role in the post-Cold War world. In this sense, the Chinese note, there was no real difference between Bush and Clinton in terms of their strategic aim (*zhanlue mubiao*), that is, to maintain the US hegemonic position (*baquan diwei*) in the international system (Li Dongyan 1996: 62–74).

Clinton's emphasis on the restoration of America's domestic capability through the strengthening of its economic power was noted by Chinese analysts. He claimed that economic issues had been ignored by his predecessors for too long and that America would not be able to lead the world into the 21st century without a sound economy (Huang Hong 1993: 31; Qian Chunyuan, Lu Qichang and Tao Jian 1993: 20–22).

Chinese scholars and analysts point out that to avert American decline as a result of what Paul Kennedy (1988) called 'imperial overstretch', Clinton substantially curtailed America's overseas commitments, including the reduction of US military presence in foreign countries and a huge cut in overseas aid. As overseas aid had always been a significant aspect of Washington's foreign policy since the introduction of the Marshall Plan in 1947, its contraction represented a major adjustment in American policy. Moreover, America became more cautious and selective in its policy of intervention, avoiding getting embroiled in regional or international conflict on its own. Instead, the US sought to encourage collective actions in dealing with crises through the UN and other security mechanisms. This policy adjustment was clearly illustrated by its limited involvement in the crises in Somalia and Bosnia-Herzegovina. Furthermore, Clinton made a great effort to revitalize the American economy, reform the health system and tackle crime and other social problems. This is, however, not to say that Clinton had given up America's self-proclaimed role of world leader or that the US had returned to isolationism. The emphasis on domestic development, according to the Chinese, was merely seen as a more effective strategy of achieving American hegemonic ambition.

During the early phase of the Clinton administration, it is argued, economic security (*jingji anquan*) was put at the top of the US foreign policy agenda (Ke Juhan, Tao Jian and Gu Wenyan 1993a: 3, 1993b: 9; Jin Junhui 1994: 1). Specifically, the American government reduced its military expenditures, scaled down its overseas security commitments, and channelled some of its resources from the military sector to the domestic economy and hi-tech research. Through these measures Clinton hoped to solve America's economic problems and enhance its competitiveness in the global economy. In addition, Chinese analysts note that the Clinton administration proposed that diplomacy, intelligence activities and scientific research should be exploited to serve American economic interests. Thus, more officials were deployed in overseas countries to assist American companies in their business operation, more diplomats were involved in the gathering of economic and market intelligence, and the intelligence services, research institutes and universities were all encouraged to collect and analyze foreign economic information. According to Chinese analysts, the Clinton administration became more assertive in promoting and defending America's economic interests. While Washington did not advocate trade protectionism, it insisted that other countries must open up their domestic markets to America. Indeed, the US adopted a tough stance in trade negotiations with its trading partners, including Japan and European nations. Clinton's economic strategy, Chinese analysts contend, was to use American economic power to dominate the world economy and to support US diplomatic and military activities with the ultimate objective of leading the post-Cold War world (Xu Heming and Wang Haihan 1997: 29).

Indeed, the Chinese observe that there were three main pillars of President Clinton's foreign policy, the most important of which was economic security. The second was to preserve robust American armed forces to protect US security interests and safeguard international peace, while the third was to encourage and spread democratic principles and systems throughout the globe. Economic growth, military power and support for democratization were viewed as inseparable parts of American strategy in the post-Cold War era. Thus, a strong and vibrant economy would enable the US to assume its global responsibilities and sustain a powerful military force without sacrificing America's domestic needs. In the meantime, the emergence of more democratic regimes in the world would hopefully lower the possibility of conflict and provide more trade and investment opportunities for the Americans. In short, America was seeking to play a leading role in uniting the community of liberal democratic nations, backing countries that were in the process of advancing marketization and liberalization, and opposing any countries that attempted to disrupt the US-led international peace and security. Clinton's global strategy was characterized by Anthony Lake, his National Security Advisor, as 'the strategy of enlargement' (*kuozhan zhanlue*) which, the Chinese assert, reflected America's intention of maintaining its hegemonic position and building a unipolar world (Qian Chunyuan, Lu Qichang and Tao Jian 1993: 20; Li Dongyan 1996: 70–72). In 1994, this strategy was further developed into a 'strategy of engagement and enlargement' (*canyu he kuozhan zhanlue*) which underscored the Clinton administration's desire to expand US interests and values through active engagement in international affairs. To the Chinese, the strategy was designed to ensure the leading role (*zhudao diwei*) of the United States in global affairs (Yang Jiemian 2000: 25).

From 1994 onwards, Chinese analysts noticed a significant adjustment in US global strategy. The change, they argued, was due mainly to the sustained economic growth in the United States. As Europe and Japan were no longer perceived as a major challenge to the US economy, the economic tensions between them abated accordingly. At the same time, Washington began to make a greater effort to strengthen its alliance relations with both Japan and European countries. This, according to the Chinese, reflected a growing emphasis on military security in US global strategy. More attention was said to be paid to traditional geopolitical thinking. While Europe remained a strategic focus for America, Chinese analysts maintained that Asia's strategic importance was increasingly appreciated by US leaders (Xiao Feng 1999: 1). Given that America's key allies and rivals were all located in Europe and Asia, it was necessary for Washington to consider the roles of the two areas in the US global strategy simultaneously (Xiao Feng 1999: 1). This was characterized by the Chinese as 'paying equal attention to Europe and Asia' (*OuYa bingzhong*).

Chinese analysts point out that the term Eurasia (*OuYa dalu*) had been used frequently by US officials in the 1990s (Song Yimin 2000: 17). The idea behind this was to establish a multi-level security network in Europe and Asia, with the US playing a central role. The network in Europe would be led by America and would include the 19 NATO countries as core members, plus 23 other countries that had joined the Partnership for Peace. In Asia, the core of the network would be built around the US-Japan security alliance and the bilateral alliances between the US and South Korea, Thailand, the Philippines and Australia, respectively. ASEAN states and possibly India could also become part of this network. Chinese analysts suspect that America had clear targets in mind when designing the security network. In Europe, the US government sought to prevent Russia from posing any major challenge to the US while keeping an eye on France and Germany as future rivals. In Asia, the US saw China as a potential threat to US security interests. Although the security network would not necessarily exclude interactions and engagement with China, the Chinese believe that the Clinton administration intended to constrain the PRC via the new US-Japan defence guidelines and the proposed development of a Theatre Missile Defence (TMD) system that would include Taiwan (Yang Jiemian 2000: 25).

In the view of many Chinese policy elites, the ultimate aim of the US global strategy was to prevent the emergence of any countries or regions that would be stronger than America economically, politically and militarily, thus threatening its perceived security interests. This aim was said to be clearly conceptualized in the 1997 *National Security Strategy* (NSS) (US Department of State 1997). The document outlined three main elements of America's national security strategy. The first was to actively shape the international environment in ways to promote and protect US security interests. This could be achieved through promoting regional stability, preventing and reducing conflicts and threats, and deterring aggression and coercion in major regions of the world. The second was to develop the capabilities of responding to a variety of crises swiftly and effectively. The final element of the strategy was to prepare for the security challenges of an uncertain and unpredictable future.

Indeed, American leaders identified various types of existent threats to their country, including regional conflicts, proliferation of weapons of mass destruction (WMD), transnational organized crime, possible attacks from terrorists and the 'rogue' states and so on. Russia and China might emerge as America's global rivals after 2015, thus posing a potential threat to the US. The Clinton administration's response to the diversity of threats, according to Chinese analysis, involved the use of economic, political, diplomatic and military means to safeguard American interests. Nevertheless, special emphasis seemed to be placed on military capabilities and the US military strategy was adjusted several times in the Clinton era, say the Chinese. In particular, a military strategy based on the NSS was published in the Quadrennial Defense Review Report in May 1997 (US Department of Defense 1997). This strategy, Chinese analysts observe, was designed to support the government in shaping a favourable international environment in times of peace and responding to any major crises that might develop. In times of war, US forces would be equipped to deal with conflicts and fight and win major wars. This strategy was thought to prepare America's military for both current needs and future requirements, thus ensuring its overwhelming superiority and leading position in different types of situations. In order to fulfil these aspirations, the Chinese note, the Clinton administration ended the cutback in military expenditure from 1999. Instead, US military spending increased from US$276.7 billion in 1999 to US$288.9 billion in 2000 and US$309.9 billion in 2001 (Sa Benwang and Shang Hong 2001).

To achieve absolute security and superiority as well as offensive and defensive capabilities, Chinese scholars assert, the Clinton administration formally proposed the plan of developing a National Missile Defence (NMD) system in January 1999, which was authorized by Congress in March. In the meantime, the US government was said to have stepped up the eastward expansion of NATO and strengthened America's military ties with its five Asian allies, especially with Japan. In addition to this, the US actively promoted bilateral and multilateral military cooperation with ASEAN states, Mongolia and many countries in Central and South Asia (Sa Benwang and Shang Hong 2001). Chinese scholars and analysts believe that the global strategy of the Clinton administration reflected America's ambition of maintaining its unipolar position in the international system. This strategy, in their view, had a strong offensive and expansionist tendency and its key elements would be likely to have a considerable impact on the strategic thinking and policy of the new administration in the early 21st century.

The significance of Europe in America's global strategy

The importance of Europe to US global strategy has attracted much attention from Chinese scholars and analysts. For over 40 years, American presence in Europe was conspicuous in terms of providing a security guarantee and a nuclear umbrella for West European countries that were concerned about the Soviet threat. After the break-up of the Soviet Union, the Chinese suggest, America's role as a defender of European security has been substantially weakened. In the absence of a common enemy, the tensions and disputes within the Western alliance could re-emerge or intensify. More significantly, the rise of a united, wealthy and powerful Germany could present an immense challenge to the United States (Wang Houkang and Jin Yingzhong 1992: 125–26; Wang Zhenhua 1996: 60–61).

However, the US is believed to be determined to fortify its hegemonic position in the new Europe through the reform and expansion of NATO. Specifically, Washington sought to continue to play a leading role in European security matters while reducing its military presence in the region. In America's view, although there still existed some ethnic conflicts and unresolved disputes in Europe, they were unlikely to turn into major wars and endanger US strategic interests. Thus, the number of American troops stationed in Europe decreased from 326,000 in the early 1990s to 100,000 by the end of the decade. In addition, some American military bases and facilities were removed from European territories. This strategy of 'Europeanization of NATO' (*Beiyue Ouzhouhua*), say Chinese analysts, was designed to maintain America's control over the Western alliance while sharing the burdens and responsibilities for the defence of Europe more equally with European countries. Given its domestic economic difficulties, the US was no longer in a position to sustain a high level of military spending in Europe (Hu Jie 1990: 15–17; Wang Naicheng 1995: 47; Zhou Rongyao 1995: 50).

During his visit to Germany in July 1994, President Clinton emphasised the growing importance of Germany in international affairs and the significance of US-German partnership in leading the post-Cold War world. The aims of this move, Chinese analysts argue, were to find a powerful and reliable partner to share America's leadership in Europe and to undermine any effort to create separate

European security arrangements. In the meantime, America hoped to constrain Germany, whose increasing power had already caused considerable apprehension in Europe. The new US-German partnership is said to have enervated both the traditional 'special relationship' between Britain and America and Franco-German collaboration. Thus, America was hoping to benefit from the differences and suspicions among West European countries (Hu Jie 1990: 15–17; Wang Naicheng 1995: 47; Zhou Rongyao 1995: 50).

To ensure that it would play a dominant role in Europe, Chinese analysts say, the US argued strongly against the dissolution of NATO. On the contrary, the Americans believed that NATO should be consolidated to perform new tasks and face new challenges (Ji Yin 1992: 4; Wan Shirong 1996: 14; Yan Xiangjun 1991: 24; Zhang Baoxiang 1991: 28). Apart from maintaining NATO's internal cohesion, the US actively advocated the enlargement of the alliance to allow such countries as Poland, Hungary and the Czech Republic to become members. Some Chinese scholars argue, however, that America's obsession with Europe must not be explained by geopolitics alone. One should also take into account the historical and cultural dimensions of US perceptions of Europe and trans-Atlantic relations (Wang Zhenhua 1996: 64).

During the Cold War years, some Americans saw the struggle against communism as a battle to protect and salvage Western civilization. President Harry Truman is reported to have said in 1949 that, as a member of NATO, the US was deeply rooted in Europe in terms of tradition as well as passion for freedom. Almost 50 years later, Madeleine Albright, former American Secretary of State, is said to have made similar remarks: 'The root of the United States, and of myself in particular, is in Europe. Our views are invariably influenced by European tradition' (Liu Jinghua, Niu Jun and Jiang Yi 1997: 58). The Americans tended to exhibit an exceptionally passionate sentiment when they talked of 'establishing a united, stable and democratic Europe'. It was this sentiment, Chinese scholars maintain, that led to American concern over the fate of Central Eastern Europe. Thus, the US found it very difficult to reject the request of these countries to join NATO. In addition, America's 'European complex' (*Ouzhou qingjie*) was reinforced by the post-Cold War foreign policy discourse among certain US elites, which stressed the clash between Western and non-Western civilizations in world politics. American politicians therefore felt that culturally they had an obligation to defend those European countries that belonged to the world of Western civilization (Liu Jinghua, Niu Jun and Jiang Yi 1997: 59).

Nevertheless, most Chinese scholars and analysts believe that America's strategy towards Europe was ultimately determined by political and security considerations, especially by its assessment of Russia's internal development and foreign policy. Following the disintegration of the Soviet Union, America provided substantial support for President Yeltsin and his government, hoping that Russia would become more liberalized economically and politically and that it could gradually be integrated into the Western world (Li Dongyan 1996: 61, p. 73).

Indeed, President Clinton encouraged Japan, Western countries, and the IMF to provide more financial assistance to Russia. He appealed to the G7 leaders to take 'bolder actions' to aid Yeltsin's reform programme, insisting that the West must make every effort to help Russia to deepen its economic restructuring and democratization. Clinton believed that the continuation of the Russian reform would make the world a safer place to live in and enable America to reduce its defence expenditure and concentrate on its own economic development. In 1995, the Chinese estimated that American loans to Russia amounted to US$8.6 billion and that the US helped privatize 17,000 large and medium Russian state enterprises. In addition, Washington provided Russia with technical advice and training in numerous spheres ranging from price reform, financial and tax reform, energy management and telecommunications to agricultural development, health and medical provisions. As for the reform of the Russian political system, American assistance in preparing for elections, drafting constitutions and establishing the rule of law was also prominent. Moreover, agreements were signed by the broadcasting companies of the two countries to let Russian people view the programmes on American satellite television. Furthermore, the US government reached a consensus with the Yeltsin government in various areas of arms control and defence cooperation, including the reduction of strategic weapons, the banning of nuclear testing and chemical weapons, non-proliferation of nuclear weapons and nuclear technology, joint peace-keeping military exercises and so on (Gu Guanfu and Tian Runfeng 1993: 2–3; Jin Junhui 1996: 22).

It is clear that the Clinton administration played an active role in transforming the Russian polity and economy. There was, however, simply too much uncertainty in Russia's domestic situation. The US government was worried, say the Chinese, that a failure in Yeltsin's reform might lead to political instability in Russia, which could have adverse effects on the relations between Russia and the US and European countries. To the Americans, the revival of Russian imperial expansionism is a distinct possibility, and Russia may one day seek to dominate Central Eastern Europe again, thus posing a potential threat to European security. Dr Henry Kissinger is said to have voiced his concern at the US Senate: 'During the Cold War period, we had to deal with communism plus imperialism [in Russia]. Although communism has been defeated, the tendency towards imperialism remains' (Jin Junhui 1996: 24).

Such latent fears explain why the US endeavours to complete NATO's eastward expansion before Russia is able to reassert its power in Europe. Based on American sources, some Chinese analysts suggest that the original aim of forming NATO was to constrain Soviet actions in Eastern Europe by military deterrence. But the US has no intention of relinquishing its influence in the region even though the Soviet Union has collapsed. In this sense, the process of NATO expansion can be said to have begun in the early 1990s, when East Germany was absorbed by West Germany and the reunified Germany was allowed to stay in the Western alliance. From America's perspective, the Chinese note, NATO expansion is the best way of ensuring that the current democratic reform in Eastern Europe will not be reversed, that the disputes among the countries in the region will not result in great power confrontation, and that Russia will remain a second-rate power in the European geopolitical structure (Liu Jinghua, Niu Jun and Jiang Yi 1997: 56, 60–62).

Through the eastward expansion of NATO, say the Chinese, the US has gained enormous geopolitical advantages and strengthened its military domination in Europe. From Russia's standpoint, however, its 'security space' (*anquan kongjian*) has been vastly reduced following the admission of Poland, Hungary and the Czech Republic into NATO (Jiang Benliang 1997: 35). Not surprisingly, Russia has been vehemently opposed to American proposals to extend NATO's boundary towards its border, as it is seen as a direct challenge to Russian security interests. Moscow's argument is that NATO is a product of the Cold War and should not continue to exist, let alone expand, in the post-Cold War era. More seriously, the Russians contend, NATO expansion could provoke Russian nationalism, cause instability in Europe, widen European division, and escalate an arms race and military antagonism in the region (Wan Shirong 1996: 15).

Despite Russia's protests, Chinese analysts conclude, the US is fully committed to the expansion of NATO because it will supposedly contribute to the building of democracy in Europe, the promotion of stability in Central Eastern Europe and the integration of former communist states into Western society. Citing George Kennan and other American critics, the Chinese warn that NATO's eastward expansion could have undesirable consequences for future European security. As a weaker power, they argue, Russia has no choice but to accept the uncomfortable reality today. But this may well be the first thing that Russia wants to overturn if and when it becomes stronger and more prosperous (Liu Jinghua, Niu Jun and Jiang Yi 1997: 50–51). Chinese analysts are convinced that the real purposes of America's efforts to bring East European countries into the orbit of NATO are to perpetuate US presence in Europe and to build a European security structure that is dominated by NATO and led by the US. Such a security arrangement would be useful in containing Russia, restraining Europe (especially Germany), and preserving America's unipolar position in the world. The American view of NATO's future, according to the Chinese, was succinctly presented by Madeleine Albright when she said in April 1997: 'If NATO does not expand ... it will face the danger of losing its significance and even of disbandment. Then our leading position in Europe will be in jeopardy, and our relations with traditional allies there will deteriorate' (Xia Yishan 1997b: 34; Xu Heming and Wang Haihan 1997: 29).

Chinese analysts suggest that America's determination to lead Europe is demonstrated by its involvement in the conflict in Bosnia-Herzegovina. At the beginning of the crisis, the United States was reluctant to get involved directly in any mediation, insisting that it was essentially a European affair and should be handled by the Europeans (Wang Haihan 1996: 24; Wang Zhenhua 1996: 63). However, US leaders soon realized that this was a great opportunity to justify the continued existence of NATO in the post-Cold War world and to strengthen the leading position of America in the new European order. The US therefore used NATO to enhance its influence in the Bosnian crisis, including the supervision of arms embargoes, the enforcement of the UN no-fly resolution, the air-raids against the Serbs and the use of military force to achieve a ceasefire in Bosnia (Wang Haihan 1996: 24). Warren Christopher, former American Secretary of

State, is reported to have said that NATO remained an important tool for the US to partake in European affairs. Indeed, NATO's military action in enforcing the no-fly resolution was its first out-of-area operation since the establishment of the alliance in 1949 (Man Bin 1997: 77).

Chinese analysts argue that America's interest in Bosnia-Herzegovina was not so much helping different ethnic groups resolve their differences, but seeking to prevent them from threatening European stability which could disrupt the US-led post-Cold War order. Another motive of American intervention was said to be to seek to dominate the Balkans, which had traditionally been within Russia's sphere of influence. In addition, the American government was said to have been biased towards the Bosnian Muslims because of the powerful Islamic pressure from Congress as well as America's wide-ranging economic and political interests in the Islamic and Arab world. Specifically, the US needed the cooperation of the Arab countries in the Middle East peace process. In the end, the high-tech based US-led military operations, combined with the large-scale attacks by the ground forces of the Muslims and Croats, forced the Serbs to the negotiation table and to eventually sign a peace agreement. To Chinese analysts, this was a 'drama of peace' directed by America, in which 'the actions of peace-keeping and the maintenance of security turned into unprecedented military attacks' (Li Zhihong 1996: 18–20; Yang Dazhou 1995: 121–31).

From the Chinese perspective, America's hegemonism (*baquan zhuyi*) was revealed most explicitly in the Kosovo crisis. The US-led NATO air strikes on Yugoslavia in March-June 1999 were severely criticized by PRC analysts who argued that it was a blatant violation of international law and the UN Charter. No country should have the right to infringe on the sovereignty of another country, they asserted, let alone launch a military attack against it. The Western notion of humanitarian intervention, the Chinese contended, was used as a smokescreen to conceal America's strategic motives (Xia Yishan 1999). They pointed out that there had been numerous internal conflicts in Africa which led to hundreds of thousands of people losing their homes, being injured or killed. But the Americans were not interested in these 'humanitarian disasters' because they had no vital interests there. Yugoslavia was different as it had been an ally of Russia in the past and could become an obstacle to NATO expansion. By launching the Kosovo attacks, Chinese analysts claim, Washington aimed to demonstrate and fortify its position as the hegemonic leader (*bazhu diwei*) in the post-Cold War world. It could also exploit the situation to further reduce Russia's strategic space (*zhanlue kongjian*), making it easier for NATO to complete its mission of eastward expansion.

According to Chinese analysis, the Kosovo crisis showed that NATO had effectively become a strategic instrument of America in achieving its national objectives in Europe. In the meantime, the role of the UN in maintaining international peace was in danger of being marginalized and its authority was seriously undermined (Jiang Jianqing 1999; Qian Wenrong 1999). These views were widely expressed by Chinese scholars and put forward most strongly by military analysts such as Zhou Bolin (1999) of the National Defence University. Not surprisingly, the Chinese did not accept the explanation that the bombing of the Chinese embassy in Belgrade was an accident. Invoking the Vienna Convention of Diplomatic Relations, most PRC scholars and analysts condemned the embassy bombing as a 'barbaric act' and a violation of Chinese sovereignty (Lu Qichang 1999: 7; Guo Shuyong 1999: 15; Chen Demin 1999: 4). They were convinced that the Kosovo war would have a profound impact on the international system and great power relations in particular.

US security strategy in the Asia-Pacific region

Given China's geographical location, US post-Cold War strategy in the Asia-Pacific region is of special concern to Chinese policy elites. Throughout the Cold War years, the US was perceived as an imperialist (*diguozhuyizhe*) who, having failed to prevent the CCP from gaining power, attempted to isolate and weaken China and other communist countries in Asia. As part of its global strategy of containment (*ezhi zhanlue*), Chinese analysts assert, Washington provided huge economic support for and established strong security ties with Japan, Taiwan, South Korea, South Vietnam, the Philippines and any Asian regimes that took an anti-communist stance, even though most of their political systems were far from democratic by American standards. Indeed, the US fought two major wars in Asia – the Korean War and the Vietnam War – with the aim of containing 'communist expansionism'. From the late 1960s onwards, the US was depicted as a hegemonist (*baquanzhuyizhe*) who engaged fiercely in a geopolitical rivalry with the Soviet Union in Asia and other parts of the world while seeking to improve relations with China in order to check the growth of Soviet power. In the 1980s the US was said to expand its economic relations substantially with Asia, gradually shifting the focus of its trade and investment towards the Pacific region. As a result, America became one of the key players in the dynamic Asia-Pacific economy. Thus, in the eyes of the Chinese, America's Asia-Pacific policy during the Cold War era was driven by ideological, strategic and economic considerations (Chen Luzhi 1992: 137–50; Shi Yinhong 1997: 7–26; Wu Guifu 1992: 56–57; Yao Chunling 1995: 110–26).

As previously mentioned, the Chinese are convinced that the US intends to preserve its hegemonic position in the international system. Any adjustment in America's post-Cold War strategy in the Asia-Pacific thus reflects its ambition of creating a unipolar world structure. When George Bush was elected as the US president in 1989, Soviet military presence in the Asia-Pacific was still formidable. The primary goal of American policy in the region therefore remained the 'containment of Soviet expansionism', Chinese analysts point out. While seeking to avoid confrontation with Moscow, the Bush administration insisted that America must strengthen its air and naval capability in North East Asia, improve the quality of US forces and weapons in the area, and request Japan and other Asian allies to increase their military spending and share more defence responsibility (Wu Guifu 1992: 57).

By the end of 1991 the Soviet Union had disintegrated, which led to a fundamental change in the security environment of the entire region. With the absence of the Soviet threat, Chinese scholars maintain, the rationale for American military presence in the Asia-Pacific no longer existed. However, the US was reluctant to withdraw from the region. As Chen Baosen (1992: 46), a researcher at the IAS in Beijing, puts it, 'the preservation of America's superpower status depends to a large extent on whether it can stay in Asia'. Bush's high-profile visit to Australia, Singapore, South Korea and Japan in January 1992, it is argued, should be seen as part of America's effort to protect its extensive economic, political and military interests in the area. Washington's Asia-Pacific strategy in the early 1990s is best summarized by James Baker III, the former Secretary of State in the Bush administration, in an article published in *Foreign Affairs* in 1991/92:

> To visualise the architecture of U.S. engagement in the region, imagine a fan spread wide, with its base in North America and radiating west across the Pacific. The central support is the U.S.-Japan alliance, the key connection for the security structure and the new Pacific partnership we are seeking. To the north, one spoke represents our alliance with the Republic of Korea. To the south, others extend to our treaty allies – the Association of Southeast Asian (ASEAN) countries of the Philippines and Thailand. Further south a spoke extends to Australia – an important, staunch economic, political and security partner. Connecting these spokes is the fabric of shared economic interests now given form by the Asia-Pacific Economic Co-operation (APEC) process. Within this construct, new political and economic relationships offer additional support for a system of co-operative action by groups of Pacific nations to address both residual problems and emerging challenges (Baker 1991/92: 4–5).

The 'architecture for a Pacific community' envisaged by Baker was founded on three aspects of which Chinese analysts are highly suspicious and critical (Guo Xiangang 1992: 41–45). The first was to establish 'a framework for economic integration that will support an open trading system in order to sustain the region's economic dynamism and avoid regional economic fragmentation' (Baker 1991/92: 3). To the Chinese, America's intention of building such a framework for trans-Pacific economic links was to dominate the future direction of Asia-Pacific economic cooperation so that it would serve US strategic needs. Specifically, America wanted to consolidate the status of APEC as an open and inclusive economic organization with the aim of obstructing any attempt by Tokyo to establish a Japan-led Asian economic community. Meanwhile, through the promotion of economic cooperation between APEC and the North American Free Trade Area (NAFTA), America hoped to increase its competitiveness in the global economy in general and with the EU in particular (Wu Guifu 1992: 61).

The second pillar in Baker's vision of a Pacific community was to encourage 'the trend toward democratization so as to deepen the shared values that will reinforce a sense of community, enhance economic vitality and minimize prospects for dictatorial adventures' (Baker 1991/92: 3). Chinese analysts saw America's attempt to further democratization in Asia as a tool of asserting political and ideological domination of the area. Wu Guifu argues that the US had, in fact, supported many pro-American dictatorial regimes in the region during the Cold War years due to the need for competing for influence with the Soviet Union. As the military value of these regimes diminished in the post-Cold War era, America's policy of unconditional support for them changed accordingly. The US therefore assisted or forced them to reform their political systems and accept American values. In addition, when offering aid to developing countries in Asia, says Professor Wu, America invariably insisted on the promotion of a market economy and democratization as pre-conditions and used 'human rights diplomacy' to interfere with the internal affairs of the recipients (Wu Guifu 1992: 61–62).

The last pillar on which a Pacific community would be founded, according to Baker, was to build 'a renewed structure for the Asia-Pacific theatre that reflects the region's diverse security concerns and mitigates intra-regional fears and suspicions' (Baker 1991/92: 3). Despite the radical change in the Asia-Pacific security environment, Wu Guifu notes, America's strategic interests in the region remained unchanged, which included protecting the US from attack, supporting its global deterrence policy, preserving its political and economic access, maintaining the balance of power to prevent the rise of any regional hegemon, strengthening the Western orientation of the Asian nations, fostering the growth of democracy and human rights, deterring nuclear proliferation and ensuring freedom of navigation (Wu Guifu 1992: 62; see also US Department of State 1990: 8).

To achieve all these objectives, Professor Wu says, the US would continue its military presence in the Asia-Pacific but some adjustment in the missions and structures of American forces in the area could be expected. Specifically, gradual reduction of US ground and air forces in Asian countries such as South Korea, Japan and the Philippines would take place in the 1990s. In the meantime, Japan and other Asian allies would be urged to increase their share of defence costs and assume more responsibilities. But Wu stresses that the essence of Bush's post-Cold War security strategy in the Asia-Pacific was to strengthen a regional security structure led by the United States and based on various types of bilateral relations. Complementary to bilateral security arrangements, America would seek to deal with some security-related issues by certain mechanisms of multilateral consultations (Wu Guifu 1992: 63).

Chinese analysts argue that there was much continuity in America's strategy towards the Asia-Pacific region from Bush to Clinton (Lin Hongyu 1997: 1). In many ways, Clinton's proposal of establishing a 'new Pacific community' (*xin Taipingyang gongtongti*) in July 1993 was based on the strategic framework laid down by the Bush administration.[3] However, given his priority of revitalizing the American economy, Clinton is believed to have paid special attention to the Asia-Pacific, which was fast emerging as a global economic powerhouse. He reportedly said in 1993 that 'half of America's employment depends on trade' and that '40 per cent of American trade depends on the Asia-Pacific region' which 'can and will become a massive source of employment, income, and growth for the American people' (Lin Hongyu 1997: 1). Closer economic links with the region could thus help revive America's economy, reduce its budget deficit, enhance its economic competitiveness, and create more job opportunities in the US (Li Dongyan 1996:

69). Indeed, when Clinton attended the 1993 APEC meeting in Seattle, he put forward his idea of building an Asia-Pacific economic community, seeking to transform APEC from a consultative economic forum to a multilateral trade organization. The aims of the US proposition, according to the Chinese, were to further promote the liberalization of trade and investment in the Asia-Pacific, to augment opportunities for American companies to enter the Asian market and, most importantly, to play a leading role in the Asia-Pacific economy (Lin Hongyu 1997: 2).

On the ideological and political aspects of America's Asia-Pacific strategy, Chinese analysts note, Bush's emphasis on exporting such American values as 'democracy' and 'human rights' to Asia was carried forward by Clinton. When Clinton elaborated his vision of a 'new Pacific community', he repeatedly stressed the importance of promoting democratic systems in the region. In his view, only when US-style democracy was advocated and established in the Asia-Pacific could American security and economic interests be adequately safeguarded (Lin Hongyu 1997: 2; Chen Shixiang and Yan Ling 1995: 20, 23). As most of the remaining socialist countries were located in Asia, it became America's main ideological target, say the Chinese (Li Dongyan 1996: 69).

In terms of security, Clinton shared Bush's view that it was essential to continue US military presence in the region. But, Chinese scholars believe, he placed more emphasis on the concept of the 'balance of power' (*junshi*), maintaining that it was in America's strategic interests to preserve the balance among the great powers – the US, Japan, China and Russia – in the Asia-Pacific, and that the presence of American forces would contribute substantially to the balance of power in the area. In other words, the US attempted to play the role of a 'balancer' (*pinghengguo*) in Asia-Pacific security (Lin Hongyu 1997: 2; Wang Wenfeng 1997: 8–10. Ma Yuan 1996: 14–19). As a self-appointed balancer, the Clinton administration was said to have become more enthusiastic about the use of multilateral consultative mechanisms to deal with Asia-Pacific security matters which, some Chinese scholars contend, represented a new tendency in America's Asia-Pacific policy (Yan Xiangjun and Huang Tingwei 1993: 2; Chen Shixiang and Yan Ling 1995: 20–21). These scholars worried that Washington would use multilateral security forums to constrain Chinese actions given its expression of growing concern over China's territorial disputes with ASEAN states over the sovereignty of the Spratly Islands. The Chinese suspected that America had changed its previous position of 'non-interference' on the South China Sea disputes as China grew stronger (Xiao Feng 1999: 1). Indeed, the expansion of US-ASEAN security cooperation in the 1990s caused considerable apprehension among Chinese analysts. This is clearly expressed in an article written by Hu Jiulong (2000), an international relations scholar at Peking University.

According to Professor Li Dongyan (1996: 70) of CASS, there are three main reasons why the Clinton administration was zealously involved in Asia-Pacific affairs. The first was to take advantage of Asia-Pacific economic dynamism to improve America's economic performance and to protect its economic interests in the region. Secondly, America sought to fortify its leading position in the

Asia-Pacific and to prevent other forces from replacing it in the area or excluding it from regional affairs. Last but not least, through the control of the process of Asia-Pacific cooperation, America wished to build up its power to compete with Europe and to strengthen its standing in leading the post-Cold War world politically and economically. In short, Clinton's policy towards the Asia-Pacific was seen as a major component of Washington's strategy of realizing its ambition of global domination (Weng Jieming, Zhang Ximing, Zhang Tao and Qu Kemin 1997: 399–400).

Japan in US security strategy

Japan is no doubt the United States' most valuable ally and has thus received huge attention from PRC security specialists. To strengthen its 'hegemonic position' in post-Cold War Asia-Pacific, according to Chinese analysis, the US needed the continued support of regional friends and allies. While Japan remained America's closest and most powerful ally in Asia, some Chinese analysts believe, there had been considerable strains in US-Japan economic relations which could undermine the foundation of the military alliance.

Throughout the Cold War years, America was able to maintain a special relationship with Tokyo. The 1951 Japanese-US Security Treaty enabled the US to retain its military bases in Japan after World War II, which became extremely useful to Washington in its rivalry in the region with the former Soviet Union. Protected by the American security umbrella, Japan is said to have got a 'free ride' on defence and saved a vast amount of defence expenditure for post-war economic reconstruction. America's wars in Korea and Vietnam are also believed to have stimulated the rapid growth of the Japanese economy in the 1950s and 1960s. In addition, the US was Japan's largest trading partner and the most important source of advanced technology. By the 1980s, Japan had reached the status of an economic superpower in the world whose strength was second only to that of America. For various domestic and external reasons, the US faced tremendous economic difficulties with huge budget and trade deficits. However, given the crucial role of Japan in America's global strategy of containment, the US government was by and large tolerant of Tokyo's unfair trading practices which gave rise to a serious US-Japanese trade imbalance. In the meantime, Japan also tried to avoid any direct confrontations with the US because of its fear of the enormous Soviet military power in the Far East (Ding Yuejin 1997: 19–20; Zhan Shiliang 1992: 1–2).

With the end of the Cold War and the disappearance of the Soviet threat, Japan was loath to be America's junior partner. Instead, Japan wished to achieve a political status commensurate with its economic power, which was viewed by the Chinese as an impregnable challenge to US attempts to shape the post-Cold War order in Asia. Indeed, many Japanese politicians and elites are said to have argued that Japan should now be an equal partner of the US, and that it should become an 'ordinary' state, that is, being a political as well as an economic power. This sort of strong nationalistic sentiment was widely expressed in Japanese publications in the late 1980s, including the highly sensational book *The Japan That Can Say*

'*No*' (Morita and Ishihara 1991), which caused much concern in the US (Wang Mingming 1996: 105–06; Zhan Shiliang 1992: 2–3; Ding Yuejin 1997: 20). As Japan's capability and confidence grow, Chinese analysts argue, it will seek to contend with the US for regional leadership in Asia and political influence around the world. In the longer term, it is said, the tension between the two countries will rise and the Americans will make every effort to keep Japan under control (Ding Yuejin 1997: 21–22, 47). Being the sole superpower in the post-Cold War era, the Chinese claim, Washington is hoping to establish a US-led hegemonic system. But it has found it increasingly difficult to dominate global affairs due to the decline of its economic strength. At the same time, Japan has gradually emerged as the number two economic superpower and is trying to remove the various constraints imposed upon it by the US and the international community for over 50 years. Chinese experts predict that a US-Japanese confrontation is unavoidable as the struggle between the existing hegemon and the aspiring hegemon intensifies.

As the revitalization of the US economy was at the top of Clinton's policy agenda, Chinese analysts believed that US leaders would strive to address the problem of trade deficits with East Asian countries, and with Japan in particular (Wang Yuan 1996: 35–39). In addition, the US and Japan are said to be earnestly competing for economic dominance in East Asia, an area of growing significance for the future development of both nations. The Americans were especially concerned that Japan had now replaced the US as the largest investor and provider of economic assistance in the Asia-Pacific region. More worrying for America was the fact that while US trade deficits with Asia-Pacific countries were huge, Japan had a substantial trade surplus in Asia (Zhao Jieqi 1992: 21–25). The Chinese thus conclude that the on-going trade disputes between America and Japan, together with their intense struggle for political and economic leadership in the Asia-Pacific, could lead to 'a qualitative change' in US relations with Japan in 15 to 20 years' time.

However, most Chinese scholars are certain that America would do its best to avoid a conflict with Japan. Economically, the Japanese market and Japan's investment in America remained important to the US economy. For example, America's export to Japan was greater than its total export to Germany, Italy and France. More significantly, the US budget deficit was largely financed by the Japanese. The Chinese maintain that politically the US needed the support of Japan in advancing America's interests and promoting its values in the Asia-Pacific. Clinton's plan to build a 'new Pacific community' would not be successful without the full cooperation of Japan, which was recognized as a key player in the region.

In the area of security relations, Chinese specialists point out, Japan was needed by America to share its defence responsibility and expenditure in Asia. In particular, the assistance of Tokyo was indispensable in America's endeavour to constrain Russia, China and other Asian communist countries. Meanwhile, the presence of US forces in Japan was useful in curbing the growth of Japanese military power. According to Chinese analysis, the US-Japan security alliance would continue to play a pivotal role in perpetuating the forward presence of American forces in Asia, maintaining the regional balance of power and protecting US economic, political and security interests in the Asia-Pacific (Ding Yuejin 1997: 22, 47; Zhan Shiliang 1992: 5–6).

In April 1996, President Clinton met the former Japanese Prime Minister Hashimoto Ryutaro at a summit meeting in Tokyo, where they signed the 'US-Japan Joint Declaration on Security Alliance for the Twenty-first Century'. The Joint Declaration stressed the need for US-Japanese cooperation in dealing with issues in Japan's surrounding areas that could threaten its peace and security. In other words, the bilateral treaty between the US and Japan had now been extended to cover the entire region, including the Korean Peninsula, the Taiwan Strait and the South China Sea which, according to the Chinese, clearly indicated America's hegemonic ambitions of dominating Asia-Pacific security matters, restraining Japan from gaining strategic independence and constraining a rising China that was perceived as a potential enemy (Zhang Dalin 1996a: 26–30, 1996b: 24–28; Li Genan, 1996: 1–3).

A rising China and US-Taiwan relations

Besides Japan, China figures prominently in America's post-Cold War Asia-Pacific security strategy. During the 1970s and the 1980s, Washington's strategic partnership with China was based almost entirely on their common concern of the Soviet threat. As one Chinese scholar points out, both US and Chinese leaders ignored the fact that the basis of their bilateral relationship was very fragile, and they did not think about any intrinsic values in Sino-American relations that were unrelated to strategic considerations. The end of the Cold War demolished the very foundation on which the relations between the two countries was established. Consequently, both sides were unprepared for the impact of such a dramatic change on their relationship and thus unable to handle the differences and frictions between them (Niu Jun 1995: 131–32).

Chinese analysts argue that as the only superpower in the post-Soviet world, the US was concerned about the challenge from any great power or group of countries to its leading position in the international system. With the rapid growth of China's 'comprehensive national strength' (*zonghe guoli*), the PRC was regarded by some Americans as the 'greatest challenger' to US interests (Ying Xiaoyan 1995: 120; Wang Haihan 1997: 6). Those who were used to the Cold War mentality and needed an enemy to define their foreign policy goals, it is noted, maintained that China was an existing or potential enemy (Wang Jisi 1996: 2). On the one hand, the Clinton administration recognized the importance of a stable Sino-US relationship to America's long-term strategic interests. On the other, it was uncertain whether China would play a 'stabilizing' or 'destabilizing' role in regional and international affairs. To US policy-makers, China was neither a friend nor an enemy. From the Chinese perspective, America was striving to integrate China into the existing international system, but was sceptical of or even hostile towards the PRC's domestic and foreign policy (Niu Jun 1998: 23).

For almost a century, Wang Jisi (1997a) argues, America's China strategy has not changed in that it has attempted to shape China's development according to US values and interests. In the view of Liang Gencheng, one of the characteristics of a highly developed capitalist state such as the United States is monopoly (*longduan*), and the nature of monopoly is that one must defeat all the rivals in a competition in order to achieve an uncontested, supreme status. Like other hegemonic powers in history, says Professor Liang, America has always sought to preserve its so-called leadership role and to prevent other great powers from endangering the US hegemonic position. Thus, the Clinton administration was believed to be pursuing a China policy that consisted of the strategies of both engagement and containment (*bian jiechu, bian ezhi*) (Liang Gencheng 1996: 15–16).[4] This policy was also explained by some Chinese analysts in terms of the impact of domestic forces in US politics. The Clinton administration was said to be under constant political pressure from many right-wing conservative Congressmen and irresponsible journalists to adopt a tougher policy towards China (Wang Jisi 1996: 5–6). More importantly, one of the characteristics of post-Cold War American foreign policy was that the influence of a wide variety of domestic institutions and actors on the making and implementation of US foreign policy had increased substantially, argue the Chinese. As a result, it became much harder for Clinton to coordinate the actions of various departments, some of which were in favour of engaging China while others advocated a hard-line anti-Chinese policy (Niu Jun 1998: 23–24).

Chinese analysts note that there were three main aspects to Clinton's policy towards China. First, from the security perspective, the US had good reasons to engage China.[5] To begin with, through the process of engagement, Washington hoped to win Chinese support in tackling the problem of the proliferation of WMD. It also needed China's cooperation to deal with security issues in the Korean Peninsula, South Asia and South East Asia, where US interests could be threatened. Moreover, engagement enabled the American military to pursue exchanges with the PLA, which would hopefully help increase Beijing's military transparency. This would, in turn, enhance the confidence of China's neighbours and reduce the possibility of armed clashes between these countries due to misunderstandings or accidents. Furthermore, by engaging China, the Clinton administration tried to encourage the PRC to participate in the US-led regional and global security systems and organizations. As a result, high-level contacts and exchanges between the Chinese and American armed forces took place in the 1990s. For example, in October 1994 William Perry, Clinton's Secretary of Defense, was invited to visit Beijing (Liang Gencheng 1996: 16, 9), while the former Chinese Defense Minister, Chi Haotian, paid an official visit to the US in December 1996 (Zhongguo Guoji Wenti Yanjiu Suo 1997: 61).

Despite various incentives to promote defence cooperation with China, Chinese analysts contend that the Americans were suspicious of the growth of Chinese military power, which was seen as a potential threat to US security interests. As China continued to grow, American leaders feared that it could challenge America's leading position in the world and in Asia in particular. This, the Chinese assert, explained US hostility to the PRC's defence modernization, limited nuclear testing for defensive purposes and purchase of a small number of weapons from other countries. The re-emergence of China as a great power was interpreted by the US as a threat to global security. In the view of Washington, a militarily powerful China would seek to alter the existing international order and would not adhere to the rules and norms of the international community created by the West. What is more, China's rise is said to have caused apprehension among its Asian neighbours. As a leading power in the world, America felt that it had responsibility to maintain the status quo in the international system and to aid the small Asian nations in resisting Chinese 'expansionism' (Liang Gencheng 1996: 16–17; Wang Jisi 1996: 3).

The Chinese believe that many of the measures adopted by the Clinton administration reflected, in varying degrees, the US intention of guarding against (*fangfan*) the growth of Chinese power and constraining (*zhiyue*) or containing (*weidu*) China.[6] This intention, it is pointed out, was confirmed by a 1994 national security strategy report emphasizing the importance of preventing China from threatening regional security in the Asia-Pacific. The former US Secretary of Defense, William Perry, reportedly said in October 1995 when referring to America's engagement with China:

> Engagement is not appeasement … engagement is perfectly compatible with the steps taken by the US to prevent any threat to the interests of America and its allies. It is precisely because of this that we will continue to maintain the forward presence of 100,000 troops in the Pacific region (Liang Gencheng 1996: 12).

Similarly, Chinese analysts and specialists suspect that the 1996 'US-Japan Joint Declaration on Security Alliance for the 21st Century' was targeted against China. Their suspicion became stronger following the publication of the revised 'Guidelines for US-Japan Defence Co-operation' in September 1997.[7] To the Chinese, the new guidelines were designed to reinforce US security ties with Japan with the aim of containing China (Xiao Feng 1998: 11–12). Indeed, the Foreign Affairs College organized a symposium assessing the nature of the guidelines and their security implications. More than 30 scholars and security specialists from various leading think-tanks and research institutes participated in the meeting. Some Chinese analysts argued that the readjustment in US-Japan security relations and the publication of the defence guidelines, together with NATO's eastward expansion, represented two main components of America's global security strategy in the post-Cold War era. The strengthening of the US-Japan security alliance, they believe, served a strategic purpose of deterring China. The Chinese also feared that the possible inclusion of the Taiwan Strait in the ambiguous 'surrounding areas' stated in the treaty and guidelines would allow Japan to interfere in a conflict across the Taiwan Strait. The widening of the geographical scope of the treaty would also make the complicated claims over the South China Sea islands even more complex.

Indeed, Taiwan has always been the most sensitive issue in Washington's relations with China (Lu Junyuan 1996).[8] The Chinese feel especially dubious of the sincerity of America in adhering to its 'one China' policy. Since 1992, they claim, the American government has sold more weapons to Taiwan, upgraded US-Taiwan relations to a semi-official level, and provided active support for

Taipei to join the GATT/WTO and other international organizations (Zhou Qi 1995: 35–37). To most Chinese elites, the Clinton administration's decisions to allow the former Taiwanese President, Lee Teng-hui, to visit the US in June 1995 (Cao Zhizhou 1996) and to send two aircraft carriers to the Taiwan Strait in March 1996 following Beijing's large-scale missile tests and military exercises in the area signalled a major adjustment in US policy towards Taiwan which had begun in the Bush era (Weng Jieming *et al.* 1997: 368–70; Zhou Zhihuai 1998: 4–5). However, Chinese analysts do not fully agree with each other on their interpretations of the policy shift. Some believe that America was willing to compromise on the Taiwan issue in the 1980s due mainly to the strategic need of gaining Chinese support against the Soviet Union. Since the collapse of the Soviet empire, US policy towards Taipei had been strongly influenced by domestic factors such as party politics and pressure from Congress. In addition, the Tiananmen events in 1989, combined with Taiwan's economic and political developments, are believed to have had an undesirable impact on Sino-American relations, which also affected Washington's Taiwan policy.

Others argue that the adjustment in the US-Taiwan relationship was merely a continuation of America's policy. Ever since the US established diplomatic relations with China in 1979, it is said that the Americans had been trying to hinder the reunification of China and Taiwan by seeking to maintain the status quo across the Taiwan Strait. Now that the Cold War was over, they wanted to ensure that Taiwan was neither independent nor reunified with China. Through its 'balancing diplomacy' (*pingheng waijiao*) America is believed to have used the 'Taiwan card' to constrain China. Still others contend that the political change and economic success in Taiwan somehow forced America to reconsider its relations with the island. Given that Taiwan made impressive progress towards democratization and became one of the largest trading partners of the United States, some Americans felt that US-Taiwan relations should be upgraded in order to protect American interests in the area (Xiao Rong 1995: 147–48; Niu Jun 1996: 154).

Nevertheless, most Chinese scholars and experts believe that the US did not wish to see a rapid deterioration in China-Taiwan relations which could lead to American involvement in a military conflict in Asia. Even if an armed confrontation across the Taiwan Strait did occur, they predicted, America would be likely to provide military advice and equipment for Taiwan and apply economic sanctions against Beijing, rather than getting embroiled in a war with China. In any case, the Clinton administration was fully aware of China's market potential and significant role in maintaining peace and stability in the Asia-Pacific, and it would not jeopardize America's long-term strategic and economic interests for the sake of Taiwan (Xiao Rong 1995: 148–49; Fan Yuejiang 1997: 36–41; Pu Ning 1997: 4–6; Zhou Zhongfei 1998: 11–13; see also the analysis in Li 1996).

In addition to Taiwan, Chinese analysts assert, the US had used the South China Sea issue to substantiate the 'China threat theory' (*Zhongguo weixie lun*) and perpetuate its military presence in the Asia-Pacific, claiming that China's disputes with South East Asian countries over the sovereignty of the Spratly Islands would become a major source of potential conflict in the region. In the meantime, America was said to have exploited the ASEAN Regional Forum to draw China into a multilateral security forum with the aim of isolating or constraining China (Chen Shixiang and Yan Ling 1995: 21; Wang Haihan 1997: 7, 9). Moreover, the Chinese are concerned about US interference with issues relating to China's national unity and territorial integrity. Although the Clinton administration recognized Tibet as part of China, it allegedly supported the Tibetan separatist movement. For example, President Clinton met with Tibet's exiled leader, the Dalai Lama, three times and allowed him to advocate the independence of Tibet in the US. In the view of many Chinese observers, the Americans also abetted the British colonial regime in Hong Kong in obstructing Beijing's reassertion of its sovereignty over the territory. All these activities were designed to weaken China's political cohesion and external power position, say Chinese policy analysts (Wang Jisi 1996: 4; Liang Gencheng 1996: 13–14; Wang Haihan 1997: 9).

Politically, America is believed to be particularly keen to engage China so as to promote 'a widespread and peaceful evolution from a communist to a democratic system' in the country. Warren Christopher, the former American Secretary of State, reportedly said in 1994: 'If we want to encourage peaceful reform and change in China, we must strengthen and broaden our engagement with it' (Liang Gencheng 1996: 14, 18). Only through 'comprehensive engagement' (*quanmian jiechu*), it was hoped, could the US effectively advance freedom and democracy in China. At the very least, China should be integrated into the 'international community' and forced to play by the 'international rules and regulations' favoured and interpreted by America. However, the American attempt to advocate US values and 'peaceful evolution' (*heping yanbian*) in China was tenaciously resisted by the Chinese communist regime. Thus, say Chinese scholars, the US government sought to contain China politically and ideologically while pursuing a policy of engagement. For example, Washington had allegedly played the 'human rights card' at various international forums and supported Chinese dissidents who aspired to overthrow the PRC government. The Clinton administration also established a 'Radio Free Asia' which aimed to help Chinese citizens 'understand what is happening within China and in the world' and to assist the people of China and other communist states in Asia to 'find their own road to freedom' (Liang Gencheng 1996: 13–14; Wang Haihan 1997: 9; Zhou Qi 1995: 33–35).

Economically, the Chinese believe that engagement of China will bring about enormous benefits for America. China is one of the biggest emerging markets in the world, and increased Sino-American economic and trade interactions would help the US revive its economy and tackle its unemployment problem. As the Clinton administration placed a great deal of emphasis on promoting and sustaining America's economic prosperity, it is argued, it felt the need to strengthen US trade relations with China. This was why Clinton extended the most-favoured-nation (MFN) status to Beijing and de-linked China's human rights record and the MFN issue despite strong criticisms from Congress. Indeed, by the end of the 1990s, the US had become China's third largest trading partner, while China was America's sixth trading partner (Liang Gencheng 1996: 8–9, 17; Wang Haihan 1997: 7; Ren Junsheng 1995: 20–23).

However, China's rapid economic development was seen by some Americans as a potential challenge to US economic supremacy in the world economy, Chinese analysts point out. If China continues to grow, its economic strength could be transferred to military power, thus posing a long-term security threat to the US. While seeking to benefit from the rapidly growing China market, it is argued, the Clinton administration took various measures to contain China economically. For instance, America claimed to support China's admission to the WTO but tried to block it by insisting on the harsh entry requirements which China found it very difficult to fulfil. Moreover, the US government is said to have used the issues of the violation of intellectual property and trade imbalance to exert economic pressure on China and to gain further access to the Chinese market (Liang Gencheng 1996: 17–18; Zhou Qi 1995: 37–38; Niu Jun 1995: 133).

Theoretical analysis

The central argument of this book is that Chinese perceptions of the East Asian powers should be understood as part of a process of identity construction. Specifically, the book argues that PRC analysts tend to view the aspirations, capabilities and strategies of other great powers in terms of how they will affect China's quest for a great power status. As the US is the sole superpower in the post-Soviet world, Chinese perceptions of the country are of particular significance to this study.

The evidence presented in the previous sections suggests that Chinese scholars and analysts are convinced that US leaders under the Bush and Clinton administrations had the ambition and determination of creating a unipolar world in which America would play a dominant role. US security strategies in Europe and the Asia-Pacific are said to have reflected such aspirations. From the realist perspective, it is not difficult to understand China's assessment of US intentions in the post-Cold War era. Classical realists have a particularly pessimistic view of human nature which is believed to be selfish, power-seeking and even aggressive. Given the opportunity, people will seek to dominate and control others. This is why the ultimate aim of international politics is seen as 'a struggle for power' (Morgenthau 1978: 29). Following the collapse of bipolarity, the US emerged as the only superpower in the world and other great powers had neither the will nor the capability to challenge America's pre-eminence in the international system. From a realist standpoint, there was nothing to discourage the Americans from preserving 'the unipolar moment' (Krauthammer 1990/91).

America's active participation in the 1991 Gulf War and President Bush's idea of establishing a 'new world order' were seen by the Chinese as clear evidence of Washington's wishes to maximize its power and dominate the world. For offensive realists like John Mearsheimer (2001), however, the major force behind competition for power in international politics is not so much the greediness of human beings but the anarchic nature of the international system. They argue that there is little incentive in the international system for states to maintain the status quo and that they will seek any opportunities 'to gain power at the expense of rivals' (Mearsheimer 2001: 21). This is certainly a view shared by PRC analysts in their examination of US global strategy after the Cold War. To the Chinese, America's decision to push for NATO expansion was a move to extend its power in Europe at the expense of Russia. Similarly, its efforts to expand US security relations with Japan and other allies in the Asia-Pacific were perceived as part of a security strategy designed to undermine China's power in the region. The interpretation of Chinese security analysts is that the US is exploiting Japan to balance against the potential threat of a rising China in East Asia. They appear to have grasped the essence of the 'off-shore balancing' strategy in offensive realism in that a distant hegemon may choose to use a local great power to prevent other great powers from dominating a far-off region (Mearsheimer 2001: 141).

Realism may have a strong influence on PRC security analysts, but they are sceptical of the arguments of defensive realists (Jervis 1978; Van Evera 1999; Walt 1987). A great power, according to Kenneth Waltz (1979: 127), will seek to maintain the existing balance of power in order to achieve a satisfactory level of security. Once this is accomplished, it is argued, there is no further incentive for the great power to accumulate more power. In their consideration of US security policy, Chinese analysts seem to have rejected this central tenet of defensive realism. Instead, they concur with the analysis of offensive realists that a country which is substantially more powerful than its rivals will continue to accumulate power until it becomes a hegemon. Even then the hegemon will not be satisfied with the situation and will continue to expand (Gilpin 1981; Mearsheimer 1990; Labs 1997). This line of thinking is running through many Chinese articles. The reasoning is this: the US was already the most powerful country in the post-Soviet world but it was not satisfied with the status quo; it was determined to seek opportunities to accumulate its power and was prepared to maximize its power at the expense of rival powers in Europe (Russia) and Asia (China). To the Chinese, the national goal of the US under Bush and Clinton was to achieve its security through the maximization of power. This assessment fits in well with the arguments of offensive realism. In the words of Mearsheimer (2001: 35), 'states do not become status quo powers until they completely dominate the system'.

So what does this realist interpretation of America's global security strategy mean for China? This study argues that China has been pursuing a great power status ever since 1949 when the PRC was established. Despite their ideological and political differences, all Chinese communist leaders seem to share a common national goal, that is, to build a strong and powerful China. In the Cold War years, China actively interacted with the US and the former Soviet Union in a 'great power triangle' in order to maximize its strategic interests (Nelsen 1989). Seen from a realist perspective, China's leaders had always paid enormous attention to the importance of polarity and balance of power in international relations. This was especially the case when China was relatively weak compared to the two superpowers. By playing the 'China card' within a 'strategic triangle', PRC leaders were seeking to elevate the status of China as a great power in the international system.

After the end of the Cold War, Chinese elites were deeply concerned about their country's position in the new security environment. The disintegration of the Soviet Union meant that the US became the only superpower on the globe and the prominent role America played in the 1991 Gulf War confirmed Chinese suspicion of its 'hegemonic ambition' in the 'new world order'. The rapid growth of America's military power and high level of defence expenditure in the 1990s, combined with its willingness to tackle crises in Iraq and Kosovo, exacerbated Chinese misgivings of the US 'benign hegemony'. This partly explains why PRC scholars are so critical of US global strategy and its Asia-Pacific strategy in particular.

If the US manages to sustain its unipolar position, the best China could hope to achieve would be the status of a second-ranking power. To Chinese leaders, this is not an acceptable option as they are determined to develop their country into a major power that would be able to compete with other great powers economically, politically and militarily. The Chinese thinking is close to the realist view that if eligible states 'do not acquire great power capabilities, they may be exploited by the hegemon' in future (Layne 1993: 12). American hegemony might turn out to be benign, but given its experience with the great powers in the 19th century, this would not be something that China would wish to risk. The fear of a US-dominated world where China's rise to a great power status would be frustrated is evident in the Chinese writings examined in this chapter. The Chinese thus take a hostile stance against unipolarity and advocate the development of a multipolar system. In this sense, Chinese elites' perceptions of the international system and US global strategy in the 1990s are shaped by their desire to construct a great power identity for China.

There is no doubt that China's security perceptions of the US are heavily influenced by realist thoughts but Chinese analysts are not oblivious of other approaches to the analysis of world politics. Indeed, they are aware of how certain aspects of US global strategy have been driven by liberal ideas. For example, Chinese scholars are able to discern the significance of ideology in US foreign policy under Bush and Clinton. This has, however, caused considerable apprehension regarding America's intentions among Chinese analysts. They resent US attempts to export liberal values such as freedom and democracy to other countries. The PRC elites feel particularly threatened by external criticisms of their regime following the Tiananmen crackdown of the student movement and the revolutions across Eastern Europe in 1989. As the unipolar system emerged from the ashes of communism and the demise of the Soviet Union, the Chinese viewed the idea of democracy promotion in US foreign policy with great suspicion. They perceive America's assistance to Russia and East European countries in reforming their political systems and command economies as a way of extending US ideological influence to Europe.

Similarly, the American policy of promoting democratization along with marketization in Asia was seen to be designed for asserting political and ideological domination of the region. America's policy of engaging China is also considered a way to foster 'peaceful evolution' (*heping yanbian*) and political change in the PRC. Behind the rhetoric of democracy, freedom and human rights, Chinese analysts maintain, is a deliberate attempt to undermine the legitimacy of Chinese communist rule. If the PRC regime were to collapse and the country degenerate into chaos and disintegration, the prospects for a rising China would be significantly diminished. Thus, the theory of democratic peace (Doyle 1983; Russett 1993) is rejected by many Chinese security analysts who suspect that the liberal argument that democracies would not fight democracies could be used to substantiate the 'China threat theory' (*Zhongguo weixielun*) because of the nature of the Chinese political system.

Another important element of liberalism is the role of trade and economic activities in international relations. Liberals generally believe that inter-state conflict can be reduced by economic interdependence (Rosecrance 1986). Chinese analysts notice that much attention was given to economic factors in Bush's and Clinton's global strategies. The links between promoting free trade and global peace and security have been discussed in many Chinese publications, but PRC scholars tend to see this from the perspective of neorealism or neomercantilism (Gilpin 1987) rather than that of liberalism. They believe that economic strength is normally deployed by political leaders to strengthen their nation's power. To Chinese scholars, America is interested in international trade because it would serve US national interest, and Clinton's proposal of a 'new Pacific community' is a case in point. The motive behind America's active participation in Asia-Pacific economic affairs, they argue, is to increase their economic competitiveness with the ultimate aim of enhancing US economic power and dominating the world economy. This is why economic security was treated as a priority on Clinton's foreign policy agenda which, Chinese analysts assert, combined with a robust military force and growing political clout, would assist America in fulfilling its hegemonic aspirations.

Similarly, Chinese analysts are sceptical of America's claim of utilizing international institutions to promote international cooperation. In this regard, they share the realists' critique of the 'false promise' of international institutions in mitigating the constraining effects of anarchy on inter-state cooperation (Mearsheimer 1994/95; Grieco 1995). Chinese scholars question the assumption of neoliberal institutionists that powerful countries could be bound by their own commitments to the rules of international institutions (Keohane 1984; Abbott and Snidal 1998). Instead, they share the realist view that institutions are used primarily to bind other states to adhere to their commitments (Ikenberry 1998/99). This is precisely how Chinese analysts interpret US approaches to the UN, the WTO and other international organizations. Both the Bush and Clinton administrations are said to have exploited various international institutions to put forward America's economic, political and security agenda. According to the Chinese, the Americans would lay down the rules for others to follow. However, if these rules no longer suit their needs, they would either ignore the rules or change them. PRC analysts refer to US actions relating to the Middle East, Iraq, Bosnia-Herzegovina and Kosovo as evidence of how the Americans refused to be bound by their commitments to the UN Charter when they did not serve US interests (see, for example, Wang Jie 2000)

To the Chinese, international institutions and international regimes are no more than instruments of statecraft for America.

While most Chinese scholars do not feel that US security strategy is constrained by international institutions, they seem to appreciate the complexity of foreign policy-making in the US. When analyzing Clinton's policy towards China, for example, they have paid particular attention to the roles of various domestic institutions and actors within the American system, especially Congress, business organizations and the media. All these domestic forces are thought to have exerted some influence on America's China policy.

Whether one looks at China's security perceptions of America from a realist or a liberal perspective, it is clear that Chinese analysts are apprehensive of US global and Asia-Pacific strategy. To understand China's intense suspicion of US intentions, it is necessary to go beyond material and institutional factors. As constructivists rightly point out, people's perception of the world is socially and historically constructed. Why do the Chinese have such a sceptical view of the United States? The answer to this question is rooted in Chinese history and culture.

During the Cold War years, America was seen as the leading Western power constantly seeking to weaken the Chinese communist regime. The US maintained strong security ties with Japan and other Asian allies that were aimed at containing Chinese communism. The two major wars America fought in Asia – the Korean war and the Vietnam war – both involved China directly or indirectly. In the 1930s and 1940s, the US government supported General Chiang Kai-shek in his battles with the Chinese communist forces until he retreated to Taiwan in 1949 following his defeat in a civil war. Since then, Washington has maintained a close relationship with the Taiwanese government, despite the normalization of Sino-US relations in 1979. It is within this historical context that Chinese scholars and analysts perceive post-Cold War US global strategy.

In addition, Chinese security discourse of America should be analyzed in terms of China's self-perception. In other words, how does China define its own identity in relation to other actors in international relations? To constructivists, a good understanding of an actor's identity is important in interpreting its interests (Wendt 1999: 231). As discussed in Chapter One, China's identity is defined within a specific cultural context in that China perceives itself as a country with a glorious past and a great civilization but also a victim of Western imperialism. For many Chinese elites and intellectuals, it is a duty to contribute to the revival of their country and to make it powerful so that the experience of the 'century of national humiliation' will not be repeated (Cheng Chaoze 1997). From a psychopolitical perspective, perceptions of history are a major dimension of national self-imagery and they may 'generate powerful needs to avoid past experiences which are felt as humiliating, dangerous, or deadly' (Kaplowitz 1990: 51). As Huang Dahui (2005), a scholar at Renmin University, puts it, 'the rise of China is the dream of several generations of Chinese'. In social identity theory this is known as a sociocognitive process of 'self-enhancement' in that 'people have a basic need to see themselves in a positive light in relation to relevant others' (Hogg, Terry and White 1995: 260).

Clearly, PRC leaders are determined to ensure that China will achieve a great power status in the international system. Any other countries that are believed to forestall their aspirations would be viewed with great suspicion. To Chinese intellectuals and policy elites, there is a psychological need to 'restore honor, dignity, and strength to the nation' and to 'demand and gain respect from the rest of the world' (Kaplowitz 1990: 52). Wendt (1999: 236) argues that 'collective self-esteem' is often considered by political elites as a national interest. The 'China threat' debate in America and Clinton's policy of 'containment plus constrainment' are thus interpreted as US attempts to prevent China from acquiring a national identity that reflects its growing significance in the international community. Indeed, Chinese elites have been haunted by their negative self-images ever since the Opium War, when China suffered from a tormenting identity crisis. Given China's unpleasant encounters and fluctuating relations with foreign powers, including the US, it is not surprising that Chinese policy analysts see a unipolar world as a potentially dangerous place.

If the conception of national identity is central to Chinese security discourse, it also informs the strategic thinking of US leaders and political elites. From a constructivist standpoint, America's identity changed dramatically following the collapse of the bipolar system and the disintegration of the Soviet Union. It emerged as the victor of the Cold War and the only superpower in the 'new world order'. It was therefore necessary for the Americans to search for a new identity that would reflect their changing position in a unipolar world. The new identity would of course be underpinned by the key components of America's 'national essence' (Dittmer and Kim 1993: 18) such as the values of liberal democracy, freedom and the free market. As constructivists argue, a country's political interests and national security policy will change as its identity changes (Katzenstein 1996: 25). In this sense, America's global and regional security strategy during the Bush Snr and Clinton presidencies was closely linked to the process of its identity construction in a new era. To Chinese security analysts, however, America's acquisition of an identity as the preponderant power would threaten China's endeavour to establish a great power identity. The thinking behind this was that it would be much more arduous for China to secure its status as one of the major powers in the international system should the 'unipolar moment' perpetuate.

Drawing from symbolic interactionism, constructivists seek to understand identity formation in terms of distinguishing between self and other (Blumer 1986). This insight is similar to that of postmodernists. Indeed, postmodernist scholars argue that the construction of a threatening other is essential to identity construction. David Campbell (1998) argues persuasively that the state often relies on 'discourses of danger' to construct its identity. Chinese analysts certainly see the 'China threat' thesis as a discourse of danger generated deliberately by US leaders and elites who perceived an ascending China as a major rival. In treating China as a latent threat to global peace and security, they argue, the identity of the American self as the leading democratic nation in the post-Cold War world can be strengthened.

In the meantime, America is considered by many Chinese scholars and security specialists as a threatening other. One can find ample evidence of discourse of danger from Chinese writings on America's global and regional strategy: US unipolarity is a threat to world peace; NATO expansion is a threat to Russia and European security; US-Japanese security alliance is a threat to China and Asian security; democracy promotion and humanitarian intervention are a threat to state sovereignty and so on and so forth. The implication of this discursive construction of an American other is that it is imperative for China to achieve a great power status so that it can withstand US pressure and challenge. As such, the discourse contributes to the process of constructing a great power identity for China. As the authors of many articles in specialist journals are respected analysts of international affairs, their security discourse is likely to have a wider impact beyond the academic and policy communities.

Conclusion

This chapter has examined the security perceptions of Chinese scholars and elites on the United States in the Bush and Clinton eras. The evidence indicates a high degree of suspicion among Chinese elites of America's global security strategy. The Chinese are sceptical of what they perceive as US 'hegemonic' ambition and America's desire to sustain its unipolar position in the post-Cold War world which began in the early 1990s during the Bush presidency. Taking advantage of the break-up of the Soviet Union and the American victory in the 1991 Gulf War, the Chinese believe, the Bush administration put forward the idea of a US-dominated 'new world order'. This was seen as the first step in establishing a post-Cold War world order based on US values and interests. This ambition was said to have been carried forward by President Clinton.

Indeed, throughout the 1990s, the Clinton administration is thought to have exploited its superior power to consolidate America's hegemonic position in the international system. Specifically, the US is believed to have developed a strategy of 'engagement and enlargement' in order to dominate both Europe and the Asia-Pacific region. In Europe, the Chinese argue, America was able to strengthen its position through the eastward expansion of NATO and its intervention in the crises in Bosnia-Herzegovina and Kosovo. As to the Asia-Pacific, Chinese scholars are particularly concerned about America's strategy towards Japan and Taiwan, which is considered as part of the US strategy of preventing the rise of a strong and united China. Nevertheless, Chinese scholars are able to discern the complexity of Clinton's China policy which had a strong element of engagement. The Chinese remain suspicious of his policy towards China, and it has been characterized as a strategy of 'containment plus engagement'.

The last section of this chapter contains an analysis of Chinese security discourse from various theoretical perspectives. This theoretical analysis shows that Chinese security perceptions of America are heavily influenced by the theory of offensive realism in that Washington is seen to be dissatisfied with the status quo and determined to maximize its power relentlessly at the expense of its rivals in Europe and Asia. The evidence also indicates that Chinese scholars are familiar with liberal theory, including the economic interdependence and democratic peace theories and neoliberal institutionalism. However, they tend to reject the validity of liberal ideas in explaining America's strategies. In addition, this analysis reveals that Chinese perceptions of US security strategy cannot be fully explicated by realism. One needs to draw upon the insights of constructivism to understand the Chinese mentality in their analysis of America. The relevance of historical and cultural factors to Chinese considerations has been shown, and an attempt has been made to understand Chinese perceptions of America from the postmodernist perspective in terms of China's discursive construction of America as a threatening other.

To conclude, the evidence examined in this chapter clearly demonstrates that Chinese security discourse of America is shaped by China's self-perception as a rising power. In this context, China's perceptions of America's security strategy are directly linked to its own identity. Whether one looks at the Chinese view of the US from a realist, liberal, constructivist or postmodernist perspective, America is perceived as a major obstacle to China's endeavour to achieve a great power status.

3 September 11, pre-emption and the Bush Doctrine

US security strategy under the George W. Bush administration

This chapter continues the analysis of Chinese security perceptions of the United States, focusing on the George W. Bush presidency. The chapter begins by looking at how PRC scholars and analysts perceive US global strategy since 2001, with special emphasis on Chinese security analysis of the impact of 9/11 and the challenge of global terrorism on US security strategy. This is followed by an examination of Chinese discourse of the nature and implications of the Bush Doctrine and America's invasion of Iraq in 2003. The chapter then goes on to consider China's perceptions of Bush's Asia-Pacific security strategy. Special consideration is given to the views of Chinese scholars on American strategy towards Japan, China, Taiwan and the Korean Peninsula. The chapter will conclude with an analysis of Chinese security discourse of Bush's global and Asia-Pacific strategy from the perspectives of realism, liberalism, constructivism and postmodernism.

'September 11', anti-terrorism and US global strategy

Given the significance of the United States in China's security considerations, the Chinese followed the US election campaign closely in 2000. By the time George W. Bush was elected as the President, Chinese analysts had been well informed of the broad policy ideas of the new administration. They did not expect any major differences between the Republicans and the Democrats in terms of the overall direction of their external policy. Like the Clinton administration, said PRC analysts, the Bush administration would continue to strengthen America's leading position in the world and defend its national interest. Where they might differ was the means of achieving these goals.

Unlike the Democrats, the Chinese pointed out, the Republican Party had a long tradition of realism in dealing with foreign affairs. To Republican leaders, the best way of defending a country's interests and preserving international peace and security was through the exercise of power, especially military power. Apart from military capabilities, it would also be important to have strong allies and to maintain a regional balance of power. However, their emphasis on realism did not mean that the Republicans would not pay any attention to ideology (Song Yimin 2001: 1).

According to Chinese analysis, there would be several features in US foreign policy under President Bush. First, the new administration would try to strengthen US military power, consolidate defence ties with allies and adjust overseas troop deployment. Moreover, America would further increase its military superiority over other countries by increasing US military budgets. The Bush administration would take a tougher stance against international terrorists who would pose a threat to America and rogue states such as Iraq, Iran and North Korea. Another emphasis of the Bush administration, according to Chinese analysis, would be on geopolitical considerations. For example, America would not ignore the potential threat from Russia just because it had been moving towards democracy. The Chinese predicted that the new administration would further reduce Russia's strategic space in order to prevent the country from regaining its previous pre-eminence (Song Yimin 2001: 1–3).

In addition, Chinese analysts believed that the Bush administration would be likely to constrain China by various means, preventing it from playing a leading role in the Western Pacific region. Meanwhile, the Republican government would seek to expand business relations with the PRC due to its close links with the business community. Despite its criticism of Clinton's China policy, the new administration would continue to engage with China, given the country's growing importance on the world stage. Although the Americans would continue to criticize China's human rights problem, this would not play a major part in the Bush administration's policy towards China, the Chinese predicted. However, a rising China would inexorably be seen by Washington as a 'strategic competitor' for America (Song Yimin 2001: 6; Yang Jiemian 2001: 26–28).

Indeed, even before 9/11, Chinese analysts were apprehensive of the Bush administration's foreign policy. In their view, there was a strong Cold War mentality among many members of the new government. They were believed to have a specific foreign policy approach based on their Cold War experience and as a result, they tended to place emphasis on how to tackle rivals and enemies. President Bush was also believed to consider traditional military issues and defence matters as his priority. This, to the Chinese, explained America's decision to increase its defence budgets, take a tougher stance against Iraq, engage in a spy war with Russia, approve massive arms sales to Taiwan, highlight the missile issue in its negotiations with North Korea and so on. There was a strong unilateral tendency in the new government's foreign policy, and America's attitude towards the Kyoto Agreement was often cited as an example of growing US unilateralism. The Chinese argued that global issues such as globalization, spread of WMD, environmental protection and other non-conventional security issues were taken more seriously by the Clinton administration. Yet, the Bush administration paid very little attention to the importance of environment issues, global interdependence and the need for countries to work with each other to solve common problems. Towards the end of the Clinton era, the US made considerable effort to promote great powers cooperation and interaction. The Bush administration, instead, focused heavily on great power rivalry and the potential threat or challenge from Russia and China (Song Yimin 2001: 2; Yang Jiemian 2001: 21–25).

Following the 'September 11' terrorist attacks on America, some Chinese analysts hoped that Sino-US relations could be improved. China's official response to the events was cautious but swift. Jiang Zemin, the then Chinese President, was among the first world leaders to send messages of condolence to President Bush. Chinese leaders decided to condemn the terrorist attacks immediately and expressed sympathy with the victims, but would not take sides in America's conflict with terrorists (Lam 2001). The PRC government also had concerns about terrorism, especially in the far-western province of Xinjiang where Muslim separatists were believed to be supported by Afghan-based groups like those of Osama bin Laden. Nevertheless, Chinese leaders were reluctant to offer unreserved support for America's anti-terrorist campaign. PRC officials urged the US to discuss anti-terrorist proposals at the UN Security Council. They insisted that any actions against terrorism should be based on international law and the UN Charter in particular (BBC 2001a). Indeed, China demanded 'concrete evidence' from America before military strikes against suspected terrorist groups were launched. Any military action, Chinese officials asserted, 'should have a clear orientation that should not hurt innocent people' (BBC 2001b).

Reliable information on public opinion is scarce in China. Western media reports suggested that Chinese citizens had mixed feelings towards the terrorist attacks. The Chinese were horrified by the scale of damage and the huge loss of lives, and most of them showed deep sympathy for the victims. In fact, there were fourteen Chinese-owned companies in the Twin Towers of the New York World Trade Center. However, they tended to blame the tragedy on America's 'hegemonic policy'. As a student at Peking University said: 'Terrorism is wrong but I personally think this was a lesson for the United States. From now on, the US won't be so arrogant and reckless.' Another student commented: 'Now they know how it feels to be bombed' – by that he referred to NATO's accidental bombing of the Chinese embassy in Belgrade in 1999. Some even went further to say: 'Heroes, brave men who liberated the world … America under attack – it deserved it!' (FlorCruz 2001). This sort of anti-American sentiment was widely expressed on Chinese websites and chat-rooms which reflected popular ambivalence towards the US. The Chinese admired America's wealth and power but resented its dominant role in world affairs, especially its alleged attempts to frustrate China's aspirations to become a great power.

Indeed, there have been lively discussions among Chinese security experts and international relations specialists on various aspects of 9/11 and their security implications. Chinese analysts invariably regard the attacks as terrorist acts and believe that they are of an extreme and evil nature which will have negative effects on both America and the world. While Chinese security specialists disapprove of many aspects of US foreign policy, they maintain that nothing could justify such barbaric acts (Shi Yinhong 2002: 45). They argue that international terrorism is rooted in an unjust international political and economic order which is largely dominated by a hegemonic power, namely, the United States. The wealth gap between the North and South, according to Chinese analysis, has widened in recent years. The situation is exacerbated by the process of globalization, which has led to further marginalization of the South, creating a political climate conducive to the growth of global terrorism (Niu Hanzhang 2001; Yang Jin 2001). Yang Yunzhong (2002a: 5), a professor at Jinan Military College, argues that 9/11 represents an extreme form of struggle between hegemonism and anti-hegemonism, rather than a clash of civilizations between Islam and the West. Some extremist non-state actors, he says, have now moved to the forefront of anti-hegemonism and they have become the most radical anti-hegemonic forces in the world. In this sense, 9/11 has set the precedent of direct attacks on a hegemonic power by non-state actors. Despite the fanatical and evil nature of these international terrorist movements, Yang asserts, their anti-hegemonic characteristics are clear.

However, other analysts argue that international terrorism should be regarded as a common problem in international politics which has challenged the entire international society and threatened the stability, peace and security of the world. As such, it must be opposed by every country including China. Nevertheless, they agree that one of the contributing factors to the rise of terrorism in the post-Cold War era is the consequence of America's 'hegemonic' policy. Washington's support for the Chechen rebels and bias towards Israel in its conflict with the Palestinians are some of the examples cited to illustrate this argument. To eradicate global terrorism, Chinese analysts suggest, the international community has to tackle the root causes of the problem, focusing in particular on changing the social and political environment that has nurtured terrorism (Pang Zhongying, Shi Yinhong, Li Jingzhi *et al.* 2001; Yang Mingjie, He Xiquan, Li Wei *et al.* 2002). Tang Zhichao (2002) concurs that the anti-American sentiments in the Arab world are the result of a failure of US policy in the Middle East and continued American military presence in the region. Given the plethora of challenges in a globalizing world, Chinese scholars like Pang Zhongying (2001) believe that it is essential to establish a new global order based on equality, justice and mutual respect. This suggestion is shared by two leading scholars of Shanghai's Fudan University, among others, who argue that 9/11 has made it more urgent to promote 'democratization of international relations' (Ni Shixiong and Wang Yiwei 2002: 24–25). In their view, the current international order is dominated by one single superpower (read America) that seeks to promote a 'unipolar hegemonic strategy' (*danji duba zhanlue*). Only by building a more democratic international society where hegemony is replaced by equality, they maintain, would it be possible to remove the root causes of international terrorism.

Soon after the 9/11 attacks, Chinese scholars and analysts were able to discern some adjustments in US foreign policy. In particular, Washington is thought to have made a special effort to improve relations with Russia, strengthen relations with Arab countries, promote the Middle East peace process and take into account some of the concerns of the Third World. There is also a greater emphasis on consultations and cooperation with other great powers. As Guo Xiangang (2002: 34–35) notes, America needs the support and collaboration of as many countries as possible to combat terrorism, which is seen as a major security threat to the US. For a short period of time after 9/11, as Chu Shulong (2001) observes, the Bush administration appeared to be willing to abandon its unilateralism. Lu Zhongwei

(2002) has noticed some active counter-terrorist cooperation among the great powers. But Chinese scholars point out that the adjustments in American policy are based on pragmatic considerations rather than a reflection of a fundamental change in US global strategy (Fu Mengzi 2002: 26).

Despite its seemingly less unilateralist stance, America's basic strategic thinking is believed to be based upon the pursuit of hegemonism (Chu Shulong 2001: 8). In his address to a Joint Session of Congress and the American People on 20 September 2001, Bush made it clear that: 'Every nation, in every region, now has a decision to make. Either you are with us, or you are with the terrorists' (Bush 2001). To the Chinese, this does not indicate any change in America's hegemonic attitudes towards other countries. Thus, they insist that any international campaign against terrorism should be led by the UN and conducted in accordance with international law. More importantly, the national sovereignty of independent states should not be violated in the name of fighting terrorism (Wang Tingdong 2002: 53; Yang Jin 2001: 57). This signals their concern that America might use the war on terrorism as a pretext to attack other states. Indeed, some scholars question the legality of America's military operations in Afghanistan without the approval of the UN Security Council. If anti-terrorism were to be led by a great power rather than the UN, they argue, it would only serve the interests of the great power, and the world order would become even more unequal and unjust (Qian Wenrong 2002: 28, 30–31).

There is a consensus among Chinese security analysts that America is the major source of global instability. The tensions between the US and other countries, they assert, lie in Washington's ambitions to build a unipolar global system in an increasingly multipolar world. By early 2002, many Chinese observers detected the domination of 'realist' thinking in foreign policy circles in America. The Quadrennial Defense Review Report (US Department of Defense 2001) and Washington's unilateral withdrawal from the Anti-Ballistic Missiles (ABM) Treaty, they argue, show that America's pre-9/11 global strategy remains largely unchanged and that its pursuit of international primacy in a world of uncertainty is seen to be desirable (Feng Shaolei 2002; Zhou Jianming 2002).

The 9/11 terrorist attacks have inflicted enormous financial damage on the US and a devastating psychological shock to the American people, Shi Yinhong (2001) concurs, but they have enabled President Bush to mobilize elite and popular support for his policies. Specialists such as Ge Lide (2002) of the National Defence University are especially concerned about America's proposed plan to develop NMD and TMD systems which could undermine Beijing's nuclear deterrent. The Chinese had hoped that the Bush administration would not continue with the NMD project in light of the non-conventional attacks on America. But they were soon disappointed by US withdrawal from the ABM Treaty with Russia in December 2001. Hence, Professor Ge concludes that the strategic aim of the US is to achieve absolute security and global dominance. Similarly, the real purpose of America's war in Afghanistan is to try to shape the future of the country rather than to capture bin Laden. The war, according to Chinese analysis, gives the Americans a golden opportunity to move into the oil-rich region of Central Asia

(Shi Lan and Li Wenjing 2002: 25; Zhang Wenmu 2002: 42–43; Yang Yunzhong 2002a: 6).

The Chinese are convinced that America's desire to dominate the world has not been deterred by the 9/11 attacks. On the contrary, according to Yang Yunzhong (2002a: 5), the tragic events have provided the US with an opportunity to expand its sphere of influence which has increased through the development of its anti-terrorist coalition. Chinese analysts assert that the coalition is useful to the US in achieving its global strategy. First, America has successfully exploited the sympathy of other countries to improve its relatively isolated position prior to 9/11. By and large, the cause of anti-terrorism has wide-ranging support from the UN and other nations including Russia and China, America's two potential rivals. Second, the Bush administration is said to be able to withdraw from the ABM Treaty without facing widespread condemnation because of the international community's preoccupation with the 'war on terrorism'. Third, the US has taken advantage of the anti-terrorist sentiment at home and abroad to discredit any anti-American or anti-hegemonic forces as forces of 'evil'. Fourth, Washington is able to have a military presence in Central Asia which, the Chinese believe, would have been impossible under any other circumstances. Fifth, 9/11 and the subsequent war in Afghanistan have enabled America to strengthen its security relations with NATO members, Japan and other allies. Lastly, to consolidate its unipolar position in the international system, it is argued that the US has made use of the post-9/11 situation to set and dominate the agenda on international anti-terrorist activities. All in all, America's influence around the world has augmented substantially after 9/11, according to Chinese analysis (Ruan Zongze 2002: 37–39).

Of particular concern to Chinese analysts is President Bush's reference to Iran, Iraq and North Korea as an 'axis of evil'. They are certain that Bush has sought to demonize these countries so as to increase his popularity, justify a massive rise in military spending and stimulate the American economy through increased arms production (Wang Hongwei 2002). More worrying for China's security specialists is the shift in America's strategic emphasis towards the Asia-Pacific (Yang Yunzhong 2002a: 5–7). Zhou Jianming (2002) and others believe that the US has tried to maintain its military presence in, and fortify its security ties with, other Asia-Pacific countries with a view to containing China which is perceived as America's main rival and potential enemy (Chu Shulong 2001; Yang Yunzhong 2002a: 7). To the Chinese, the swift removal of the Taliban regime in Afghanistan has demonstrated unambiguously US determination and capability of using its superior military power to eradicate any perceived threat to American security interests. Chinese elites are increasingly worried that the Bush administration will exploit the post-9/11 security situation to enhance America's global position. This is why former Chinese Foreign Minister, Tang Jiaxuan, warned at the UN in September 2002 that 'efforts should be made to prevent the arbitrary expansion' of the war on terrorism (CNN 2002).

If China had any suspicions of America's anti-terrorist motives after 9/11, they were confirmed by the publication of the US *National Security Strategy* (NSS) (US Department of State 2002b). Chinese analysts have paid a great deal of attention to the report. They feel that the NSS has validated their assessment of America's 'hegemonic' ambitions. The assertion in the document that the US possesses 'unprecedented – and unequaled – strength and influence in the world' (US Department of State 2002b: 1) is said to reflect both America's formidable power and its arrogance. Chinese analysts see the report as the most explicit exposition of the Bush administration's global strategy. They argue that America's strategic aim remains the consolidation of its unipolar position in the international system, using US superiority to seek absolute security. As the NSS puts it, 'Today, the United States enjoys a position of unparalleled military strength and great economic and political influence.' (US Department of State 2002b). To the Chinese, this implies that the US would not allow any other countries, friends or foes, to challenge its position, and that any attempts to do so would be futile. But the US government recognizes that the 'gravest danger' America is facing lies at 'the crossroads of radicalism and technology'. Thus, the most pressing task is to prevent international organizations or states that sponsored terrorist activities from gaining or using WMD.

In order to do this, Chinese analysts point out, the US needs to maintain good relationships with other great powers. The NSS acknowledges that Russia is 'in the midst of hopeful transition' and that Chinese leaders are 'discovering that economic freedom' is the 'only source of national wealth'. Great power cooperation was clearly important to the Bush administration in its war on terrorism. Not surprisingly, America's intention of leading the cause of promoting democracy, development, free markets and free trade throughout the world is viewed with great suspicion. What worries Chinese leaders and elites most is the inclusion of the Bush administration's new strategic doctrine in an official document, signifying a fundamental shift from the Cold War strategy of deterrence to a new doctrine supporting pre-emptive strikes against terrorist groups and any states sheltering them and/or possessing WMD. This doctrine, they fear, could be used to justify any military actions in the name of self-defence and anti-terrorism. Chinese analysts argue that it would be against international law and the UN Charter to launch pre-emptive attacks on other countries which, in their judgement, would seriously undermine international stability and world order. Judging from the NSS, Chinese scholars such as Guo Xiangang (2003: 22) conclude that the Bush administration's foreign policy was a unilateral policy packaged as one of multilateralism.

The Bush doctrine, pre-emption and the Iraq war

Since 2001, US global strategy has been shaped and guided by what has come to be known as the Bush Doctrine (Daniel, Dombrowski and Payne 2005; Heisbourg 2003; Jervis 2003, 2005; Kaufman 2007; Singh 2006). The main elements and rationale of the Bush Doctrine have been articulated in various official documents and addresses given by President Bush and his colleagues. Essentially, the Doctrine consists of a number of key components. The most well-known and contentious one is probably the legitimization of 'pre-emptive action' in eradicating any actual or potential threat to American security whenever and wherever it emerges. A related element of the Doctrine is combating global terrorism, which has shaped US policy considerations since the 9/11 terrorist attacks. This is closely linked to the emphasis on preventing 'rogue states' and terrorist organizations from obtaining or producing WMD that may be used against the United States and its allies. In the view of the US government, the threat to American security does not have to be current or imminent to justify military actions. The growing threats of WMD combined with the challenge from states that are connected to or supportive of terrorist movements have necessitated a rethinking of the effectiveness of deterrence in protecting US national security. America will work with international organizations or other countries to deal with global and regional security problems if possible, but will not hesitate to act unilaterally to safeguard its interests. As President Bush put it in his 2002 West Point speech: 'Our security will require all Americans to be forward-looking and resolute, to be ready for preemptive action when necessary to defend our liberty and to defend our lives' (Bush 2002).

To some Chinese analysts, Bush deliberately obscures the difference between pre-emptive actions and preventive wars (Liu Aming and Wang Lianhe 2005). They argue that pre-emption is a response to the threat of an imminent offensive or invasion while a preventive war is usually launched to prevent possible external attacks. Under certain circumstances, pre-emptive wars could be justified. A preventive war, on the other hand, is a matter of choice on the part of political leaders. As such, this type of war is said to be of an aggressive nature, challenging international law and making it more difficult to resolve conflict peacefully. Chinese scholars also contest the Bush administration's argument that pre-emption is the most effective way of removing potential threats to US security. They contend that it would be very difficult to obtain accurate intelligence about one's adversary and that most people's analysis of potential enemies would be biased. Even with reliable intelligence, they note, it would not be easy to know the real intentions of leaders of other countries. Equally difficult would be an objective assessment of the capabilities and past behaviour of one's adversary (Hao Yufan 2005: 8–9). If all other countries were to follow Bush's approach to the prevention of possible threats, they said, the world would become chaotic and lawless.

Another component of the Bush Doctrine is related to the promotion of liberal democracy and free markets around the world, especially in the Middle East, that are believed to be essential to the enhancement of global peace and security. Indeed, fostering 'regime change' in countries that are considered domestically repressive and externally aggressive is an integral part of the Doctrine. Democracy promotion is, of course, rooted in the traditions of US foreign policy, and the belief in freedom and democracy is not confined to the Bush administration (Monten 2005). However, its conviction in the linkage between peace and democracy has arguably surpassed that of previous administrations. More importantly, the passion in advocating 'democratic peace' has been buttressed by an extraordinary resolve to sustain US military superiority over all other nations, which is seen as the best guarantee of peace, democracy and freedom. 'In the unipolar world we inhabit', argues Charles Krauthammer (2004), 'what stability we do enjoy today is owed to the overwhelming power and deterrent threat of the United States'. Thus, the mission of promoting liberal democratic ideas and systems worldwide cannot be accomplished without the realist means of military capabilities.

The notion of 'democratic realism' (Krauthammer 2004) or 'moral democratic realism' (Kaufman 2007) is clearly conveyed in the 2002 NSS document: 'At present the United States faces no global rival. America's grand strategy should aim to preserve and extend this advantageous position as far into the future as possible' (US Department of State 2002b). Not surprisingly, the Bush administration's aspirations of spreading American values through military means have led to considerable anxiety among PRC scholars. They believe that the US government has exaggerated the connections between terrorism and the 'rogue states' intentionally in order to legitimize pre-emptive attacks against countries whose regimes are disapproved by the American government (Liu Aming and Wang Lianhe 2005). The Bush Doctrine, in their view, is an offensive, adventurous and expansionist doctrine (Sa Benwang 2003). As such, the US 'mission' of using extraordinary military power to promote democracy and maintain peace and stability is only a façade for establishing an American empire in the 21st century.

Towards the end of 2002, Chinese security specialists were increasingly concerned that the Bush administration was building up a case for applying the doctrine of pre-emption to Iraq. In the view of the Chinese, US leaders had wanted to remove Saddam Hussein from power ever since the end of the 1991 Gulf War. They regarded 'regime change' as the key to the solution of the Iraq problem. This explained America's portrayal of Saddam as a tyrant who had connections with the Al-Qaeda network. The Iraqi regime was also portrayed as a totalitarian country that posed a serious threat to America and its allies. Another reason for America to attack Iraq, according to Chinese analysis, was to use Iraq as a 'negative example' sending a clear signal to other members of the 'axis of evil' that the US had both the will and the capability to take on any perceived enemies. In addition, the US saw the establishment of a 'democratic' Iraq as a first step towards the democratization of the Middle East and, in the longer term, the entire Muslim world. Deposing Saddam would, Chinese analysts believe, help enhance the security of Israel and force the Palestinian leaders to democratize their country. But democracy promotion was not the only motive for invading Iraq, say the Chinese. Another consideration for the Bush administration was America's energy security. Control over Iraq's oil resources, it is argued, would ensure a stable supply of energy for the US. Chinese scholars and security analysts seem to agree that a successful US invasion of Iraq would bring about substantial geopolitical and economic advantages for America, which would in turn help fortify its hegemonic position in the post-Cold War world (Liu Jianfei 2003; Zhang Youxia 2003; Liu Jinzhi 2004).

The approach taken by the PRC leaders in handling the Iraq crisis seemed to have been informed by Chinese analysts' analysis of US intentions. In November 2002, China voted along with other permanent Security Council members on resolution 1441 in the hope that the US could be dissuaded from tackling the crisis unilaterally. As Zhang Qiyue, a PRC Foreign Ministry spokeswoman, put it: 'I think our position is extremely close to that of France' (CNN 2003a). In a telephone conversation with President Jacques Chirac, former Chinese President

Jiang Zemin reportedly said that 'the Iraq issue should be resolved through political and diplomatic means within the framework of the UN' (CNN 2003b).

Although Chinese scholars and commentators were critical of US approaches to Iraq, the official media had by and large refrained from publishing reports that expressed strong anti-American sentiments. However, from January 2003 onwards, Chinese analysts became much more outspoken and there were noticeably more articles criticizing US policy. When two UN arms inspectors, Drs Hans Blix and Mohamed ElBaradei, informed the Security Council that they were unable to find evidence of WMD in Iraq (Blix 2004: 175–78), former Chinese Foreign Minister Tang Jiaxuan joined his French and Russian colleagues in pressing for continued UN inspection. He argued that 'to intensify inspections is for the purpose of seeking a peaceful solution to the Iraqi issue, we are obliged to try our best and use all possible means to avert war' (CNN 2003c).

In the build-up to war, the CCP's Leading Group on National Security (LGNS)[1] met regularly to discuss how China should respond to the situation. The LGNS was deeply concerned about the tendency of 'US unilateralism' and America's global ambitions, and their implications for Chinese security interests (Lam 2003b). After President Bush asserted that it would no longer be possible to disarm Saddam Hussein peacefully, Chinese officials, including Premier Wen Jiabao and Foreign Minister Li Zhaoxing, continued to express their opposition to military attack on Iraq without UN approval (CNN 2003d) but did not wish to confront Washington directly. Critical of the US-led military actions, Chinese officials called for an end to the war, emphasizing the consequences of civilian casualties and humanitarian catastrophe. The invasion had, in the words of Li Zhaoxing, 'trampled upon the UN Constitution and international law'. The war was also condemned by China's parliament, the National People's Congress (NPC) and the advisory Chinese People's Political Consultative Conference. Chinese leaders were warned by their advisers that America could become more assertive in Asia in pursuing its interests following a successful operation in Iraq (Lam 2003a). A group of Chinese intellectuals was permitted to organize a conference that condemned US 'hegemonism' (Lam 2003b). Meanwhile, numerous articles were published in the state media which vehemently criticized the US invasion.

The US invasion of Iraq, according to Professor Liu Jinzhi (2004) of Peking University, should be understood in the context of the Bush administration's attempts to build an American empire (*Meiguo diguo*). He argues that the Iraq war can be seen as a practice of Bush's imperial foreign policy (*diguo waijiao*) and that it would be used as a model for America's imperial expansion in future (see Tonnesson 2004 for a critical review of the debate among Western scholars on America's 'imperial temptation'). Liu's view is shared by many Chinese scholars who concluded that the war in Iraq would have undesirable consequences for international relations, and global peace and security in particular (Gao Zugui 2004; Zhu Kun 2004). The US is said to have launched the war on false pretences which, they judge, has set a very bad precedent of great power invasion of a small country. When America failed to obtain UN approval for military action, it chose to form a 'coalition of the willing' with a group of countries and push ahead with the invasion. This, to the Chinese, has revealed America's disdain for international law. In order to justify its hegemonic policy, the Chinese argue, the Bush administration has produced a whole range of jargons or 'theories' to discredit potential targets such as 'the rogue states', 'failed states', 'the axis of evil', 'regime change' and so on (see Stephen Chan 2005 and Mel Gurtov 2006 for critical analyses of the axis of evil). PRC analysts reject the Bush administration's claim that the Iraq war is part of the war on global terrorism, arguing instead that the war has actually stimulated more terrorist activities against America and its allies. Some Chinese specialists assert that Bush's Middle East policy is essentially based on the theory of 'clash of civilizations', and its ideological focus on reforming the Islamic world would only result in greater tension in the region (An Huihou 2004).

Most Chinese writers are of the opinion that the Iraq war has seriously damaged the world order and that the philosophy of 'might makes right' may now prevail in international affairs (Li Jingzhi 2003a). Some argue that the Iraq war represents the beginning of a process whereby the US attempts to reshape the international order based on its new security strategy. The doctrine of pre-emption, they predict, may well be applied to other countries making certain states vulnerable. To Chinese analysts, America's 'pre-emptive strike' on Iraq reflects its unilateral position, total disregard of world opinion and contempt for the UN. Iraq posed no imminent threat to America, they contend, nor did it possess any WMD. The real motive behind the invasion was to fortify US economic, political, and military dominance in the world (Wang Jian 2003). Some Chinese policy elites predicted in 2003 that the Bush administration would become more conservative and hawkish in its foreign policy after the success of US military occupation of Iraq. A 'democratic' Iraqi regime is seen to be central to the neoconservative agenda of democratizing the Middle East that is also closely linked to America's anti-terrorist strategy. The Iraq 'project', the Chinese conclude, would help enhance US economic and strategic interests in the region which, combined with America's growing influence in other areas, would ensure its global dominance in the post-9/11 world (Li Jingzhi 2003a).

More recently, Chinese analysts contend that the invasion of Iraq has not helped the Bush administration in achieving its mission of democracy promotion in the Middle East. On the contrary, the situation in Iraq has become very unstable since the removal of Saddam Hussein's regime, with suicide-bombing incidents regularly occurring. The stability and peace that the American government had promised to bring to the Iraqi people when invading the country have not materialized, say the Chinese. As a result of the foreign policy disaster in Iraq, they assert, the influence of the Bush Doctrine began to wane in 2004 (Zhou Qi 2007).

PRC scholars note that the Bush Doctrine is underpinned by the ideas and policies advocated by the neoconservatives, including pre-emption, regime change, unilateralism and benign hegemony. Neoconservatives tend to believe that American interest is best served by military expansion and worldwide democratization. Indeed, a number of core members of the neoconservative think-tank, Project for the New American Century, such as Donald Rumsfeld, Dick Cheney and Paul Wolfowitz, occupied prominent positions in the first Bush administration. However, some neoconservative figures were replaced by the more pragmatic ones in Bush's second term in office. This, according to the Chinese, signifies the decline of neoconservativism's dominance in US foreign policy. Towards the end of his presidency, Bush no longer saw pre-emptive strike as an effective means of dealing with the other two states within the 'axis of evils', namely Iran and North Korea (Zhou Qi 2007: 25).

To many Chinese security analysts, the demise of the Bush Doctrine is inevitable for a number of reasons. First, the US invasion of Iraq is regarded as an illegal action by many countries around the world and it has seriously undermined international law and the authority of the UN. The second problem for the Bush administration, it is argued, is its inability to find any WMD in Iraq, which rendered America's attack on the country indefensible. The third is the failure of US efforts to rebuild a stable Iraqi society and establish a democratic system there. This, PRC analysts contend, has proved that democracy cannot be imposed on other countries externally through military means. They conclude that Bush's foreign and security policy has led to an intense anti-American sentiment in various parts of the world and widespread rejection of America's 'benign hegemony' (Zhou Qi 2007: 26–27).

Bush's Asia-Pacific security strategy

As discussed in the previous section, Chinese scholars and analysts are highly suspicious of the Bush administration's global strategy. In their view, US security strategy towards the Asia-Pacific reflects both America's global interests and the changing security situation after 9/11 (see Beeson 2006 and Gurtov and Van Ness 2005 for perspectives from other Asia-Pacific countries on Bush's security strategy).

In terms of overall geopolitical considerations, PRC analysts believe that Bush has accepted Clinton's assessment that it is important to consider the roles of Europe and Asia simultaneously in US global strategy. To the Americans, Eurasia (*OuYa dalu*) is a region of geostrategic significance where the US has long-standing allies, as well as emerging rivals, including China, Russia and India (Song Yimin 2001: 3–4). While Europe remains a key strategic area for America, Chinese specialists maintain that the Bush administration has gradually shifted its strategic focus towards the Asia-Pacific. This is because Washington is thought to be less concerned about the security environment in Europe. According to the Chinese, America has greater military and political control over Europe via NATO. Subsequent to NATO's eastward expansion, it is argued, US influence on European security affairs will increase further. Although Russia is seen as a potential challenger to America's global dominance, its national strength has declined substantially in recent years. At the same time, it is in the process of integrating itself into the West politically and economically. Thus, Russia will not present a direct challenge to the US, at least not for the time being. In addition, there are no regional flashpoints in Europe that would threaten America's national security and global interests, say the Chinese. With the exception of the Balkans, Europe is in peace. Even in that area, the conflict in the former Yugoslavia does not constitute a threat to US security (Yang Yunzhong 2002a: 8).

In the Asia-Pacific, however, America is believed to have more security concerns. Despite its military presence in the region, the US has not established a military alliance similar to that of NATO, nor does it have alliance relations with the majority of Asian countries. As US troops are stationed primarily in North East Asia, the Chinese observe, its military presence in South East Asia is far from adequate. On the whole, America's military influence in the Asia-Pacific is relatively weak. However, this is a region with a number of major security issues that could present an immense challenge to US global and regional security interests. Of particular concern to the United States is the status of Taiwan, the tension on the Korean Peninsula and the territorial disputes in the South China Sea. Chinese analysts point out that America may well be dragged into any of these issues should they develop into a major conflict. Related to these regional security issues is the emergence of China as a great power whose rapid economic growth and rising military capabilities are seen as a tremendous challenge to the US. From the Chinese perspective, America has always wanted to dominate Asia-Pacific security affairs but is frustrated that it may not be able to realize its ambition.

PRC security experts believe that Bush has been more proactive and assertive than Clinton in shaping the Asia-Pacific security environment. By exaggerating the security threat in the region, they argue, the Bush administration has tried to find some justification for strengthening America's military power and developing and deploying the TMD system in Asia. The Chinese predict that Bush would encourage Japan to play a more significant role in Asia-Pacific security matters. They also expect the US to be more active in tackling security issues in North East Asia while cultivating relations with South East Asian countries. What the Americans intend to do, the Chinese suspect, is to organize a 'coalition of the willing' to deal with the challenge of a rising China (Song Yimin 2001: 5).

Most Chinese security analysts believe that 9/11 has not altered the trend in America's strategic shift towards the Asia-Pacific, but it has had a considerable impact on the focus of the Bush administration's strategy in the region. Prior to 9/11, the geographical focus of US strategy in the Asia-Pacific was on the Western Pacific area, including North and South East Asia (see Map 2). After 9/11, this has been broadened to encompass Central and South Asia (see Map 3) and certain parts of the Middle East. In terms of strategic priority, the Chinese note, American leaders were more concerned about traditional security issues in East Asia before 9/11, especially the security implications of the rise of China. In the post-9/11 era, however, the most pressing task for the US government is to combat terrorism and achieve its strategic objectives in Central Asia. Indeed, as PRC scholars point out, Central Asia is a very important area in Eurasia because of its strategic location and rich resources.

The war in Afghanistan has fundamentally changed the geopolitical situation in the region which, according to Chinese analysis, has led to major adjustments in the foreign policy and security strategy of various countries. The most obvious outcome of this geopolitical realignment, the Chinese note, is the growing influence of the US in Central Asia. They lament the fact that America has gained substantially from the new regional balance of power. With Russia's agreement, US forces were able to use the military bases of some Central Asian states for their military operations in Afghanistan (see also the analysis in Malik 2002). Apart from its strategic gains in Central Asia, say the Chinese, Washington has benefited hugely from the cooperation of both Pakistan and India in its 'war on terrorism', thus strengthening the US strategic position in South Asia (Yang Yunzhong 2002a: 9–10).

Nevertheless, PRC analysts recognize the diversity and complexity of security threats that the US is facing. They agree that anti-terrorism has become a major element of America's Asia-Pacific security strategy. To the US leaders, South East, North East, Central and South Asia are all parts of a single and interrelated entity in terms of its counter-terrorist strategy. America is said to have handled its political and economic relations with the countries in all these areas on the basis of the nature and degree of their cooperation in the war on terrorism. For example, the US government has paid greater attention to South East Asia where certain terrorist groups are suspected to be linked to the Al-Qaeda network. In its struggle against terrorism, the US has received wide-ranging assistance from regional leaders, although the motives for and level of their support differ (Zabriskie 2001). Indeed, Chinese security analysts observe that America has made a special effort to upgrade and restructure its alliance relations with Japan, South Korea and Australia so as to support US security strategy in the post-9/11 era. The US-Japan-Australia trilateral strategic dialogue is a good example, illustrating how traditional bilateral security alliances are coordinated to meet new challenges. Australia announced in 2003 that it would be involved in the development of America's TMD system. According to Chinese analysis, the US government intends to supplement bilateral alliances with multilateral 'coalitions of the willing' to enforce America's anti-terrorist and anti-proliferation measures in the Asia-Pacific and beyond. While maintaining its forward military presence in the Asia-Pacific, Washington has reconfigured its forces in the region as part of US global military adjustments (Liu Xuecheng 2004b; Tao Wenzhao 2005).

In the eyes of the Chinese, America's fundamental strategic aim in the Asia-Pacific is to maintain its leading position and the balance of power in the region, preventing the emergence of any regional hegemon from threatening US interests. Nevertheless, given the priority of anti-terrorism, the Chinese observe, America has placed considerable emphasis on great power relations in the Asia-Pacific and seeks to prevent the escalation of any regional flashpoints from disrupting US global strategy. Meanwhile, the promotion of liberal democratic values and political reform in the region is not treated as a priority compared to the need to form anti-terrorist alliances. This, say PRC analysts, explains why America has no hesitation in improving its security relations with such countries as Pakistan, Indonesia and Malaysia, whose human rights records may not be acceptable by American standards. The emphasis is on the construction of a series of formal and informal multilateral security alliances, which is believed to be the third pillar of the Bush administration's Asia-Pacific security strategy in addition to bilateral alliances and forward military arrangements (Wu Xinbo 2007: 14–15).

Japan and US security strategy

As discussed in Chapter Two, Japan has played a pivotal role in US policy towards Asia since the end of World War II, and the US-Japan security alliance has been strengthened considerably after the two countries signed a joint declaration in 1996. When Bush came into office in 2001, he criticized Clinton for paying too much attention to developing a 'strategic partnership' with China, thus neglecting valuable allies like Japan. The Bush administration has made it clear that it wishes Japan to play a more prominent role in regional security affairs. On many occasions, US leaders have emphasized the indispensable role of Tokyo in maintaining US security interests in Asia, making a genuine effort to strengthen and expand the US-Japan security alliance.

Unsurprisingly, the greater importance of Japan in America's security strategy in the Asia-Pacific has caused much anxiety among Chinese elites and analysts. They argue that the real motive behind America's effort to enhance US-Japanese security relations is to constrain China which is seen as a 'strategic competitor' (Li Xiao 2001). China's concern has been exacerbated by the Japanese government's response to 9/11. After initial hesitation, Koizumi Junichiro, the Japanese Prime Minister, decided to offer the US all the necessary support in its 'war against terrorism'. On 19 September 2001, Koizumi announced a seven-point assistance plan, which was followed by the passage of counterterrorism legislation by the Diet in October of the same year.

This was appreciated by Bush who called Japan 'the bedrock for peace and prosperity in the Pacific' during his visit to Tokyo in February 2002. In 2002, the Japanese government also expressed its willingness to back America if it were to attack Iraq but it was constrained by Article 9 of its constitution, which would prevent the Self-Defence Forces (SDF) from taking part in US military operations (Hughes 2004b). Initially, the Japanese government was in favour of finding a peaceful solution to the Iraq crisis. After America, Britain and Spain set a deadline for disarming Iraq through diplomatic channels, Koizumi announced Japan's support. He expressed his regret for the UN's failure to deal with the crisis peacefully, but noted that military operations could be legitimized by past UNSC resolutions (Berkofsky 2003).

Nonetheless, Koizumi did not hide the fact that his government backed the US invasion because of the necessity of maintaining the US-Japan security alliance. 'To lose trust in the Japan-US security relationships', as he explained in March 2003, 'would be against Japan's national interests' (CNN 2003d). This was particularly true when nuclear development in North Korea was considered as an escalating threat to Japan. The Japanese government might have had some reservations over Washington's strategy of military pre-emption in tackling regional issues, but it stood shoulder to shoulder with the Bush administration in its decision to attack Iraq. The need for closer Japan-US security cooperation, especially in the area of missile defence, was reiterated in Japan's third National Defense Program Outline in December 2004 (Japanese Defense Agency 2004).

To the Chinese, 9/11 and the war on terrorism have provided America with the opportunity to deepen its alliance relations with Japan in order to achieve various security objectives in Asia and beyond (Fu Mengzi and Yang Wenjing 2004). Indeed, Japan will be expected to play a prominent role in America's comprehensive restructuring of its military forces overseas in the coming decade, Chinese analysts argue. According to the plan announced by President Bush in August 2004, most of the troops to be withdrawn from Asia were stationed in South Korea. Washington did not reveal how many US troops would be withdrawn from Japan at that stage. PRC strategic analyst Wang Chiming (2005: 57–58) has speculated that American troops in Japan may not be reduced at all. In any case, he does not expect any significant reduction in US military bases and facilities in Japan. Professor Wang notes that a second aircraft carrier battle group would be deployed in the Pacific, and that more air force bombers and other advanced strike assets would be stationed in Guam, along with the transfer of military personnel from Washington State to Japan (see Map 2).

As the White House puts it, America will work with its strongest allies to restructure its military presence and command structures, while simultaneously improving capabilities in the Asia-Pacific (US Department of State 2004). Chinese security specialists thus expect Japan to play an enhanced role within the new command structures following America's force realignment (Sun Cheng 2005). This will help integrate Japanese forces more closely with US forces. Given the strategic locations of Okinawa and Guam, the US will have to rely heavily on Japan to respond to any potential crises in the Taiwan Strait and the Korean Peninsula (see Map 2). But Chinese analysts believe that the American government has a much broader agenda, aiming to transform US-Japan security relations from a bilateral alliance that focuses on 'the situation in Japan's surrounding areas' to a global security partnership similar to the special relationship between America and Britain. In order to achieve this, they predict that Washington will persuade the Japanese government to redefine the nature of the US-Japan alliance again, and to revise Japan's constitution accordingly (Wang Chiming 2005: 59). From China's perspective, such a US-Japan alliance will put the United States in a much stronger position to pursue its 'hegemonic policy' throughout the world.

China, Taiwan and Bush's China policy

During the Clinton era, the relationship between the United States and China was characterized as one of 'strategic partnership' (*zhanlue huoban guanxi*). However, Chinese policy elites remained wary of US policy towards China and believed that it consisted of elements of both engagement and containment. In the view of many PRC analysts, there is no serious difference between the Democrats and Republicans in terms of their perceptions of a rising China. They are all concerned that an economically and militarily powerful China would almost certainly challenge America's security interests around the world, especially in the Asia-Pacific (Song Yimin 2001: 6). Nevertheless, the Bush campaign is said to have placed more emphasis on the containment aspects of America's China policy, arguing that Beijing should be regarded as a 'strategic competitor' (*zhanlue duishou*) rather than a strategic partner (Yang Jiemian 2000: 26–28).

This view of the PRC was well articulated by Condoleezza Rice (2000: 55–57) in her article 'Promoting the National Interest' in *Foreign Affairs*. She argued that China was not a status quo power and that it would present a potential threat to Asia-Pacific security. Indeed, immediately after taking office, President Bush took steps to strengthen America's security relations with friends and allies across the Asia-Pacific. This heightened China's negative perceptions of US security intentions. The mid-air collision of an EP-3 spy plane and a Chinese fighter jet over the South China Sea, and the subsequent unauthorized emergency landing of the American plane on China's Hainan island in April 2001, led to a major diplomatic crisis between the two countries. Meanwhile, Bush approved the sale of a significant arms package to Taipei and said in public that the US would do 'whatever it took to help Taiwan defend herself' (Sanger 2001).

However, the Chinese note, many Americans recognized the potential benefits from trading with China, whose market was growing rapidly, and the importance of maintaining a stable US-China relationship. Chinese analysts discerned an adjustment in Bush's China policy in mid-2001 (Xia Liping 2004: 5). When Colin Powell, the former US Secretary of State, visited China in July, he had abandoned the talk of 'strategic competition' in America's relations with the PRC. Instead, Powell advocated the development of a 'constructive cooperative relationship' between the two nations. PRC scholars and security analysts seem to agree that both engagement and containment are central to the Bush administration's China strategy, although the emphasis on one or the other varies depending on the circumstances or policy areas. They also believe that the two dimensions of America's policy towards China should not be considered in isolation. Instead, they are intertwined and mutually reinforcing. The real purpose of engagement, it is argued, is to change China in ways that would make it less likely to contest US interests in future.

Economically, this strategy is designed to make China more dependent on and interdependent with America and the West so that the Chinese leaders would have vested interests in preserving the existing international order. Politically, engagement would allow the US to spread the ideology of Western liberal democracy to China which, over time, could help transform its political system. Through engagement, Chinese analysts contend, America hopes to gain from China's market, foster political change in the PRC, shape and constrain Chinese behaviour and bring China into the orbit of an international system dominated by the United States. This is characterized by Professor Hao Yufan (2005) as 'restrictive engagement' (*xianzhixing jiechu*). At the same time, the US is believed to have put in place a variety of strategic plans and military measures to guard against a China that might challenge America's 'hegemonic position' if and when it becomes stronger.

To Chinese analysts, America's policy of 'engagement plus containment' is evident in all areas of the Bush administration's China strategy. To begin with, Bush's security policy towards Beijing is thought to have exhibited elements of containment and engagement prior to 9/11. This policy has continued into the post-9/11 period, according to the Chinese, although they have expressed considerable concern over the security implications of America's war on terrorism for China.

PRC analysts recognize that the 9/11 terrorist attacks have provided a new opportunity for Sino-American cooperation, as both sides share a common interest in fighting terrorism. Indeed, in October 2001, Chinese and US leaders agreed to establish an anti-terrorist consultative mechanism, and four high-level consultative meetings had taken place by the end of 2004. In October 2002, China agreed to let the Federal Bureau of Investigation (FBI) set up an office in Beijing, which became operational in April 2004. In October of the same year, the FBI announced that it would collaborate with China in providing security for the 2008 Olympics in Beijing, given the potential threat of global terrorism. The challenge of terrorism, the Chinese observe, has emerged as a major threat to US security after 9/11 and the Bush administration needs the support and cooperation of other countries, including China, to combat terrorism (Sun Jinzhong 2005: 16).

Indeed, China's willingness to cooperate with the US in fighting international terrorism was welcomed by President Bush. When attending the October 2001 APEC meeting in Shanghai, Bush referred to the US and China as 'two great nations'. He assured the then Chinese President Jiang Zemin that 'we will always deal with our differences in a spirit of mutual respect'. More significantly, he said that America wanted 'to seek a relationship [with China] that is candid, constructive and cooperative' (US Department of State 2001). In December, the US government granted China permanent status as a normal trading partner which, according to the White House, marked 'the final stage in normalizing US-China trade relations' (BBC 2001c).

However, America and China seem to have different views on the origins of terrorism, the approaches to fighting it and the expected outcomes of anti-terrorist cooperation. PRC security analysts admit that the two countries disagree on how to conduct the 'war on terrorism'. They maintain that Washington considers the anti-terrorist war as essentially a war of ideas, and the spread of American values and democracy around the world as the best guarantee of winning the war against terrorism. America's preferred strategy of eradicating terrorists is to destroy them through military means, using pre-emptive strikes in particular. All this is rejected by Chinese elites and analysts who are convinced that the US has exploited the war on terrorism to reconstitute the international order and fortify its 'leading position' in the international system. In this sense, anti-terrorist campaigns based on traditional military intervention and invasion are said to have become a new instrument for America to implement its global strategy in the 21st century (Sun Jinzhong 2005).

Chinese scholars and analysts believe that the need to have the PRC's cooperation in tackling terrorism has contributed to the increasing prominence and visibility of the engagement aspect of the Bush administration's China policy, thus stabilizing Sino-US bilateral relations. Nonetheless, they argue, anti-terrorism has not changed the 'structural contradictions' (*jiegouxing maodun*) between the two countries (Sun Jinzhong 2005: 18; Yang Yunzhong 2003a: 9). By this, they mean the clash of America's geopolitical interests with China. The majority of Chinese scholars are of the view that Washington views China as a potential strategic competitor that must be contained or at least guarded against. Their assessment was reinforced by a Central Intelligence Agency (CIA) report in 2002 that estimated China's ballistic missiles would increase several-fold by 2015, and that they would be deployed primarily against the US (CIA 2002).

Moreover, the Americans worry that the PRC's rapidly expanding military power, especially its nuclear capabilities, would present an immense challenge to the US. Concerns about China's military modernization and its potential threat to Asia-Pacific security and US security interests have been expressed in several Pentagon reports (see, for example, US Department of Defense 2005, 2006a, 2006b, 2007). To most Chinese analysts, the war on terrorism has enabled the US to consolidate its defence ties with traditional allies and develop new security relations across Asia. They are convinced that America's growing military presence in the Asia-Pacific and enhanced alliance relationships with a range of countries surrounding China are aimed primarily at encircling China. As a result, Beijing's peripheral security environment is thought to have deteriorated after 9/11 (Yang Yunzhong 2003a: 8–9; Gao Zichuan 2004: 9–10; Sun Jinzhong 2005: 18).

Many Chinese scholars believe that America's Asia-Pacific strategy revolves primarily around its assessment of the significance and implications of a rising China. In other words, US perception and policy in the region are often shaped by China's activities and interactions with other countries, particularly its Asian neighbours. For example, Washington is thought to have exhibited an ambiguous attitude towards the East Asian Summit, hoping that it would be led by ASEAN states rather than driven by a major power like China (Ren Xiao 2007: 51–52).

According to Wu Xinbo (2007) of Shanghai's Fudan University, there are three core concepts that underpin the Bush administration's China policy. The first one is dissuasion, which is said to have informed US strategic thinking relating to major and emerging powers, particularly China. This concept has been employed in the 2001 and 2006 Quadrennial Defense Review Reports as well as the NSS published in 2002 and 2006. Professor Wu believes that the US government is determined to dissuade any countries that may have the technological potential to develop their military power and challenge US military supremacy in future. PRC security analysts are convinced that the main target of America's strategy of dissuasion is China, whose defence capabilities are developing rapidly. However, they reject the US assessment that 'the pace and scope of China's military build-up already puts regional military balances at risk' (US Department of Defense 2006a: 29). Although the Bush administration has somewhat downplayed this strategy since 9/11, argues Wu Xinbo (2007: 11), it remains a major component of US policy towards China. Thus, Washington's force realignment and military activities in the Asia-Pacific region are seen to be closely linked to the dissuasion of China from competing with America militarily.

In various US official defence and security documents, the strategy of hedging has been mentioned in discussing America's response to future strategic uncertainty. This is considered by Wu Xinbo (2007) as the second core concept in the Bush administration's China policy. There are both competitive and cooperative elements in this concept. To many Chinese security analysts, the hedging strategy is designed to prepare for the worse-case scenario in US-China relations, that is, a military confrontation between the two countries. The 2006 Quadrennial Defense Review Report has made this quite clear: 'Shaping the choices of major and emerging powers requires a balanced approach, one that seeks cooperation but also creates prudent hedges against the possibility that cooperative approaches by themselves may fail to preclude future conflict' (US Department of Defense 2006a: 30).

Why has the US government placed more emphasis on hedging than dissuasion in its China policy during Bush's second term? This, according to Chinese analysis, is a result of Washington's assessment that China has not been dissuaded from developing its great power potential. On the contrary, its economic strength, military power and international influence continue to grow while the US is preoccupied with the situation in Iraq and the war on terrorism. Therefore, America needs to prepare for the possibility that China will one day possess the military capability to challenge its dominant position in the international system (Wu Xinbo 2007: 12–13). Indeed, the hedging strategy reflects the Bush administration's concern about the 'uncertainty surrounding China's future and the path it will take' (US Department of Defense 2006b: 7). To implement its hedging strategy, say the Chinese, the Bush administration introduced a series of military and security measures to impose 'structural constraints' on China, including the development of various formal and informal multilateral security alliances with America's friends and allies in the Asia-Pacific (Wu Xinbo 2007: 14–15). In the view of Wu Xinbo (2007), the third core concept that shapes the Bush administration's policy towards China is deterrence, which is clearly reflected in Washington's Taiwan policy.[2]

Despite their apprehensions regarding Bush's policy towards China, PRC analysts recognize that the US government has become more pragmatic in its response to China's growing power (Chen Dongxiao 2006). US leaders and officials in the Bush administration have described the US-China relationship as a candid, cooperative, constructive and complex relationship. The Chinese acknowledge the positive aspects of Bush's China strategy which was clearly outlined by Robert Zoellick (2005), the former US Deputy Secretary of State, in his speech at the National Committee on US-China Relations on 21 September 2005. In this speech, Zoellick reiterated Secretary Rice's (2005) comments that the United States welcomes 'the rise of a confident, peaceful, and prosperous China'. He also noted that 'China is big, it is growing, and it will influence the world in the years ahead'. 'For the United States and the world', he asked, 'how will China use its influence?' Zoellick's (2005) answer was to encourage China to become a 'responsible stakeholder' in the international system. By that, he meant that China may collaborate more closely with the US to tackle major international issues such as the threat of global terrorism and the spread of WMD. It is also important, he said, for the two countries to work together to sustain the current international system. Indeed, as a high-level US Task Force has recommended: 'The United States needs to invest heavily to maximize the areas of cooperation with China and minimize the likelihood of conflict' (Council on Foreign Relations 2007: 97).

The Bush administration's recognition of China's significant role in the operation of the international system is by and large welcomed by Chinese scholars. Nevertheless, they remain sceptical of US strategy towards China. Specifically, the decision to urge China to act as a 'responsible stakeholder' is said to be based on the need to preserve the US-led international system and America's hegemonic position in particular. They believe that the Bush administration, like its predecessors, wished to change China's social and political system according to US interests and values. Moreover, China's America specialists have criticized Washington for shifting all the responsibilities to China for the uncertainty in US-China relations. As China is considered as a rising power with an undemocratic system and uncertain strategic intentions, it can only be treated as a 'responsible stakeholder' rather than a strategic partner. In this sense, Chen Dongxiao (2006: 42–43) contends, Washington seeks to maintain its dominance in the discourse of Sino-American relations.

This view is shared by Ma Zhengang (2007), the CIIS Director, who argues that the subtext of the 'China responsibility theory' (*Zhongguo zeren lun*) is that China is not a responsible power and that it needs to be integrated into the international system and constrained by its rules and norms. The reason for this is simple, says Ma, because the existing international system is dominated by the West and America. The US and Western countries will set the agenda for China and decide how China should meet the criteria of a responsible power. While China is given the status of a 'responsible stakeholder', he asserts, Washington is actively pursuing a strategy of hedging against China. To Chinese analysts, behind the 'China responsibility theory' is still the old policy of 'containment plus engagement' (Ma Zhengang 2007: 3).

Washington's relations with Taiwan have always been a prime concern to Chinese leaders and policy elites. Despite the necessity to secure China's support for the war against terrorism, the US government has not abandoned its commitments to Taiwan (Tsang 2004). If anything, it has developed closer defence ties with the Taiwanese military. Indeed, Bush expressed more sympathy towards Taiwan than any of his predecessors, publicly indicating that America would do 'whatever it took' to assist Taiwan in defending itself. A leaked Pentagon report allegedly suggested that nuclear weapons could be used against China in the event of a conflict across the Taiwan Strait (BBC 2002a). Some Chinese analysts believe that the US has effectively changed its policy of 'strategic ambiguity' to 'strategic clarity' (Su Ge 2001: 4; Wu Xianbin 2004: 17). Specifically, they point to the high-level interaction between Washington and Taipei via various unofficial avenues, such as granting transit visas to Taiwanese leaders and officials, including former Taiwanese President Chen Shui-ban. For example, the US government allowed Taiwan's former Defence Minister, Tang Yiau-ming, to attend a Florida defence conference that was sponsored by US arms manufacturers. During his visit, Tang allegedly had private meetings with senior officials from the State and Defense Departments (Xu Shiquan 2003: 4).

Having achieved the 'internationalization' (*guojihua*) of the status of Taiwan, PRC security analysts argue, the US government attempts to 'militarize' (*junshihua*) the issue by fortifying its security relations with Taipei through a variety of channels (Yang Yunzhong 2002a: 6–7). In April 2002, the Bush administration offered Taiwan a massive arms package that included four *Kidd*-class destroyers, eight diesel-electric patrol submarines, 12 P-3 Orion maritime patrol aircraft, submarine- and surface-launched torpedoes and other naval systems. Together, they would enhance Taiwan's capability to break potential Chinese blockades, although it would take some time for Taiwan to receive these systems and to absorb the sophisticated US equipment (Li 2002).

If Chinese security experts are wary of US arms sales to Taipei, they are even more concerned about Washington's plan to include Taiwan in its TMD system in Asia. In their view, TMD would help raise the quality of Taiwan's military technology and equipment and integrate Taiwanese defence with the US-Japan security system. Consequently, this would 'open up a shortcut for foreign countries to intervene in the Taiwan problem' (Wu Xianbin 2002: 48), thus further 'internationalizing' what the Chinese government considered as its 'internal affairs'. From China's perspective, a TMD system that includes Taiwan would make it more difficult for the PRC to achieve its national goal of reunification. It would also increase the possibility of a conflict between China and the US. To the Chinese, the development of missile defence systems is part of America's strategy of nuclear deterrence against a rising China, which is a core concept in Bush's China policy. An important component of the deterrence strategy is the closer military cooperation among the US, Japan and Taiwan in recent years (Huang Yuerong 2007: 20–21; Wu Xinbo 2007: 17–19).

Most Chinese scholars agree that Taiwan drifted further away from the mainland under the leadership of Chen Shui-bian, the former Taiwanese President (Zhou Zhihuai 2007: 4; Zhu Weidong 2006: 4–5; see also the analysis in Li 2003c). They are convinced that Bush's closer links with and arms sales to Taipei had given a greater impetus to the independent forces on the island (Liu Jianfei 2003: 28). Chinese leaders have stepped up their military pressure on Taiwan, and their resolve to use force to thwart Taiwanese independence was stated unambiguously in China's National Defense White Paper published in December 2004 (Xinhua 2004). China also passed an anti-succession law in March 2005, which threatened to achieve 'reunification' with Taiwan through military means should peaceful negotiations fail. The PRC's military threat against Taiwan has led to considerable concern among Western scholars and analysts (Christensen 2002; Friedman 1997; Lieberthal 2005; Tsang 2005).

As the former US Deputy Secretary of State Richard Armitage acknowledged in 2004, Taiwan was the biggest landmine in US-China relations (PBS 2004). Nevertheless, the United States would not wish to have a military engagement with China, as it is preoccupied with fighting the global war on terrorism which is likely to last for many years (Li 2006). At any rate, the political, economic and human costs of fighting a war with China would be incalculable. The nature and extent of support from its allies in a US-China military confrontation would also be uncertain. Thus, while opposing the use of force against Taiwan, US officials have exerted more pressure on Taiwanese leaders not to alter the status quo and risk provoking China. Towards the end of Bush's first term, the Chinese observed that he had moved closer to the position of 'strategic ambiguity' adopted by his predecessors. But Chinese analysts believed that the Bush administration would not change its strategy of 'using Taiwan to constrain China' (*yiTai zhiHua*) or its policy of maintaining the status quo where Taiwan is neither independent nor reunified with the PRC (*budu butong*) (Wu Xianbin 2002: 49; Wu Xianbin 2004: 19; Zhu Weidong 2006: 5).

Nevertheless, some scholars argue that the sensitivity of the Taiwan issue in Sino-US relations has reduced considerably, as maintaining 'relative peace' in the Taiwan Strait is said to have become a major element of Washington's China policy (Guo Zhenyuan 2007). They believe that it is not in America's interest to have a military confrontation with China, even though it has 'the military capabilities to threaten Chinese national security' (Liu Jianfei 2007: 3).

The Bush administration and the North Korean nuclear crisis

Another area that has attracted much attention from Chinese security analysts is America's policy towards the security situation on the Korean Peninsula. In the early 1950s, China supported North Korea in the Korean War. For over 50 years, the PRC and the Democratic People's Republic of Korea (DPRK) had a close relationship of so-called 'lips and teeth'. Although their relationship is no longer based on ideological convergence, they remain close allies. With Pyongyang's increasing isolation in the international community, it has become more and more dependent on China as its main source for energy and food supplies.

Following North Korea's withdrawal from the Treaty on the Non-Proliferation of Nuclear Weapons (NPT) and its admission of possessing nuclear weapons in 2003, the US, Russia, China, Japan and South Korea have actively engaged in a variety of diplomatic activities with a view to finding a solution to the nuclear crisis (Li 2003b). However, most Chinese analysts believe that America is the primary source of instability on the Korean Peninsula (Piao Jianyi 2003b: 42). Soon after coming into office, they argue, Bush ended Clinton's limited engagement policy towards the DPRK and was critical of South Korea's 'sunshine policy' aiming at the improvement of North-South relations. Instead, Bush is said to have adopted a much tougher stance against North Korea (Pu Guoliang 2004).

Even before Pyongyang's acknowledgement of a clandestine programme for producing highly enriched uranium in October 2002, Chinese analysts assert, Washington had identified the DPRK regime as a potential target for pre-emptive attack. They maintain that America's hostile attitude towards North Korea has been expressed consistently by US officials since President Bush gave his 'axis of evil' speech in January 2002 (Wang Hongwei 2002). The Chinese seem to appreciate Pyongyang's fear of a potential US pre-emptive strike which, they contend, has little to do with issues relating to terrorism or WMD. Rather, the Bush administration has allegedly used the threat from the 'rogue states' to justify military actions against countries whose leaderships or political systems are disapproved by the Americans (Piao Jianyi 2003a: 24).

According to Chinese analysts, North Korean leaders were alarmed by America's invasion of Iraq and the rapid removal of Saddam Hussein's regime. After US attacks on Afghanistan and Iraq, say the Chinese, the DPRK government believed that North Korea might well be the next target of America's 'pre-emptive strikes' (Zhang Liangui 2004). North Korea is said to have learnt several lessons from Iraq. The first is the importance of possessing nuclear weapons in deterring a hostile great power such as the US from invading the country. The second is the disastrous consequences of allowing foreign countries to conduct weapons inspections in one's own territories (Zhang Liangui 2004; Gao Hui 2005). From the Chinese perspective, it is America's menace to the DPRK regime's survival and its refusal to engage in a direct dialogue with Pyongyang that has led North Korea to play the 'nuclear card'.

Why does the United States refuse to tolerate a North Korea with nuclear weapons? According to Chinese analysts, a nuclearized North Korea would pose a significant challenge to the US-dominated international order, and the existing East Asian security order in particular. As the hegemonic power in the region, say the Chinese, America feels that it has to demonstrate the will and capability to protect its regional allies such as Japan and South Korea. The nuclearization of the Korean Peninsula could also lead to a regional nuclear arms race, thus undermining the stability and economic prosperity of East Asia from which America has benefited immensely. In addition, the Chinese argue that Washington is not really worried about a nuclear attack from North Korea. Its fear is that Pyongyang would export its nuclear technology and material to terrorist organizations, which would then be used against America. In this sense, a North Korea with nuclear ambitions, observe the Chinese, would threaten America's hegemonic position and national security (Zhang Liangui 2004).

Chinese analysts are able to discern the US perception that a democratized North Korea would be less threatening to America, which explains the Bush administration's desire to promote regime change in Pyongyang. However, the US is unwilling to invade North Korea or launch a 'surgical attack' on the DPRK's nuclear and missile bases. Unlike Iraq, the Chinese point out, North Korea is in a stronger position in that both China and Russia are opposed to pre-emptive actions against Pyongyang. Clearly, Washington cannot ignore the views of these two major powers on the Korean situation. The Chinese speculate that America may not even receive full support from Japan and South Korea for a pre-emptive attack on the DPRK. Moreover, America has to take into account the geographical conditions of North Korea, where its mountains and forests would make it difficult for America to launch high-tech military operations. Sending ground troops to North Korea is also not an easy option as it could result in heavy casualties, as shown by the Korean War. In any case, Washington cannot preclude the possibility of a North Korean nuclear retaliation on American bases in Japan. For all these reasons, the Chinese believe, the US has decided to deal with the North Korean nuclear crisis through the six-party talks (Gao Hui 2005).

To the Chinese, a fundamental change in America's North Korean policy is essential to the solution of the problem. What is needed, they suggest, is a comprehensive package to address North Korea's security concerns and economic problems, the normalization of US-DPRK relations, the denuclearization of the Korean Peninsula and other relevant issues (Piao Jianyi 2003a: 26). Despite

Pyongyang's nuclear test in July 2006, some progress has been made through the six-party talks in reducing tensions on the Korean Peninsula.

The expansion of US security network and 'strategic encirclement' of China

From the Chinese perspective, Taiwan is not the only player exploited by the US to constrain Chinese actions. Since 2001, they assert, the US government has actively sought to construct a security network surrounding the PRC that could be used to prevent China from challenging America's hegemonic position. Apart from consolidating the US-Japan alliance, the Chinese contend, Washington has strengthened its alliance relations with South Korea and Australia (Hu Ning 2004). In South East Asia, America's security role is said to have been enhanced by various types of military cooperation with Indonesia, the Philippines and Singapore (US Department of State 2002a). In August 2002, the US and South East Asian countries signed an anti-terrorism agreement which was referred to by former Secretary of State Colin Powell as 'a political declaration that brings ASEAN and the United States together in a more intimate relationship' (BBC 2002d). The Chinese assert that the US is using the 'war against terrorism' as a pretext to perpetuate its military presence in South East Asia with the aim of guarding against a rising China (Cao Yunhua 2001; Xia Liping 2002).

Moreover, America is said to be concerned about the growth of China's maritime power, which could obstruct freedom of navigation in the South China Sea (Cao Xiaoyang 2006) (see the analysis on China and the South China Sea disputes in Tonnesson 2000). According to the Chinese, America's aim in South East Asia is to establish a US-led multilateral security mechanism based on the two sets of alliances between the US and the Philippines and Thailand, respectively, and security cooperation with Singapore, Malaysia, Indonesia and Vietnam. Washington is also believed to have exploited the ASEAN Regional Forum (ARF) to constrain Chinese actions in the area (Fu Mengzi and Yang Wenjing 2004).

However, some Chinese scholars contend that there are positive effects of enhanced US military presence in South East Asia. First, it can help maintain the balance of power in the region where a 'power vacuum' has emerged following America's withdrawal from its military bases in the Philippines. Second, Washington's decision to strengthen security cooperation with South East Asian states may encourage them to reduce their defence spending. Third, America's military presence would be helpful to South East Asian governments in tackling terrorism and radical Islamic forces, thus contributing to the enhancement of regional security. In this respect, it is argued, China and America share similar strategic interests (Cao Yunhua 2003).

In South Asia, the Bush administration was able to secure Pakistan's military cooperation in removing the Taliban regime in the Afghanistan. Given the PRC's close military and strategic relations with Pakistan, Chinese analysts feel uneasy about the warming of US-Pakistan relations. Although Pervez Musharraf, the former president of Pakistan, repeatedly assured Chinese leaders that US-Pakistani cooperation on fighting terrorism would not harm the friendship between China and Pakistan, the Chinese suspect that a pro-American regime in Islamabad could help the US extend its influence to Central Asia (Ma Jiali 2001b: 35), thus undermining China's security interests in the region. Meanwhile, Chinese analysts are apprehensive of America's improved relations with India, particularly since 9/11. Knowing that New Delhi has the desire to become a dominant power in South Asia and the Indian Ocean, and that it is suspicious of China's great power aspirations, they argue, Washington has tried to use India to constrain China (*yiYin zhiHua*) (Ma Jiali 2001a: 3).

Indeed, Chinese analysts were wary of Bush's visit to South Asia in March 2006 and the 'upgrading' of US-India relations. They are particularly critical of the nuclear cooperation between the two countries. Washington's agreement to provide New Delhi with nuclear technology is said to be equivalent to acquiescing to the development of nuclear weapons in India. A good relationship with India, the Chinese assert, would help America tackle the challenge of global terrorism and Islamic extremism in South Asia, promote the values of democracy in the areas surrounding India, ensure smooth energy supply from the Middle East through the Strait of Malacca and the Indian Ocean and, most importantly, weaken Russia's traditional influence in the region and balance against a rising China (Hu Zhiyong 2006; Li Haidong 2006).

To PRC defence analysts, the most worrying development is America's entry into the Central Asian region. They believe that the US has been trying to exert its influence on Central Asia through the development of political links, economic assistance and military penetration ever since the early 1990s. The decisions of some Central Asian countries to open their air space and military bases to America have therefore caused tremendous anxiety in China. According to the Chinese, Central Asia is important to their country in many respects. First, over 30 percent of China's oil supply is imported from the region. Beijing has actively cooperated with Central Asian countries on oil exploration and construction of oil pipelines. The presence of US forces in Central Asia is thus seen as a serious threat to the PRC's energy security (Deng Hao 2002; Dai Chaowu and Li Chunling 2002; Yang Yunzhong 2003a: 11–12; Zhao Huasheng 2007: 23).

Second, Western entry into Central Asia could affect China's economic interests, as Western China has been targeted by the PRC government as a new area of development in the early 21st century. Third, Central Asia's growing political links with the West could push it away from China. The Chinese also fear that Western forces in Central Asia would help the separatist movements in Xinjiang, although the US government referred to the East Turkistan Islamic Movement as a terrorist organization in August 2002 as a result of Chinese pressure. Should the US gain a foothold in Central Asia, Chinese military analysts warn, it would pose an immense challenge to China's national security. They point out that, for example, there are only about 300 kilometres between American troops stationed in Kyrgyzstan and the Chinese border. The most serious concern is the proposal that NATO's eastward expansion should be extended to Central Asia (Deng Hao 2002; Dai Chaowu and Li Chunling 2002; Yang Yunzhong 2003a: 11–12; Zhao Huasheng 2007: 23).

Finally, Chinese analysts maintain that America's involvement in Central Asian affairs would weaken the Shanghai Cooperation Organization (SCO), which consists of China, Russia, Kazakhstan, Kyrgyzstan, Tajikistan and Uzbekistan (Deng Hao 2002; Dai Chaowu and Li Chunling 2002; Yang Yunzhong 2003a: 11–12).[3] The overall judgement of Chinese analysts is that America's 'greater Central Asia strategy' will lead to a more intense rivalry among the major powers, thus having a destabilizing effect on the region (Xu Heming 2007). This would undermine the strategic stability of Central Asia, which is seen to be extremely important to Chinese security (Zhao Huasheng 2007: 23).

To many Chinese scholars, the US is seeking to constrain China's actions through the formation of various security networks and the expansion of its military relations with China's neighbouring countries (Xu Ping and Zhao Qinghai 2007: 29).

Theoretical analysis

As established in the previous chapter, Chinese analysts' views of the United States in the Clinton era were strongly influenced by the way they perceived the identity of their country in the international system. Their discourse on the global and regional strategies of the United States clearly reflects their concern of how American policy may impact on China's efforts to achieve the status of a great power. The data presented in this chapter indicates that this apprehension was exacerbated during the Bush administration. PRC scholars and security specialists are in agreement that the US government under President Bush is more determined to maintain America's unipolar position in the world. In their view, 9/11 has enabled the US government to consolidate its hegemonic power and extend its geostrategic influence. The 'war on terrorism' is said to have provided US leaders with the justification to adopt a more assertive external policy. More alarming to the Chinese is America's willingness to launch a military attack on Iraq in the absence of UN approval and broad international support.

To many Chinese analysts, America's strategic aims and foreign policy behaviour in the Bush era are best explained by the realist theory. Realists see the world in terms of anarchy in which states constantly engage in competition for power and influence, and they tend to believe that the majority of problems in the world can be resolved through military means (Morgenthau 1978). This interpretation of US security strategy was found in most Chinese writings when Bush first came to power. Indeed, Chinese analysts pointed to the Republican Party's realist tradition in foreign policy, arguing that this tradition would be carried forward by the Bush administration. They cited America's tougher stance towards Russia, China and North Korea together with its reluctance to support the Kyoto agreement as evidence of realist tendencies in US foreign policy.

There is a consensus among Chinese analysts that America's response to 9/11 is a reflection of its realist approach to international relations. In their view, the US government could have learnt something from the terrorist attacks in terms of the changing nature of world politics and security threats. After all, the attacks were coming from non-state actors rather than any particular state. However, they assert that the Bush administration chose to use traditional military means to tackle non-conventional security challenges. That explains why Washington launched a military operation in Afghanistan soon after 9/11 and has since focused heavily on the military approach to combat international terrorism.

Indeed, many Chinese analysts believe that realism has dominated the thinking of US leaders and officials in the post-9/11 era. From the 2001 Quadrennial Defense Review Report to the 2006 NSS (US Department of State 2006), the Chinese see an America that is zealously seeking to exploit the anti-terrorist campaign to pursue an assertive global security policy. To Chinese analysts, the admission of America's extraordinary military power and political and economic influence, and the declaration of its intention of taking pre-emptive actions against suspected terrorists and 'rogue states' in the NSS, demonstrate clearly the realist orientation of US global strategy. Despite the tremendous challenge of 9/11, PRC scholars believe that the Bush administration was firmly committed to its realist policy agenda. Instead of collaborating closely with other countries to confront the challenge of international terrorism, they say, Washington has decided to take advantage of the historic opportunity to strengthen its military power and widen its global reach (Pang Zhongying 2006b; Yang Mingjie 2006). American actions seem to be consistent with the logic of realism that great powers would strive to maximize their relative power whenever and wherever possible. Despite the immediate threat of terrorism to US security, according to some Chinese analysts, terrorist movements are unlikely to threaten America's hegemonic position. The only political entities that can challenge America's status in future are believed to be sovereign states or alliances that consist of sovereign states (Hao Yufan 2005: 20). America's efforts to expand alliance relations, its decision to develop missile defence systems and its invasion of Iraq are all used as examples to illustrate their assessment of Bush's realist security strategy.

To Chinese scholars, achieving its hegemonic position in the world is the overriding aim of the US and must not be distracted by the war on terrorism. Many Chinese scholars have applied the main tenets of offensive realism to the analysis of America's global strategy (Ye Jiang 2003; Li Yongcheng and Zhang Yan 2004). According to offensive realists, the world is a dangerous place where great powers have offensive capabilities and their future intentions can never be certain. The only way to ensure a state's security and survival in an anarchic international system is to maximize any opportunities to increase its power, at the expense of rivals if necessary (Mearsheimer 2001: 30–31). But the United States is already the most powerful country in the world and its survival is not under threat. The US appears to be seeking to preserve its global pre-eminence, achieve maximum security in an uncertain environment, and spread American values of liberty, democracy and free market across the world. In this sense, the Bush administration's foreign policy cannot be fully explained by offensive realism which posits that 'survival is the primary goal of great powers' (Mearsheimer 2001: 31). This also explains why Professor Mearsheimer, a leading offensive realist, is critical of the neoconservative agenda and the invasion of Iraq in particular. In his view, the ambition of democratizing Iraq and other countries in the Middle East and promoting democracy around the world is unrealistic and does not serve US security interests (Mearsheimer *et al.* 2002; Mearsheimer and Walt: 2003).

Chinese scholars often claim that the US has the ambition of achieving global hegemony. However, Mearsheimer (2001: 40–42) argues that it is practically impossible for any great power to become a global hegemon unless it has 'clear-cut nuclear superiority' over all other states. The best one can expect, he states, is to achieve regional hegemony with the possibility of dominating another region adjacent to it. But the existing regional hegemon would not wish to see the rise of a hegemon in another region which may eventually be able to challenge its interests. To prevent this from happening, says Mearsheimer, the existing hegemon should encourage aspiring hegemons within the same region to balance against each other. In this way, they will focus all their energy on regional balancing rather than challenging the distant hegemon. Failing that, a great power can practise what is known as 'offshore balance', that is, seeking to prevent a threatening state from emerging as a hegemon in another region. As the regional hegemon in the Western Hemisphere for over a hundred years, the US has played a prominent role as an 'offshore balancer' in preventing imperial Japan, Wilhelmine Germany, Nazi Germany and the Soviet Union from rising to regional ascendancy.

Whether US unipolarity should be interpreted as global hegemony or regional hegemony, Chinese elites and analysts are deeply concerned about American policy. As a rising power in the Asia-Pacific, China is thought to have become the target of America's 'offshore balance'. The fear of US 'strategic encirclement' surrounding China since 9/11 is widespread among PRC defence specialists (See, for example, Yang Yunzhong 2003a: 8–9; Gao Zichuan 2004: 9–10; Sun Jinzhong 2005: 18). They are of the view that the Bush administration's attempts to fortify its position in Central and South Asia, upgrade the US-Japan security alliance, strengthen its security ties with Taiwan, South Korea, Australia and ASEAN states, and improve relations with virtually all of China's neighbours were part of its Asia strategy designed primarily to constrain Chinese actions and prevent it from becoming a regional hegemon that may contest US position in the Asia-Pacific. Here Kenneth Waltz's (1979) balance of power realism may also be used to explain the Chinese concern that America is trying to strengthen alliance relations and develop security links with the PRC's neighbouring countries with a view to balancing China.

However, it can be argued that it is not so much Chinese power that needs to be balanced, as Beijing's overall power, however measured, is still far behind that of the United States. In this regard, Stephen Walt's (1987) theory of balance of threat may be more appropriate, given America's threat perception of China. Either way, the Chinese see a conscious attempt on the part of America to balance against a rising China. US global and regional strategies are thus perceived as major obstacles to China's pursuit of a great power status in the 21st century. They do not believe that American hegemony can be benign, as the neorealist theory of hegemonic stability would suggest (Gilpin 1987: 72–80, 85–92). Rather, they have a different conception of hegemony (*baquan*) that is associated with domination, control and subjugation. They tend to use the term 'hegemonism' (*baquan zhuyi*) that has a much more negative connotation to describe US foreign policy behaviour. With few exceptions (see, for example, Wang Jisi 2003), Chinese scholars and analysts are not very interested in exploring the complexity of the concept and practice of hegemony within the context of US culture, history and ideology. They would concur with Layne's (2006a: 27) observation that '[I]n international politics there are no benevolent hegemons'. Indeed, most are convinced that the Bush administration is seeking to build an American empire stretching from the Americas to the Asia-Pacific and Europe to the Middle East. US ambition, they fear, would make it much more arduous for China to fulfil its great power aspirations. As Chinese analysts put it, the security threat posed by America on China's periphery directly affects the 'great cause of the revival of the Chinese nation' (Gao Zichuan 2004: 10; Sun Jinzhong 2005: 18).

Chinese analysts seem to treat the liberal element of the Bush Doctrine as a pretext of expanding US political and military power. They see Bush's mission of democracy promotion as yet another exercise of imposing American values and systems on other countries. Many PRC scholars are critical of the theory of democratic peace (Doyle 1986; Russett 1993) which is said to have provided the ideological justification for criticizing or seeking regime change in countries whose political systems are considered as undemocratic and disapproved by the US government (see, for example, Liang Tao and Ding Liang 2005). They argue that the removal of Saddam Hussein's regime by invasion is a blatant violation of international law, and that the threat of regime change in North Korea has increased tensions on the Korean Peninsula. The Chinese reject Charles Krauthammer's (2004) theory of 'democratic realism' which posits that America can and should utilize its superior military power to promote liberal democratic ideas around the world.

Chinese security analysts consider this argument to be both unrealistic and dangerous, in that democracy imposed by outside forces would not be welcomed by local people and military attacks on other sovereign states would only lead to conflict and instability. Behind the façade of democracy promotion, the Chinese contend, is America's ambition of empire-building and global dominance. What is needed in the post-Cold War world, it is argued, is 'democratization of international relations' based on respect for sovereignty and equality among states (Pang Zhongying 2001; Ni Shixiong and Wang Yiwei 2002). This idea is similar to the concept of 'cosmopolitan democracy' (Archibugi and Held 1995: 4) advocated by some Western scholars who have noted that 'the increase in the democratic states has not been accompanied by a corresponding increase in democracy *among* states' [the authors' emphasis].

In addition, Chinese analysts are critical of the liberal claim of the effectiveness of international institutions in mitigating the constraining effects of anarchy on international cooperation (Abbott and Snidal 1998). Although the Chinese appear to have defended the role of the UN in maintaining international peace and security, they have shown little faith in international institutions in promoting world peace. Nowhere has this sentiment been more clearly expressed than in their disappointment at the UN's failure to stop America from launching a war against Iraq. Indeed, they reject the neoliberal institutionalists' argument that the rules of international institutions can constrain the actions of the great powers (Keohane 1984). To Chinese analysts, Washington's disregard of the role of the United Nations Security Council (UNSC) in its decision to invade Iraq shows how fragile international institutions are in restraining the actions of powerful states. Their critique echoes the realist view of the 'false promise' of international institutions (Mearsheimer 1994/95). Moreover, they find it hard to share the liberal faith in the efficacy of international law in regulating great power behaviour. Again, America's invasion of Iraq is seen by the Chinese as an unabashed defiance of the international legal order. In short, PRC scholars are unconvinced that the US would behave as a liberal or benevolent hegemon acting with self-restraint and multilaterally as suggested by some defensive realists (Ikenberry 1998/99; Walt 2002: 141–52; Walt 2005: 223–32).

However, Chinese analysts appreciate the relevance of the liberal elements of trade and economic interdependence to US global strategy. This is, of course, related to the core arguments of the 'democratic peace' theory which provides the rationale for the American policy of engagement of China. The Chinese also recognize that America's attempts to expand economic interactions with the PRC are part of a strategy of ensuring that the rise of China would not threaten US interests. Chinese analysts are aware that few, if any, mainstream politicians and elites in Washington have advocated the application of the Bush Doctrine of military pre-emption and regime change to China (Hao Yufan 2005: 19). One of the main reasons for this is China's growing economic and trade interdependency with the United States. But the Chinese view international economic relations primarily from the perspective of neorealism or neomercantilism, in that trade and economic activities should serve the purpose of strengthening state power. In this sense, America is said to have perceived China as a potential threat to its economic dominance as Chinese economic power augments.

If Chinese analysts are apprehensive of the Clinton administration's global strategy, their suspicion of US security intentions under Bush is even greater. Why are they so concerned about US hegemony and why do they see growing American power as a threat to their national interest? This is related to our hypothesis that China perceives other great powers in relation to its self-identity. Realism and liberalism have offered useful insights into the material dimension of Chinese perceptions. They have helped explain the structural and institutional factors that shape Chinese interests. But as constructivists argue, it is difficult to understand an actor's interest without reference to its identity. If 'anarchy is what states make of it' (Wendt 1992), we need to know why states see anarchy in a particular way.

It is clear that Chinese security discourse is heavily influenced by realist thoughts. Most Chinese analysts do perceive the international system as one of anarchy within which great powers compete with each other relentlessly. Their realist perceptions are clearly demonstrated by their analysis of America's foreign policy and the Bush Doctrine in particular. As discussed in previous chapters, Chinese leaders and elites have long had the desire of developing their country as a great power. They tend to perceive American power within the context of their search for a great power identity. It is therefore important to show how China's interests are influenced by its self-identity. Of course, identity has not been ignored by neorealist and neoliberal scholars, but they tend to treat it as a given in their analysis of Chinese security perceptions. It is necessary to go beyond this type of rationalist thinking to explore the historical and cultural contexts within which Chinese identity is formed (Katzenstein 1996: 25–26).

The evidence presented in this chapter shows that China's views of America are shaped not only by material considerations, especially America's formidable military and economic power, but also ideational factors such as the concept of hegemony. The Chinese conception of *baquan* or hegemony is rooted in its history where *bazhu* or *bawang* (hegemonic leader) is usually seen as someone who is arrogant and ruthless in dominating others. To most Chinese intellectuals and elites, the best way to avoid the 'century of shame and humiliation' (*bainian chiru*) when China was invaded and subjugated by foreign powers is to become a great power rather than placing their hope on a benign US hegemony. Their view is that the Bush administration's global strategy is detrimental to the achievement of China's national goal. On many occasions, Chinese writers have used the phrase 'gunboat diplomacy' to depict Bush's foreign policy. 'Gunboat diplomacy' is the term that is widely used by the Chinese to describe Western policy towards China in the 19th century. From a psychological perspective, PRC elites' determination to shake off China's negative national self-images is indivisible from their endeavour to enhance collective self-esteem and develop a positive self-identity (Kaplowitz 1990: 51–52; Mercer 1995: 241).

Many Chinese scholars and analysts believe that the Bush administration is seeking to build an American empire (*Meiguo diguo*) based on the ideology of neoconservatism. Having consolidated its unipolar position by 2001, they argue, the US was resolute in preserving this supreme status. In their view, Washington's global ambition has not been deterred by the 9/11 terrorist attacks. On the contrary, it has capitalized on the new security situation in expanding US influence and augmenting American power. Indeed, America's 'unprecedented – and unequaled – strength and influence in the world' were emphasized in the 2002 NSS (US Department of State 2002b: 1). Underpinned by the theory of 'democratic realism', the Bush Doctrine is said to be the manifestation of a desire to establish an American empire in the 21st century. This, according to Chinese analysis, explains why the US has attempted to increase its influence in the Middle East and Asia and impede other great powers from challenging its unrivalled position.

Although Chinese international relations specialists have rarely used the concept of 'identity' to explicate Bush's foreign policy, their analysis is consistent with the constructivist perspective on identities and interests (Katzenstein 1996; Wendt 1992). A clear theme can be discerned in most Chinese publications: the US is striving to acquire the identity of an imperial power or hegemonic power; the American empire may or may not be benign but it is built on US values that are expected to be accepted and absorbed by other countries. Chinese analysts have pointed to the doctrine of pre-emption, regime change and other elements of the

Bush Doctrine in illustrating America's hegemonic aspirations. For constructivists, states are social actors and their interests, including security interests, will change as a result of their changing identities (Jepperson, Wendt and Katzenstein 1996: 61). Seen from this theoretical angle, America's 'imperial foreign policy' (*diguo waijiao*) mirrors its changing identity and interests in the Bush era.

It is within this context that many PRC scholars believe that the US does not wish to see China rising to the status of a great power, but that is precisely what the Chinese wish to accomplish. For this reason, they feel that their aim of constructing a great power identity is being obstructed by the Americans. That is why Chinese security analysts are especially critical of Bush's Asia-Pacific strategy, which is believed to include a strong element of 'strategic encirclement' of China aiming to prevent the PRC from using force to achieve 'reunification' with Taiwan and regain its 'rightful place' in the world. Indeed, the status of Taiwan is arguably the single most important issue that unites all Chinese leaders and elites. The occupation of Taiwan by Japan before 1945 is seen as part of the 'shame and humiliation' that China suffered while it was weak. As long as Taiwan is separate from mainland China, PRC policy elites and analysts believe, it will be exploited by the US and Japan to constrain China. Control over Taiwan and its surrounding areas would strengthen China's military position immensely and allow China to dominate the adjacent water that is extremely important to other great powers economically and strategically. If Taiwan were to be peacefully incorporated into the PRC, its human and financial resources could add additional strengths to Chinese economic power. Reclaiming Taiwan is therefore an integral part of China's efforts to construct its great power identity (Wu Xianbin 2002: 49; Yang Yunzhong 2003a: 10). This type of realpolitik discourse may be explained by what Alastair Iain Johnston (1999: 300) calls 'identity realism' in the sense that the in-group identity needs to be fortified in the light of the 'potential dangers of the external environment'.

In understanding Chinese security perceptions of America during the Bush era, it is also useful to draw upon the theoretical insights of postmodernism. David Campbell (1998) and Richard Jackson (2005), among others, have argued that a 'discourse of danger' is important to the construction of a state's identity. There is general consensus among Chinese scholars and analysts that the Bush administration has exploited the 'China threat' and 'China collapse' discourses to exaggerate the security challenge of a rising China. They are also sceptical of the US government's attempts to make China a 'responsible stakeholder'. In foreign policy practices, argues Michael Shapiro (1989: 15), 'various forms of global otherness' can be created. From a postmodernist perspective, what the Americans are trying to do is to deprive China of its subjectivity and mould China's development in such a way that it will help strengthen US identity as a benign hegemon. This is no more than the creation of a different form of a threatening other that is objectified in order to sustain the dominant position of the American self.

If PRC scholars feel that China is treated as a menace by the US, the Chinese writings examined also indicate a discursive construction of America as a threatening other. There is a clear sense of an American threat running through Chinese articles on US global and Asia-Pacific strategy. This sentiment is expressed directly or indirectly in the publications. Some articles attempt to balance the threat with opportunities for cooperation, others highlight explicitly a US threat to China's security and its prospects as a rising power. For example, one article provides graphic details of how America threatens China's peripheral security environment and its long-term future as a great power (Gao Zichuan 2004: 9–10). Another article asserts that the threat from America must not be underestimated, and that it is a persistent threat aiming to destroy China so long as China is determined to attain a great power status (Yang Yunzhong 2002a: 9). The implication of such an external 'threat' is clear: the Chinese people must unite to resist America's pressure and its attempts to thwart China's rise to a global status. This process of othering is very powerful in asserting the identity of the self. The dichotomy of the construction of self and other may contribute to the formation of a distinctive Chinese identity, thus reinforcing the confidence and resolve of the Chinese in achieving what they consider as a common objective of the nation.

Conclusion

This chapter has examined the security perceptions of Chinese scholars and elites on the United States in the Bush era. The evidence shows that China's suspicion of US global ambitions has increased substantially since 2001. America's declared aim to achieve global pre-eminence is seen as a direct threat to China in the sense that it has the potential of obstructing China from achieving its goal of becoming a great power in the post-9/11 world. In the view of the Chinese, the Bush administration exploited the 'war on terrorism' to expand America's influence around the world and in the Asia-Pacific in particular. Chinese scholars are especially wary of the Bush Doctrine of pre-emption and America's plan to develop NMD and TMD systems which, they fear, could seriously undermine China's nuclear deterrence and strategic position in Asia. The Chinese have come to the conclusion that America's appetite to dominate the world has increased, and the Iraq war is used as the key example to support this argument.

Specifically, Chinese scholars believe that the US has been actively seeking to establish close security ties with all the countries surrounding China. The strengthening of the US-Japan security alliance after 9/11 is of particular concern to China. America's alleged 'strategic encirclement' of the PRC is said to be designed to constrain Chinese actions with a view to frustrating China's great power aspirations. But Chinese analysts do recognize that the US is willing to collaborate with China in a variety of areas, including anti-terrorism and the resolution of the North Korean nuclear crisis through the six-party talks.

The final section of this chapter analyzes the security perceptions of PRC scholars on America from a number of theoretical standpoints. The theoretical analysis clearly indicates that China's security discourse on the US is influenced by realist thinking, especially offensive realism. Indeed, many PRC scholars are familiar with the arguments of Mearsheimer and have referred to his work in their analysis of US foreign policy. They are convinced that China is the target of America's 'off-shore balance' in that Washington is actively seeking to prevent

China from emerging as a hegemon in the Asia-Pacific. Chinese perceptions of America's enhanced security relations with Japan and other Asian countries can also be explained by structural realism. They have little faith in the United States' 'benign hegemony'. They have also dismissed the liberal aspects of the Bush Doctrine arguing that the promotion of democratic peace is only a façade for US expansionism. The Chinese analysts' discussion on the failure of the UN to prevent America's invasion of Iraq reflects their scepticism of the liberal theory of international institutions.

In addition, the relevance of constructivism to the analysis of the PRC's perceptions of the US has been considered, which shows how Chinese views are shaped by ideational factors such as the Chinese conception of 'hegemony' and China's historical encounters with Western powers. Finally, the postmodernist theory is used to illustrate the link between the 'discourse of danger' in Chinese writings and the construction of China's great power identity. To conclude, the Chinese writings reviewed in this chapter demonstrate the intensity of PRC policy elites' apprehensions of US global strategy and its security implications for China.

4 Security, identity and strategic choice

Japan's quest for a great power status

The focus of this chapter is to examine Chinese perceptions of both Japan's global strategy and its security strategy in the Asia-Pacific region. The first part of the chapter deals with the views of PRC scholars and security specialists on Japan's political aspirations in the post-Cold War world within the context of its changing domestic political environment. This is followed by an analysis of Chinese perceptions of Japan's Asia-Pacific strategy with special reference to Japanese-US security relations, Japan's strategy towards ASEAN, China and the Taiwan Strait, North Korea and Russia. Drawing on the insights of realism, liberalism, constructivism and postmodernism, the final section provides a theoretical analysis of the security discourse of Chinese analysts on Japan.

Japanese political aspirations in a changing global context

The end of the Cold War has had a profound impact on the global political environment, which has forced every single country to reconsider its position in the international system. Japan, like other great powers, has been trying to advance its status in the hierarchy of the newly emerging international structure. In China's view, Japan's endeavour to play a more active role in world affairs can be traced to 1982, when Nakasone Yasuhiro became the Japanese Prime Minister. This national strategy (*guojia zhanlue*) is said to have been carried forward by Nakasone's successors, especially in the post-Cold War era.

Indeed, the collapse of the bipolar structure has, according to Chinese scholars and analysts, provided Japan with a favourable international environment to fulfil its aspirations of becoming a political power (*zhengzhi daguo*). First, following the break-up of the Soviet Union, the rationale for maintaining a rigid, hierarchical, and US-led Western alliance was shaken. At the same time, in the absence of the Soviet threat, Japan's strategic environment has improved considerably which has helped alter its essentially subordinate position in US-Japan security relations. Second, while the bipolar system was established largely on the basis of the superior military capability of the two superpowers, the post-Cold War international structure is shaped not only by traditional military power, but also by other factors such as economic strength and scientific achievement. As an economic superpower, Japan is uniquely positioned to play a prominent role in global politics. The Japanese vision of the post-Cold War world, say the Chinese, is one of tripolarity based on Western values and led by the United States, Europe and Japan (Xi Runchang and Gao Heng 1996: 105–107; Du Gong and Ni Liyu 1992: 314–18).

To raise Japan's international profile, Chinese analysts argue, the Japanese government has been fervently seeking to exert its influence on global and regional affairs. In the early 1990s, Japan assisted the US in promoting economic and political liberalization in the former Soviet Union and Eastern Europe, as well as offering substantial economic assistance and expert advice to the countries that are in the process of reforming their command economies. In 1991, Tokyo provided US$13 billion for the UN operation in the Gulf War. Another aspect of Japan's 'great power diplomacy', the Chinese note, is to maintain and improve its relations with other major powers in the world. Thus, despite its condemnation of the way that the Chinese regime handled the 1989 student demonstrations in Tiananmen Square, Japan was the first nation to end its economic sanctions against China and to resume normal relations with Beijing. Similarly, Japan has made a considerable effort to ameliorate its relations with Russia, although their disputes over the Northern Territories remain unresolved. In addition, Japanese politicians and officials have made frequent visits to leading EU member states such as Britain, France, Germany and Italy. Japan has also sought to consolidate or extend its influence through diplomatic activities and economic aid in various parts of the world, including the Middle East, Latin America and Africa.

In the view of Chinese analysts, there are two main strategic aims (*zhanlue mubiao*) in Japan's foreign policy. The first is to safeguard the national security and prosperity of the country. In the context of the post-Cold War security environment, Japan has strengthened its security alliance with the United States while seeking to build up its own defence capabilities. In the meantime, the Japanese government is said to have placed greater emphasis on multilateral security arrangements which, in the longer term, may replace the bilateral security alliance with the US. In terms of economic development, Japan has been actively involved in East Asian economic cooperation, although its trade and economic ties with America remain strong. What Tokyo intends to do, according to the Chinese, is to establish various free trade areas with ASEAN countries, South Korea and Taiwan. This would be extended to the PRC and, eventually, to Australia and New Zealand. The Chinese suspect that Japan aspires to play a leading role in East Asian economic cooperation (Liu Shilong 2003: 24–25).

Japan's second strategic aim, the Chinese believe, is to become an 'ordinary nation' in the sense that it should be an economic, as well as a political and military, power (Yang Yunzhong 2003b). By 2003, observe the Chinese, a consensus was reached by various political forces in Japan that becoming an 'ordinary nation' is the path that should be followed. This is said to be related to Japan's quest for the status of a political power (*zhengzhi daguo*). From the Japanese perspective, to become a political power it is necessary to develop its economic strength and military capabilities accordingly. This is thought to be the rationale behind Japan's active involvement in the US-led 'war on terrorism' and the diplomatic activities related to the North Korean nuclear crisis (Liu Shilong 2003: 26–27; Yao Wenli 2003: 47, 49).

According to Chinese security analysts, Japan's 'UN diplomacy' (*Lianheguo waijiao*) is an integral part of its attempts to reach the status of a political power. Many Japanese politicians are said to be deeply unhappy with Japan's current position in the United Nations and feel that it does not fully reflect Japan's economic power and rising political status in the world. Despite the fact that Japan makes a significant financial contribution to the UN, it has been excluded from the 'great power club'. The Japanese government therefore wants to have the 'enemies' clause deleted from the UN Charter (Article 107) and to become a permanent member of the UNSC (Lu Yi 1997; Liu Shilong 2003: 28–29). To achieve its objectives, say the Chinese, Tokyo has increased its contribution to the UN's total expenditure from 11.4 per cent in 1989 to 19.5 per cent in 2004. From July 2003 to June 2004, Japan contributed US$53 billion to the UN's peacekeeping budget. In addition, the Japanese government has argued that it has made enormous contributions to various types of UN activities, including UN peacekeeping operations, anti-terrorism, arms control, poverty reduction and so on. Indeed, there is a consensus among Japanese politicians of all parties that Japan should become a permanent UNSC member. The Chinese note that Japan was encouraged by former General Secretary Kofi Annan's support for UN reform in 2004. Tokyo is said to become more active in promoting the reform and expansion of the Security Council with other countries having the same ambitions, such as Germany, India and Brazil.

To PRC analysts, Japan is seeking to play a more prominent role in the UN because of national pride – it wishes to be able to interact with the five permanent Security Council members on an equal footing. This is also said to be related to Japan's motive of revising its pacifist constitution. Being a permanent member of the UNSC, Japan would be expected to be responsible for maintaining international peace and security, which would include authorizing military operations and participating in UN peacekeeping. This, the Chinese assert, would provide the best justification for Japan to amend its constitution, paving the path towards its destination of political power. Finally, Chinese scholars and analysts maintain that Japan is keen to play a major part in preserving the existing international order, which has served Japanese interests. Japan's eventual aim, argue the Chinese, is to establish itself as a truly 'ordinary nation' having an equal relationship with the United States (Liu Shilong 2003: 29; Zhang Jing 2005: 89–91).

In addition to its UN diplomacy, Japan is believed to be actively involved in other types of multilateral diplomacy. In particular, it has advocated a greater degree of trilateral cooperation between the US, Japan and Europe. Tokyo is also said to have paid more attention to the role of G7/G8 summits in international cooperation. To the Chinese, this reflects Japan's desire of seeking to be involved in the reconstruction of the post-Cold War world order at global, regional and bilateral levels. In the Asia-Pacific, Japan is also said to be active in promoting multilateral security dialogues with a view to raising its position and playing a leading role in regional security affairs. Multilateral security mechanisms, the

Chinese contend, would enable the Japanese government to reduce its level of dependence on the US. In the meantime, Tokyo is hoping to integrate the socialist countries in Asia (China, North Korea and Vietnam) into a multilateral security framework in order to enhance regional stability and Japan's own security (Liu Shilong 2003: 29–32).

Like other countries, Japan's foreign policy is determined by external forces as well as domestic factors. Most Chinese analysts believe that the political environment within Japan has made it easier for the Japanese to adopt a more assertive posture around the world and in the Asia-Pacific in particular.

First, the Chinese observe that Japanese politics has been dominated by conservative forces since the early 1990s. The liberals, they believe, are no longer in a position to constrain the activities of the right-wingers. In particular, most of the people who belong to the so-called 'new generation politicians' (*xinshengdai zhengzhijia*), including the former Japanese Prime Minister Hashimoto Ryutaro, are said to have strong conservative tendencies (Wu Jinan 2002). Many of them have published books that advocate ideas such as the revision of Japan's pacifist constitution. The new generation politicians are not afraid of putting forward their views on sensitive issues, nor are they restrained by traditional party or factional allegiance. As they have little wartime experience, say the Chinese, they do not have a guilty conscience towards other Asian countries that suffered from Japanese imperialism. Without such a historical burden, they tend to subscribe to the view that Japan should assume more responsibility in world affairs and make a full contribution to the international community. Their ambition is to become regional, and even global, politicians. The influence of this group of politicians on Japanese politics and foreign policy is increasing rapidly, according to Chinese observation (Wu Jinan 1996).

To Chinese analysts, the strength of conservative forces in Japanese politics is clearly illustrated by the growing number of incidents in recent years where Japanese politicians and officials have attempted to justify Japan's actions during World War II. For example, in May 1994, Nagano Shigeto, Japanese Minister of Justice, said that the Pacific War was a war 'for the liberation of colonies in order to establish the Greater East Asian Co-prosperity Sphere' and that 'Japan did not want to occupy those territories'. Three months later, Sakurai Shin, Director-General of the Environmental Agency, made similar remarks, saying that Japan did not want to launch an aggressive war. Instead, it helped Asian countries 'to gain their independence from European colonial rule'. In August 1995, Shimamura Yoshinobu, Minister of Education, stated that 'whether it was a war of aggression was a question of differing points of view'. 'As two-third of the Japanese were born in the post-war years', he went on to say, 'they were not familiar with the wartime period at all.' 'Is it sensible to mention the past constantly and make apology all the time?' he asked. In October of the same year, Eto Takami, Director-General of the Management and Co-ordination Agency, asserted that 'Japan did some good things during its colonial rule in Korea.' All these Japanese ministers withdrew their statements later and apologized publicly. With the exception of Shimamura Yoshinobu, they were forced to resign (Liu Jiangyong 1996a: 3).

Chinese scholars and analysts point out that other worrying signs of the conservative tendency in Japanese politics are the visits by many Japanese politicians, cabinet ministers, and former Prime Ministers such as Hashimoto and Koizumi to the Yasukuni Shrine. As the dead in the shrine include 14 class A and over 1,000 classes B and C war criminals executed by the Allied Powers, these visits are interpreted as a move to whitewash the crime committed by Japanese imperialists which is 'hurtful to the feelings of the peoples in China and other Asian countries' (Liu Jiangyong 1996a: 4–5; Gao Haikuan 2006; Jiang Lifeng 2006).

Moreover, Chinese specialists note that there has been a discernible change in Japan's foreign policy-making process. In the past, the making of foreign policy decisions was dominated by the Liberal Democratic Party (LDP), the financial sector and the Foreign Ministry. However, such a tripartite pattern is said to be changing as the role of the Japanese parliament, other political parties and ministries has increased. This is due to the diversity and complexity of the international issues in which Japan is involved today. The financial sector has always had close relations with the LDP, and the decline of its influence on Japanese foreign policy is seen to be an inevitable result of the end of the LDP's one-party dominance. But Japan's growing involvement in global political issues has also rendered the financial sector less relevant in foreign policy making. Even the Foreign Ministry, say the Chinese, is ill-prepared to make major political decisions. Meanwhile, the power of the Cabinet, especially the Prime Minister, in the making of Japanese foreign policy has been augmented substantially (Liang Yunxiang 1997). For example, Hashimoto's speech on Japan's new Russia policy in July 1997 was written by the Prime Minister's office rather than the Foreign Ministry (Fang Baihua 1998: 51).

The new pattern of foreign policy making, according to the Chinese, will make the Japanese government more vulnerable to the pressures of various groups in society that want to see their country playing a more prominent role in international affairs. In particular, the Chinese suggest that Japanese Defense Agency (upgraded to Japanese Ministry of Defense in January 2007), which is said to represent the interests of the Japanese military, has been much more forceful in exerting its influence on Japan's foreign policy since the early 1990s. It has succeeded, for example, in persuading the Japanese government to lift the ban on the participation of the Self-Defense Forces (SDF) in the UN-sponsored peace-keeping operations, and to approve the provision of direct support for US military forces in peace time (Fang Baihua 1998: 53).

Apart from the conservative trend in Japanese politics, an intense nationalistic sentiment is believed to be prevalent in post-Cold War Japanese society. At a seminar organized by the Foreign Ministry and the Japanese Diplomatic Association in March 1997, a group of students from Tokyo University and other leading universities in Japan allegedly advocated a policy of containment towards China. Other manifestations of Japan's neonationalism include the repeated attempts of some right-wing groups to erect a lighthouse and Japanese flags on the disputed Diaoyu/ Senkaku islands (Downs and Saunders 1998/99; Deans 2000) who, the Chinese suspect, were abetted by the Japanese authorities (Fang Baihua 1998: 53–54; Chen Benshan 1997: 92; Li Ye 1998: 33).

In addition, support for Japan's permanent membership of the UNSC among Japanese citizens increased from 45 per cent in 1992 to 70 per cent in 2004 (Zhang Jing 2005: 90). Indeed, a rising number of Japanese people have accepted the view that Japan should become an 'ordinary nation', assume a leadership role in Asia and participate fully in global affairs. In this sense, Japan's global security strategy is said to have widespread support from its people. Overall, Chinese scholars believe that there is a strong conservative and right-wing tendency in Japan's politics and society in recent years which, combined with rising Japanese nationalism, has led to the emergence of what they call 'nationalistic conservatism' (*minzu baoshou zhuyi*) (Lu Yaodong 2006; Zhang Jinshan 2007).

Japan's more assertive approach to global and regional security issues, coupled with the conservative tendency in its domestic politics, have given rise to much uneasiness in China. To the Chinese, the most crucial question is whether there will be a resurgence of Japanese militarism in the near future. However, as Glenn Hook (1996: 6) argues, there is a distinction between the concept of 'militarism' and that of 'militarization'. The former is used to describe excessive use of military power while the latter refers to 'a dynamic process of increasing military influence'. Chinese scholars seem to believe that militarization in Japan will inevitably lead to militarism.

Although some Chinese analysts appreciate the difficulties and disincentives for Japanese politicians to fulfil their political aspirations through military means (Wang Houkang and Jin Yingzhong 1992: 152–53; He Fang 1996: 19–20; Zhao Dawei 1999: 54), the possibility of Japan becoming a military power (*junshi daguo*) has not been ruled out. They assert that Japan's conventional capability is comparable to that of European countries, and that its naval and air forces are the most advanced forces in Asia. It is also suggested that Japan possesses the technology and material to produce nuclear weapons within a very short period of time if it wishes to do so. Quoting the IISS publications, Chinese analysts strongly criticize Japan's high level of military spending, which has exceeded the limit of 1 per cent of its Gross Domestic Product (GDP). The talk of the 'China threat theory', they argue, is merely used as a pretext for Japan to further expand its military forces. The Chinese are particularly worried that Tokyo may get involved in any future conflict across the Taiwan Strait (Chen Benshan 1997: 93; Lu Guozhong 1997: 42–43; Xi Runchang and Gao Heng 1996: 116–17).

Indeed, Japan's growing military power and its responses to the events since 9/11 have caused much trepidation among Chinese scholars and security specialists (Yang Yunzhong 2002b; Hu Rongzhong 2004). On 29 October 2001, the Japanese government passed an Anti-Terrorism Special Measures Law. Although the legislation had a two-year limit, it allowed the SDF to provide logistical, rear-echelon support to the American and British forces in the Indian Ocean. From 2002 to 2004, the counter-terrorism legislation passed by the Diet was revised four times. Meanwhile, the government approved the dispatch of Japanese C-130 transport planes to provide relief supplies to Afghan refugees in Pakistan. In November 2001, Tokyo decided to send two destroyers and a supply ship to the Indian Ocean. A year later, Japan's government decided to offer further surveillance and logistical support to American and British naval forces by sending an Aegis-equipped destroyer to the area (IISS 2001/2002: 279; IISS 2002/2003: 255).

More significantly, the Koizumi government decided to support America's military actions in Iraq, despite negative public opinion and opposition from the leaders of its coalition partners, the new Conservative Party and the new Komei Party, as well as members of its own party, the LDP. However, Koizumi promised that Japanese forces would not take part in the US-led invasion of Iraq. Instead, they would contribute to the rebuilding of post-war Iraq which was made possible by the passage of a Law Concerning Special Measures on Humanitarian and Reconstruction Assistance by the Diet on 26 July 2003. In December, the Japanese government approved a plan to dispatch several hundred non-combat troops to Iraq for a period of one year. Even though the main task of the troops was to provide humanitarian assistance, it aroused intense debate as the move was widely seen as a violation of Japan's pacifist constitution. Only nine per cent of the population showed their support for the plan, and critics pointed to the dangerous situation in Iraq and the possibility of the troops being drawn into combat (CNN 2003e).

In 2004 Japanese troops did not suffer any casualties in Iraq, but Japanese civilians became the targets of Iraqi militants who demanded the withdrawal of the 550-strong Japanese troops in Southern Iraq. A number of Japanese nationals were abducted and one of them was killed. Two Japanese freelance journalists were also shot dead. One Japanese tourist was abducted and beheaded after Japan refused to concede to the demand of Iraqi insurgents (*Mainichi Daily News* 2004). Despite these shocking incidents, the government decided in December 2004 to extend the SDF mission for another year. Koizumi was fully aware of public divisions and debate on the issue but he stressed that the troops were deployed in a 'non-combat' zone (*Asahi Shimbun* 2004).

Not surprisingly, Japan's reactions to 9/11 and the 'war on terrorism' have been followed closely by Chinese security specialists. They are convinced that the Japanese government has exploited the fear of terrorism to push legislation through the Diet that allows the SDF to be deployed beyond Japanese waters and air space. Tokyo's active diplomacy in the Arab world, Central and South Asia before and during the Afghan war, coupled with generous Japanese financial support for the post-war reconstruction of Afghanistan, have increased apprehension in Beijing. Many Chinese scholars believe that Japan's 'anti-terrorism diplomacy' (*fankong waijiao*) is designed to expand the areas of its security cooperation with America and to elevate its international status more generally (Wang Shan 2001; Jin Xide 2002: 6). They also argue that Japan's decision to support America's invasion of Iraq and dispatch SDF abroad signifies its intentions of expanding Japanese military activities, which will inexorably lead to the revision of its pacifist constitution (Zhang Jinshan 2003; Hu Rongzhong 2004). Indeed, former Prime Ministers Koizumi and Abe are both said to be active in using Japan's 'rights of collective self-defence' (*jiti ziweiquan*) to enhance its military ties with America, thus paving the way for a joint US-Japanese interference into any future conflict in the Taiwan Strait (Wu Huaizhong 2007).

In December 2004, Japan published its third set of National Defense Program

Guidelines (Japanese Defense Agency 2004)[1] which would enable Japan to play a broader role in international security. Specifically, it would allow the SDF to defend Japanese security interests and carry out anti-terrorist missions around the world. This again heightened Chinese concerns about Tokyo's future strategic intentions (Hu Jiping 2005). Some PRC security analysts believe that Japan's defence capabilities are developed for the purpose of launching offensive or 'pre-emptive' actions in future. Lu Chuan (2006) argues that a major pattern in Japan's strategic thinking is to promote its national interest through military means. The Chinese are wary of the Japanese government's 'pro-American foreign policy' (*qinMei waijiao zhengce*), which is seen as part of a strategy of pursuing the status of a 'political power'. They are also concerned about Japan's increased bilateral military cooperation with other Asian countries and its alleged attempts to establish an 'Asian version of NATO' (*Yazhouban Beiyue*) with the US, South Korea, Australia, India and other countries.

Chinese elites were particularly critical of Koizumi's assertive stance on various issues, ranging from his repeated visits to the Yasukuni Shrine and Japan's bid for permanent membership of the UN Security Council to Japanese policy towards China, Russia and North Korea (Zhou Yongsheng 2006). The tensions between China and Japan that had built up in the Koizumi era reduced considerably soon after former Prime Minister Abe Shinzo took office in September 2006. Abe decided to make China the destination of his first overseas trip (Kahn 2006; Fan 2006). Following this 'ice-breaking visit' to Beijing, he emphasized the importance of building a 'mutually beneficial, strategic relationship' with China in his New Year statement in 2007 (Pilling 2007; Associated Press 2007).

In response to Abe's positive moves, the Chinese Premier Wen Jiabao made an 'ice-thawing' trip to Japan in April 2007, where he gave an address to the Japanese parliament thanking Japan's 'support and assistance' in China's economic modernization. Wen also acknowledged the 'apologies' made by Japanese leaders and politicians over various historical issues, while urging Japan to 'show in concrete ways their expressed attitudes and promises' (Onishi 2007). Interestingly, both of the major points in Wen's speech were suggested by Chinese scholars and intellectuals who advocated 'new thinking' in Sino-Japanese relations.[2]

However, Chinese analysts were apprehensive of Prime Minister Abe's efforts to promote Japan's 'value-oriented diplomacy' (*jiazhiguan waijiao*), to expand the scope of Japanese external military activities, and to seek permanent membership of the UNSC (Zhou Yongsheng 2007). In a speech at the North Atlantic Council on 12 January 2007, Abe (2007) emphasized the significance of 'freedom, democracy, human rights and the rule of law' in Japanese foreign policy and his government's commitments to 'reinforcing the stability and prosperity of the world' based on these 'fundamental values'. This, to the Chinese, provided the ideological foundation for Japan to fortify and extend its strategic relations and political cooperation with the US, Australia, India and EU and NATO members, thus helping to raise Japan's profile on the global stage (Liu Jiangyong 2007: 47).

What is more worrying to Chinese policy elites is the Abe government's desire to establish 'the arc of freedom and prosperity' along the outer rim of Eurasia on the basis of the universal values of democracy, freedom, human rights and market economies. They believe that Abe's 'value-oriented diplomacy' in North East, South East and South Asia, the Middle East, Central and Eastern Europe and the Baltic States could be seen as an attempt to employ America's neoconservative ideology and geopolitical strategy to constrain a rapidly ascending China (Liu Jiangyong 2007: 47–48). Related to value-oriented diplomacy was Abe's pledge to build 'a beautiful country, Japan' which, in his own words, should be 'trusted, respected, and loved in the world' and able to 'demonstrate leadership' (Abe 2006). It is this global aspiration, combined with Japan's active diplomacy to forge closer strategic ties with other liberal democratic countries in the Asia-Pacific, that perturbs Chinese security analysts.

This is why Chinese scholars expressed a more optimistic view of Japan's global and regional security strategy after Prime Minister Fukuda Yasuo came into office in September 2007 (Lian Degui 2007b). They have detected a significant difference between Fukuda's more pragmatic foreign policy and Abe's 'neoconservative approach' that combined values such as 'freedom' and 'democracy' with an assertive defence posture. The Chinese welcomed Fukuda's (2007a, 2007b, 2007c) 'peace diplomacy' that emphasized the promotion of 'peace', 'stability' and 'prosperity' of Asia and the world. They were also pleased to find that he was not active in pushing for the revision of the Japanese constitution, which was seen as a reflection of Toyko's ambition of becoming a 'military power'. Nevertheless, it is uncertain whether the optimism in Chinese perceptions of Japan's external policy can be sustained following Prime Minister Fukuda's unexpected resignation on 1 September 2008.

Japan's security strategy in the Asia-Pacific region

While Japanese ambitions in the international arena have attracted much attention from Chinese scholars and analysts, it is Tokyo's Asia strategy that causes the greatest concern in China. After all, Japan and China are historical rivals in East Asia. Many Chinese experts believe that Japan is gradually 'returning to Asia' (*huigui Yazhou*), having been a close friend and ally of America for over 50 years (Zhao Jieqi 1993: 29–34, 49; Zhao Guangrui 1996: 30–37). Others, however, contend that Japan has always placed a great deal of emphasis on Asia and that it has regarded the region as its backyard. Its post-war economic development was, to a certain extent, dependent on the resources and markets of Asia, especially South East Asia. As the only developed country in Asia, say the Chinese, Japan has often acted as if it were Asia's spokesperson in international forums (He Fang 1996: 22; Lu Guozhong 1997: 41). Following the debate in the 1990s over whether Japan should 'leave America to join Asia' (*tuoMei ruYa*) or 'leave Asia to join America' (*tuoYa ruMei*), Chinese scholars note that Japan has chosen the external strategy of 'joining America and Asia simultaneously' (*ruMei ruYa*) (Wang Gonglong 2002: 26). In any case, Japan's Asia strategy is seen to be inseparable from its global aspirations.

In recent years, apart from maintaining a high level of economic and trade interaction with Asian countries, Japan has been developing closer political and security relations with its Asian neighbours and with the ASEAN states in particular. More significantly, Japan is believed to have taken a higher profile and more assertive stance on a whole range of security issues in Asia. This is partly due to Japan's apprehension about the uncertain security environment in the Asia-Pacific despite the end of the Cold War. From the Japanese perspective, the Asia-Pacific is a region of complexity and diversity in terms of its history, culture, political system and level of economic development. Within this region, there are also divergent security perceptions, which may lead to tension and conflict. Chinese security analysts recognize Japan's concern about regional flashpoints relating to the Korean Peninsula, the Taiwan Strait and the South China Sea, as well as unresolved territorial disputes between Japan and China, Japan and South Korea, and Japan and Russia, respectively. Tokyo is also said to be troubled by the rise of defence budgets in many Asian countries and military development in the region. This is particularly destabilizing given the lack of established multilateral security mechanism in Asia (Yao Wenli 2003: 45).

Overall, Chinese policy analysts believe that Tokyo's Asia-Pacific security strategy reflects and serves its global strategy, that is, to enhance Japan's international profile and achieve the status of a great power. To this end, they argue, Japan has adopted a more proactive and assertive policy in the Asia-Pacific, with the aim of dominating East Asian security affairs. This explains the Japanese government's decision to strengthen the US-Japan security alliance and defence cooperation, establish a 'strategic global partnership' with India (Zhang Weiwei 2007), create a two-plus-two security dialogue with Australia,[3] conduct military exercises with the US, India and Australia, and initiate quadrilateral dialogue with the three countries emphasizing the 'shared values' in their strategic relations (Liu Jiangyong 2007). Indeed, the conception of establishing a 'four-nation alliance' (*siguo tongmeng*) between these countries has caused considerable concern among PRC security analysts. If such an alliance were to be formed, they fear, it could provide a basis for establishing an 'Asian version of NATO', which would alter the Asia-Pacific balance of power fundamentally and put enormous strategic pressure on China (Zhao Qinghai 2007).

In the meantime, Chinese policy analysts maintain, Japan has become more active in promoting the idea of an East Asian community since 2002 (Wu Huaizhong 2006a). While acknowledging Tokyo's growing interest in promoting closer regional cooperation, especially in the area of trade and economic activities, they are critical of Japan's 'Cold War mentality' in treating the US-Japan security alliance as the precondition for its involvement in regional security cooperation. Not surprisingly, the emphasis on Japanese national interest that includes such values as freedom and democracy in Japan's vision of an East Asian community (Council on East Asian Community 2005: 4–5) has attracted Chinese criticism.

According to some PRC scholars, Japan has attempted to transform the East Asia Summit (EAS) into a 'community of democratic countries' (*minzhu guojia gongtongti*), using it as 'a tool for guarding against and containing China'. Specifically, Japan is said to have advocated the use of 'common values' of democracy, freedom and human rights as the basis for the EAS. Another Japanese move, say the Chinese, is to enlarge EAS membership to include such 'democratic countries' as the US, Australia, New Zealand, India and so on (Liu Shaohua 2007). Moreover, PRC security specialists are sensitive of the suggestion put forward by some Japanese politicians and scholars that China is exploiting the development of sub-regional cooperation to exert 'Chinese hegemony'. In their view, Japan's Asia-Pacific security strategy, including its strategy of promoting an East Asian community, revolves around the aims of constraining or hedging against a rising China and playing a dominant strategic role in the Asia-Pacific region (Wu Huaizhong 2006a).

However, Chinese scholars became more sanguine about Japan's regional security policy after Abe's departure (Lian Degui 2007b). Indeed, Prime Minister Fukuda (2007b) had been pursuing what he called 'an active diplomacy vis-à-vis Asia' that emphasized the importance of stability and peace to the region. He had held substantive talks with US, Chinese, Indian, South Korean and ASEAN leaders on a whole range of bilateral and multilateral issues. Chinese analysts believe that the Fukuda government intended to enlarge the scope of its Asia policy to encompass wider areas such as Central and South Asia. While advocating the development of a peaceful, prosperous and open Asia through regional cooperation, Fukuda (2007b) stressed that the US-Japan alliance remained the 'firm lynchpin of Japan's foreign policy'. To the Chinese, what distinguishes Fukuda from Abe is that Fukuda avoided using sensitive language like 'value-oriented diplomacy' to package Japanese policy (Lian Degui 2007b: 60).

Japanese-US security relations

During the Cold War years Japan was a staunch ally of the United States in Asia, and it played an indispensable role in America's strategy of containing the Soviet Union and other communist states in the region (Liu Shilong 2006). In return, the Americans provided Japan with a security umbrella so that it could concentrate on its economic development. America's wars in Korea and Vietnam in the 1950s and 1960s, respectively, are also believed to have stimulated the rapid economic growth of the Japanese economy. Economically, the US offered a huge market and advanced technology to the Japanese, making it possible for Japan to achieve its 'economic miracle'. Since the end of the 1980s, however, Japan is no longer satisfied with its status as America's 'junior partner'. On many issues the Japanese are beginning to say 'no' to the United States (Morita and Ishihara 1991).

Despite their economic competition and trade disputes, Chinese scholars and analysts argue that there is still a high level of strategic dependence between Tokyo and Washington. They need each other to face the rapidly changing and uncertain security environment in the Asia-Pacific region.[4] In particular, they both see the rise of China as an immense challenge to regional security and Russia's unstable domestic situation as a major source of uncertainty. Other regional issues, such as the situation on the Korean Peninsula, the South China Sea disputes, and the tension across the Taiwan Strait, are also considered potential threats to Japanese and US security interests. Thus, a strong Japanese-US security alliance is crucial to Asia's stability and will serve the interests of both countries (Lu Guozhong 1997: 41). It is because of this consideration, according to Chinese observation, that Hashimoto Ryutaro, the former Japanese Prime Minister, met former US President Bill Clinton in April 1996 in Tokyo where they signed the 'Japanese-US Joint Declaration on Security Alliance for the Twenty-first Century' (for the English text, see CSIS 1996).[5]

The Joint Declaration stressed the need for bilateral cooperation in dealing with situations in areas surrounding Japan that would threaten its peace and security. In other words, the bilateral treaty between Japan and the US, the Chinese suspect, has now been extended to the entire region, including the Korean Peninsula, the South China Sea and the Taiwan Strait (Zhang Dalin 1996a, 1996b; Li Genan 1996: 1–3). Their concern heightened substantially when the revised 'Guidelines for US-Japan Defense Co-operation' were published on 23 September 1997 (for the English version of the guidelines, see *Journal of East Asian Affairs* 1998). Indeed, the Foreign Affairs College immediately organized a symposium to assess the nature of the guidelines and their implications for Asia-Pacific security. Over thirty scholars and security experts from the major Chinese think-tanks and research institutes in Beijing took part in the meeting. Some participants believed that the adjustment in US-Japan security relations and the publication of the defence guidelines would be detrimental to China's security environment. Other scholars, however, argued that the US-Japan alliance would help constrain Japan in developing its own military power, thus contributing to the preservation of regional stability in the Asia-Pacific (Su Hao 1998: 143, 145, 146).

Nevertheless, Chinese analysts argue that the original guidelines are quite sufficient in ensuring US-Japan defence cooperation if Japan were to be invaded. At any rate, the possibility of external military attack against Japan is virtually non-existent at present. The real aim of the new guidelines, they contend, is to shift Japan's security policy towards a new direction, that is, to integrate Japanese policy into America's Asia-Pacific strategy and to enable Japan's SDF to get involved in regional conflict legitimately (Liu Jiangyong 1997: 8). Indeed, the Japanese government has made specific agreements with the US in responding to situations in areas surrounding Japan. First, either government may conduct and initiate cooperation in certain activities, including measures to deal with refugees, relief activities, search and rescue operations, non-combatant evacuation operations and activities for ensuring the effectiveness of economic sanctions for the maintenance of international peace and stability. Second, Japan has agreed to provide support for US Forces activities if needed, which includes the provision of rear area support and the use of Japanese SDF facilities and civilian airports and ports. Third, should Japan's peace and security be affected by situations in its surrounding areas, the SDF will conduct activities, such as intelligence gathering, surveillance and minesweeping, to protect lives and property and to ensure navigational safety.

According to the guidelines, Japan's rear area support will be provided primarily in Japanese territories and on the high seas and in international airspace around Japan, rather than in areas where combat operations are being conducted. However, the Chinese contend that by providing US Forces with support while they are conducting operations in the Asia-Pacific, Japan would, in effect, be involved in joint military operations with America without being attacked by other countries (Hook, Gilson, Hughes and Dobson 2001: 136–46). In China's view, the new defence guidelines, together with the 1996 US-Japan Joint Declaration, are said to reflect the two allies' strategic intention of dominating Asia-Pacific security in the 21st century. As a rising power, it is argued, China is viewed by both Japan and the US as a formidable challenger to their desire. Although China is not considered as an immediate threat, they fear that in 20 years' time it could become a strong military power in the Pacific region. By then neither Japan nor the US would be able to prevent it from using force to deal with regional issues and territorial disputes.

Chinese analysts are convinced that the US has decided to help Japan to enhance its military capability and to reinforce the security ties between the two nations while China is relatively weak. For its part, Japan is said to be pleased to collaborate with the Americans in order to gain US support for its bid for permanent membership of the UN Security Council, and to achieve its ambition of becoming a 'political power' (Liu Jiangyong 1997: 8). Thus, the Chinese conclude that the redefinition of the US-Japan alliance has upset the balance among China, Japan and the United States in the Asia-Pacific in a way that will be detrimental to the development of Sino-Japanese and Sino-US relations, respectively (Jin Linbo 1999: 38–9). They believe that the joint declaration and the new defence guidelines signed by Tokyo and Washington are targeted primarily against the PRC (Zhu Zinchang and Shi Xiaojie 1999: 15; Lin Xiaoguang 1998a: 9–10).

In the view of Chinese analysts, Japan-US security cooperation has been strengthened substantially since 9/11. The various anti-terrorism legislations passed by the Diet, it is argued, have enabled the Japanese government to collaborate more closely with the US in achieving its security objectives. From the Japanese perspective, a solid security relationship with Washington is essential to Japan's quest for a more significant role in the world. This explains why the Koizumi government acted against public opinion in supporting Washington on the Iraq war (see the analysis in Li 2006: 78–80, 81–83). To the Bush administration, Japan's backing for the US invasion of Iraq was vital, even though Japanese contributions to the war were essentially symbolic. As former Prime Minister Koizumi commented at a news conference in December 2004: 'Japan's support activities in Iraq are the implementation of policies for the Japan-US alliance and international cooperation ... such implementation is a national interest of Japan' (*Asahi Shimbun* 2004).

What Japan seeks, Chinese analysts argue, is to achieve the status of an 'ordinary nation' through the expansion of the US-Japan security alliance (Liu Shilong 2003: 34–35). In the meantime, Japan has been encouraged by US politicians such as Colin Powell and Richard Armitage to amend its constitution, which has restricted Japan's international peacekeeping activities (BBC 2004). Many observers agree that Japan is considered America's most valuable and trusted ally in the Asia-

Pacific region (Marquand 2005). Japan's widening security role has certainly had the blessing of the US, as both share a range of common security concerns, particularly their apprehension about the rise of Chinese power.

Although the PRC is Japan's biggest trade partner, the Japanese are acutely aware that a stronger China would present a huge challenge to Tokyo's position in the Asia-Pacific. Especially worrying are Beijing's growing military capabilities (Drifte 2003: ch. 2). Indeed, this anxiety was conveyed in Japan's recently published defence guidelines where, for the first time, China was named as a potential threat (Japanese Defense Agency 2004). The Koizumi government also shared the Bush administration's concern over the PRC's threat of using force against Taiwan. In a joint US-Japan security statement published on 19 February 2005, both countries agreed that encouraging 'the peaceful resolution of issues concerning the Taiwan Strait through dialogue' should be one of their 'common strategic objectives'. They also agreed to 'encourage China to improve transparency of its military affairs' (Japanese Ministry of Foreign Affairs 2005a). Ono Yoshinori, Director General of Japan's Defense Agency, is reported to have said: 'While we should maintain good relations with China, we must also pay attention to its military moves' (Kyodo News 2005). The Japanese saw the intrusion of a Chinese nuclear submarine into Japanese territorial waters in November 2004 as evidence of a growing China threat.

Chinese scholars accept that the 'China threat' is not the only basis on which Japan maintains its alliance with the United States. From a Japanese standpoint, they point out, no other security relations can be more important than the US-Japan alliance in terms of ensuring Japan's security. The alliance is also seen to be vital in securing American involvement in tackling any potential regional crisis. More broadly, Japan hopes that the alliance would play a stabilizing role in Asia-Pacific security and contribute to the preservation of international peace (Yao Wenli 2003: 45). Chinese analysts are convinced that Tokyo has tried to exploit America's recent force realignment[6] to strengthen the Japanese-US alliance and enhance Japan's security role, with the ultimate aim of achieving the status of a military and political power (Wu Huaizhong 2006b).

To the Chinese, the most worrying aspect of Japan-US security cooperation is arguably Tokyo's involvement in the development of the TMD system in Asia. In December 1998, Tokyo and Washington agreed that their joint research on the TMD would begin in 1999, involving expenses of 200–300 billion Japanese yen. Japan indicated in December 2003 that it would procure an off-the-shelf ballistic missile defence system from Washington (Hughes 2004a: 108–09).

Not surprisingly, the Chinese are sceptical of the claim that the TMD is designed solely to deal with potential missile attacks from North Korea. They argue instead that the project reflects a wider agenda between Japan and America in coordinating their missile defence activities in East Asia and deepening their military cooperation in the region and beyond. Japan's motive, say the Chinese, is to utilize the joint development of the TMD to enhance its position within the alliance and to raise its profile in regional security affairs (Yao Wenli 2003: 51–53). But China's main concern is the possibility that the TMD would be exploited by Japan and America to help Taiwan defend itself in the event of a cross-strait conflict. Full-scale anti-missile defence cooperation between Tokyo, Washington and Taipei would be a nightmare scenario for Chinese defence planners (Wu Xinbuo 2003: 47–48).

Japanese strategy towards ASEAN

Apart from strengthening bilateral defence cooperation with the United States, Japan has, over the past few years, been active in promoting multilateral security in the Asia-Pacific region. In particular, Japan has been closely involved in the activities of the ARF, which is the most important official channel of security dialogue in Asia (Liu Jiangyong 1993: 6–7). Japan's support for the ARF is, however, viewed by Chinese scholars and analysts as an indication of a strategic adjustment in Japanese policy towards ASEAN (Wang Gonglong 1997: 55–68; Qiao Linsheng 2006).

According to Chinese observation, Japan has been zealously expanding its economic, political and security relations with the ASEAN states. The new relationship between Japan and ASEAN is characterized by the Japanese as one of 'equal partnership' (Jia Chaowei 1997: 8–9). Economically, ASEAN figures significantly in Japan's development in terms of both resources and markets. Indeed, ASEAN is Japan's third largest trading partner, and Japan is the biggest investor in ASEAN. For example, Japanese investment in Indonesia, Malaysia, the Philippines and Thailand in 1995 amounted to US$ 61.9 billion. In addition to the huge profits from trading with the ASEAN countries, Chinese analysts argue, the Japanese intend to use ASEAN as a base to penetrate into the emerging markets in Indochina, particularly Vietnam. Ultimately, they hope that ASEAN would play a prominent role in a Tokyo-led East Asian economic community that is capable of competing with other trading blocs in Europe and North America (Jia Chaowei 1997: 8; Wang Gonglong 1997: 61–62).

Similarly, Japan's attempts to improve political relations with ASEAN have caused much anxiety among Chinese specialists. They believe that Japan's efforts to gain more trust from the ASEAN states are designed to increase its political influence in South East Asia and to elevate its standing as an Asian power. For a long time, it is argued, Japan has employed such means as trade, investment, economic aid and technology transfer to eliminate its aggressive image in the mind of ASEAN elites. The Japanese government is particularly pleased with the backing rendered by some ASEAN states to its quest for permanent membership of the UN Security Council. Given ASEAN's rising status as an independent force in the Asia-Pacific, its support is essential to Japan in achieving its political aims in the region and beyond (Wang Gonglong 1997: 63–64; Bai Ruchun 2004).

In recent years Japan has been engaged in security dialogue with ASEAN which, according to Chinese analysis, aims at safeguarding Japanese security interests in South East Asia. It can be said that Japan's economic security is largely determined by its geographical location. Eighty per cent of the oil that Japan needs passes through the waters in the South China Sea. Thus, a vital part of Japanese security strategy is to ensure that freedom of navigation in the area is not disrupted by any potential conflict. Maintaining security dialogue with ASEAN, some Chinese analysts note, will contribute to the promotion of regional peace and security, which will in turn protect the lifeline of the Japanese economy. Others, however, argue that Japan's close association with the ARF reveals its aspirations to create an Asia-Pacific security system in which Tokyo will play a central role (Wang Gonglong 1997: 64–65; Jia Chaowei 1997: 9; Qiao Linsheng 2006).

A major concern of Chinese scholars and analysts is Japan's alleged collaboration with ASEAN to constrain China. As China's comprehensive national strength increases and its international status rises, they argue, some people in the US and Japan are deliberately spreading a 'China threat theory' (*Zhongguo weixie lun*) that assumes that China is keen to fill the power vacuum in Asia left by the two superpowers, and that it will present a threat to Japan and other Asian countries. The fear of an increasingly powerful China is shared by some ASEAN states that have unresolved territorial disputes with the PRC in the South China Sea. They have sought to 'internationalize' the issue, hoping that a solution favourable to them could be found with external intervention. This, say the Chinese, has provided an opportunity for Japan to entice ASEAN's support to curtail China's influence in the region (Wang Gonglong 1997: 65–66; Qiao Linsheng 2006).

Given the mutual suspicion between Japan and China, Tokyo was said to be displeased by the announcement made by Chinese and ASEAN leaders in November 2002 that they would establish a China-ASEAN Free Trade Area by 2010, which could become the world's third largest trading bloc. In response to China's economic diplomacy, Japan has become more proactive in developing relations with ASEAN states (Bai Ruchun 2004: 88). At the 2002 ASEAN-Plus-Three Summit, Japan launched a new initiative, Japan-ASEAN Comprehensive Economic Partnership, which would involve the negotiation of a series of bilateral trade agreements with individual ASEAN states (Dent 2003: 89, 2006). Apart from its economic diplomacy, many Chinese analysts believe that Japan has expanded relations with ASEAN countries in political and military spheres with the aim of establishing a leading position in South East Asia and preventing other great powers from dominating the area (Qiao Linsheng 2006).

Japan, China and the Taiwan Strait

In addition to the ASEAN region, China suspects that Japan is seeking to challenge Chinese interests in the Taiwan Strait. Indeed, the extension of the geographical areas covered by the 1996 Japanese-US Joint Declaration and the revised Guidelines for US-Japan Defense Co-operation has led to considerable apprehension among Chinese policy elites. Their greatest worry is the possible inclusion of the Taiwan Strait in the ambiguous 'surrounding areas' mentioned in the treaty and guidelines (Xiao Feng 1998: 8–9). According to a Taiwanese newspaper, the former Japanese Prime Minister Hashimoto admitted at a private meeting in April 1997 that the areas of security collaboration between Tokyo and Washington would include not only the Korean Peninsula, but also the Spratly Islands and the Taiwan Strait. The allegation was denied by Hashimoto at once (*Zhongguo shibao* 1997). But a few months later, the Japanese Chief Cabinet Secretary Seiroku Kajiyama said on the Asahi television network that the Taiwan Strait naturally fell within the scope of Japanese-US security cooperation. This statement was supported publicly by several senior Japanese officials, although the Japanese government later explained that 'the situation in Japan's surrounding areas' in the defence guidelines referred to 'the nature of the situation' rather than 'specific geographical locations' (Xiao Feng 1998: 10–11). The Chinese are convinced that in collaboration with America, Japan is exploiting the Taiwan issue to impede the reunification of China and Taiwan.

Indeed, since the early 1990s, Chinese analysts contend that Japan has upgraded its relationship with Taiwan significantly. During the Cold War era, Japan-Taiwan relations were confined mainly to the sphere of economic cooperation. Over the past decade, it is said that greater emphasis has been placed on political interactions. More official and high-level contacts between the two sides have taken place (Ma Yuan 1997: 18–22; Yang Yunzhong 1996: 24–38). According to Chinese observation, there are a variety of explanations for Japan's increasingly pro-Taiwan stance. First, from a geopolitical perspective, Japan is a small country with few natural resources and a limited domestic market. Its economic survival is dependent largely on the shipping lanes in the area of which the Taiwan Strait is an important part. Thus, Japan is worried that its national security will be threatened should China take over Taiwan and gain full control of the Taiwan Strait (Lu Junyuan 1995: 16–24; Ma Yuan 1997: 19–20). Second, an intimate relationship between Tokyo and Taipei will aid Japan in establishing a dominant position in Asia-Pacific security. In this sense, the Japanese are believed to be encouraged by the growing strength of the independence movement in Taiwan since the election as president of Lee Teng-hui, who had exceptionally close ties with Japan and Chen Shui-bian, the pro-independence Democratic Progressive Party (DPP) leader (Huang Yuerong 2007: 21; Ma Yuan 1997: 20; Yang Yunzhong 1996: 34, 36)

Third, Taiwan was ceded to Japan following China's defeat in the Sino-Japanese War in 1894 (Jiang Weiqing 1995). During the 50 years' Japanese occupation, the Chinese complain, Taiwan was subjected to a process of 'Japanization'. Even after Japan's forced departure from Taiwan in 1945, some Japanese are reluctant to accept that Taiwan is part of Chinese territory, and try to glorify their colonial rule over the island. It is claimed that throughout the post-war years, Japan has never ceased to support Taiwanese independence forces. Indeed, the overseas offices of some pro-independence organizations are said to be located in Japan. This historical legacy explains Japan's continued interests in Taiwan (Ma Yuan 1997: 20; Yang Yunzhong 1996: 35). Fourth, Japan has had strong trade and economic links with Taipei since the 1950s. Japanese companies and financial institutions have extensive business interests in Taiwan, and over the years they have benefited tremendously from the Taiwanese market. The Chinese argue that to maintain Japan's share of this lucrative market in the face of fierce competition from the US, Germany and France, Japan desperately needs to fortify its official relations with Taiwan (Ma Yuan 1997: 20; Yang Yunzhong 1996: 35–36).

Japan's evolving relationship with Taiwan through various channels of informal politics is characterized by Phil Deans (2001) as 'virtual diplomacy'. To Chinese security specialists, however, the ultimate aim of Japan's post-Cold War Taiwan policy is to use the 'Taiwan card' to constrain China, perceived as its principal rival in the Western Pacific region (Fan Yuejiang 1999: 24–36; Lian Wen 1998: 29–30). A united China that combines the economic strengths and strategic advantages of the PRC and Taiwan will present Japan with a huge challenge in the 21st century. As long as Beijing and Taipei remain divided, it is said, they will not be able to take effective measures to deal with the issue of sovereignty in the Spratly and Diaoyu/Senkaku islands. It is therefore in Japan's interests to maintain the status quo across the Taiwan Strait. This is why Japan has been exaggerating China's potential threat to regional security, say the Chinese. During 1995 and 1996, when China held a series of large-scale military exercises and missiles tests in the East China Sea, Japan's media were highly critical of the Chinese actions, and some Japanese politicians expressed deep concern over the security of Taiwan. This, the Chinese conclude, reflects Japanese displeasure at Beijing's decision to use military means to deter the activities of the 'separatist elements' on the island, as it frustrates Japan's ambition of pursuing regional dominance in Asia (Ma Yuan 1997: 19, 21; Lu Junyuan 1996: 35).

In the view of Chinese analysts, Japan has continued to fortify its relations with Taiwan since the mid-1990s with the aim of 'using Taiwan to constrain China' (*yiTai zhiHua*). It is possible, they predict, that Tokyo would provide military support for America in a Taiwan conflict in future. During the presidency of Chen Shui-bian, the Chinese assert, Japan maintained close links with the DPP government. Japan is also believed to have increased its influence on the island through 'economic penetration', political interactions, high-level defence and security dialogues and the development of the TMD system. Increasingly, Japan, America and Taiwan are engaged in regular trilateral strategic dialogues, say the Chinese (Yang Yunzhong 2004; Wu Wanhong 2005). Tokyo's decision to issue a visa to former Taiwanese President Lee Teng-hui to visit Japan in December 2004 was interpreted as another attempt to challenge China on the Taiwan issue. The Chinese therefore reacted strongly to the February 2005 US-Japan security statement that listed Taiwan as one of their common security concerns (Japanese Ministry of Foreign Affairs 2005a). It was the first time that the Taiwan issue had been mentioned publicly by both Japan and America in their bilateral security statement. This is perceived by the Chinese as an indication of US-Japan collaboration to interfere with China's 'internal affairs', despite the Japanese government's reassurance that Japan does not support Taiwan's independence. The first US-Japan-Taiwan joint military exercise in March 2007 was seen as indicative of Japan's intention in the Taiwan Strait (Zhou Yongsheng 2007: 63–64).

Taiwan is not the only issue that Japan is worried about. PRC security analysts recognize that Japan does have broader concerns over China's policies and activities. Central to Japan's security considerations are, say the Chinese, China's rapid defence modernization, strong nuclear capabilities and its non-transparent defence budgets. China's involvement in various unresolved territorial disputes, such as those in Taiwan, South China Sea and East China Sea, has also troubled

Japanese defence planners. The fact that China has become increasingly powerful, and that it is not willing to rule out the use of force to resolve border disputes, means that there may be future conflict in the Asia-Pacific that could affect Japanese security. However, according to Chinese observation, Japan has an ambivalent attitude towards a rising China. On the one hand, it is uncertain of the PRC's future development and therefore feels the need to guard against China. On the other, Japan sees China's economic growth as an opportunity for Japanese businesses. Japan's China policy is said to have reflected this ambivalence (Yao Wenli 2003: 46; Liu Shilong 2003: 32).

According to the Chinese, there are two dimensions to Japan's strategy towards China. In terms of regional security, the Chinese note, the two countries have common interests as well as differences. The Japanese hope to establish a multi-lateral security framework that can be used to constrain Chinese actions without antagonizing it. In terms of economic cooperation, Japan needs China's participation but is wary of its growing economic power in the region. Essentially, the Japanese government is believed to try to influence China's behaviour through engagement and dialogue, but it is unsure of Beijing's security intentions. This is why Tokyo has strengthened its alliance relations with the US while engaging in security dialogue with China. At the same time, Japan is seeking to develop its relations with China's neighbouring countries in order to balance an increasingly powerful China. This strategy, the Chinese observe, has been written into Japan's strategic documents (Liu Shilong 2003: 33–34). It is within this context that Chinese security analysts are apprehensive of the recent debate on the 'sea power theory' (*haiquan lun*) in Japan. Their interpretation of the debate is that some Japanese defence specialists are deliberately trying to portray Japan as a maritime state that should ally with other maritime powers, such as the US, to face the challenge of a rising continental state, that is, China (Guan Xi 2006).

Nevertheless, Chinese scholars have noticed positive signs in the development of Sino-Japanese relations following the election of Fukuda as Japan's prime minister. Fukuda appeared to be determined to improve Japan's ties with China. He used the phrase 'spring has come' to describe Japan-China relations before his visit to Beijing in December 2007 (BBC 2007). In his speech at Peking University, Fukuda (2007c) expressed the hope that Japan and China would become 'creative partners' in developing a 'mutually beneficial relationship based on common strategic interests'. He highlighted three pillars of Japan-China relations: mutually-beneficial cooperation, contributions to international society, and mutual understanding and mutual trust.

The proposed areas for bilateral and multilateral cooperation included the battle against terrorism, climate change, security in North East Asia (especially denuclearization of the Korean Peninsula), UN reform, poverty alleviation in Africa and so on. Fukuda also suggested specific measures to advance 'mutually-beneficial cooperation' and bring about 'the virtual cycle of dialogue, understanding, and trust' between the two nations. Speaking on historical issues, Fukuda stated the need for 'remorse' for Japan's 'mistakes' and 'proper regards' to the 'feelings of people who suffered'. During his visit to China, he also 'reiterated Japan's opposition to Taiwanese independence' (BBC 2007). These remarks, together with Fukuda's pledge not to visit the Yasukuni Shrine, have made some PRC scholars more hopeful for a better relationship with Japan, at least in the short term (Lian Degui 2007b).

Japan, North Korea and Russia

In North East Asia, North Korea and Russia are seen as potential adversaries who could pose a grave security threat to Japan. Indeed, in the recent editions of the Japanese Defense White Paper, they were invariably treated as the main targets of Japan's strategic defence. Chinese scholars and analysts point out that while Japan is wary of the security challenges from the two countries, it has been trying to improve relations with them (Yang Yunzhong 1995: 36).

In terms of history, culture and geographical proximity, Japan is very close to the Korean Peninsula. During the Cold War years, however, Japan's relations with North Korea were seriously affected by the hostility between the two Koreas and between Pyongyang and Washington. Since the end of the 1980s, both the US and South Korea have been more flexible in their policy towards North Korea, say the Chinese. This has made it possible for Tokyo to normalize its relations with Pyongyang. In the view of Chinese analysts, the Asia-Pacific is an important region in Japan's global strategy, and an improvement in Japanese-North Korean relations will be useful to the elevation of Japan's status in East Asia. Thus, Japan has made a significant adjustment in its North Korea policy, including a high-profile visit by leading Japanese politicians to Pyongyang, and the signing of a joint declaration between both sides in 1990. Between 1991 and 1992, eight rounds of negotiation on normalization took place but were suspended in 1993, due mainly to domestic political problems in Japan (Ding Yingshun 1996: 68–74, 1998: 93–98).

Since 1995, the Japanese government has been once again engaging North Korea. Although Japan expresses support for the four-way talks between the US, China and the two Koreas on the Korean situation, the Chinese note that it is not pleased with the arrangements initiated by Washington, as the exclusion of Japan from the talks meant that the Japanese would not be directly involved in an influential mechanism that is likely to shape the future of the Korean Peninsula. In December 1996, Japan proposed to North Korea that a 'North East Asian Forum for Security and Defence Dialogue' could be established to complement the work of the four-way talks, but the suggestion was rejected by North Korea. Therefore, the only way that Japan can influence events on the Korean Peninsula is to end the abnormal state of its relations with Pyongyang. This, according to the Chinese, will not only be essential to the preservation of Japanese security, but propitious to the expansion of Japan's overseas market. In the longer term, it is argued, Japan will try to bring North Korea into an East Asian economic circle led by Tokyo.

As far as Japan's policy towards inter-Korean relations is concerned, Chinese analysts believe that it has changed from an entirely pro-South Korea stance to one of keeping equal distance from both sides. The priorities of the Japanese government are to ensure stability in its surrounding areas and to enhance its capacity to intervene, should a conflict arise. Tokyo encourages security dialogue between the two Koreas, as it would contribute to the relaxation of tension and the prevention of nuclear proliferation in the area. In the meantime, the Japanese have offered substantial economic aid to North Korea for fear that the regime may collapse as a result of famine and economic disaster, which could have dire consequences for Japan. However, the Chinese claim that Japan does not wish to see the reunification of Korea in the near future but would like to maintain the status quo on the Korean Peninsula. A reunified Korea, it is suggested, could become a rich and powerful nation, thus constituting a potential military threat to Japan's security and a tremendous challenge to its economic supremacy in East Asia (Ding Yingshun 1996: 74–80, 1998: 99–107).

However, North Korea's nuclear programmes and ballistic missile activities pose a tremendous threat to Japanese security, given the geographical propinquity between the two countries. North Korea's missile launch in August 1998 is a vivid reminder of how vulnerable Japan is to a missile attack. Despite the difficulties in dealing with North Korea, Japanese leaders have been trying to develop a stable relationship with Pyongyang. They do not wish to see a military confrontation on the Korean Peninsula, nor face the consequences of a sudden collapse of the North Korean regime. Chinese security experts agree that Koizumi's historic visit to Pyongyang, and his meeting with the North Korean leader Kim Jong-il in September 2002, demonstrated Japan's desire to engage with North Korea through diplomacy and dialogue (Jin Linbo 2003).

To Tokyo, a desperate North Korean communist regime could fire missiles at Japan and South Korea, where US troops are stationed. Both Japan and the US regard a peaceful resolution of the North Korean issue as a 'common strategic objective', as outlined in their recent joint security statement (Japanese Ministry of Foreign Affairs 2005a). In the meantime, the Koizumi government agreed to collaborate with the Bush administration to maintain 'preparedness for any situation' (Japanese Ministry of Foreign Affairs 2005b). But Chinese analysts argue that Japan's alliance with America has constrained Japanese actions regarding the Korean Peninsula and could actually undermine Japan's security. Japan can only play a positive role, they believe, in handling the North Korean crisis if it has the support of its neighbouring countries (Wang Chuanjian 2005).

In order to find a diplomatic solution to the recent nuclear crisis, Japan has been involved in the six-party talks with North Korea, South Korea, China, the US and Russia. However, PRC security specialists assert that Japan has exploited Pyongyang's nuclear test in July 2006 to elevate its security role in East Asia. They point out that immediately after the test, Japan put together a draft UN resolution on imposing economic sanctions against North Korea and actively sought the support of the US, UK, France and other countries for such a resolution. To the Chinese, this was an attempt to please Western powers, reduce the influence of China and Russia, enable Japan to play a leading role in East Asian security affairs and, most importantly, raise its international profile and great power status (Zhou Yongsheng 2006: 34–35).

Prior to the Gorbachev era, there were serious strains in Japan's relations with

Russia/the Soviet Union due to various factors, including the Cold War political climate, historical animosity between the two countries and their disputes over the Northern Territories (Li Fuxing 1995: 30–33). Since the mid-1980s both sides have been more willing to improve their relationship. In particular, Japan has revised its previous policy that the issue of territorial disputes could not be separated from the development of economic relations. In 1993, Japan decided to de-link the issues of the Northern Territories and economic assistance to Russia, and invited President Boris Yeltsin to attend the forthcoming G7 summit in Tokyo. The Japanese government has also provided substantial aid to Russia and supported its entry to APEC.

According to Chinese analysis, this signifies a major adjustment in Japan's Russia policy. It aims to create a relaxed atmosphere through economic cooperation, which will hopefully be more conducive to the resolution of territorial disputes. In early 1997, Japan broadened its policy to one of 'multi-level engagement' covering territorial negotiations, economic, political, security and international cooperation with Russia. The emphasis of the policy is to promote mutual trust so that both countries would benefit from the new relationship (Lin Xiaoguang 1998b: 31–37).

Chinese specialists contend that Japan's post-Cold War strategy towards Russia must be understood within the context of a changing global and regional environment. In terms of strategic considerations, Japan needs Russia to face new challenges and uncertainties in North East Asia, such as possible conflict on the Korean Peninsula and the security implications of a rising China. In addition, Japan is concerned that its position in Asia may be weakened following a considerable improvement in Sino-US relations and Russia's relations with America and China respectively. In any case, Russia is thought to have moved towards political democratization and economic liberalization (Wang Qinghai and Zhou Zhenkun 1997: 14–18; Jin Xide 1998: 15–32).

Consequently, Moscow no longer constitutes a major threat to Japanese security as it did during the Soviet era. Politically, the backing of Russia is indispensable in Japan's endeavour to become a permanent member of the UN Security Council. From an economic point of view, Tokyo hopes to benefit from energy cooperation with the Russian government. In the eyes of the Chinese, the adjustment in Japan's Russia policy is part of a national strategy of attaining the status of a world political power (Wang Qinghai and Zhou Zhenkun 1997: 14–18; Jin Xide 1998: 15–32). Nevertheless, Chinese security analysts point out, Japan remains apprehensive of the presence of the Russian military forces in the Far East and Moscow's stance on the territorial disputes over the Northern Territories (Yao Wenli 2003: 46). Despite an expansion of economic and security cooperation between the two countries,[7] the Koizumi government is said to have taken a rather inflexible and uncompromising approach to the resolution of their territorial disputes (Zhou Yongsheng 2006: 37).

Theoretical analysis

The evidence presented in this chapter suggests that the majority of Chinese policy analysts perceive Japan as a major challenge to Asia-Pacific security and to the security of China. Chinese specialists believe that Japan is in a transitional period from an economic power to a political power. To be a true political power, Japan has to increase its military strength and raise its profile in the international arena. Its Asia policy is thus seen as an inseparable part of this global strategy.

The Chinese view of Japan's post-Cold War global aspirations clearly reflects the realist perspective on international relations in that Japan seeks to increase its global economic and political influence in order to advance its national interests in the international system. Chinese analysts tend to see Japan as a unitary actor seeking to compete with other great powers in the world, and with China in particular. Their interpretations of Japan's post-Cold War security strategy in the Asia-Pacific are shaped largely by the consideration of great power competition and the balance of power in the region (Morgenthau 1978; Waltz 1979).

It can be argued that Japanese intentions and actions are perceived by the Chinese primarily through the realist lens. In the eyes of the Chinese, Japan is an ambitious nation seeking to become a 'political power' in the world and a regional power in the Asia-Pacific. Thus, the decision of the Japanese government to renew its security treaty with the United States is thought to be motivated by a desire to strengthen Japanese power so as to dominate Asia-Pacific security matters. Japan's attempts to develop a better relationship with Russia are also believed to serve the purpose of offsetting any undesirable effects of improved relations among other great powers. Similarly, the efforts made by Tokyo to improve political relations with Taiwan, North Korea and the ASEAN states are interpreted as a vital part of Japan's strategy to establish its status as an East Asia power whose influence on the future of the Asia-Pacific region should not be ignored.

In addition, it appears that China's perception of Japan's post-Cold War security strategy is shaped by the views of structural realism. Seen from this perspective, Japan's desire to play a more significant role in the world and in East Asia is largely driven by the changing structure of the international system. The end of bipolarity has arguably given Japan the opportunity to reassert itself as a more significant player in world politics. This is why some Chinese security analysts argue that Japan is seeking to become a more equal partner of America within the US-Japan security alliance. It can also explain why the Chinese believe that Japan has become more assertive in its pursuit of a 'political power' status. As Kenneth Waltz argues, it is inevitable that the current international structure will shift from unipolarity to multipolarity. He believes that Japan will inexorably develop into a great power because of its economic capability and its fear of vulnerability to other great powers, especially China (Waltz 2000: 32–34). The structural realist theory can therefore be used to explicate the Japanese government's concern of growing Chinese military power and Japan's recent activities in UN peacekeeping, anti-terrorist operations, the Iraq conflict and cooperation with America on missile defence programmes. The Chinese may ponder over Waltz's (2000: 34) question with some trepidation: 'How long can Japan live alongside other nuclear states while denying itself similar capabilities?'

In the view of many Chinese security specialists, Japan has the ambition of becoming a political power, with or without the potential 'threat' from China. They believe that Japanese politicians have merely used the 'China threat' theory to justify Japan's high defence spending, military development and enhanced security cooperation with America. Tokyo's ultimate aim, according to the Chinese, is to become a political and military power possessing the capability of exerting regional hegemony in East Asia. In this sense, the Chinese perception of Japan can be explained by offensive realism, which argues that states would exploit any opportunity to maximize their relative power. In an anarchic international system, according to this theory, all great powers are non-status quo powers (Mearsheimer 2001: 21). Seen from this theoretical perspective, it is not too difficult to comprehend why some Chinese analysts believe that Japan's security strategy is of an offensive rather than defensive nature. If Japan were to become a regional hegemon in East Asia, it would be in a position to prevent China from acting assertively in the Taiwan Strait and South China Sea. For PRC leaders and elites, reclaiming their 'lost territories' is an integral part of China's great power aspirations. Thus, Japan's 'ambition' is perceived by Chinese analysts as a major obstacle to their construction of a great power identity for China.

However, Chinese scholars are not oblivious of the variety of traditional and non-conventional security challenges that Japan faces. They appreciate the relevance of other dimensions of security to Japanese strategic thinking. In particular, they have recognized the linkage between economic development, energy security and strategic considerations. Japan's policy towards the Middle East is said to be closely related to its strategy of ensuring energy supply in an unstable environment (Jin Xide 2006). PRC analysts have also pointed out that one of the main reasons Japan is interested in the territorial disputes in the South China Sea and the Taiwan Strait is its concern over the impact of potential regional conflict on the Japanese economy. As freedom of navigation in these areas is of utmost importance to Japan in terms of oil supply and trade activity, it does not wish to see any developments that might be detrimental to Japanese interests.

An area where Japan and China have been competing for access to potentially rich deposits of natural gases is the East China Sea. This is linked to their territorial dispute over the sovereignty of the Diaoyu/Senkaku islands (Liu Jiangyong 1996b; Zhu Fenglan 2005). Given the growing demand for energy in both countries, their rivalry will only intensify in the coming years. There has been some discussion on joint development between the two countries, but it has not led to any tangible results due to disagreements over the nature and operation of the joint development (Drifte 2008; Valencia 2007).

Moreover, Chinese analysts maintain that Japan is actively seeking to dominate the Strait of Malacca, a major shipping channel between the Indian Ocean and the Pacific Ocean, through anti-piracy and anti-terrorist activities and humanitarian assistance. A main consideration of the move, it is argued, is to protect Japan's strategic sea lanes, which are the lifelines of its economy (Li Bing 2006).

Chinese analysis is clearly informed by the neorealist security perspective and the mercantilist theory of International Political Economy, in that state is seen as the primary actor in international relations and economic activity should not be separated from state interests (Gilpin 1987).

Chinese security analysts are aware of the Japanese apprehension that successful resolution of the disputes over the sovereignty of Taiwan and the South China Sea islands hinges largely upon the future policy of the PRC. Hence, the Japanese perceive China as a challenge, if not a potential threat, to Asia-Pacific security. It is precisely because of these concerns, Chinese specialists note, that Japan has decided to maintain close security ties with the United States. At the same time, Tokyo is keen to promote security cooperation with its Asian neighbours (Liu Shilong 1998; Yang Yunzhong 1998). In particular, the Japanese government sees the ASEAN Regional Forum as a useful channel of security dialogue, through which suspicion could be reduced, mutual understanding enhanced and confidence built among the key regional players. Chinese analysts observe that like China and other Asian nations, Japan needs a stable and peaceful environment to sustain its economic growth. That is why Japan has pursued policies to help maintain regional stability, such as the provision of economic assistance to North Korea and Russia. All this indicates Chinese awareness of Japan's intention of enhancing its security through multilateral institutions and cooperation. In this regard, Chinese analysis is consistent with the theory of defensive realism, which posits that cooperation is possible in an anarchic international system (Jervis 1978). This can also be explained by the theory of neoliberal institutionalism, which is widely used to explain why and how states can cooperate through international institutions.

Chinese experts have also noted Japan's fear that arms proliferation and territorial conflict may intensify in post-Cold War Asia, which could undermine the stability of the entire region. As China is involved in many unresolved territorial disputes in East Asia, they admit, its growing economic strength and military capability are viewed with considerable concern by Japan. This apprehension has not prevented Japan from accelerating the development of its trade relations with China. Despite their mutual suspicions on security matters, Sino-Japanese economic relations have continued to grow. Chinese security specialists have clearly grasped the essence of Tokyo's strategy of achieving regional peace through trade and economic interdependency. In this sense, they could be regarded as liberals rather than realists. Indeed, the Chinese recognize the liberal elements in Japan's policy towards China.

In their analysis of the relationship between Japan's domestic politics and its security strategy, Chinese analysts seem to have moved further away from their realist position. They have demonstrated an understanding of the impact of domestic factors on Japan's foreign relations. Specifically, they have discerned the changing balance of power between various institutions within the Japanese foreign policy-making process. In addition, Chinese scholars have noticed the rising influence of conservative forces on Japan's foreign and security policy since the 1990s. The rise of neonationalism in Japanese politics and society, in their view, has led to a more assertive security strategy and unstable Sino-Japanese relations.

However, they have placed a great deal of emphasis on the strength of conservative groups in the Japanese system. It is true that some people in Japan have found it difficult to come to terms with history and have sought to deny the war crimes committed by Japanese imperialists. But it does not necessarily follow that right-wing forces will always dominate Japan's foreign policy agenda. There exist numerous peace movements and groups that for many years have campaigned against the revival of Japanese militarism. In a pluralist society like Japan, the views of various domestic actors cannot be disregarded by policy-makers. Specifically, the business community that has benefited enormously from a peaceful trading environment in East Asia has a powerful voice in the policy process.

Despite their negative security perception of Japan, few, if any, Chinese analysts suggest that China should adopt a confrontational stance towards Japan at the expense of economic and commercial benefits. It is clear that China has much to gain from Japanese investment and Sino-Japanese trade (Taylor 1996). Indeed, China has benefited immensely from Japan's Official Development Assistance (ODA) programmes over the years (see Fig. 4.1), although the Japanese government has decided to end its loan aid to the PRC by 2008 (Drifte 2006). Chinese scholars acknowledge the need to pursue further economic and security cooperation with Japan. They accept that China and Japan are both great powers and close neighbours, and that they have a shared interest and responsibility in maintaining peace and stability in the Asia-Pacific region (He Fang 1998: 16–18; Wang Sheng 1999: 12–14; Xu Ping 2007: 16–17). This view seems to reflect the perspectives of defensive realism and neoliberalism in that cooperation is perfectly possible under anarchy.

Nevertheless, realism and liberalism alone cannot adequately explain the complexity of Sino-Japanese relations. While material factors are pertinent to the analysis of China's security perceptions of Japan, one has to take into account the ideational aspects of Chinese discourse. From the constructivist standpoint, the interests of a state are generated and shaped by its identity (Jepperson, Wendt and Katzenstein 1996: 60). It appears that Chinese analysts are fully aware of the tendency among Japan's politicians and elites to redefine its post-war identity in recent years. Toyko's growing interests in playing a more prominent role in regional and global security affairs are believed to be a reflection of its desire to become a 'normal nation' or what the Chinese call a 'political power' (*zhengzhi daguo*). The Chinese analysis is consistent with the constructivist view that 'states can develop interests in enacting, sustaining, or developing a particular identity' (Jepperson, Wendt and Katzenstein 1996: 60).

Moreover, constructivists argue that history and culture are important in shaping an actor's identity which in turn influences what the actor considers as its interests (Berger 1996; Johnston 1996). In the case of Japan, history plays a significant role in shaping its identity and how other countries perceive it. Indeed, the way Chinese analysts view Japan's security thinking and foreign policy behaviour is overshadowed by Japan's modern history. They tend to emphasize the militaristic tendency in Japanese security discourse on the basis of Japan's wartime behaviour.

The Chinese are particularly sensitive to Japanese actions that may trigger their historical memory, the most prominent example of which is the visit of senior Japanese politicians to the Yasukuni Shrine. Former Prime Minister Koizumi's regular visits to the shrine, where executed war criminals are venerated along with other war dead, were seen as a sign of Japanese reluctance to accept the past (Jiang Lifeng 2006). Another example illustrating the relevance of history to China's perception of Japan is the dispute over how Japan's actions during World War II is presented in Japanese history textbooks which, according to the Chinese, have been deliberately distorted. The textbook issue is of course not just a matter of interpretation of history (Rose 1998). As the issue is seen to be an indication of Japan's attitudes towards its national goal and military policy, a 'correct view of history' becomes directly relevant to how the country is perceived by its neighbours. Thus, Professor Li Jingzhi (2006) of Renmin University has called for a region-wide discussion on issues relating to World War II, led by US scholars with participation of scholars from America, China, Japan, Korea and other Asia-Pacific countries.

Indeed, the Chinese (and the Japanese) are constantly reminded of Japan's invasion of China in the 1930s by the phrase *qianshi buwang, houshi zhishi* (past experience, if not forgotten, is a guide to the future). The recent row over the Japanese government's approval of eight highschool history textbooks which had allegedly downplayed the magnitude of Japan's wartime crimes led to widespread public protests in China in April 2005 (BBC 2005).[8] In December 2006, a joint research project between Chinese and Japanese scholars was established to facilitate collaborative research on historical issues (Japanese Ministry of Foreign Affairs 2006; *People's Daily Online* 2006, 2007). Whether this state-sponsored project produces any significant outcomes remains to be seen.

To many Chinese elites and analysts, the history of Japanese invasion reminds them of the invasion and division of China by foreign powers during the 'century of shame and humiliation'. For example, their conjecture of Japanese support for the pro-independence forces in Taiwan is linked to the history of Japanese occupation of the island before 1945. There is a tendency among Chinese writers to view Japanese security strategy through a historical lens. For many years, the Chinese population, including Chinese intellectuals and analysts, have been socialized into viewing Japan's foreign policy in terms of its historical record. This kind of discourse underpins the argument that Japan should not be allowed to develop its military capabilities, play a leadership role in Asia, assume the responsibilities of a permanent member of the UNSC and become a 'normal nation'.

China's perception of Japan is also shaped by cultural factors in the sense that the Japanese language and culture are in many ways influenced by China. This explains why the Japanese tend to show more restraint in dealing with China. Despite its concern over the implications of a rising China and its close security ties with the US, the Japanese government has been loath to take a confrontational approach to China. On the contrary, it seeks to reassure China of its benign intentions while working closely with Washington to minimize the potential 'threat' of a powerful China to Japanese interests. This has been noted by the Chinese and is sometimes exploited effectively to put pressure on the Japanese government to show more 'understanding' of China's position. Nevertheless, Japan's deference towards China has not altered Chinese analysts' perception of Japanese security intentions. As Reinhard Drifte (2003: 170–72) argues, it has actually exacerbated Chinese suspicion that Japan may be trying to conceal its real motives and will confront China when the time is right. This demonstrates how difficult it is to change ideas and perceptions that have been historically and socially constructed, as the constructivists argue.

Related to constructivist thinking is the notion of strategic culture, which has been explored by Western scholars in relation to East Asian security (Johnston 1995; Booth and Trood 1999). It is interesting to note that Chinese scholars are beginning to analyze Japanese foreign and security policy within the context of Japan's cultural traditions. Lian Degui (2007a) argues that Japanese national security strategy should be understood in terms of Japan's 'consciousness of position' (*weizhi yishi*), which is deeply rooted in its culture and national characteristics.

Essentially, *weizhi yishi* derives from the Confucian concepts of *he* (harmony) and *dengji* (hierarchy). Harmony does not necessarily mean equality and justice, but a hierarchical structure is often required to achieve harmonious relations. In this context, a country may occupy a superior or inferior position in relation to other countries, depending on its strength. The constant changes in Japanese relations with other great powers, especially China and the US, says Lian, can be seen as the outcome of Japan's regular assessment of its *weizhi* (position). Historically, Japan is said to have a 'consciousness of inferior position' (*xiawei yishi*) vis-à-vis China and Western powers. But this *xiawei yishi* started to change in the 19th century when the Chinese empire began to decline. Forming alliances with powerful nations such as Britain, Germany, Italy and, more recently, the US, is also believed to be driven by Japan's *xiawei yishi*. Lian Degui (2007a: 104) contends that Japan's 'consciousness of superior position' (*shangwei yishi*) has become much stronger in recent years, particularly in the post-Cold War era. This is reflected by its desire to achieve the status of a great power (*daguo*) through various means.

It is clear that Chinese scholars and analysts perceive Japan's security strategy as a major obstacle to the formation of China's great power identity. Postmodernist scholars would argue that the discursive construction of Japan as a threatening other serves to unite the Chinese people in achieving their common goal. The general view presented in most Chinese writings is that a politically and militarily powerful Japan is detrimental to the security of Asia and of China in particular. This assessment is based largely on Japan's behaviour during World War II and its 'unrepentant attitudes' towards its history.

What is more 'threatening' to the Chinese is the supposition that Japan is working closely with America to frustrate China's great power aspirations. The extension of the scope of Japanese-US security cooperation to include 'the situation in Japan's surrounding areas', Japan's involvement in the development of the TMD system and the dispatch of Japanese SDF to Iraq, are but a few examples cited in Chinese writings to illustrate the growing 'Japan threat'. Japan's gravest 'threat' to China's core interests would be a US-Japan-Taiwan collaboration in preventing

China from using force to 'reunify' with Taiwan. This type of discourse of danger (Campbell 1998; Jackson 2005) is useful in reminding the Chinese population of the importance of building a strong and powerful nation. Both China and Japan have the ambition and the potential to achieve the status of a great power, but are uncertain of each other's future intentions. In this sense, their competition may be interpreted as a clash of identity. Seen from the postmodernist perspective, Chinese writers' construction of the self seems inseparable from the construction of the other, that is, a threatening Japan.

Conclusion

This chapter has examined Chinese security perceptions of Japan in the post-Cold War era. The Chinese believe that Japan's primary strategic aim is to become a political power. To this end, Japan is said to have actively pursued its 'UN diplomacy', participated in UN peacekeeping operations, promoted and taken part in various multilateral economic and security forums and expanded its security relations with America. Chinese security specialists are of the view that Japan has exploited the situation after 9/11 to pass a series of anti-terrorist legislation allowing the Japanese SDF to be deployed overseas. To the Chinese, the aim of Japan's 'anti-terrorism diplomacy' is to develop closer security ties with Washington and to raise its international profile.

In the Asia-Pacific, Chinese scholars have also noticed that Japan is taking various measures to increase its influence in North and South East Asia and other parts of the region. Japan's Asia-Pacific security strategy is also seen by PRC scholars as a challenge to China because the Japanese government is suspected of collaborating with America to prevent China from attaining a great power position in the world. The expansion of US-Japan security relations since the 1990s is said to have allowed Tokyo to play a more prominent role in East Asian security affairs. To the Chinese, Japan's involvement in America's development of a TMD system in Asia is indicative of Japanese security intentions.

In addition, 9/11 and the Iraq war have enabled Japan to extend its military activities beyond Japanese territories. Chinese suspicions of Japan are exacerbated by the memory of Japan's past wartime behaviour, historical animosity between the two countries and their unresolved territorial disputes in the East China Sea. Most worrying to PRC security specialists is the possibility that Japan may provide support for the US in its intervention in a cross-strait conflict in future. Many PRC elites believe that Japan does not wish to see a united and powerful China that would become a formidable rival in East Asia.

The theoretical analysis in the final section has shown that Chinese suspicion cannot be fully explained by one single theoretical perspective. Realism has, no doubt, offered some useful insights in helping us to make sense of China's apprehensions towards Japanese security intentions. Structural realism can be used to explain the rise of both Japan and China after the collapse of bipolarity and the mutual suspicion between the two Asian powers. Moreover, Chinese concern of Japan's hegemonic ambition in East Asia fits in with the analysis of offensive realism that great powers would maximize their relative power at the expense of their rivals.

However, Chinese analysis of Japan's domestic politics, its foreign economic relations and Tokyo's involvement in regional security dialogues reveals some clear signs of influence of liberal theory. In addition, China's perceptions of Japan's attitudes towards its wartime behaviour and the history textbook issue are best explained by constructivism, which takes into account cultural and historical factors. Finally, one may use the theory of postmodernism to account for China's discursive construction of Japan as a threatening 'other'. Indeed, Japan's post-Cold War security strategy is viewed by many Chinese analysts with anxiety, as it is seen to present an obstacle to China's attempts to fulfil its great power aspirations.

5 A key player in an emerging multipolar world

Russia and East Asian security

This chapter examines the perceptions of Chinese scholars and security analysts of Russia's post-Cold War global strategy and its security strategy in East Asia. The chapter begins with a detailed analysis of Chinese perceptions of Russia's global strategy since the break-up of the Soviet Union and the evolution of Russian external policy from Yeltsin to Putin. It then moves on to an examination of Chinese views on Russia's strategy towards East Asia, focusing in particular on Russian strategy towards China, Japan and the Korean Peninsula. In the final section, the discourse of PRC scholars and Russian specialists is analyzed from a number of theoretical perspectives, including realism, liberalism and constructivism.

Russia's global strategy in the post-Cold War era

The standing of Russia in the international system has been dramatically altered by the political upheaval across Eastern Europe in 1989 and the disintegration of the Union of Soviet Socialist Republics (USSR) in 1991. These changes have had a profound impact on Russia's domestic political and economic development, as well as its external power position.

The shrinking of Russia's territory and the loss of its 'buffer zone' in Eastern Europe, according to Chinese analysis, have resulted in incalculable economic loss and considerable vulnerability along its borders. As the 'loser' of the Cold War, Russia lost its superpower status in the world in the early 1990s. The dissolution of the Warsaw Pact Treaty Organization and the Council for Mutual Economic Assistance (Comecon) exacerbated the decline of Russia's influence on European affairs. Even traditional friends and allies in Asia, such as Cambodia, Laos, Mongolia and Vietnam, gradually moved away from Moscow,[1] which led to its further political isolation. Chinese analysts observe that the national pride and self-esteem of the Russians were badly damaged by all these developments (Wang Shi 1993: 16–17, 21).

However, the most pressing problems Russian leaders confronted were the serious economic crisis and the instability of the political situation within the country. A rapid improvement of the Russian economy, it was believed, would help Russia regain its great power status in the international arena. The priority of the Yeltsin government was therefore to seek assistance from the West so as to reform Russia's ailing economy. Without such support, the economic problems in Russia could deteriorate which would threaten the political position of President Boris Yeltsin. As a result, Russia sought to promote an international environment conducive to the reconstruction of its economy. The Chinese argue that this laid the foundation for Moscow's pro-Western foreign policy in early 1992. Western recognition of Russia's international status was also seen to be useful in strengthening its leading role in the newly established Confederation of Independent States (CIS) (Shun Jianshe 1993: 17).

In 1992, Russia's diplomatic activities focused almost entirely on Western advanced nations. During the first few months of the year, President Yeltsin visited all the major Western countries, signing various agreements and joint declarations with the leaders of the United States, Canada, Britain, Germany, France and Italy. In all the speeches during his visits, Yeltsin invariably emphasized the importance of Russia's relations with Europe. In addition, he openly declared that America would no longer be seen by the Russians as their 'potential enemy' and that the two nations would strive to establish a relationship 'based upon friendship and partnership' (Shun Jianshe 1993: 17; Zhang Yueming 1993: 3).

Indeed, to ensure that Russia would become a friend and partner of the West, it was willing to make concessions to Western countries, especially the United States, on a host of domestic and international issues, including the reduction of strategic weapons, withdrawal of troops from the Baltic states and sanctions against Serbia and Iraq. However, these concessions did not bring the economic benefits that the Russians had expected, say the Chinese. For example, of the amount of US$24 billion promised by the G7 countries, only half was realized. The US$6 billion fund that the IMF was supposed to provide for stabilizing the Russian currency was never released because Russia failed to control its inflation. Investments from Western companies were even more disappointing, given Russia's poor investment environment. At the same time, the West did not fully open its market to the Russians. Chinese scholars maintain that to protect its strategic and economic interests, the US tried to prevent the Russians from selling weapons to other countries, which was one of the few remaining sources of income for Russia (Ni Xiaoquan 1993: 56).

The lack of whole-hearted Western economic support for Russia, the Chinese contend, reflects their differing aims of cooperation. For Russia, Western aid was seen to be crucial to the success of the economic and political transformation of the country. This would hopefully provide the conditions for the revival of Russia in the longer term. For the West, however, economic assistance to Russia merely served the purpose of strengthening President Yeltsin's political position and preventing major upheavals in the former Soviet Union. The collapse of the Yeltsin government could mean a reversal of the process of marketization and democratization, which could result in the return of an autocratic regime in Russia. Such a regime could once again present an immense challenge to the West politically and militarily. Another undesirable outcome of the defeat of Yeltsin's 'democratic forces' could be a situation of anarchy in Russia, possibly followed by a massive influx of Russian refugees into Europe, with which Western governments would find it impossible to cope. Nevertheless, the West did not wish to see the re-emergence of Russia as a superpower in the post-Cold War world, according to Chinese analysis (Shun Jianshe 1993: 18; Ni Xiaoquan 1993: 57).

Initally, President Yeltsin did not fully appreciate the implications of adopting a Western-oriented reform agenda, say the Chinese. In order to gain Western confidence in his programme, he introduced a series of radical measures. Politically, Western pluralism and multiparty competition were promoted. Economically, he decided to transform the Russian economy through 'shock therapy', hoping to establish a free market economy based upon private ownership within a short period of time. However, the Yeltsin leadership failed to provide the expected improvements in the economic situation in Russia. For example, in the first half of 1992, the price of daily goods rose by a magnitude of 10–20, while the average wages only increased 6.8 times. One-third of a worker's salary was usually used to buy food, and the retired spent about three-quarters of their pension on food. Another result of Yeltsin's radical reform, Chinese analysts note, was the rapid growth of the unemployment rate. By the end of 1992, four million people were unemployed in Russia, and one-third of the population lived below the poverty line. Most factories were half-closed, with a 13–15 per cent fall in industrial output in the first six months of 1992 compared with the same period of time in the previous year. Disillusioned by the new regime, hundreds of thousands of well-educated Russians, including many artists, scientists and top specialists in various fields, emigrated to the West. In 1992 Russia's budget deficit reached 950 billion roubles, and its Gross National Product (GNP) fell by 20 per cent compared to that of 1991 (Zhang Yueming 1993: 1–2; Ni Xiaoquan 1993: 56; Xing Guangcheng *et al*. 1993: 22).

Apart from its poor economic performance, Chinese scholars point out that the Yeltsin government also faced enormous domestic political challenges. There were numerous ethnic conflicts, both within Russia and between Russia and other former Soviet Republics. The political turmoil following the break-up of the USSR led to the emergence of a variety of political forces and movements in Russia, and the fierce contests between them caused enormous political instability within the country. This, coupled with a rapid decline in people's living standard, weakened President Yeltsin's position in Russian politics. Indeed, Yeltsin faced strong criticism from his political opponents and the media, as well as the Russian people. He was criticized for relying too heavily upon 'fictitious Western assistance' in reforming the economy and allowing Russian foreign policy to be 'dominated by Western forces', thus leading the nation towards disaster (Zhang Yueming 1993: 1–2; Ni Xiaoquan 1993: 56; Xing Guangcheng *et al*. 1993: 24–26).

Under the circumstances, Chinese analysts observe, President Yeltsin found it difficult to continue his radical economic programme and pro-Western stance in external affairs. From the autumn of 1992, he was forced to pursue a more independent policy on various international issues. In a speech to the Foreign Ministry in October 1992, Yeltsin is reported to have admitted that a lot of mistakes had been made in Russia's foreign policy. At the same meeting he allegedly said that there was considerable discrepancy in the words and deeds of

Western countries in offering economic aid to Russia (Ni Xiaoquan 1993: 57). From the second half of 1992 onwards, Russia began to redress the imbalance in its diplomatic attention by developing closer links with Asian countries.[2]

Indeed, between 1992 and 1995, a serious reassessment of Russia's global strategy was believed to have taken place. In the immediate post-Cold War period, Russian leaders were under the impression that Russia would be welcomed by Western nations as a 'family member' as long as a Western liberal democratic system and the free market economy were introduced. With the support of the West, it was hoped that Russia would be able to achieve social stability and economic prosperity, and eventually, national revival. The West was thus seen as a 'natural ally' that would be indispensable to Russia's integration into the 'world of Western civilization'. However, according to the Chinese, Russia's efforts were not rewarded by the West. In spite of the adoption of many conciliatory measures by Moscow, it remained a prime target of Western suspicion. The West is said to have sought to guard against Russia and constrain its activities wherever possible. The attachment of harsh political and economic conditions to financial aid to Russia was often cited as an example of the Western ulterior motive of subduing the country. By 1993, Chinese scholars suggest, the Russians had concluded that a blind imitation of the Western development model and the policy of 'leaning towards the West' had led to a further deterioration of economic conditions in Russia, thus damaging Russia's national interests and contributing to the continued decline of its great power status. In a document entitled 'The Fundamental Principles of Russia's Foreign Policy Conception' published in April 1993, three principal aims of Russian foreign policy were advocated – reviving Russia, upholding its national interests, and regaining its great power status (Xia Yishan 1997a: 22).

Chinese analysts discerned a number of significant changes in Russia's strategic thinking. First, Russia's pro-Western foreign policy was said to be replaced by one that was independent and more balanced in geographical focus. Second, Russia was seeking to become an 'independent member' of the international community rather than a member of the 'Western democratic world'. Third, Russia's relationship with Western nations, including the US, was now regarded as 'a partnership based upon equality and pragmatism' instead of one of 'strategic allies'. Meanwhile, Russia had developed 'strategic partnerships' with such countries as India and China. Fourth, in handling Russia's relations with other states, emphasis would be placed upon the consideration of national interests rather than ideology. Fifth, Russia's attitude towards its previous sphere of influence in the former Soviet Union had changed from a strategy of 'comprehensive retreat' to one of active involvement. Finally, Russia no longer tacitly accepted a unipolar world dominated by the United States. On the contrary, it had enthusiastically encouraged the development of a multipolar system, in which Russia sought to become a major player (Xia Yishan 1997a: 23).

To achieve the aim of reviving the nation, the Yeltsin government was said to have made several policy adjustments. The first major step that had been taken was to promote further integration of the CIS, which would strengthen Russia's presence and influence in the areas of the former Soviet Union. In security terms, the geographical location of the CIS was thought to be extremely important to Russian defence after the 'loss' of Central Eastern Europe. Economically, Russia has close links with CIS countries, and the level of their trade and commercial interactions would have a direct impact on Russian economic development. Politically, a large number of Russians reside in the CIS, while numerous CIS ethnic groups could be found in Russian territory. The domestic and foreign policies of CIS countries could therefore affect the national interests and social stability of Russia. In terms of international relations, Russia hoped to create a CIS that would be similar to NATO militarily and to the EU economically. It could also be developed as a federal entity under Russian political leadership. Thus, the CIS was believed to be vital to Russia's endeavour to reclaim its great power position on the world stage (Xia Yishan 1997a: 23; Yu Sui 1998: 4; Song Yimin 1994: 13).

Chinese scholars note that another adjustment in Yeltsin's foreign policy was to obstruct, or even oppose, NATO's eastward expansion. At the outset, Russia's attitudes towards NATO enlargement were rather ambivalent, reflecting its desire to join the Western community. In September 1993, however, President Yeltsin wrote to the leaders of the United States, Britain, France and Germany expressing his concern over the proposed expansion of NATO. At the same time, Russia's position on the issue hardened. Yeltsin reportedly said in 1994 that NATO's eastward expansion would lead to the emergence of two camps that could bring about a 'cold peace' or even war in Europe. Moreover, Russian political and military leaders repeatedly warned that Russia might respond to NATO expansion by establishing an opposing military alliance, repealing various arms control agreements with the US and Europe, and placing strategic weapons along its Western borders. More alarming was the threat from the Russian military to conquer the Baltic states if they were to be included in NATO's expansion plans. All of these warnings were, however, ignored by the West (Xia Yishan 1997a: 23–24).

When Russia realized in late 1995 that it was impossible to halt the process of NATO's eastward expansion, it came up with three specific proposals. The first proposal was based upon the so-called 'French model', which suggested that Central East European states could be allowed to join NATO's political organizations, but not the military ones. In other words, these countries could follow the French approach by maintaining political links with NATO without being involved in its military cooperation. The second proposal was that Russia would accept NATO expansion, provided that no NATO forces were stationed in areas close to Russian borders. More importantly, it was suggested that NATO must not have any military bases or nuclear weapons in Central Eastern Europe. The third proposal was one of 'limited enlargement' in that NATO's expansion should not be extended to the Baltic states, which would be interpreted as a direct challenge to Russia's national security interests (Xia Yishan 1997a: 24). Nevertheless, all of Moscow's efforts to impede NATO expansion ended in failure.

NATO's successful expansion had, argue Chinese security experts, assisted the Russian leadership in understanding where Russia stood in the post-Cold War world, Russia had come to recognize that it was merely treated by the US as a regional power with nuclear capability rather than an equal partner in global politics. This was thought to have reinforced Russia's resolve to thwart US attempts to create a unipolar system and to advocate multipolarity, which would enable Russia to take what it perceived as its rightful place in the world (Yu Sui 1998: 1–2, 4).

Chinese analysts assert that the third adjustment in Yeltsin's security strategy, which was not unrelated to its trepidation of NATO expansion, was to maintain a strong military capability. While Russia did not have the ability to achieve a military balance with the US, retaining a relative balance in strategic nuclear forces remained a major goal in its national defence. To Russian leaders, it was said, the possession of nuclear weapons was a symbol of great power and an effective means of defending the country from external threat. It was also less expensive to maintain and develop nuclear forces than conventional ones. Russia's willingness to collaborate with the US and other Western countries on the indefinite extension of the Nuclear Non-Proliferation Treaty, and to sign the Comprehensive Test Ban Treaty was, in the view of Chinese analysts, a reflection of its intention of consolidating the nuclear power status of Russia. In the meantime, a greater effort had been made to rationalize Russian conventional forces, with the aim of increasing the morale and efficiency of the army. Another measure of preserving Russia's status of military power, say the Chinese, was to retain a robust defence industry, which would be essential for the 'regeneration of military strength' in the future. Thus, one of the main tasks of Yeltsin's foreign policy was to help defence industries explore foreign markets. Indeed, Chinese security specialists claim that following the admission to NATO of Poland, Hungary and the Czech Republic in 1999, Moscow was more determined than ever to develop all dimensions of its military capability, which was thought to be indispensable to upholding the great power standing of Russia in the globe (Xia Yishan 1997a: 25; Liu Guiling 1999: 31–32).

However, the Russians were well aware that the strength of a great power was not measured purely by its defence capability. Without a healthy economy, Russia's aspirations to regain its great power status would never be fulfilled, Chinese scholars maintain. The elevation of economic diplomacy (*jingji waijiao*) to a significant level in Moscow's foreign policy thus reflected another major adjustment in its global strategy. As mentioned previously, Russia had abandoned its hope that the West would be a primary source of succour for the revival of the Russian economy. Nevertheless, Russia had to continue to develop economic and trade relations with Western advanced nations. In particular, it sought to remove the obstacles and restrictions that had hindered the entry of Russian products into the Western market, albeit without much success. In the meantime, Russia struggled to recover traditional markets in Cuba, Iraq, Yugoslavia and CIS countries, and to explore new ones in Asia. It put more efforts into the export of military and high-tech products, seeking to alter its 'colonial position' as a provider of primary materials. For instance, Russia has sold weapons to Iran, Malaysia, South Korea and some East European states, despite American protests. But, to Russian leaders, the best way for Russia to integrate into the global economy was, say the Chinese, to become a member of the major regional and world trade organizations.

Indeed, having joined APEC, Russia was actively involved in various bilateral and multilateral economic cooperation in the Asia-Pacific region. It had also developed a closer economic relationship with the EU. In addition, Russia had begun negotiations for its admission to the WTO through which, it was hoped, the door of the world market would be opened for the Russians (Xia Yishan 1997a: 24–25; Yu Sui 1998: 5).

The final element of Yeltsin's great power strategy was a conscious attempt to pursue an independent foreign policy, and to play a more active role in international affairs, Chinese analysts suggest. Specifically, Russia no longer followed the West in its foreign policy, as it did in the early 1990s. Instead, it was said to have tenaciously resisted alleged Western and American coercion on issues such as the Bosnian crisis and US sanctions against Cuba, Iraq and Yugoslavia. The Russians were especially critical of American bombing of Iraq and NATO's alleged disregard of Russian interests in its eastward expansion. Following the NATO air campaign against Yugoslavia in March 1999, Russia's attitudes towards the US had become more confrontational. At the same time, Moscow paid particular attention to its traditional areas of influence, note the Chinese. For example, senior Russian officials visited Cuba, India, Mongolia, North Korea and Vietnam, and Russia's relations with these countries had in varying degrees been strengthened. Moscow also increased the level of its economic, political and military interactions with Central East European states. In the Middle East, Russia tried to change its image of an 'outsider' by playing a conspicuous mediating role in the peace process (Xia Yishan 1997a: 25–26; Liu Guiling 1999: 32).

However, the ultimate aim of the Yeltsin government was, Chinese scholars observe, to rejoin the 'great power club' (*daguo julebu*) at both regional and global levels. To this end, Russia played a prominent part in ending the conflict in Bosnia-Herzegovina, participated in the discussion of political issues at G7 summits, hosted a great power conference on security and nuclear weapons in Moscow, participated in ARF meetings, expressed an interest in joining the Asia-Europe Meeting (ASEM) and proposed the establishment of collective security systems in Europe and Asia, respectively, among other high-profile diplomatic activities (Xia Yishan 1997a: 26). To project its great power image, Russia also expanded economic, political and military relations with many developing countries in Africa, Asia, Latin America and the Middle East (Yu Sui 1998: 4–5).

To many Russian leaders, according to Chinese analysis, a multipolar world would be propitious to the pursuit of Russia's national interests. Yeltsin was said to be convinced that the US and its allies did not welcome the revival of a Russia that would be capable of competing with them economically, politically and militarily. The Western perception of Russia as an existing or potential enemy, it was believed, had not changed with the end of the Cold War. The West had allegedly done its utmost to debilitate Russia's military strength and curtail its political influence around the world. NATO's eastward expansion was but one example of Western attempts to ensure that Russia would never be able to reassert itself in Europe. Russian leaders were particularly suspicious of the leading role played by the US on European security matters, which was seen to be a reflection of America's 'hegemonic' ambition. In this regard, the Russians shared Beijing's fear of a unipolar world dominated by the United States. One Russian politician was reported to have said in 1996 that Russia should not be dependent upon a certain 'pole' (i.e. the US) politically because it would soon become a pole itself. From 1996, the Yeltsin government was said to begin to pursue an 'omnidirectional diplomacy' (*quanfangwei waijiao*) (Dai Dezheng and Zhang Yuhua 1998).³ The emphasis in the new policy was on the expansion of relations with the widest possible range of countries in the world so that Russia could assume its role as a 'major global actor' (*shijie zhujiao*) as soon as possible.

In the light of the changing security environment, Chinese scholars observe, the Yeltsin government formulated a set of responses that included several elements. First, it was decided that Russia should oppose unipolarity while seeking to raise its international status and develop the capability of becoming a major player in a multipolar world. The second element of the strategy was to focus on the prevention and resolution of regional conflict, with a view to enhancing the security in Russia's border areas. The third element was to seek to achieve integration among CIS states and the fourth was to promote a kind of European security arrangement that would be compatible with Russian interests. The final element of Russia's external strategy was to advance Russia's economic interests (Zhao Huirong 2004: 52).

When President Putin came into office in 2000, Chinese analysts note, he reiterated the fundamental aim of Russia's external strategy, that is, to preserve its great power status in the world. Putin was quoted to have said: 'Russia's only realistic choice is to be a major power and a strong and confident country' (Xu Zhixin 2004: 50). To the new administration, say the Chinese, the key to ensuring Russia's status was to revive the domestic economy. Putin emphasized that the gravest threat to Russia was its economic backwardness. In this sense, Moscow's foreign policy is shaped largely by its desire to retain the external power position of Russia and to revitalize the Russian economy. Indeed, multipolarity is central to Russia's foreign policy thinking. Many Russian policy elites are in agreement that their country should become an influential 'pole' in a multipolar world. Their arguments are thought to be based on the assumption that Russia possesses huge economic, technological and military potential and that it enjoys a unique strategic position in Europe and Asia. Russia's multipolar discourse, say the Chinese, is a response to the changing international environment since the collapse of bipolarity. In the view of Chinese scholars, Russia is facing a variety of external threats, including the decline of its international status, the weakening of international security mechanisms such as the UN and the Organization for Security and Co-operation in Europe (OSCE), NATO's eastward expansion and the entry of NATO forces to Central Asia. The Chinese argue that the most serious menace to the Russians is America's ambition of building a unipolar system.

According to China's Russia specialists, there has been a heated debate among Russian scholars and elites over the desirability and viability of a global strategy based on the promotion of multipolarity. Some believe that Russia's interests can be better safeguarded and that it will gain more respect from other countries if it is willing to stand up to US hegemony. In this view, it is important to identify potential partners and seek to cooperate with them in the face of American assertiveness. Others, however, believe that multipolarity should not be seen as a panacea to all the problems in the world. On the contrary, it may lead to instability and intense rivalry among the great powers. It is also argued that the promotion of multipolarity implies anti-Americanism, and that Russia may be exploited by other countries to oppose the US.

Chinese scholars have discerned some 'contradictions' in Russia's conceptualization of multipolarity. The problem with the concept, they argue, is that Russia is opposed to US hegemony and yet reluctant to confront America. Meanwhile, Russia needs the support of other countries but is unwilling to form alliances against Washington. Another 'contradiction', the Chinese argue, is the incompatibility between Russia's objective of becoming an influential 'pole' in the world and the limits to the means by which this can be achieved.

Despite the disagreements among Russian elites on multipolarity, Putin was believed to have accepted its relevance to Russia's global strategy. This was consistent with his desire of fulfilling the 'great power dream' (*qiangguomeng*) of Russia in the 21st century. Chinese analysts have noticed the continuity in Russian foreign policy from Yeltsin to Putin (Sun Changdong and Yang Xianghong 2000; Geng Lihua 2000). First, both leaders were said to have pursued a non-ideological foreign policy with an emphasis on seeking to build a strong and powerful Russia. Second, like Yeltsin, Putin practised a 'pragmatic diplomacy' (*wushi waijiao*), focusing on ensuring a peaceful security environment for domestic economic development. Third, Yeltsin's 'omnidirectional diplomacy' that emphasized broadening and deepening relations with countries in all the regions of the world was carried forward by Putin.

However, the Chinese believe that Putin became more pragmatic and flexible in dealing with Russia's relations with the West and with the US in particular. First, while the Putin government remained critical of America's 'hegemonic policy', it was thought to have focused more on cooperation with Western countries. According to Chinese observation, Putin's government downplayed Russia's multipolar aspirations in its interactions with the Western world. In particular, Putin sought to present an image of Russia as a sincere partner, by stressing the significance of international political and economic cooperation and its willingness to integrate Russia into the global economy. To Russia, Chinese scholars note, America, the EU, China and other actors were all important partners in achieving its goal of strategic balance (*zhanlue pingheng*). The Chinese point out that the thinking behind this approach was that it did not matter whether the future international system would be unipolar or multipolar. What matters was to seek market and investment opportunities for Russia in an increasingly globalized world. Indeed, some Chinese scholars believe that Putin's foreign policy reflected his appreciation of the significance and implications of globalization (Liu Jun 2004a: 55–56; see also the analysis in Ferdinand 2007a).

•   Second, the Putin government's approach to international cooperation was further developed after 9/11, according to Chinese analysts. Putin appeared to have changed his security perceptions in that terrorism, separatism, border security and military conflict were now regarded as the primary threats to Russian national security. The differences between Russia and the West, observe the Chinese, were no longer treated as 'threats'. Rather, they were 'problems' that could and should be dealt with through diplomatic channels, and Russia should be prepared to compromise on certain issues if necessary. Moscow's responses to the war in Afghanistan and the entry of US forces into Central Asia are often cited as examples to illustrate this point. Another distinctive characteristic of Putin's foreign policy was, in the view of Chinese scholars, his emphasis on great power cooperation and the development of a strategic environment based on a network of partnerships between Russia and other nations.

The Chinese note that the role of geopolitics seems to be declining in Russia's security considerations. Despite his criticisms of NATO expansion, it is argued, Putin did not adopt a confrontational stance on the issue. Instead, Moscow expressed its wishes to join NATO. The Chinese have also noticed the enhanced role of Europe in Russia's foreign policy. At the same time, Putin was said to have pursued active diplomacy in Asia. The ultimate aim of Putin's global strategy, say the Chinese, was to cultivate an international environment that would allow Russia to maintain its great power status without having to confront America and other European powers. A related aim of Russia's global strategy was to elevate its status by playing a more prominent role in international organizations and regimes. (Zhao Huirong 2004: 54, 56).

However, some Chinese scholars question whether the Putin government's external strategy actually helped enhance Russian interests. They believe that Russia's strategic adjustments after 9/11 were a big mistake, contending that Russia had made excessive compromise to the Americans without gaining much in return. Chinese analysts are especially critical of Putin's decision to allow US forces to enter CIS states. Putin was said to have justified his concession by claiming to abandon 'Cold War mentality' in Russian foreign policy. To Chinese security analysts, however, Russia was not the one who initiated confrontation with the West. It was the West, they suggest, that should abandon its 'Cold War mentality'. Russia's voluntary geopolitical retreat, the Chinese contend, has not brought any real benefit to Russia. For example, America unilaterally withdrew from the ABM Treaty in 2001 and started the development of its NMD system soon after 9/11. Despite Russia's concession, the Chinese point out, the process of NATO expansion continued, with membership extending to the Baltic states in 2004. They recognized the economic motives of Russia's collaboration with America in the 'war on terrorism' but have serious doubt over the actual benefits of the trade-off. The Chinese have concluded that Russia has been further marginalized in European security affairs and that it will face greater geopolitical pressure from the West in future.

In the view of some Chinese scholars, the Putin government was mistaken in thinking that international terrorism had altered the nature of world politics and that the interest of Russia and that of the West would converge through anti-terrorist cooperation. Putin is said to have realized this when America revealed its intention of invading Iraq towards the end of 2002. The Russian government therefore insisted on resolving the Iraq crisis through diplomatic means. This, according to the Chinese, was ignored by the Bush administration, which decided to launch a 'pre-emptive' attack on Iraq without UN approval. When the war started, Putin criticized America's military actions and the Russian Duma passed a number of resolutions condemning the 'aggressive' acts of the US. Nevertheless, the Chinese point out, Russia was in a better position to negotiate with Washington after the Iraq war due to America's increasing difficulties in post-war Iraq. The Putin government was believed to have seized this opportunity to readjust its external strategy taking a more assertive stance on what it considers as its vital interests (Wang Zhenhua 2004; Xu Zhixin 2004: 55–57).

Indeed, Chinese scholars have discerned a significant change in Russia's external strategy since October 2004, when the 'colour revolutions'[4] (*yanse geming*) took place in the Ukraine. The Russian leaders are said to have finally realized that the strategic compromise they had made earlier did not change America's intentions of weakening Russia at all. Having completed its enlargement into the Baltic states of Estonia, Latvia and Lithuania, NATO was thought to be advancing towards the CIS. Indeed, both Georgia and the Ukraine expressed their wishes to become NATO members. US and NATO leaders also made it clear that they would support the efforts of any CIS countries to join the organization. In addition, Poland and the Czech Republic have been actively involved in America's missile defence systems since 2007. According to Chinese analysis, the Putin government was convinced that US 'penetration' into the CIS through the 'colour revolutions', combined with NATO's continued eastward expansion, posed a tremendous threat to the security and survival of Russia (Feng Yujun 2007; Wu Dahui 2007).

In response to US assertiveness, Chinese analysts argue, Russia has become much more forceful in safeguarding its security interests on a variety of issues including arms control, European security and Kosovo. Meanwhile, Russia is believed to have taken various measures to strengthen its political influence and military presence in the CIS. All this indicates that Russia is determined to change its previous strategy that relied on concession and compromise to maintain an amicable relationship with the US, say the Chinese. Given Russia's concern about the security implications of America's missile defence systems, it may not be possible to sustain the existing arms control mechanisms. This, according to some Chinese scholars, could lead to a new round of arms race between the two countries, with significant repercussions on their future relations. At the moment, the Russians are said to be reluctant to confront America but they have taken a non-cooperative stance on certain issues in order to demonstrate their displeasure. They have also exploited various multilateral forums or mechanisms to constrain US unilateralism (e.g. over the Iran nuclear crisis). At the same time, Moscow is actively developing its own missile defence systems (Shi Ze 2007; Wu Dahui 2007).

To China's Russian specialists, Russia is desperate to reclaim what it considers its rightful place in the world. Chinese scholars believe that Russia is seeking to alter its asymmetrical relationship with Washington and play a more prominent role in the international system. This is thought to reflect Russia's 'great power complex' (*daguo qingjie*). The Chinese predict that Russian-American relations may enter into a period of uncertainty (Shi Ze 2007).

In the eyes of Chinese scholars, Russia is rapidly re-emerging as a key player in world affairs, although there is still a long way to go for it to regain its status of a 'strong world power' (*shijie qiangguo*). Economically, Russia is believed to have recovered from its economic crisis and is maintaining a steady economic growth. Russia's FDI is rising and it has enjoyed an average of six per cent GDP growth since 2000. Meanwhile, President Putin has paid special attention to the strengthening of Russia's military forces. Both Russian defence spending and weapon acquisitions are said to have increased considerably in the past few years. In addition, more emphasis has been placed on military training and research and weapons exports. Despite some temporary setbacks, many Chinese scholars claim, Russia's potential to re-emerge as a strong power must not be underestimated (Wang Haiyun 2007).

Russia's security strategy in East Asia

According to the Chinese, the security strategy of Russia in post-Cold War East Asia must be understood within the context of Russian leaders' assessment of and response to their changing domestic situation and external environment. Specifically, it is said to be closely linked to the major adjustments in Moscow's global strategy following the end of the Cold War.

Chinese scholars believe that by mid-1992 the Russian government realized that its 'pro-Western' policy had placed Russia in a disadvantageous position in the evolution of Asia's strategic environment. During the Cold War years, it is argued, Russia was a great power in the Asia-Pacific and played a dominant role in shaping the strategic structure (*zhanlue geju*) of the area. With the gradual decline of the significance of military factors in international relations and the changing balance of power in East Asia, Russia lost the pivotal role that it had previously enjoyed in the region. Russian leaders feared that their country would become vulnerable and isolated, should the West withdraw their support. Thus, there was a discernible shift in Moscow's diplomatic activities towards Asia during the second half of 1992, Chinese analysts note. Indeed, the visits of President Yeltsin to China and South Korea marked the beginning of Russia's new oriental policy (*xin Dongfang zhengce*), which is characterized as one of a 'double-headed eagle' (*shuangtou ying*) capable of facing the West and the East at the same time. The strategic importance of the Asia-Pacific in Russia's endeavour to regain its great power status was further confirmed in the April 1993 document 'The Fundamental Principles of Russia's Foreign Policy Conception'. Since then, the Russian government has paid a great deal of attention to the Asia-Pacific region while maintaining its relations with Western nations, observe the Chinese (Liu Guiling 1998a: 29; Shi Ze 1995: 1; Zhang Yueming 1993: 3). In the words of a senior advisor to Yeltsin: 'We must pay special attention to the strengthening of our place in the East, as such a major shift will enable Russia to recover its leading position in the world and to play the role as a bridge between East and West' (Wang Anqi 1993: 33).

To Chinese scholars, the changes in Russia's Asia-Pacific policy are based on a variety of strategic, political and economic considerations. To begin with, the post-Cold War geopolitical change has increased the salience of Asia in Russia's strategic calculation. Following the break-up of the USSR, Russia is said to have become more of an Asian country. Its direct links with European countries have been somewhat broken as a result of the emergence of independent states in the former Soviet Union. It has also lost the control of the major ports in the North and South, which are strategically important to Russia. Under the circumstances, the significance of the ports along the Pacific in the East has increased substantially. Moreover, two-thirds of Russian territory lies in Asia, and seven of ten CIS countries are located in the region. According to Chinese sources, Russian officials have repeatedly stressed that Russia is at the centre of the European and Asian continents, and that it is a global and European power as well as an Asia-Pacific power (Xu Zhixin 2005: 13). Yeltsin has allegedly claimed that Russia is an Asian country and has responsibility towards the Asia-Pacific region (Li Zhongcheng 1996: 13; Gu Guanfu 1996: 13; Shi Ze 1995: 1; Wang Anqi 1993: 38; Shun Jianshe 1993: 18).

Related to these strategic considerations is Moscow's desire to use the 'new oriental policy' to alter its subordinate position vis-à-vis the West. The Russians are deeply unhappy with their role as a 'junior partner' of Western countries, say the Chinese. Russian commentators have reportedly asserted: 'In order to gain true respect from the West Russia must be more independent [in its external affairs], including establishing a long-lasting relationship with the East' (Li Zhongcheng 1996: 13). Thus, through a closer link with Asia-Pacific countries, and with China in particular, it is argued, Moscow seeks to demonstrate its independence in foreign relations, raise the profile of Russia in world affairs and balance its position against the dominance of the United States in post-Cold War international politics (Shu Xiangdi 1994: 39; Wang Anqi 1993: 38; Wang Xiaoquan 2005: 51–52).

Another explanation for the shift in Russian strategy towards East Asia is, according to the Chinese, the need to promote a more stable and secure external environment, which is vital to the success of Russia's economic reform. In the view of Russian leaders, the possibility of having a global war within 10 to 15 years is rather remote. Citing Russian material Chinese scholars note that the main sources of threat to Russian security are regional conflicts and armed confrontations and separatist forces in Russia that might undermine the country's political cohesion and territorial integrity. Apart from growing ethnic tension within the CIS, the Russian government has to face the increasingly strong challenge of Islamic fundamentalism from Turkey, Iran and some CIS countries in Central Asia. This fear has increased following the 9/11 terrorist attacks (Xu Zhixin 2005: 15). Thus, Russia needs to have a good relationship with other regional powers to tackle these potential problems. From the Russian perspective, it is said, the most secure area at present is East Asia, especially North East Asia. It is therefore in Russia's interests to focus more on the region (Gu Guanfu 1996: 13–14; Wang Anqi 1993: 37–38).

Nevertheless, arguably the strongest motive for Russia to develop a closer link with East Asia is the consideration of potential economic benefits, the Chinese claim. Russian leaders are said to be particularly interested in exploiting the rich resources in the Russian Far East and Siberia. Through its involvement in the process of economic integration in East Asia, it is hoped that the Russian Far East could be developed more rapidly (Xu Zhixin 2005: 16). Chinese scholars note that in the eyes of Russian leaders, cooperation with the vibrant and dynamic economies of Pacific Asia will enable Russia to achieve the economic success essential to the revival of the Russian nation. Most Asia-Pacific countries possess abundant capital, technology and labour, but limited natural resources. Hence, the geographical proximity between Russia and East Asia combined with their economic complementarity are said to be conducive to mutually beneficial collaboration (Shun Jianshe 1993: 18–19; Wang Anqi 1993: 37; Shu Xiangdi 1994: 39; Shi Ze 1995: 1, 4; Li Zhongcheng 1996: 13; Gu Guanfu 1996: 13; Yu Sui 1996: 55; Zhang Shuxiao 1998: 33–35). The Asia-Pacific is also an important market in Russia's arms trade, which is particularly useful for the Russians to earn badly needed hard currency. Since the early 1990s, the Chinese observe, Russia has exported a wide variety of weapons to such Asian countries as China, India, Malaysia and South Korea. In addition, Moscow has been trying to explore new defence markets in the ASEAN region (Li Zhongcheng 1996; Hou Baoquan 1999). However, Western analysts believe that Russia's efforts to tap the ASEAN defence market have not been very successful (Huxley and Willett 1999: 36).

Moreover, the Russians are attracted to the remarkable success of East Asia's development model. According to Chinese observation, an increasing number of Russian politicians and scholars subscribe to the view that the oriental developmental model (*Dongfang fazhan moshi*) is more suited to Russia in terms of its historical traditions and cultural characteristics. While Russia is a European nation, it is said, it has more similarities with oriental countries than with its European neighbours, in that it has a long history of centralized and authoritarian rule. The Russians are impressed by the approach adopted by such countries as Japan, South Korea, Taiwan and Singapore, where outstanding economic performance is achieved by a combination of the market economy and government intervention. In particular, they are believed to be keen to learn from the Chinese experience of economic reform. Indeed, some Chinese analysts argued that the oriental path to economic growth would help President Yeltsin transform the Russian economy under his centralized political leadership (Wang Anqi 1993: 37; Shun Jianshe 1993: 19).

Chinese scholars have no doubt that Russia would like to be a full participant in Asia-Pacific affairs (Shu Xiangdi 1994: 40; Gu Guanfu 1996: 13). Economically, the Russian government has strived to utilize East Asian capital and technology to explore the potentially rich resources in the Russian Far East and Siberia, and to develop 'free economic zones' (*ziyou jingjiqu*) in these areas. Indeed, since the opening up of the Russian Far East, it has attracted a great deal of foreign investment and technology which, the Chinese believe, has contributed to the modernization of the region (Yin Jianping 1999: 54). At the same time, the level of trade and economic interactions between Russia and East Asian countries has increased considerably. More importantly, the Russians have been closely involved in bilateral and multilateral economic cooperation in the Asia-Pacific, the Chinese observe (Wang Xiaoquan 2005: 52). For example, Russia is now a member of various regional economic organizations including APEC, and has hosted a number of high-profile conferences on the promotion of trade, investment and economic cooperation in North East Asia. And its attitudes towards multinational development projects in the region, such as the UN-sponsored Tumen River project, are also positive (Shu Xiangdi 1994: 41–42; Shi Ze 1995: 3–4; Li Zhongcheng 1996: 17, 38; Liu Guiling 1998a: 33; Yu Guozheng 1998: 22). Increasingly, Russia is said to be paying more attention to its energy cooperation with its North East Asian neighbours, especially China (Tian Chunsheng 2005).

In terms of security cooperation, Russia has been consistently engaged in bilateral and multilateral security dialogue with East Asian countries through numerous official and unofficial channels, Chinese analysts point out. The Russian government has withdrawn its troops from Mongolia, reduced the number of soldiers stationed in the 'Northern Territories', scaled down its military forces in the Far East and around the Pacific, signed agreements on arms control and confidence building measures with its Central Asian neighbours, and advocated peaceful resolution of regional conflict and the prevention of the proliferation of WMD in Asia. Russia's involvement in the six-party talks aiming to resolve the recent North Korean nuclear crisis is a good example showing Moscow's intention of playing an active part in resolving regional security issues. As a result of these efforts, the Chinese believe, most Asia-Pacific nations no longer perceive Russia as a military threat to their national security. Instead, they have taken Russian ideas of promoting regional peace and security more seriously (Shi Ze 1995: 2, 3; Li Zhongcheng 1996: 17; Liu Guiling 1998a: 33; Xu Zhixin 2005: 15; Yu Sui 1996: 55–56).

In addition, Chinese security specialists have noticed Russia's various suggestions on the establishment of inclusive collective security mechanisms in the Asia-Pacific over the recent years, including a 'Centre for Regional Conflict Management', a 'Centre of Regional Strategy', and a 'North East Asian Multilateral Consultative Mechanism' covering the entire Asia-Pacific region and its sub-regions. Being a participant of the ASEAN Regional Forum, the Chinese also note, Russia has played an active part in the discussion of major political and security issues in the Asia-Pacific that could affect the future of the region (Shu Xiangdi 1994: 41; Shi Ze 1995: 3; Liu Guiling 1998a: 33).

However, Russia has not rejected the utility of military force as a means of preserving regional peace and security, say the Chinese. Indeed, it has maintained a substantial military presence in the area in order to ensure strategic stability and regional balance of power. While seeking to reduce the arms race and the possibility of military confrontation, it is pointed out that Moscow still upholds the strategy of nuclear deterrence, insisting that it needs to have considerable military power to cope with potential threat to Russian security and to prevent any particular country from pursuing 'special interests' in the region (Shi Ze 1995: 2; Li Zhongcheng 1996: 17).

Despite its growing interest in multilateralism, the consideration of bilateral relations remains central to Russia's East Asian strategy, according to the analysis of Chinese specialists. Indeed, since 1992, a huge effort is said to have been made to develop and improve the bilateral relations between Moscow and virtually all other countries in East Asia (Shi Ze 1995: 2, 3). By improving its relations with East Asian states, regardless of their social and political systems and ideological orientations, Chinese scholars argue, Russia has made a positive contribution to the reconceptualization of security in the Asia-Pacific, helping to enhance regional peace and stability (Liu Guiling 1998a: 33; Song Kui 2007).

Russia and China

The mutual suspicion and antagonism between China and the Soviet Union during the Cold War years are well documented by both Western and Chinese scholars (Zagoria 1962; Griffith 1964; Gittings 1968; Hinton 1976; Ellison 1982; Su Chi 1992; Ni Xiaoquan and Luobote Luosi 1993). In the early 1980s, both countries began to improve their relations, culminating in the Deng–Gorbachev summit in May 1989 (Segal 1985; Nelson 1989; Dittmer 1992; Ross 1993). Significantly, Beijing's newly 'normalized' relationship with Moscow was not altered by the collapse of the Soviet communist regime and the break-up of the USSR. On the contrary, Sino-Russian relations are said to be at their best today since the CCP came to power in 1949 (Xu Kui 1996: 4; Yu Sui 2007: 10, 69).

According to Chinese analysts, the normalization of Sino-Soviet relations provided a solid foundation for the development of the 'strategic partnership' between the two nations in the post-Soviet era. During the period of political upheaval in the former Soviet Union in the late 1980s and early 1990s, they argue, the leaders of both countries handled their relations on the basis of their national interests, rather than ideological considerations. Indeed, in 1990 and 1991, former Chinese leaders including Jiang Zemin and Li Peng visited Moscow in order to strengthen Sino-Soviet relations. Since the demise of the Soviet Union, Russian and Chinese leaders and senior government officials have met frequently, and numerous joint declarations and documents have been signed by the two countries. In the words of China's Russian specialists, the Sino-Russian relationship has developed from one of friendship to a 'constructive partnership' (*jianshexing huoban guanxi*), and finally to a 'strategic coordinative partnership' (*zhanlue xiezuo huoban guanxi*) (Shu Xiangdi and Wang Lijiu 1995: 10; Liu Qingcai 1995: 24–25; Shi Ze 1996: 1–4; Li Jingjie 1997: 3–5; Liu Dexi 1997: 33–37, 50).

Not surprisingly, Russia's post-Cold War strategy towards China has attracted substantial interest from Chinese scholars and policy elites. In their analysis of the rationale behind Russian China policy, they have considered both strategic and economic factors.

First, Chinese analysts argue that the growing significance of China on Moscow's foreign policy agenda is closely linked to the adjustments in Russian strategy in the Asia-Pacific, and in the world more generally. In the early 1990s, Russia was said to realize that Western powers would not wish to see a revival of the Russian nation. Its decision to cultivate a closer relationship with China was therefore seen as a result of disillusionment with Western financial assistance and political recognition. Chinese security specialists also claim that the West has sought to weaken Russia while expanding its geostrategic influence, with the aim of bringing the country into the orbit of a Western-dominated international system. Chinese support was thus seen to be useful for Russia to resist Western pressure (Shu Xiangdi and Wang Lijiu 1995: 12; Xu Kaixin 1996: 59; Liu Guiling 1998b: 20). However, as Western technology and investment are central to Russia's economic reform, the Russian government is particularly keen to join the Western world. Indeed, President Putin has defined Russia as a European country which, together with its liberal-oriented political system, means that Moscow is willing to be integrated into the Western society. This worries the Chinese because the value of China's cooperation may decline.

Despite the rhetoric of Sino-Russian friendship in most Chinese publications, China's policy analysts admit that it is the common strategic need of the two countries that has driven them in the direction of collaboration. Like China, Russia is deeply suspicious of US global aspirations. To the Russians, Washington is exploiting its superior economic strength and military power to dominate world affairs. The ultimate aim of the United States, the Chinese assert, is to create a world of unipolarity in which no other major powers would be able to challenge its 'hegemonic position' (*baquan diwei*). Thus, the US is believed to endeavour to impede the rise of China and to prevent Russia from re-emerging as a great power in the international system. Indeed, Russia has clashed with the US on a range of global and regional issues since the end of their 'honeymoon period' (*miyue shiqi*) in the early 1990s. To safeguard its 'security space' (*anquan kongjian*) in the post-Cold War world, Chinese scholars contend that Russia would need to join China in promoting a multipolar system. Given that China is a permanent member of the UN Security Council and a nuclear power whose 'comprehensive national strength' is growing steadily, it is noted that a close relationship with Beijing would assist Russia in balancing against US dominance (Shu Xiangdi and Wang Lijiu 1995: 13; Liu Qingcai 1995: 29; Xu Kaixin 1996: 59, 60; Li Jingjie 1997: 9; Liu Guiling 1998b: 19–20). In July 2001, the two countries signed a high-profile Treaty of Friendship which was clearly directed at the US.

Nonetheless, Chinese security specialists have noticed that the Putin government has been less enthusiastic about advocating multipolarity for fear of offending the Americans. Russia wants to be seen as a cooperative partner of the West, rather than a challenger of the existing international order. The Chinese argue that Russia continues to maintain a good relationship with Beijing so that it can use the 'China card' to strengthen its position vis-à-vis the US. Indeed, the American factor has always been a major consideration in Sino-Russian relations (Li Jingjie 2000). This explains why Chinese elites and analysts are disturbed by Russia's active support for the war in Afghanistan (Zhu Feng 2001: 24–25). They fear that an improved relationship between Moscow and Washington would jeopardize the Sino-Russian 'strategic partnership' (Yang Yunzhong 2002a: 13). Undoubtedly, the nuclear arms treaty signed by Putin and Bush in Moscow in May 2002 was viewed by the Chinese with misgivings (BBC 2002b). Indeed, Sergei Ivanov, the former Russian Defence Minister, made a special visit to Beijing at the end of May 2002 to reassure Chinese leaders that Russia's improved relations with the US and its closer links with NATO would not be detrimental to Sino-Russian relations (BBC 2002c). This did not alleviate Chinese uneasiness of a Russia that was seen to be moving closer to the West.

Chinese analysts have discerned other broader geopolitical considerations in Russian strategy towards China. Since the disintegration of the USSR, it is pointed out, Russia has had to face an adverse geostrategic environment. Not only have Russia's previous allies in Eastern Europe moved away from Moscow, but other former Soviet republics have become independent. Russia's relations with these newly independent states are rather complex, especially over territorial and nationality issues. At the same time, Russia is confronted with the challenge of NATO's eastward expansion. In addition, the growing strength of Islamic fundamentalism and military conflict in Central Asia are increasingly perceived by the Russians as potential threats to its stability and security. What is more worrying is that the US and other Western countries are said to have penetrated into the area through the provision of economic assistance to Central Asian states. This would, according to Chinese scholars, enable them to benefit from potential oil supply in Central Asia and to weaken Russian influence in the region. Under the circumstances, it is in Moscow's interests to maintain a stable and harmonious relationship with China which is, after all, Russia's biggest neighbour. Indeed, the two nations share a common border of over 4,000 kilometres. Strategic collaboration with China is therefore thought to have helped improve Russia's security environment (Shu Xiangdi and Wang Lijiu 1995: 12; Xu Kaixin 1996: 59–60; Li Jingjie 1997: 5–6, 8–9, 10; Liu Guiling 1998b: 18–19).

But the changing strategic landscape since 9/11 has had a considerable impact on Sino-Russian partnership. Chinese security analysts are alarmed by Putin's decision to allow Central Asian countries to open their military bases and air space to the US in its war in Afghanistan. The Chinese are also aware of Russia's increasing tolerance of NATO's eastward expansion which, in their view, has exceeded what was previously accepted by the Russians as their bottom line. To Chinese analysts, Russia's 'strategic contraction' (*zhanlue shousuo*) indicates its intention of trying to create a more conducive environment for economic and trade cooperation with the West. From China's perspective, however, this has enabled America to build its 'new empire' with significant implications for the world order (Zhao Mingwen 2004). It may also affect the strategic cooperation between Beijing and Moscow. In particular, they are worried that the role of the SCO in regional cooperation may be reduced, and even marginalized, as a result of growing US influence in Central Asia. However, China's concern may have been eased slightly by the agreement of Russia and the four Central Asian states in June 2002 to adopt a charter making explicit the aim to 'fight terrorism, prevent conflicts and promote security in Central Asia' and to create a permanent secretariat in Beijing (Gorshkov 2002).

In addition to strategic factors, Chinese analysts note that Russia's China policy is shaped by economic considerations (Shu Xiangdi and Wang Lijiu 1995: 12–13; Liu Qingcai 1995: 27–28; Zhang Shuxiao and Li Chunyan 1996: 29–32;

Xu Kaixin 1996: 60; Xu Kui 1996: 9; Li Jingjie 1997: 9, 2000: 5–6; Liu Guiling 1998b: 19). To the Russian leaders, a successful economy is a prerequisite for the revival of Russia. As mentioned in the previous section, Russia is attracted by the economic dynamism of the Asia-Pacific. Given China's growing economic importance in the region, it is believed that it makes sense for Russia to develop a good relationship with Beijing. Indeed, Russia has sought and received Chinese support for its successful application for APEC membership. Russia also hopes that Chinese participation and assistance will aid the development of the Russian Far East and Siberia. As well as showing considerable interest in Chinese experience of economic reform, the Russians are keen to trade with China because of their economic complementarity, say the Chinese. For example, China offers a huge market for Russia's industrial products which are not normally welcomed by the Western market. Meanwhile, China's textile, light industrial and consumer goods can satisfy the need of the Russian market. Geographical proximity between the two countries also makes it relatively easy for Russia to develop closer trade and economic links with China. In recent years, Russia's cooperation with China is said to have expanded into the area of scientific and technical collaboration. Energy cooperation is another area that has attracted growing attention from Russian and Chinese leaders (Feng Yujun 2004; Ren Jingjing 2005).

Despite Russia's desire to establish closer economic ties with the PRC, Sino-Russian economic cooperation remains rather limited in terms of mutual investment, insurance and finance. Although their trade activity has increased, China's overall trade with Russia represents a relatively small proportion of its foreign trade (see Fig. 6.2). There have also been difficulties in developing the Sino-Russian oil pipeline project (Li Quanyi 2004: 76). Still, Russia was China's seventh largest trade partner in 2007 (US-China Business Council 2008). The Chinese understand that the future of Russia's economic development depends more on Western technology and investment than Chinese trade.

The problems with Sino-Russian economic relations may also be seen as a reflection of Russia's apprehensions of an ascendant China. Chinese scholars are conscious of the increasing suspicion of China in Russia, which has been labeled as the Russian version of the 'China threat theory'. Some Russian commentators are worried that growing Chinese activities in Central Asia will undermine Russia's traditional influence in the area, and that Russian security interests may be jeopardized in the longer term. The 'China collapse theory' is also said to be popular among some Russian writers. They have expressed the fear that the numerous domestic problems in the PRC will sooner or later result in economic stagnation and possibly the collapse of the Chinese economy. Some Russian commentators even predict that a serious political crisis may emerge in China as a result of the contradictions between economic pluralism and the CCP's monopoly of power. Another prediction is a conflict across the Taiwan Strait that may lead to a Sino-US military confrontation. An unstable political situation and a disintegrating China, it is argued, could cause massive Chinese migration into neighboring countries, thus affecting the stability of Russia (Hu Jian 2006). Not surprisingly, Chinese analysts have criticized the Russian media for producing 'incorrect and irresponsible' reports that exaggerate the 'dark side' of Chinese society and the 'misbehaviour' of some Chinese people in Russia (Li Chuanxun 2004).

Some Russian scholars, intellectuals and politicians are said to have expressed their concern of the 'negative impact' of rising Chinese power on Russia. According to Chinese analysts, there are different types of theories of 'Chinese expansionism', including China's 'demographic expansion' in the Russian Far East, the offensive nature of the Chinese economic strategy and Beijing's military threat to Russia (Yu Guozheng 2002: 60–62; Li Chuanxun 2004: 7–9). What concerns the Chinese most is that some Russian military officials are apprehensive of Beijing's defence modernization and growing military strength and regard China as a potential threat to Russia's future security (Sun Jian 2001: 32–33). This might explain Russia's reluctance to offer Beijing cutting-edge weapons systems (Bilveer 1998: 501), although Moscow is China's biggest arms supplier. Indeed, Chinese security specialists are fully aware that the weapons systems Russia has exported to India are more advanced, sophisticated and wide-ranging than those supplied to China. They have noted Russia's intention of maintaining military superiority over the PRC due to its scepticism and anxiety about China's 'peaceful rise' (Hu Jian 2006).

Nevertheless, Chinese analysts believe that it is in Russia's interest to maintain a robust Sino-Russian 'strategic partnership'. Despite the talk of a 'China threat' in Russia, they point out that the two countries signed a friendship treaty in 2001, established the SCO in the same year and settled their border disputes in 2004. More significantly, China and Russia staged their first joint military drill in October 2005, involving about 10,000 soldiers from the air, naval and ground forces on both sides. Known as 'Peace Mission 2005', the exercise was organized under the auspices of the SCO to combat the 'three forces' of terrorism, extremism and separatism. To promote mutual understanding among their people and further develop bilateral cultural, political, economic and trade cooperation, the two countries organized the 'year of Russia in China' in 2006 and the 'year of China in Russia' in 2007 (Li Jingjie 2006; Yu Sui 2007).

Sino-Russian defence cooperation was further strengthened through another SCO-sponsored military exercise, 'Peace Mission 2007'. Unlike previous joint military exercises, this drill, held in August 2007, involved the armed forces of all the SCO member states. It was truly unprecedented in terms of the scale, length and coordination of the operations. Some of the best units of each country were dispatched and the PLA's military capability was vividly displayed. The exercise was covered widely by the Chinese and Russian media. While the leaders of both countries stressed that the high-profile drill was not targeting any third party, Washington could hardly miss its significance. Indeed, the US was not among the 80 countries that were invited to observe the rehearsals (Yu 2007). On the whole, Chinese scholars and analysts are optimistic about the prospects for deeper and more extensive cooperation between China and Russia (Feng Yujun 2007; Li Jingjie 2006; Yu Sui 2007). But they warn that Sino-Russian collaboration should not be driven by Moscow's changing strategic agenda. As the Russians will be likely to face greater strategic pressure from the US, it is argued, they may seek further support from China. However, Chinese analysts point out that it is not in China's interest to turn the Sino-Russian strategic partnership into an anti-American force, and that China must manage its great power relations cautiously (Wu Dahui 2007: 54–55).

Russia and Japan

Japan's importance in Russia's external strategy has increased considerably in recent years, despite the strain in their relations during the Soviet era (Li Yonghui and Ping Zhanguo 2000). According to Chinese analysis, Russia is keen to develop economic ties with Japan mainly because of its economic power. As an economic superpower, Japan is thought to be able to provide Russia with advanced technology and rich investment. Without the collaboration of Japan, it is argued, Russia would find it more difficult to explore its oil in Siberia, construct its oil pipeline towards the Pacific and, most importantly, develop the economy in the Russian Far East. Another important reason for Moscow to establish good neighbourly relations with Japan is to raise the status of Russia in the international community. Among all the great power relations, say the Chinese, the Russo-Japanese relationship is the least developed, both economically and politically. Moreover, a good rapport with Japan would be useful to Russia in constraining a rapidly growing China. Finally, a closer link with Japan would be helpful in reaching a consensus on the North Korean nuclear crisis, thus strengthening Russian influence on this matter (Li Yonghui 2004, 2005; Liu Guiling 2005).

In the view of China's Russian specialists, Putin has made a special effort to enhance confidence between Russia and Japan. First, the Russian government expressed a willingness to make some compromise on their territorial disputes over the Northern Territories. This message was conveyed through the media by the Russian Foreign Minister Sergey Lavrov in November 2004. Putin is quoted to have said that Russia would do its best to resolve the territorial disputes with Japan (Liu Guiling 2005: 41–42; Li Yonghui 2005: 70). Second, in January 2003, Moscow signed a document with Tokyo (Russia-Japan Action Plan), which included detailed and concrete plans on how to improve their bilateral relations. The document was very wide-ranging and went beyond pure economic cooperation to encompass aspects such as political dialogue, international cooperation, defence and security relations and cultural and educational collaboration (Li Yonghui 2004: 62).

Third, Chinese analysts observe that of particular significance to Russo-Japanese relations is the establishment of various confidence-building measures (CBM) and their security cooperation. In September 2000, soon after he came into office, Putin paid a visit to Japan. In his meeting with former Japanese Prime Minister Obuchi, Putin was said to have emphasized the geopolitical significance of high-level contacts between the two countries (Liu Guiling 2005: 40–41). Indeed, between 2000 and 2003, Russian and Japanese leaders visited each other five times. In addition, there has been regular interaction between government officials and parliamentarians of the two countries. The Chinese have noticed the expansion of Russo-Japanese military cooperation, including regular meetings of their defence ministers and military leaders, as well as contacts of the military colleges of the two countries (Li Yonghui 2004: 60–61).

Fourth, Chinese scholars have discerned huge progress in Russo-Japanese economic and trade relations. Their trade volume reached a historic record of US$85 billion in 2004. What bothers the Chinese is Japan's enthusiastic involvement in the construction of oil pipelines in Siberia and their cooperation in the use of nuclear power. Finally, Putin is believed to have paid particular attention to non-official diplomacy, aiming to build confidence at the societal level. There have indeed been a wide variety of interactions between academics, professionals, business leaders and non-governmental organizations of the two nations since 2001 (Li Yonghui 2005: 71–72).

While Chinese analysts appreciate the positive effects of improved Russo-Japanese relations on Asia-Pacific security, they are wary of the implications for China of these closer links. After all, one of the factors driving their collaboration is thought to be the rise of China. Given China's suspicion of Japan's strategic intentions and their economic competition in the region, Chinese security specialists have viewed the changing Russo-Japanese relationship with some misgivings (Liu Guiling 2005: 43–44).

Russia and the Korean Peninsula

Prior to the end of the Cold War, North Korea was an ally of Russia. But their alliance ended with the collapse of the bipolar system. Chinese analysts note that Russia placed more emphasis on its relations with the West in the early 1990s. The situation began to change in the mid-1990s, when Russian leaders were said to have decided to strengthen Russia's relations with its East Asian neighbours. Through a series of treaties, the relations between Moscow and Pyongyang improved substantially which culminated in President Putin's visit to North Korea in July 2000. In return, the North Korean leader, Kim Jong-il, paid two visits to Moscow in 2001 and 2002, respectively. During his visit to Russia in August 2002, Kim Jong-il was believed to have reached a consensus with Putin on a range of security issues, including the situation on the Korean Peninsula. They also explored opportunities for economic cooperation between the two nations. This, say the Chinese, provided the foundation on which Russia was able to play a useful role in tackling the recent North Korean nuclear crisis (Wang Bingyin 2003a: 11–12).

According to Chinese analysis, Russia has specific interests in the Korean Peninsula. First and foremost is the economic consideration in Russia's policy towards the area. As one of the 'four little tigers' in East Asia, South Korea is believed to have a lot to offer in Russia's struggle to revive its economy. In particular, Russia can benefit considerably from South Korea's capital, information technology and experience in production and management skills. Putin is reported to have said in Seoul that it is important to improve Russia's investment environment in order to attract South Korean investment. PRC scholars have noticed an improved relationship between Russia and South Korea, which has developed rapidly since the early 1990s. Quoting Russian statistics the Chinese pointed to the increase in their trade volume from US$6 billion in 1990 to US$16.89 billion in 2001. But it is not just South Korea that is considered economically useful to Russia. North Korea also has some economic value to Moscow. Apart from its cheap labour, Pyongyang is potentially an attractive market for Russian weapons export. With the decline of the military-industrial complex in Russia, observe the Chinese, Moscow is desperately trying to increase its revenue through export of military equipment and military technology (Wang Bingyin and Zhou Yanli 2001: 26; Wang Bingyin 2003a: 12).

Chinese scholars point out that there is a great potential for energy cooperation among Russia, North Korea and South Korea. Russia is known to be rich in oil reserves, whilst North and South Korea are both reliant on oil imports for their economies. Russia's proposal of repairing and constructing the Siberian network connecting the two Koreas is particularly welcomed by both countries. The Russian government is also said to have proposed the construction of an oil pipeline running from Russia through Mongolia and China to the two Koreas. If these plans were to be successfully implemented, say the Chinese, Russia would certainly be able to increase its energy exports, and North Korea, South Korea, China and Japan would all receive stable, secure and cheap energy supplies (Wang Bingyin and Zhou Yanli 2001: 25–26).

Chinese scholars argue that another consideration behind Russia's interest in Korean affairs is related to geopolitical factors. Because of the geographical proximity between Russia and North Korea, the stability on the Korean Peninsula is of utmost importance to the Russians. This point is said to have been stressed by President Putin on several occasions. Such a concern explains the reason for Moscow's strong advocacy for its inclusion in the four-party talks. The 2002 North Korean nuclear crisis was said to have provided a golden opportunity for Russia to achieve its aim. Indeed, since 2003, both Russia and Japan have been involved in a series of six-party talks with America, China, South Korea and North Korea. Chinese security analysts believe that Russia has exploited its position as a mediator between North Korea and the West to gain more respect from other G8 members. Through its direct participation in the process of reducing tension on the Korean Peninsula, say the Chinese, Russia hopes to be able to exert a greater influence on North East Asian security matters and, more importantly, to maintain its great power status in the world (Wang Bingyin 2003b: 71–72; Wang Bingyin 2003a: 13–15; Pan Guanghui 2003: 65).

Theoretical analysis

The data presented in this chapter clearly demonstrates that Chinese elites and security analysts perceive Russia to be a key player in what they consider an emerging multipolar international system. Although they acknowledge that the Russian economy is relatively weak, the potential of Russia as a major power is not in doubt. Russia is not perceived by the Chinese as an obstacle to China's pursuit of a great power status. This is not to say that they do not have disagreements over specific security issues, nor does it suggest that mutual suspicion between the two countries is entirely absent. Nevertheless, Russia is considered by PRC analysts as China's 'strategic partner' rather than strategic rival.

Chinese analysis of Russia's position in the post-Cold War world is based primarily on the realist theory of international relations. Specifically, the role of Russia as an international actor is perceived within the conceptual framework of polarity. In the early 1990s, many Chinese scholars believed that the world was in a transitional period from a bipolar system to one of multipolarity. But they were not certain as to how long this transitional period would last. Following the break-up of the USSR, the United States emerged as the sole superpower in the world. This led to the reference to 'a unipolar moment' by some US writers (Krauthammer 1990/91). Not surprisingly, the Chinese were uncomfortable with this geopolitical situation, with the prospects of an international system dominated by the US. This is why they were reluctant to accept the advent of unipolarity. In a sense, their conceptualization of multipolarity is more a reflection of preference than a recognition of the reality. It is within this context that they view the role of Russia in the post-Cold War world.

In a way, their perception of the international structure is not dissimilar to that of some Russian scholars and intellectuals. The Chinese are correct in identifying the significance of multipolarity in shaping Russian foreign policy in the Yeltsin era. They have discerned considerable suspicion among the Russian politicians and analysts of America's pre-eminence in the world. Chinese analysts tend to see relations among great powers through a realist lens, in that international relations is shaped largely by the balance of power among a number of major players. This kind of perception is informed by the analysis of structural realism, which posits that unipolarity cannot be sustained forever. According to structural realists such as Kenneth Waltz (1979) and Christopher Layne (1993, 2006a), countries with great power potential will pursue great power status and they will rise to challenge the predominance of the dominant power in the international system. This is a structural-driven phenomenon that cannot be prevented. Thus, Russia, along with other great powers, will challenge America's current position sooner or later. This is because, as the Chinese would argue, Russia possesses many key features that would enable it to become a great power again, if it is not already regarded as one. It is the only country located in both Asia and Europe and still has enormous military strength, including nuclear capabilities. Structural realists would also point to the size, population and resources of Russia in supporting their argument that Russia should be taken seriously as a great power.

The Chinese view of Russia's security strategy can be best explained by defensive realism, which argues that a great power is more interested in ensuring its security than expansion, and that the primary concern of states is survival (Jervis 1978; Walt 1987; Van Evera 1999). The Chinese would contend that Russia has no expansionist intent, at least not for the time being. On the contrary, Russia has accepted the 'loss' of a vast amount of territories that previously 'belonged to' it. Russia is also said to have opted for a 'strategic contraction', allowing America to have a military presence in its backyard in Central Asian countries and NATO to extend its membership to include the Baltic states. In this regard, Russia's global strategy cannot be explicated by offensive realism, which contends that all great powers are non-status quo powers seeking to maximize their relative power at the expense of rivals (Mearsheimer 2001).

Chinese discourse of Russia's global security strategy can also be explained by Waltz's (1979) structural realism, in that Russia seeks to maintain a careful balance of power with the US on the one hand and China on the other. This is of course not something new in Russian foreign policy, as it reminds us of the strategic triangle among the Soviet Union, China and America during the Cold War years. However, Chinese security analysts are aware that Russia is loath to form a military alliance with China, despite its apprehensions of unipolarity. They seem to understand Moscow's preference for a 'soft balancing' strategy, given its inability to confront America's preponderance (Pape 2005) and its reluctance to be constrained by a rigid alliance relationship with China. David Kerr (2005) has argued persuasively that despite the collaboration between Beijing and Moscow in preventing the US from dealing with the North Korean nuclear crisis unilaterally, the Sino-Russian partnership should not be interpreted as a counter-hegemonic alliance.

Chinese analysts have recognized the importance of economic factors in Russia's national goal and external strategy. They are right in pointing out that the primary concern of Russian leaders is to revive their country's economy, especially in the Putin era. In their writings, they have discussed the economic motives behind the Russian government's decisions to collaborate with America on the 'war on terrorism', its muted response to US withdrawal from the ABM Treaty, its tacit agreement on US presence in Central Asia and NATO's eastward expansion towards its borders. This discourse seems to be consistent with the neorealist theory of international political economy in the sense that economic activity is directly related to the pursuit of state interest (Gilpin 1987).

On the other hand, Chinese discourse of Russia's external strategy can be elucidated by liberal theory, which tends to emphasize the importance of economic cooperation in international relations. From this perspective, one can argue that Russian leaders have become more interested in improving the economic performance of their nation than following the traditional path of geopolitical rivalry with other great powers. Russia's interest in developing economic cooperation is captured by Chinese scholars in their consideration of Moscow's relations with Japan, North Korea, South Korea and other Asian countries. Liberal institutionalism (Keohane 1984) is also prominent in Chinese scholars' discussion on Russia's efforts in pursuing economic and trade cooperation with its neighbours through such economic institutions as APEC and its desire to join the WTO.

Indeed, PRC scholars are well aware of Russia's activities in promoting regional integration in the Asia-Pacific. The Chinese have grasped Russia's intention of utilizing economic interactions as a means of reducing regional tension in North East Asia. They have cited Russia's proposal of energy cooperation with China, Japan and other East Asian countries to support their argument. Other examples that can be used to illustrate Chinese discussion of the liberal-institutional tendency in Russian external strategy include Moscow's increasing interests in involving itself in multilateral security mechanisms in Asia, such as the ARF and the six-party talks. On the other hand, these initiatives could be explained by defensive realism in that cooperation is possible under anarchy (Jervis 1978).

Another explanation for Russian foreign policy may be found in the theory of democratic peace (Doyle 1983; Russett 1993). Russia has adopted a liberal democratic political system, however imperfect, which encourages the free market and allows multi-party competition, freedom of the press and so on. If one accepts the basic tenets of the democratic peace theory, it is not difficult to understand why Russia has become more interested in international cooperation than confrontation. In this sense, the liberal argument that democracies do not fight with democracies has been validated, but this is not a view widely shared by Chinese analysts.

No doubt, realism and liberalism offer some useful insights into Chinese discourse of Russia's global security strategy. However, they seem to have ignored the link between identity and interests. To constructivists, a sound understanding of an actor's identity is important in interpreting its foreign policy (Kubalkova 2001). They argue that social reality is a product of 'social construction' and can change according to changing circumstances (Alagappa 1998, p. 665). From a constructivist perspective, Russia's security thinking and strategy reflect its changing identity from a former superpower to a 'normal' great power. As such, Russian leaders have had to redefine their interests. As they no longer perceive their country as a superpower in the world, there is no reason why Russia should engage in a global rivalry with the United States on issues that do not threaten Russian security and survival. In this respect, Putin's comments that it does not matter whether the future international system will be unipolar or multipolar, as long as Russia is able to develop itself into a strong and prosperous country, are particularly instructive. This can be contrasted with China's self-identity as an emerging power that should be able to compete with other great powers economically, politically and militarily.

It is also important to consider the ideational aspects of Russia's foreign policy behaviour. In the constructivist view, international relations should not be explained purely in terms of balance of power among state actors in an anarchic system. Instead, it is shaped by a cognitive process of socialization through which states acquire and define their identities and interests (Wendt 1992, 1999). As such, state behaviour can be constrained, and indeed influenced, by intersubjectively shared ideas and values, as well as institutions and norms (Onuf 1989). 'The practice of diplomacy', as Theo Farrell (2002: 49) notes, 'enacts and thereby reproduces accepted international beliefs about state capacity'.

This is especially relevant to Chinese perception of Moscow's tolerance of NATO's continued expansion and American activities in Central Asia. PRC analysts appear to have problems with understanding why Russia has voluntarily relinquished control over its previous spheres of influence. What they fail to see is that Russia's idea of a great power has changed radically since the mid-1980s. In the pre-Gorbachev era, Russia's conception of a great power was one that should possess unrivalled military capabilities and be able to extend its power and influence around the globe. This of course led to the decline of the Soviet Union's domestic economy and eventually the collapse of its political system and the Soviet empire.

Built on the ideas of Mikhail Gorbachev, the present Russian leaders are seeking to redefine the role of Russia as a great power. Apparently, there is a significant change in their national role conceptions (Holsti 1970; Walker 1987). They have reached the conclusion that a great power should have a great economy, rather than a vast quantity of weapons and strategic ambitions that cannot be fulfilled or sustained. Russian leaders and policy elites have clearly learnt from their predecessors' mistake of 'imperial overstretch' (Kennedy 1988). This is a good example illustrating the constructivist argument that 'change in identity can precipitate substantial change in interests that shape national security policy' (Jepperson, Wendt and Katzenstein 1996: 61). Chinese scholars are fully aware of the (re)construction of Russian identity since the end of the Cold War. Nonetheless, as a rising power with global aspirations, China seems to have found it difficult to fully appreciate Russia's changing conception of its great power status. This is why Chinese scholars tend to believe that Russia cannot tolerate its 'strategic retreat' forever and that it will seek to regain the identity of a world power sooner or later.

Conclusion

In this chapter, Chinese security perceptions of Russia since the collapse of the communist regime in the former Soviet Union have been examined. Chinese analysts believe that the primary goal of Russia's leaders is to revive the Russian nation in the light of their 'strategic loss' after the Cold War. The main focus of their energy is said to have been placed on the reform and revitalization of the Russian economy. The Chinese observe that although the Russian elites are deeply dissatisfied with the changing geopolitical landscape, they are reluctant to engage in a strategic rivalry with the US. Thus, the Russian government has tolerated NATO's eastward expansion and pursued a policy of 'strategic retreat'. The key objective behind all this, according to Chinese scholars, is to ensure that Russia will be able to build a strong economy in order to maintain its great power position in the world.

Russia's East Asian security strategy is seen by Chinese scholars as a reflection of its global strategy in the sense that the emphasis of Russian policy in the area is on economic considerations. Indeed, the Chinese note that it is primarily the economic dynamism of the Asia-Pacific that has attracted Russia to the region. This explains Russia's enthusiasm to develop closer relations with China, Japan and South Korea. The Chinese have also discerned Russia's motive of retaining its influence in East Asia as a great power. This is by and large welcomed by PRC leaders and policy elites, as they see Russia as an important player in an emerging multipolar world. Indeed, China has been developing a 'strategic partnership' with Russia to counterbalance the augmenting power of America.

Russia's security strategy by itself is not perceived as a major challenge to China, at least not in the foreseeable future. On the contrary, Russia and China have common strategic interests in that they are both sceptical of US global aspirations. But any major change in Moscow's relations with America will impact on its relations with China. In other words, if Russia moves closer to America (as it did after the 9/11 terrorist attacks), the Chinese would feel rather uncomfortable. In fact, Russian security strategy in the Putin era has caused some concern to China. Specifically, Russia's 'strategic contraction' is believed to have inadvertently undermined Chinese interests. For example, Moscow's decision to allow US forces to enter Central Asia has presented a considerable challenge to China's security. From the Chinese perspective, American presence in the region threatens China's military and energy security. It may also weaken or marginalize the role of the SCO, of which the PRC is a founding and leading member. In the longer term, Chinese security analysts suspect that Russia may play the 'American card' or 'Japan card' in dealing with China. This explains why Russia's improved relations with Japan have led to some misgivings among Chinese scholars.

The final section of the chapter analyzes China's security perceptions of Russia from the perspectives of various international relations theories. This analysis shows that realism, especially structural realism, has had a considerable impact on Chinese study of Russia. PRC analysts and security analysts tend to look at Russia's changing position in the international system in terms of the balance of power theory. Their preoccupation with polarity is evident in most Chinese publications. Moreover, Chinese analysis of Russia's 'strategic contraction' is informed by defensive realism, which posits that great powers are more concerned with security than expansion. Furthermore, Chinese discussion on the Russian strategy to strengthen its great power position through economic revival can be explained by the neorealist international political economy theory.

However, Chinese discourse on Russia's participation in global and regional economic institutions and multilateral security mechanisms can be explicated by neoliberal institutionalism. In addition, constructivism offers some useful insights into Chinese scholars' analysis of Russia's changing identity from a former super-power with extensive global reach to a great power that has voluntarily accepted a strategic retreat. This shows that an actor's interests are shaped by its identity. As the great power identity of Russia is redefined, its geopolitical interests have changed accordingly. Finally, there is no evidence indicating any influence of postmodernist thoughts on Chinese security perceptions of Russia in that it is not considered as a threatening other by PRC scholars and analysts. To conclude, Russia's security interests in the post-Cold War era are not seen to clash with those of China. If anything, Russia could play a useful strategic role in assisting China to promote a multipolar system in a unipolar world.

6 China's response to the security challenge of the major powers in East Asia

Identity construction and great power aspirations

The previous chapters have examined Chinese security discourse of the three major powers in East Asia, namely, the United States, Japan and Russia. The purpose of this chapter is to analyze the discussion and debates among Chinese scholars and analysts on how China should respond to the security challenge of the three East Asian powers. This debate is complex and wide-ranging and is extremely important to our understanding of how Chinese elites seek to construct a great power identity for their country. China's response to the security strategies of the major powers should be understood within the context of its overall assessment of the changing international security environment in the post-Cold War era.

The chapter begins by offering a brief review of how Chinese security specialists perceive the nature and significance of the security challenge of the East Asian powers to China. This is followed by a second section on the analysis of Chinese perceptions of the changing structure of the international system, focusing on the Chinese debate on the extent to which the post-Cold War system should be regarded as a one of unipolarity or multipolarity. It also considers PRC specialists' assessment of China's changing security environment. The chapter goes on to discuss Chinese views of how China may fulfil its great power aspirations through the development of great power diplomacy. Specific attention is paid to PRC scholars' analysis of the importance of various types of 'partnerships' and the relevance of a grand strategy to China's pursuit of a great power status.

The fourth section looks at China's debate on its strategy in East Asia and, more importantly, its changing attitudes towards multilateral security cooperation. The fifth section examines the debate among Chinese analysts on how China should rise to a great power status peacefully. This debate is significant because it deals with how China should relate itself to other great powers and to the international community in general. Finally, China's response to the challenge of the major powers is analyzed from the perspectives of realism, liberalism and constructivism.

The security challenge of the major powers in East Asia

The evidence from previous chapters indicates that Chinese analysts perceive a variety of challenges from the security strategies of the three East Asian powers. First, all three major powers are former, existing or aspiring great powers with global aspirations. In the case of the United States, it is currently the sole superpower in the world and, as far as the Chinese are concerned, is determined to sustain its unipolar position, extending its military presence and economic and political influence across the world. Indeed, the defence spending of America is enormous compared with that of other East Asian powers. In 2005, American military expenditure reached US$495.3 billion. In the same year, the defence spending of China, Japan and Russia was US$104 billion, US$43.9 billion and US$58 billion, respectively (see Fig. 6.1).

In the eyes of Chinese security analysts, Japan is already an economic superpower but has a long-standing desire to become a 'political power' and a military power. It wishes to achieve the status that is commensurate with its economic strength. As such, Japan is believed to have striven to raise its international profile, and more importantly, to be accepted as a permanent member of the UN Security Council. The Chinese are convinced that Japan is moving rapidly in the direction of becoming an 'ordinary nation'. Similarly, Russia is also seen to have great power ambitions. After all, it was a superpower for almost 50 years, but has declined since the end of the Cold War. Chinese analysts recognize that Russian leaders are seeking to regain Russia's previous pre-eminence through economic revival. Although Moscow seems to be pursuing a policy of 'strategic contraction', according to the Chinese, its ultimate aim is to re-emerge as a global power.

As all three major powers have global aspirations and interests, the Chinese believe that they fear a rising China may undermine or challenge their positions. Thus, they may pursue policies to forestall China's rise to a great power status. Given their capabilities, these powers are believed to be able to obstruct China's attempts to reach its national goal. The challenge for China is therefore how to manage a competitive yet stable and non-confrontational relationship with the major powers during a time when China is developing its 'comprehensive national strength'. After all, China has strong economic and trade relations with these countries (see Fig. 6.2). In 2007, the US was China's largest trade partner and Japan was its second largest (US-China Business Council 2008).

Second, all three powers have strong interests in East Asia. The Chinese believe that the US wishes to dominate the Asia-Pacific region, where it has wide-ranging economic and security interests. Indeed, Washington is the ally of Japan, South Korea and other Asian countries, and their alliance relations have been strengthened since 9/11.

Japan is an East Asian power in its own right. The Chinese suspect that Japan aspires to play a more significant role in regional security affairs, partly to protect its economic and security interests, and partly to achieve its ambition of a 'political power'.

Russia is both a European and Asian power. Its security interests in East Asia lie in the preservation of a stable environment, as it shares a long border with China, has unresolved territorial disputes with Japan and is geographically close to the Korean Peninsula. Apart from these security concerns, the Chinese recognize that Russia is hoping to tap into the economic resources of East Asia in its development of the Russian Far East.

East Asia is a region of economic dynamism, but it is also an area where China may clash with the US, and possibly Japan, over certain security issues. The most prominent one is Taiwan, although the South China Sea disputes may re-emerge in coming years. The tension on the Korean Peninsula is another regional flashpoint where the great powers have a common interest in achieving the denuclearization of the peninsula, but they may have different views of how to handle North Korea (Li 2003b).

On some regional issues China's interests coincide with those of other great powers, while on other issues they have divergent perceptions. East Asia has always been the strategic focus of China despite its global aspirations. As East Asia is considered by the Chinese to be their traditional sphere of influence, it is imperative for China to be able to play a dominant role in regional affairs. China feels that it needs a stable peripheral environment in order to concentrate on its domestic economic development which, to the Chinese, is essential to the achievement of a great power status. The problem from the Chinese perspective is that America's security strategy in East Asia has made China feel insecure. In particular, Washington's enhanced alliance relations and military presence in the areas surrounding China are seen as a threat to Chinese security. Japan, another major power in the region, is perceived by Chinese analysts to be a partner of the US in constraining Chinese actions. The greatest fear for China is that America and Japan would support Taiwan to break away from mainland China. A conflict across the Taiwan Strait may lead to military confrontations between the PRC and the US, and possibly also Japan. Thus, an important challenge for China is how to manage various regional security issues in such a way that it would not escalate into conflict with other great powers.

Third, the military capabilities of other major powers are perceived by Chinese analysts as a significant security challenge. The challenge comes primarily from the US and Japan. The Chinese are well aware of America's superior military power, which has been demonstrated graphically by recent US military operations in Afghanistan and Iraq. What is worrying to the Chinese is that America has gained a foothold in Central Asia, close to Chinese borders. They are also concerned about the expansion of the US-Japan security alliance, the geographical focus of which has been broadened in recent years to include areas that are not clearly defined. Of the greatest concern to Chinese strategists is the development and deployment of America's TMD system in Asia, which involves Japan and, most likely, Taiwan. America's missile defence systems, if successfully deployed, would be seen as a major challenge to China's national defence. It would not only negate China's limited nuclear deterrence, but would also make it more difficult for the Beijing government to threaten to use force to take over Taiwan. Russia's military capabilities are not perceived by Chinese specialists as a challenge to China's security because of their close strategic relations. In fact, Russia is the biggest arms supplier to China. Chinese threat perceptions may of course change in future, but for the time being, Russia's military power is not viewed with fear.

Fourth, the three major powers seem to regard a rising China as a potential threat to their security interests. This is particularly the case with the US and

Japan. Their apprehensions are expressed directly or indirectly in their official documents, and by their leaders and policy elites. To the US and Japanese defence planners, China is an uncertain factor and its security intentions are viewed with suspicion. Chinese analysts are fully aware that the security strategies of the two countries have taken into account the possibility that PRC leaders would become more assertive and less compromising in advancing Chinese security interests, if and when China possesses its 'comprehensive national strength'. The American and Japanese governments thus feel that it is only prudent to prepare themselves for a China challenge.

More broadly, America and Japan, along with other Western countries and China's neighbours, are unsure of the behaviour of an economically and militarily powerful China. Specifically, they are not certain that China would respect the rules and norms of the international community in future. Would a strong China seek to challenge the existing order? Would it resort to the use of force to resolve the Taiwan issue and other territorial disputes? These and other questions are constantly raised by scholars and officials in Washington, Tokyo and other capitals. Even in Russia, a 'strategic partner' of China, PRC analysts have noticed a 'China threat' debate. A major challenge for China is to convince other great powers that it has no aggressive intent, does not wish to contest their interests and is willing to conform to the rules and regulations of the international system. Of course, the Chinese government has repeatedly said that China would never become a hegemon, but this fails to dispel external concerns of the security implications of an ascending China.

The changing international structure: unipolarity, multipolarity and China's security environment

To understand the views of Chinese analysts on how to respond to the security challenge of the major powers of East Asia, it is necessary to discover their assessment of the changing international environment in the post-Cold War era. A useful starting point is to consider their debate on the structure of the international system. This is important because how China responds to the challenge presented by the three East Asian powers is directly related to their relative power, capabilities and position within the international hierarchy. Ever since the collapse of bipolarity, Chinese scholars have been debating on whether the post-Cold War system is one of multipolarity or unipolarity. A crucial consideration in their discourse is America's power vis-à-vis that of other countries.

Indeed, the question of American 'decline' (*shuai luo*) was the subject of an intense debate in China in the late 1980s and the early 1990s. The dominant view in the Chinese international relations community was that America had been declining, both economically and politically. Some even argued that a long-term decline in American power was inevitable, given the growing economic challenge from Japan and Europe (Huang Suan 1992: 164–70; Zhao Jieqi 1992: 21–25; Feng Tejun 1993: 62–67, 70–73, 86–87; Wang Fengwu and Xing Aifen 1993: 103–10). Others contended that there was no evidence to suggest that the growth of countries such as Japan and Germany would continue into the future or that America's alleged decline was irreversible (Yao Wang *et al.* 1992: 8–9). By the mid-1990s, however, most Chinese specialists agreed that despite a relative decline in US capabilities, America's comprehensive national strength remains formidable.

In terms of what Joseph Nye (1990, 2004) calls traditional 'hard power resources',[1] Chinese scholars note that the United States is much stronger than its competitors. America has a large territory, rich natural resources and a huge population with low density, which cannot be found in any other developed countries. In a world of scarce resources, rapid population growth and environmental degradation, America's advantages become even more prominent. At the same time, the industrial and agricultural sectors in the US are highly developed, and America is at the cutting edge of technology and the information revolution. In the areas of medicine, engineering and advanced science and technology, the US is likely to remain the world leader for years to come.

Chinese scholars point out that America's economic growth has risen steadily since the end of its economic recession in 1991. In addition, America's economic competitiveness is said to have been greater than that of Japan and Germany. Various economic and financial indicators, such as the US exchange rate, industrial outputs, global market share, foreign investments, business profits, share prices and consumer purchasing power, have demonstrated US economic strength and vitality (Li Dongyan 1996: 74–75; Wang Jisi 1997b: 9–11, 15; Chen Dezhao 1998: 21–23; Zhen Bingxi 1998a: 9–12; Gu Wenyan 1998: 7–10).

The pattern of US economic development is characterized by some Chinese scholars as that of a 'new economy' (*xin jingji*) that emphasizes the production and distribution of knowledge and information. In such a new economy, knowledge and technology provide the sources, as well as the dynamics, of economic growth. Moreover, the United States is believed to be changing from an industrial economy to an information economy. Information, communication and other related industries and service sectors are playing a dominant role in the development of the US economy. Production, consumption and communication in American society are increasingly driven and dominated by computer technology and the Internet. The US government and enterprises, it is argued, have been responding to the challenge of information technology positively, and taking the opportunity to strengthen America's economy and increase its competitiveness in the world market (Zhen Bingxi 1998b: 42–44).

However, even before the Asian Financial Crisis in 1997–98, some Chinese scholars maintained that it was quite possible that the US could not sustain its robust economic performance. Rapid economic growth, a rise in employment rate and wage increases have all stimulated consumer spending which, according to Chinese analysis, could result in high inflation and serious debt problem in America. They also predicted that share prices might fall sharply after their dramatic upsurge in the mid 1990s, which could undermine investors' confidence and cause a downturn in the American economy. Other problems such as the US trade deficit and economic inequality in American society have been identified as negative factors that could have a detrimental effect on America's economic progress (Gu Wenyan 1998: 10–11; see also Song Yuhua and Lu Huajun 1997). Indeed, America's economic performance has been somewhat affected the events since 9/11. Nevertheless, most Chinese scholars believe that the US economy will continue to grow, albeit at a slower pace, and that unemployment, inflation and budget deficit in America can be kept at a relatively low level. More significantly, the US is said to have firmly established its dominant position in the areas that will determine economic growth and competitiveness in the 21st century, namely telecommunications, information and computer technology. It will maintain its leading role in the development of advanced science and technology. The US will continue to provide the biggest market for the world and retain its position as the leading global economic actor for the foreseeable future (Gu Wenyan 1998: 11).

As far as defence capability is concerned, most Chinese security experts agree that America remains the most powerful country in the world. Specifically, the US has a solid defence industry and the most advanced military technology. After the break-up of the USSR, it is said, America's status as a military superpower is second to none. Although US defence expenditure was reduced in the 1990s, it remained much higher than that of other major powers. The contraction in America's defence budget, strategic nuclear weapons and armed forces was compensated for by the rapid development of military technology, with an emphasis on the research and production of high-tech conventional weapons. Chinese analysts note that the 9/11 terrorist attacks and the challenge of global terrorism have enabled America to increase its defence budgets substantially and further strengthen its military capabilities, especially in the area of missile defence. The ability of US forces to respond to regional conflict is also believed to have increased. Indeed, since the end of the Cold War, the Chinese argue, America has frequently used military threats or forces to deal with conflicts around the world, such as Iraq, Bosnia-Herzegovina, the Korean Peninsula and the Taiwan Strait. The war in Afghanistan and the invasion of Iraq are said to have demonstrated America's military superiority over all other countries (Li Dongyan 1996: 75; Wang Jisi 1997b: 16–17; Liu Xuecheng 2004b; Tao Wenzhao 2005).

While most Chinese analysts and scholars accept the fact that the US possesses abundant 'hard power resources', they believe that it lacks sufficient 'soft power resources' to dominate or lead the world (Wang Jisi 1997b: 34). First, they maintain that the social cohesion in American society has been weakening in recent years. During the Cold War era, it is argued, the American people had a relatively clear strategic opponent in the former Soviet Union. With the demise of the Soviet empire, the American nation as a whole has lost a sense of direction. But the threat of Islamic terrorism since 9/11 is said to have regenerated a strong cohesion among Americans. Nevertheless, Chinese scholars argue that there are a number of interrelated social and political problems, such as rising racial tension, social and economic inequality and political apathy. These problems are believed to have seriously shaken the foundations of US society (Wang Jisi 1997b: 19–22).

The second element of America's 'soft power resources' is its ideological and cultural attraction which, the Chinese maintain, is also declining. Immediately after the collapse of the communist regimes in the former Soviet Union and Eastern

Europe, 'history' seemed to have ended in the sense that the American model had replaced the Soviet one as the final form of human government and the only viable path of economic and social development. This simplistic and arrogant view which is based essentially on American political values, Chinese scholars contend, has been shaken by the growing challenge of non-Western values and development models around the world.

To support their argument, Chinese analysts point to the resurgence of Islam in the Middle East, Central Asia, South and South East Asia. In particular, 'Islamic fundamentalism', which sees Islam as a political ideology that should be guiding foreign and domestic policy-making, has gained more influence in recent years. In addition, many elites in East Asia are critical of Western/American economic and political systems, which are believed to be responsible for the break-up of nucleus families, the intensification of social conflict, and the decline of economic performance in Western societies. Instead, respect for authority, emphasis on collectivism and acceptance of traditional values, it is argued, would help ensure sustained economic development and political stability. East Asian elites are said to be increasingly reluctant to follow American or Western models in terms of political systems, social norms, economic models and foreign policy orientations. On issues such as human rights, arms control and the international economic order, developing countries tend to take a stance that differs to that of Western countries (Wang Jisi 1997b: 22, 30).

Indeed, America's image in the world has become rather negative, according to the Chinese. Individualism and excessive freedom in American society have led to considerable social chaos and moral decay, substantially undermining America's position of moral leadership in the world. It is true that global culture is heavily influenced by US products such as Coca Cola, Hollywood, MTV and the Internet. But Chinese analysts have serious doubt that these are useful in constructing a positive image of America in the minds of political elites in other countries (Wang Jisi 1997b: 22–24).

Nevertheless, Chinese scholars recognize that the US possesses the 'soft power resources' of establishing the rules and norms of international regimes and dominating the decision-making process of international organizations. Indeed, America is believed to have played a central role in shaping the agenda of the NPT, the Comprehensive Test Ban Treaty, G8 Summits, WTO, NAFTA, APEC and so on. The existing rules and regulations in most international mechanisms are believed to have been laid down in such a way that would serve US interests (Li Dongyan 1996: 75; Wang Jisi 1997b: 24). America would have no hesitation in ignoring or bending the rules, if and when they do not suit its needs, say the Chinese.

On the whole, Chinese analysts' assessment of America's capabilities is realistic. Some scholars even reject the thesis that the US is suffering from a 'relative decline'. First, they argue that the 'declinists' tend to use America's unique position in the immediate post-war years as a starting point for assessing US capabilities in subsequent years. But the circumstances in those years were very special and should not be employed as a reference point when analyzing America's world standing. Second, while US economic status did decline for a while, the Americans have made the necessary economic adjustments to successfully revive their economy. Third, the rise and fall of America's status varies from one dimension or one region to another and cannot be easily generalized. As there is no evidence of a general decline in American power, they contend, it is both inaccurate and misleading to use the word 'decline' to describe US capabilities (Jin Canrong 1995: 145). However, many Chinese specialists argue that America's 'pre-emptive attack' on Iraq without UN authorization has weakened Washington's 'soft power'. From a historical perspective, Wang Jisi (2004) argues, all great powers will eventually decline no matter how strong they are.

For the moment, most Chinese international relations experts agree that the US is the sole superpower in the world, and that its superior standing will last for a considerable period of time. No other forces, they maintain, will be in a position to challenge, let alone replace, America in the international system in the near future (Jin Canrong 1995: 145). However, the recognition by Chinese analysts of Washington's formidable 'comprehensive national strength' does not necessarily lead to a conclusion that the post-Cold War world is one of unipolarity (Li Dongyan 1996: 77; Song Yimin 1997: 16; Yu Sui 2004: 20).

According to Chinese observation, it is no longer possible for America to benefit from a common threat perception among its allies (Li Dongyan 1996: 77–78). PRC analysts maintain that the cohesion of the Western alliance has been weakened since the disintegration of the USSR. America's recent success in strengthening NATO and the US-Japan security alliance does not guarantee that its leading role within the two military alliances will never be questioned. Japan and the member states of NATO are thought to have attempted to fortify their own positions through the US-Japan security treaty and NATO expansion, respectively (Song Yimin 1998: 8–9). While the US and its NATO allies were united in the face of international terrorism after 9/11, PRC scholars contend that the hope of unity began to dissipate when the Bush administration decided to launch an attack on Iraq. Although there are many common interests between America and other Western countries, other countries are said to be increasingly willing to challenge Washington. This was clearly revealed in the disagreement between Washington and some of its European allies, especially France and Germany, over the 2003 Iraq war (Liu Jun 2004b; Sun Suyuan 2004).

Indeed, the Chinese argue that EU members are making a greater effort to deepen European integration, and that Japan is seeking to develop a more equal relationship with the US. The fact that America's economic performance has been better than that of Europe and Japan in the past decade does not mean that the US will not be surpassed by other developed economies in future. On the contrary, say the Chinese, a more united Europe, together with Japan, will present a greater economic challenge to the United States in the 21st century. Meanwhile, the United States is encountering considerable challenges from China, whose economic strength and political influence are rapidly increasing. Despite a temporary decline in its national strength, Russia is seen as a potential long-term rival of the United States. Finally, there are other rising powers across the world, including India, South Africa and Brazil, that will not be prepared to accept US dominance (Wang

Jisi 1997b: 31; Ni Feng 2004: 4–5). In this sense, America is 'lonely at the top' and 'incapable of leading the world' (Wang Jisi 1997b: 34).

To the Chinese, America's ephemeral predominance has not altered the general trend of the transition of the international system from bipolarity to multipolarity (Song Yimin 1998: 7; Liu Shan 2001). The current international structure is characterized by most Chinese international relations scholars as one of *yichao duoqiang* (one superpower and several great powers). They argue that the world is undergoing a process of multipolarization (*duojihua*) but do not expect any significant change to America's superior position in the hierarchy of the international system for some time (Yu Sui 2004: 16). To them, multipolarity is a desirable yet distant goal that cannot be achieved overnight. This view is shared by many other Chinese scholars including Li Zhongjie (2002), a research director at the Central Party School. Professor Li argues that multipolarization refers to a trend rather than a reality. He criticizes those who thought that multipolarity would soon arrive as being over-optimistic. In his view, multipolarity should be understood in terms of the existence of a number of major forces in the world that are able to constrain each other, thus creating a relatively balanced and stable situation. As the world has not yet reached that stage, he believes that it is better to consider multipolarity as something to be desired. In contrast to the views of other PRC scholars, Li Zhongjie contends that the world looks more like one of unipolarity than multipolarity.

Professor Li is convinced that the US is still in a uniquely superior and powerful position, whether this is interpreted in terms of America's capabilities or its influence. Other countries or groups of countries with considerable 'comprehensive national strength', such as Russia, China, Japan and the EU, cannot be compared with America in terms of their power or status. In this sense, they cannot be regarded as significant 'poles'. Rather, they should only be seen as great powers. It is precisely because multipolarity has not yet been achieved that all the great powers are seeking to develop various aspects of their capabilities. Each actor tries to increase its competitiveness and its intenational status in the world. This is a situation characterized by Li Zhongjie as *duoyuan zhengji*, or rivalry for achieving the status of a 'pole' within the international structure. Most Chinese analysts agree that it will be some time before the arrival of a truly multipolar world, but few can predict with confidence when this might happen. This is because the power and capabilities of other potential contesters to US supremacy remain rather limited. For example, Russia is struggling with its economic revival; Japan is heavily dependent on America for its security; China is developing its comprehensive national strength; the EU, despite its successful integration, does not always speak with one voice on international issues. Nevertheless, Professor Qiao Mu (2002: 13) of the Institute of International Studies at Qinghua University, predicts that a multipolar system will emerge in the next 20 to 30 years.

It is within this global context that China assesses its security environment. Most PRC scholars believe that, on the whole, China's security environment has improved substantially since the end of the Cold War. They have reached a conclusion that the possibility of a world war or an external invasion of China is very slim. However, the danger for China to get involved in regional conflicts has risen, especially in the Taiwan Strait and on the Korean Peninsula. This view is a reflection of their assessment of China's international environment. The international system that consisted of 'one superpower and several great powers' in the 1990s remains largely unchanged today.

In the view of Yan Xuetong (2000), the relatively stable international environment explains the absence of major global conflict. In the meantime, he notes that strategic relationships among the great powers have changed considerably. Following the end of the Cold War, the US was said to be concerned about Russia's nuclear capabilities, Japan's growing economic power and the EU's potential challenge. But Washington did not have a clear strategic rival, says Professor Yan. By the end of the 1990s, he asserts, America clearly saw China as its strategic competitor. According to his observations, the 'strategic contradictions' (*zhanlue maodun*) between America and Japan and Europe, respectively, were primarily in the sphere of economic competition. The 'strategic contradictions' between America and Russia were related mainly to security issues. However, the US is believed to have serious 'contradictions' with China in their political, economic and security relations. Thus, America's global strategy and its security perceptions of China figure prominently in China's assessment of its security environment. As such, how China responds to the security challenge of the major powers in East Asia, and the US in particular, is intimately linked to Chinese discourse of the changing structure of the international system and the broader international environment.

In 2000, Yan Xuetong predicted that China's future security environment would be less favourable than that of the 1990s. The main source of growing security threat was said to be a result of the structural factors in Sino-American relations and the tensions in the Taiwan Strait. Indeed, Taiwan's independence movement had increased the possibility for the PRC to be involved in local wars. Despite this grim prediction, Yan did not think that any regional conflict, including a military confrontation over Taiwan, would lead to a global war or an outright invasion of China. While recognizing the rising challenge of non-conventional security threats, he did not regard this type of threat as more significant than China's traditional security concerns. Five years later, Chen Xiangyang (2005) of CICIR offered a similarly pessimistic assessment of China's geostrategic environment, arguing that China was facing more challenges than opportunities along its periphery. Other scholars are, however, more hopeful that China's security environment can be improved through bilateral and multilateral cooperation and great power diplomacy.

Great power aspirations, great power diplomacy

It is clear that China's response to the perceived challenge from other major powers should be understood within the context of its self-aspirations as an emerging power as well as its perceptions of the wider international security environment. From the PRC's perspective, an effective way of dealing with the challenge is to establish what the Chinese call 'partnerships' (*huoban guanxi*) with other countries and actors. In the view of PRC analysts, the most appropriate response to unipolarity is to promote a Chinese diplomatic strategy based on various types of partnerships with a variety of countries around the world. In this way, China would not have to confront the United States directly, while having the flexibility of maintaining stable relationships with a whole range of countries. If this strategy is successfully implemented, Chinese scholars believe that it would help hasten the process of multipolarization. In the meantime, by forming various partnerships, China would be able to advance its image as a responsible power, thus contributing to China's efforts to construct a great power identity. For Chinese leaders and policy elites, the ultimate aim of the partnership strategy is to safeguard China's national interest and achieve its great power status in the 21st century (Jin Zhengkun 2000).

According to Ning Sao (2000), a Peking University professor, China has developed four kinds of partnerships. The first is known as 'strategic partnership' (*zhanlue huoban guanxi*), which refers to the partnership between China and the US that was first established in October 1997. This sort of partnership reflects both competition and cooperation with three main elements. First, the two countries are partners rather than rivals. Second, their relationship is based on overall strategic considerations. Third, the relationship is 'constructive' rather than aiming at other countries or seeking 'hegemony'.

The second type of partnership is referred to as 'strategic consultative partnership' (*zhanlue xiezuo huoban guanxi*). This sort of partnership was first established between China and Russia in April 1996. A similar partnership, known as 'comprehensive partnership' (*quanmian huoban guanxi*), was established between China and France in May 1997. In addition, China and the UK established a 'comprehensive partnership that faces the future' (*mianxiang weilai di quanmian huoban guanxi*) in October 1998. In November of the same year, China and Japan established a 'friendly partnership that aims to promote peace and development in the twenty-first century'. In April 1998, China and the EU decided to establish a 'long-term and stable constructive partnership'. Despite different wordings and emphasis in these partnerships, Professor Ning Sao points out, they are all designed to promote multipolarity and offset the negative aspects of Sino-American relations.

The third type of partnership is 'good neighbourly partnership' (*mulin huoban guanxi*). In December 1997, China and ASEAN countries announced the establishment of such a partnership, designed to promote mutual trust and development between China and its neighbours, focusing in particular on regional economic and security issues.

The final type of partnership is labelled 'basic partnership', which is used to describe partnerships between China and developing countries, such as that established between China and Mexico at the end of 1997.

Another way of looking at China's partnerships is to place them at different levels as suggested by Su Hao (2000) of CIIS. The first category includes partnerships of a strategic level, such as those between China and the US, Russia and France, respectively. The second category includes partnerships at a regional level such as the partnerships between China and the EU, ASEAN, Britain, Japan, India, South Africa, Brazil and other regional powers. The third type of partnership is built on bilateral agreements, including those between China and South Korea, Pakistan, the Ukraine, Kazakhstan, Canada, Mexico and other countries. This category of partnership is known as friendly cooperative partnership.

Despite different labels, Su Hao argues that these partnerships represent several types of China's relations with other countries. The first type of partnership is thought to be the most significant in that China shares strategic aims and common interests with its partners. Their views on major issues are close and there is no fundamental disagreement between them. They can also cooperate over a wide range of areas, especially in the more sensitive sphere of military cooperation. On major international, regional and bilateral issues, they tend to consult each other and coordinate their actions. The Sino-Russian partnership clearly belongs to this type of relationship.

Another type of partnership, according to Su Hao, is characterized by mutual benefits and friendly cooperation. Again, the countries within the partnerships share broader common interests and are interested in deepening their bilateral or multilateral cooperation. China's partnerships with South Korea, Thailand, Canada, Mexico, and the Ukraine belong to this category. The third type of partnership is usually labelled 'consultative partnership' that includes partnerships between China and Britain, Germany, ASEAN and other regional organizations. While they have many common interests and are able to cooperate with each other on the basis of mutual respect, mutual benefit and equality, they may still have considerable differences on certain issues. The level of mutual trust in these partnerships remains to be improved.

The final type of partnership is known as 'constructive' partnership. In this case, there are still some serious disagreements between China and its partners that need to be resolved through a process of constructive dialogue before a real partnership can be established. Su Hao uses China's partnerships with America, Japan and India as examples for this type of relationship. He points out that these countries have, in varying degrees, treated China as their potential strategic rival. Despite some common interests in maintaining global and regional stability, they have serious differences on certain major issues and their strategic aims are different.

Chinese analysts argue that China's partnerships with various countries represent a clear departure from Cold War thinking. These types of relationships, they assert, are not based on military alliances. Instead, they are established to resolve differences and disputes through consultation, dialogue and other peaceful means. More importantly, they are not designed to target a third party. Countries within each partnership are free to develop their relations with any other countries.

China's 'partnership diplomacy' should be seen as part of its diplomatic strategy. This type of great power diplomacy has been advocated by many PRC scholars. For example, Professor Ye Zicheng (2000) of Peking University has argued strongly for a 'great power diplomatic strategy' (*daguo waijiao zhanlue*). He believes that such a strategy is essential for China to achieve its aim of modernization. The focus of the strategy is obviously on China's relations with the major powers, which is important due to China's great power aspirations. A great power must have a great power diplomatic strategy, according to Professor Ye. He argues that China should adopt the foreign policy posture of a great power if it wishes to become one. He believes that China already possesses many of the ingredients of a great power. Economically, it is the largest developing country in the world with huge market potential. It is also a permanent member of the UN Security Council. On many international issues, China is able to exert considerable influence. All this, says Professor Ye, indicates that China is in a position to practice great power diplomacy. If middle-ranking powers such as France and Britain can play the role of a great power in international affairs, Ye asks, why should China be hesitant in adopting a great power strategy?

Like other Chinese scholars, Ye Zicheng (2000) argues that China should change its diplomatic mentality (*waijiao xintai*). More specifically, it should shake off the shadow of the 'diplomacy of shame and humiliation' that was imposed by foreign powers from the 19th century. He goes on to say that China needs to come out of its 'victim mentality' and the mentality of isolation and anger. Instead, it should have a normal and rational mentality and self-confidence associated with a great power. Only then will China be able to achieve its great power status and assume great power responsibilities in the international community.

In debating China's great power strategy, some Chinese scholars have paid attention to its grand strategy (*dazhanlue*). In his article in *Zhanlue yu guanli*, Tang Shiping (2000) of the Institute of Asia-Pacific Studies at CASS has elaborated his ideas of a grand strategy that China should adopt. He believes that Chinese leaders should have a clear global strategy to create an ideal security environment for China, in order to achieve its national goal. In terms of China's global security strategy, he argues, it is important to maintain an effective strategic deterrence, so that any potential hostile forces are not able to threaten China. Secondly, it is in China's interest to promote a multipolar world that differs from the one in European history. However, Tang contends that China's grand strategy should not be determined by any specific international structure, be it unipolarity, bipolarity or multipolarity. This is because historically the change in the structure of the international system is not a result of conscious actions.

As far as the regional dimension of China's grand strategy is concerned, Professor Tang suggests that the Chinese government should pursue the following. First, the most important strategic aim for China is to make sure that no external forces are able to undermine its economic development. This requires strong defence capabilities. It is particularly important to protect the security of the coastal areas, which are vital to China's economy. To Tang, no other countries would pose a more significant threat to China's coastal areas than the US and Japan. Thus, Beijing must try to maintain a stable triangular relationship between the PRC, America and Japan.

Second, while the coastal areas are central to China's economic progress, Tang argues, it is essentially a continental power. As such, preserving China's land security is a major consideration for Chinese leaders. As Russia is said to be capable of posing a threat to Chinese land security, it is in China's interest to maintain good strategic relations with Moscow. The aim is to ensure that if and when Russia re-emerges as a great power, it remains China's partner.

Third, Tang believes that it is necessary for Chinese leaders and elites to convince the outside world that the status of Taiwan is taken very seriously by China. He believes that it would be a major task to explain to the Americans that 'a China without Taiwan will no longer be a "China"'. In this sense, 'the importance of Taiwan to China is equivalent to the importance of democracy and freedom to America'. Tang suggests that PRC leaders should seek to achieve peaceful 'reunification' with Taiwan. But he says that they should signal to Washington that China would be willing to become a status quo power only after its completion of the reunification mission. The above regional strategic aims are considered by Tang as the most important aspects of China's grand strategy. Other components of China's regional strategy include the following (Tang Shiping 2000):

- Preventing the deterioration of the security situation on the Korean Peninsula and ensuring that a united Korea would not have any negative impact on China's security environment.
- Preventing any hostile forces from influencing South East Asia's policy towards China and seeking wide-ranging cooperation with ASEAN countries.
- Ensuring regional stability of Central Asia; preventing religious extremists and separatists in the area from threatening the security of Western China; and seeking to secure energy supplies from Central Asia.
- Preventing a rising India from treating China as its enemy.
- Seeking to secure energy supplies from the Middle East through the development of relations with various countries in the region.

This regional focus of China's grand strategy is not inconsistent with the thinking of other Chinese scholars. For example, when discussing China's diplomatic strategy, Professor Xu Kaiyi (2004: 54) argues that it is more realistic to regard China as a regional great power because its influence is largely confined to Asia. This does not mean that Chinese analysts do not think that China should have great power ambitions. Indeed, many of them argue that China should use the current 'period of strategic opportunity' (*zhanlue jiyuqi*) to develop a great power mentality and pursue great power diplomacy. As Professor Xu asserts, too much emphasis has been placed on 'hiding our capabilities and biding our time' (*tao guang yang hui*) in the past. In the next 20 years, he suggests, China must make a greater effort to 'accomplish something' (*you suo zuo wei*).[2]

Regional strategy and multilateral security cooperation

As mentioned in the previous section, East Asia remains China's primary concern despite its great power aspirations. In the meantime, other East Asian powers also have a strong interest in the region and their security strategies have undoubtedly had a significant impact on China's security discourse in the region. For historical and geopolitical reasons, many of China's neighbouring countries are suspicious of its strategic intentions. This worries Chinese leaders and elites. From their perspective, Asian countries can be exploited by other great powers to act against Chinese interests. For instance, the Chinese believe that the 'China threat' theory in South East Asia has been generated by the US and Japan so as to stimulate suspicion among China's neighbours.

Many PRC analysts feel that China's peripheral environment (*zhoubian huanjing*) has, on the whole, improved since the early 1990s. Indeed, Beijing has established close economic and diplomatic relations with all its neighbours, especially Russia. Nevertheless, they recognize many uncertainties around China's surrounding areas. Among their concerns are the Taiwan issue, the North Korean nuclear crisis, the South China Sea disputes, the nuclear tests in South Asia and the disputes over the Senkaku/Diaoyu islands. Added to these are the growing threat of Islamic fundamentalism in Xinjiang and America's presence in Central Asia since 9/11 (Li Jingzhi 2003b). This is why China needs to have an effective regional strategy to enhance its peripheral security. Most Chinese analysts believe that if China cannot secure its borders and exert considerable influence in its surrounding areas, this will seriously undermine its claim to achieve a great power status in the world. Thus, China has been pursuing a 'good neighbourly policy' (*mulin zhengce*) aiming at establishing and improving relations with its peripheral countries (Ya Yan 2001). More recently, China has expanded its concept of periphery (*zhoubian*) to encompass a wider range of countries. This is known as 'greater peripheral diplomacy' (*dazhoubian waijiao*) which includes relations with two types of countries. The first are China's traditional Asian neighbours, while the second encompasses China's diplomacy towards such countries as Russia, America and EU countries (Ruan Zongze 2001).

The most significant development in China's security strategy is arguably its changing view of multilateral security cooperation. Prior to the mid-1990s, China was very sceptical of multilateral security forums, fearing that they would be exploited by the US and other Asian countries in order to constrain Chinese actions. But these perceptions have changed substantially in recent years, as Chinese leaders have discovered that it is in China's interests to take part in multilateral security cooperation (Hughes, 2005). Indeed, PRC officials and security experts have participated in a variety of Track-I and Track-II security meetings in East Asia, such as the ARF and Council for Security Cooperation in the Asia-Pacific (CSCAP).

A major change in China's attitudes is that it has actually been involved in the creation of multilateral security mechanisms, playing a leading role in both the SCO and the six-party talks on the North Korean nuclear crisis. Chinese scholars stress the depth and breadth of China's involvement in multilateral security cooperation in the past decade. A related development is that the PRC has become more active in promoting military cooperation with other states, including conducting joint military exercises with neighbouring countries. In October 2004, the ARF's security policy conference was held in Beijing, which signified the transformation of China's perception of the nature and utility of multilateral security forums (Sun Ru 2005). Indeed, some PRC scholars argue that China should play a more prominent role in developing multilateral economic and security cooperation. This would help strengthen China's influence on its surrounding security environment, as well as reduce the concern of China's neighbouring countries over the growth of Chinese power. They argue that it is in the interests of both China and its neighbours to find common grounds in their security cooperation (Tang Shiping 2000: 47–48).

Many Chinese scholars have argued that China should actively participate in regional security cooperation organizations (Yan Xuetong 2000). Sa Benwang (2004), the Deputy Head of the China Committee of CSCAP, argues that closer security cooperation among Asia-Pacific countries is an inevitable trend despite numerous obstacles. Shi Yinhong (2000) of Renmin University has written a very important article arguing that the creation of East Asian security mechanisms will benefit all countries in the region, including China. His view is based on the analysis of the 'security dilemma' (Herz 1950) in East Asia. Professor Shi points out that the security situation in East Asia is a classic example of the 'security dilemma' widely discussed in IR literature (Glaser 1997; Booth and Wheeler 2007). With the rise of China, the balance of power in the region is expected to change significantly at some point in future. This has led to considerable apprehension in the US and Japan. American and Japanese leaders feel that they have to respond to the power transition (Organski 1958) in East Asia due to the uncertainties of China's security intentions. The three major powers are thus locked into a vicious circle of suspicion. Similar suspicions also exist between China and India, and China and certain South East Asian countries. The only way out of this 'security dilemma', according to Shi, is to establish East Asian security mechanisms. Such mechanisms would reduce the possibility of regional conflict and help improve China's security environment, Professor Shi maintains.

A similar view is held by Feng Yongping (2005) who argues that the Sino-Japanese security dilemma has been exacerbated by China's ascendancy as a great power. He believes that the only solution to the problem is to replace the Hobbesian culture of security dilemma by the Kantian culture of security community. From a constructivist perspective, he says, the intersubjective knowledge of mutual distrust between China and Japan can be changed through the development of a security community (Wendt 1995). Specifically, Feng suggests that the six-party talks should be upgraded to a formal security cooperation mechanism in North East Asia equivalent to the ARF in South East Asia. Similarly, the ASEAN-Plus-Three mechanism should be used by China and Japan as an avenue for further cooperation, with the ultimate aim of establishing an East Asian community.

Qin Yaqing and Wei Ling (2007) of the Foreign Affairs College have proposed a process-driven model of regional cooperation in East Asia, the essence of which is to foster change through intersubjectivity. In other words, the model aims to promote gradual socialization of power by involving the key actors in the process of regional cooperation. This process, it is hoped, would help socialize power, nurture rules and norms, and cultivate a collective identity in the region. The utility and limitations of what Professors Qin and Wei call 'process-oriented constructivism' (*guochengxing jiangouzhuyi*) have been explored via a case study of the first East

Asia Summit. They note that further tests of the model need to be conducted as East Asian cooperation continues to evolve.

Other scholars such as Zhang Tiejun (2005) of the Shanghai Institute of International Studies have argued for the creation of an East Asian community (*Dongya gongtongti*) that draws upon the analytical insights of realism, liberalism and constructivism. This approach is shared by Wang Hongfang (2004) of the Institute of International Relations at Nanjing University who argues that East Asian security cooperation can be analyzed from the perspectives of power, institutions and identity. It is possible, in her view, to construct some sort of regional security complex (Buzan, Weaver and De Wilde 1998: 12) in East Asia based on three aspects of security cooperation – common security, comprehensive security and the creation of multilateral security mechanisms. In the longer term, the deepening of cooperation among East Asian states through such a security complex may overcome the security dilemma that currently exists in the region. Chinese scholars agree that there are different models through which an East Asian Community can be created, and that the search for the most appropriate model is likely to be a lengthy process. To Zhang Xiaoming (2006) of Peking University, it is in China's interest to establish one or more regional communities with its neighbouring countries that are open, inclusive, based on a common regional identity and transcend traditional geopolitics.

Nevertheless, Chinese scholars appreciate the difficulties of establishing multilateral security mechanisms in the Asia-Pacific. Sun Ru (2005: 103, 112) of the CICIR, for example, has pointed out the lack of concrete achievements in multilateral security cooperation and the slow progress of the institutionalization of security mechanisms. Professor Sun argues that there are numerous obstacles to the elimination of the 'security dilemma' between China and America due to various historical and structural factors. Within this dilemma, according to Sun, their attitudes towards cooperation are likely to be influenced by the consideration of 'absolute gains' and 'relative gains'. While the neoliberal institutionalists believe that the motives behind interstate cooperation are 'absolute gains', the neorealists are more concerned about 'relative gains'. As Professor Sun has rightly pointed out, if a state suspects that its 'relative gains' are limited in relation to those of other countries, it may be reluctant to engage in cooperation. Whether the creation of Asia-Pacific security mechanisms would be conducive to the development of a collective identity, as the constructivists predict, remains to be seen.

Some Chinese scholars have argued that China's embrace of multilateralism is related to its 'new security concept' (*xin anquanguan*). This concept was first announced by Jiang Zemin in his speech at the UN in October 1995. Since then, it has been reiterated by Chinese leaders on many occasions and included in various major official documents, such as China's defence white papers. There are four main elements of the new security concept, the first of which emphasizes 'mutual trust, mutual benefit, equality and cooperation'. The second element states that the political foundation underpinning world peace should be the 'Five Principles of Peaceful Coexistence and other universally recognized norms governing international relations'. Third, the economic guarantee for peace is based on 'mutually beneficial cooperation and common prosperity'. Finally, conducting 'dialogue, consultations and negotiations on an equal footing' is believed to be 'the right way to solve disputes and safeguard peace' (Kong Fanhe and Ma Qian 2005).

Kong Fanhe and Ma Qian have provided an in-depth analysis of China's new security concept. They criticize the traditional realist concept of security for focusing almost exclusively on military security. China's new security concept, they argue, is based on the notion of 'comprehensive security' (*zonghe anquan*) that encompasses economic, energy, environmental and other dimensions of security. In terms of the nature of the concept, they maintain that China has moved beyond the traditional security discourse accepting the idea of 'common security' (*gongtong anquan*). This is said to be a reflection of an understanding of an increasingly interdependent and globalizing world. As a result, security relations among different countries are perceived as positive-sum rather than zero-sum relations.

As to the types of security threat facing the world, Kong and Ma (2005: 76–78) contend that it is necessary to break away from the conceptual constraints of the 'security dilemma' prevalent in international relations thinking. They agree with other Chinese scholars that it is important to recognize the growing challenge of non-traditional security issues, especially religious conflict, global terrorism and transnational organized crime (Liu Xuecheng 2004a). In this regard, China's security interests are identical to those of the wider international community. Finally, they argue that China's security practice is underpinned by a new security concept focusing on 'cooperative security' (*hezuo anquan*). This means that in promoting international security cooperation, China supports a model that emphasizes trust rather than suspicion, dialogue rather than confrontation, negotiation rather than conflict, mutual understanding and compromise rather than competition and rivalry, and universal security of humankind rather than the security of specific alliances. The extent to which Beijing adheres to the principles of this model in its security interactions with other countries will require further empirical studies.

China's 'peaceful rise' to great power status

China's response to the security challenge of the major powers in East Asia is closely linked to its efforts of constructing a great power identity. To Chinese leaders, the US and Japan have used the 'China threat theory' to generate negative perceptions of the growth of Chinese power. This is due to their reluctance to accept a rising China that might be able to challenge their positions in the international system and their perceived security interests. From the Chinese perspective, the 'China threat theory' is part of the strategy pursued by America and Japan to undermine China's security interests and prevent it from rising to great power status. It is therefore vitally important to devise a strategy to dispel fears of a China threat among the PRC's neighbours and trade partners. The emergence of the 'theory of China's peaceful rise' (*zhongguo heping jueqi lun*) should thus be understood within this context.

Well before the theory of peaceful rise was officially pronounced by Zheng Bijian, a former executive vice-president of the CCP's Central Party School, at the Boao Forum for Asia in November 2003 (Zheng 2003), there had already been discussion among Chinese scholars on how to respond to the changing international environment and the security challenge of other great powers, especially the US and Japan. As Tang Shiping (2000) of the IAPS puts it, China's development has altered its own security environment as well as the environment of other countries. In order to shape a country's ideal security environment, says Tang, it is necessary to influence other states' security policies (p. 47). Professor Tang's concern of external perceptions of an ascendant China is shared by many other PRC analysts who believe that it is important to present a positive image of China to the outside world.

However, the debate among Chinese writers is not just about how to present a better image to the world. Behind the rhetoric of 'peaceful rise' is a serious discourse on what path China should follow, how it should relate itself to the international community and what China's ultimate goal should be. To liberal scholars like Wang Yizhou (1999), China should seek to become a constructive and responsible power that actively contributes to the preservation of regional stability and security and the promotion of mutual trust and cooperation.

There is no question that all Chinese scholars support the national goal of achieving a great power status for China. But some of them, such as Tang Shiping (2001: 31), argue that status must not be separated from responsibilities. A related question is whether China should integrate itself into the US-dominated economic and political system or challenge the existing system. This has led to much debate among Chinese international relations specialists. Tang is of the view that China's integration into the current international system and its attempts to shape it are not mutually exclusive.

In the past 20 years, Tang asserts, the Chinese people have benefited enormously from China's integration into the international system. Any attempts to sever this process of integration would meet with serious challenges. In any case, he argues, China is not in a position to establish a different international political and economic system, either in terms of its capabilities or external constraints. More importantly, China relies more on other countries for its economic development than they do on China. Thus, Tang Shiping (2001: 31–32) concludes that China's ability to influence the international system, let alone establish its own, is very limited.

Other scholars are more optimistic about China's ability to exert some influence on the current international system. Xu Kaiyi (2004: 57) argues that by actively participating in a variety of international mechanisms, China would gradually be able to shape their rules and norms. Indeed, Jiang Xiyuan (2005: 9–10) of the Shanghai Institute of International Studies argues that China should be more proactive in integrating into the existing international system with a view to reforming it. He proposes that China must not be constrained by the thinking of offensive realism. Instead, it should adopt a constructivist approach to its relations with the international community, that is, seek to develop intersubjective understanding among members of the community.

He even suggests that China should reconsider its previous foreign policy thinking and related concepts, strategies and policies, including the 'Five Principles of Peaceful Co-existence'. He argues that if China were to be integrated into the current system, and to seek to reform it and even become a leading member of the system in future, it must go beyond the concept of 'peaceful co-existence'. He goes on to argue that China must be prepared to break away from the conceptual boundaries of realism, adopting a new strategic thinking in guiding its interactions with the dominant powers in the international system. This is an extremely bold suggestion, given that the Five Principles of Peaceful Co-existence have long been regarded as the guiding principles for Chinese foreign policy. Clearly, an increasing number of PRC scholars are critical of the realist theory that has dominated China's foreign policy discourse for a long time.

Indeed, the rise of China to a great power status poses a significant challenge to both China and the outside world. From the Western perspective, it is important to ensure that China will rise peacefully and that its ascendancy will not disrupt international stability. Chinese leaders and elites seem to have understood the concerns of the outside world. They are fully aware of the misgivings of the great powers in East Asia over the potential challenge to their interests by China. Thus, the Chinese have responded to the security strategies of the East Asian powers by accommodating the existing regional and global order, rather than attempting to overturn the Western-dominated system (Yang Wenjing 2004: 35). As Ruan Zongze (2004: 29), the CIIS Deputy Director, puts it, a rising China is not aiming to 'challenge or replace the world hegemonic power'. It simply wants to gain the status of a great power equal to that of other great powers. Ruan argues that China's rise is intimately linked to the process of globalization. Like other countries, China is seeking to adjust its development strategy in order to adapt to the changing challenge of globalization. As China has benefited from the existing international regimes and mechanisms, he goes on to say, it is willing to accept certain constraints on Chinese behaviour. This is because the behaviour of other great powers is also subject to similar constraints.

Ruan Zongze (2004: 32) maintains that the current international order is far from perfect, but he admits that China has benefited from it. For this reason, China will not seek to transform the existing order by radical means. Pan Zhongqi (2007) of Fudan University believes that China has changed from an opponent and critic of the world order to a participant and supporter of the current system. In this sense, China is no longer a revisionist power. Rather, says Professor Pan, it should be regarded as a quasi status quo power. Meanwhile, Ruan thinks that China may use its influence to promote constructive reform of the international system. This view is shared by Men Honghua (2004), a professor at the CCP's Central Party School, who argues that as a rising power China should make an active and positive contribution to the gradual transformation of the international order.

What Chinese scholars suggest is that China should not respond to the security challenge of the US and Japan in an aggressive way. Instead, they advocate great power diplomacy on the one hand and closer cooperation with neighbouring countries on the other. The aim is to convince the outside world that the rise of China represents the arrival of a new type of great power interested in pursuing peace and development rather than expansion and confrontation. This is why many of them are critical of offensive realism for focusing heavily on the impact of the international structure on state behaviour. They argue that the strategic intentions of great powers should be taken more seriously by politicians and security analysts.

Of course it is difficult to be entirely sure about the intentions of any country. This explains the concern of China's neighbours over its future behaviour. Some PRC scholars emphasize the link between the rise of China and that of Asia. If the rise of China cannot be accepted by its neighbouring countries, they argue, it would be very difficult for this to be accepted by the wider international community. Thus, China must take steps to allay the fear of its neighbouring countries that a powerful China would seek to establish hegemony in East Asia. Tang Shiping (2001) uses China's participation in the ARF as an example showing that ASEAN states' trust of China has increased immensely, despite their apprehensions of the potential implications of China's rise. In the meantime, China should help other countries in its surrounding areas to develop and be prepared to accept the rise of other emerging powers in the region, such as India and Indonesia (Jiang Xiyuan 2005: 10–11). The key argument here is that China's rise should not be at the expense of its peripheral countries. Instead, China should actively promote regional integration in East Asia, focusing in particular on developing close economic and security cooperation with all its neighbours (Ruan Zongze 2004: 30–31).

To China, the most significant challenge is how to handle its relations with other major powers in East Asia, especially the US and Japan. For the liberal scholars, economic development is paramount compared to any other tasks. As one leading Chinese analyst puts it, China has no intention of challenging America's hegemony and its leading position in the international system, so long as it is willing to behave as a 'benign hegemon'. In any case, China will not be in a position to challenge US supremacy for a long time (Ruan Zongze 2004: 31).

At a Track-II dialogue held in Beijing in September 2005, Wang Jisi, Director of Peking University's Institute of International Relations, stated that China's rise would not clash with America's hegemony. In his view, China's re-emergence had never prevented the US from growing strong. He outlined four reasons for his assessment. First, China would not constitute a challenge to America's 'institutional hegemony'. Second, economically, China would not be able to challenge America's leading position. Third, on the issue of ideology, the PRC is in a defensive position. Finally, the growth of China's military capabilities could not be compared with Soviet military power in the Cold War era. He believed that, apart from Taiwan, there were few regional flashpoints that would bring America into a military confrontation with China. Professor Wang recognized the mutual suspicion between the two countries over each other's strategic intentions in the Asia-Pacific. China should, he said, make America aware that it can and should play a more significant role in the region. Meanwhile, China should accept America as a legitimate Asia-Pacific power. He proposed that the US and China should strengthen their cooperation at the global level, and that they should try to abandon the thinking of traditional great power politics when dealing with regional issues (Lu Ning 2005).

Wang Jisi's suggestions for responding to US unipolarity are representative of the views of the majority of liberal scholars in the PRC, who believe that it is not in China's national interest to challenge US pre-eminence. Instead, they tend to think that China should acknowledge America's position in the international system, but at the same time try to secure a propitious environment for China to achieve its great power status. They appreciate that China has benefited immensely from the capitalist-oriented global economy, and that the success of its modernization programme depends heavily on a stable and peaceful international environment.

Some Chinese scholars, such as Tang Shiping (2001) of the IAPS, suggest that China should find a way of 'strategic compromise' (*zhanlue tuoxie*) with the US in order to avoid a Sino-American confrontation. He believes that China is essentially a continental power and that it is unrealistic to compete with America for maritime supremacy. He points out that China does not have control over any island in the entire Pacific Ocean that could be used as a naval base. On the other hand, the US has access to Japan, the Philippines and possibly Singapore and Vietnam, even if it were to lose its domination over Taiwan and the Korean Peninsula. America also has military ties with Australia and New Zealand and is in control of other islands like Guam (see Map 1 and Map 2). Thus, America's maritime domination in the Pacific would seriously constrain any actions of the Chinese navy. Under the circumstances, Tang argues, it would be rather futile for China to try to extend its maritime power, as this would be interpreted by America as a direct challenge to its position. It would also make other Asian countries feel uncomfortable about China's ambitions. They would therefore be more likely to ally with a distant power (the US) against what they perceive to be a threatening neighbour (China). Tang utilizes Stephen Walt's (1987) balance of threat theory to substantiate his argument.

Professor Tang further argues that China should reach some sort of agreement with America over their respective spheres of influence. He asserts that the concept of sphere of influence (*shili fanwei*) has no direct link with that of 'hegemonism'. Historically, it is perfectly acceptable for great powers to have their spheres of influence. For a rising China, says Tang, the question is how to define its own sphere of influence, respect other great powers' spheres of influence and establish 'compromise mechanisms' to prevent and resolve conflict in areas where China's interests may clash with those of other powers. He contends that it is no longer possible for China to regain its previous spheres of influence that were lost during the 'century of shame and humiliation'. He warns that it is not easy for many Chinese people to accept the fact that it is unfeasible for China to regain its glorious past, especially when the country is growing rapidly and nationalistic sentiment is rising. For this reason, Tang Shiping (2001: 34) points out that it would be a huge task for Chinese leaders to make an appropriate strategic choice, while persuading their people to recognize the changing reality.

To Tang, this realistic approach to the pursuit of great power status is important because it would send a clear signal to China's peripheral countries that it has no expansionist intent. Rather, China is seeking to reach some kind of strategic understanding with other great powers to maintain global and regional stability.

In his view, apart from the Taiwan issue, over which China may find it difficult to reach a strategic understanding with America and potentially Japan, it is perfectly possible to avoid conflict with all great powers in the region, including Russia, Japan and India, through the establishment of compromising mechanisms. Tang warns that the real test on whether Beijing and Washington can reach a meaningful strategic compromise is how they handle the Taiwan question. If America is still reluctant to accept the emergence of 'a united, open, democratic and powerful China' after China's recognition of America's maritime dominance in the Pacific, a Sino-US military confrontation would seem inevitable. He points out that most American elites do not accept the 'reunification' of the PRC and Taiwan as China's legitimate interest. They tend to interpret China's desire to reunify with Taiwan as a challenge to America's position in the Asia-Pacific. What they fail to understand, Tang believes, is that the Chinese government will be under greater pressure from its population to take over Taiwan as China becomes more democratized (Tang Shiping 2001: 34–35).

So what type of great power status should China aim to achieve? Tang's answer to this is that China should seek to become a global economic power, play a prominent role in regional security affairs and exert political influence on global issues. He emphasizes that China should not aspire to become a global military power, which would involve too many responsibilities and risks that it would not be able to undertake. He believes that China should have 'a global political voice', but should not become a 'global political power'. China's global influence, he argues, should derive from its participation in a variety of international organizations, its strategic partnerships with countries in different parts of the world and its relations with other developing countries. His conclusion is that China should not become a maritime power, but should aim to become a regional military power. This would enable China to safeguard its security interests, as well as maintaining peace and stability in the Asia-Pacific through bilateral and multilateral security cooperation (Tang Shiping 2001: 35).

Tang's views have generated heated debate among Chinese scholars as to whether China should develop itself as a continental power or a maritime power. Professor Ye Zicheng (2007a, 2007b) agrees with Tang that it is not in China's interest to compete with the US for maritime supremacy. Instead, he argues that China should continue to develop its power within what he calls a 'continental space' (*ludi kongjian*). Professor Liu Zhongmin (2007) agrees that China's geopolitical environment makes it impossible for the country to develop its sea power globally and contest US maritime hegemony. This is not to say, he asserts, that China should not maintain a strong naval capability, but the development of China's sea power should be based on the need of self-defence rather than the desire to seek hegemony. For example, Liu points out that while China should have sufficient naval forces to defend its sovereignty over Taiwan, the Diaoyu and the South China Sea islands, it must avoid any potential maritime conflict with surrounding countries. Otherwise, China's economic development and peaceful image as a responsible power could be jeopardized. In any case, America's maritime presence in the Asia-Pacific is a reality that cannot be altered. To some extent, says Liu,

American presence in the Asia-Pacific plays a positive role in maintaining regional balance of power and freedom of navigation in the Pacific Ocean.

However, other scholars, such as Ni Lexiong (2007), profoundly disagree with the views of Ye and Liu. He contends that China has no option but to become a maritime power. This is because China's trade and economic activities depend heavily on external resources. Zhu Fenglan (2006) points out that 90 per cent of China's imported oil passes through the Strait of Malacca, which is, in effect, the lifeline of the country. If this strategic sea lane were to be controlled by the US and Japan, China's economic development and national security would be under serious threat. Without the naval power to dominate the water adjacent to China, Ni Lexiong (2007) concurs, the future of the country would be in jeopardy. According to Ni, the experiences of the two world wars show categorically that maritime states have a distinct advantage over continental states in terms of their ability to mobilize the necessary resources in times of war. China does not wish to fight a war, he says, but it may be forced to confront its enemies at sea. Thus, Ni concludes that China would suffer a miserable defeat, as Germany did, if it were to be afraid of developing its sea power. In the words of Zhang Wenmu (2003: 86), 'without a powerful navy China will certainly not have a great future'.

Another area of fervent debate among Chinese scholars and analysts is how to respond to a Japan that has become more confident in defending and expanding its regional security interests and achieving the status of an 'ordinary nation'. To most PRC scholars, a major consideration in Japan's security strategy is to prevent China from threatening its security interests and challenging its position in East Asia. Japan is also believed to have been collaborating with Washington to thwart China's attempts to fulfil its great power aspirations.

In 2002 Ma Licheng (2002: 44, 47), a commentator of *Renmin ribao* (*People's Daily*), published a controversial article on Sino-Japanese relations in the influential journal *Zhanlue yu guanli* (*Strategy and Management*).[3] In this article, he strongly criticized nationalistic writings on Japan and the irrational behaviour of some Chinese citizens, arguing that China needed to have 'new thinking' (*xinsiwei*) towards Japan. He pointed out that successive Japanese Prime Ministers had already apologized for Japan's wartime behaviour, and that China should not endlessly wrangle over the issue of apologies. Instead, China should forgive Japan for its past actions, focus on the common interests of the two countries and cooperate with each other to build a stable and prosperous Asia.

Ma Licheng (2002: 44–46) was particularly critical of irrational anti-Japanese sentiment in China which, in his view, was detrimental to Chinese interests. This sort of nationalistic emotion was said to have been fuelled by anti-Japanese reports and publications produced by some irresponsible media organizations. He contended that historically it was impossible to prevent a defeated country from regaining its status of a normal nation. China should therefore be prepared to accept a Japan that would sooner or later become a major political and military power. There was a difference, said Ma, between the development of Japan's military capabilities and the revival of Japanese militarism. This argument is similar to the point that Professor Glenn Hook (1996: 6) made regarding the distinction between 'militarism' and 'militarization' in Japan. According to Ma Licheng, China needed to learn from the experience of European countries which, having fought bloody wars with each other for years, were now able to achieve successful regional integration with a common currency.

The publication of Ma's article immediately stimulated intense debate among Chinese intellectuals and scholars on how to handle the PRC's relations with Japan. Central to this debate was the question of how to respond to Japan's global and regional security strategy as China rises to a great power status. There is no doubt that many Chinese analysts are wary of Tokyo's strategic intentions and its China policy in particular. Is it possible to maintain a stable and cooperative relationship with Japan while China is developing its great power capabilities? Should Japan be treated as a partner or as a long-term rival? How is China's Japan strategy related to its broader aim of 'peaceful rise'?

In support of Ma Licheng's arguments, Professor Shi Yinhong (2003a: 71–72) of Renmin University published an article in the same journal, where he proposed a 'diplomatic revolution' (*waijiao geming*) in Sino-Japanese relations. He argued that China and Japan should become closer to each other, thus alleviating their 'security dilemma'. His view was based on the argument that China could not afford to face a hostile Japan while dealing with hostility from America, Taiwan and possibly India. In developing a closer relationship with Tokyo, said Professor Shi, China would be able to concentrate on handling the pressure and potential threat from America and preventing Taiwan from gaining independence. Shi concluded that a stable relationship with Japan would help improve China's peripheral security environment.

He believed that Japan might also be interested in having a closer relationship with China. This was due to Japan's geographical proximity to China and the resultant fear of a hostile neighbouring power. Economically, China is said to have provided Japan with huge investment and trade opportunities. Thus, a hostile relationship with a China whose economic influence was rising rapidly would not be in Japan's national interest. In addition, Shi pointed out that there was considerable concern in Japan regarding certain aspects of America's assertive China policy. Finally, establishing closer relations with China would help Japan 'return' to Asia.

Specifically, Shi Yinhong (2003a: 73–74) recommended the adoption of five main strategies in relation to his 'diplomatic revolution'. First, China should not allow historical issues to undermine its overall security strategy. Second, Chinese leaders should express their gratitude to Japan for the enormous amount of economic assistance given to China since the beginning of the reform era. Third, China should not repeatedly express its concern over the possibility of a Japanese remilitarization. Fourth, Japan should be welcomed as a great power to participate in multilateral meetings dealing with regional economic, political and security issues. Fifth, on the issue of reforming the UNSC, China should treat Japan in the same way as it would treat other countries. In due course, China might even consider supporting Japan's membership of the Security Council.

Not surprisingly, the articles by Ma Licheng and Shi Yinhong generated a huge response from other scholars. For example, Feng Zhaokui (2003b, 2003c, 2003d, 2004), a well-respected specialist at CASS's Institute of Japanese Studies, published four lengthy articles on the 'new thinking' in Sino-Japanese relations, exploring the issues raised in Ma and Shi's articles. The journal *Zhanlue yu guanli* (*Strategy and Management*) published a special issue on Sino-Japanese relations. The CASS journal *Shijie jingji yu zhengzhi* (*World Economy and Politics*) also organized a special seminar on China's strategic thinking towards Japan. A number of prominent scholars and commentators were invited to participate in the seminar, including the journal's editor Wang Yizhou (2003), Shi Yinhong (2003b), Feng Zhaokui (2003a), Pang Zhongying (2003), Ling Xingguang (2003), Zhang Tuosheng (2003) and Yang Yanyi (2003).

Many scholars supported the argument of Ma and Shi that China should consider its political and security relations with Japan within its overall security strategy. They agreed that a confrontational relationship with Japan would undermine China's security environment and its efforts to pursue a great power status. Some scholars argue that China should not apply a double standard in judging Japan. As Zhou Guiyin (2003: 20) put it:

> If we believe that a rising China is entitled to become an important member of the international system, then we have no reasons to object to Japan's attempts to gain a similar status given that it is playing an increasingly important role in the international system.

Professor Zhang Wang (2003: 26–27) questioned the widely accepted assumption that Japan's participation in UN peacekeeping and other activities indicated the revival of Japanese militarism. Such security discourse, he warned, could turn into a self-fulfilling prophecy. Similarly, Professor Xue Li (2003: 33) of Qinghua University suggested that the Chinese should try to transcend the historical issue in Sino-Japanese relations. It might be wise, he said, to shelve historical issues (e.g. formal apologies, visits to the Yasukuni Shrine, etc.) and not to overreact to the textbook issue, discussion on the revision of the Japanese constitution, the dispatch of Japanese SDF to overseas countries and Japan's desire to become an 'ordinary nation'.

While accepting the strategy proposed by Ma and Shi, some scholars took issue with them on several arguments. For example, they contended that the responsibilities for resolving historical issues rested with Japan rather than China, because of repeated attempts by some Japanese politicians to distort history. They questioned the sincerity of the apologies by certain Japanese Prime Ministers, including Koizumi. It was also argued that trying to become closer to Japan in order to deal with potential threats from America was wishful thinking, given Tokyo's alliance relations with America (Ling Xingguang 2003: 19–20). Still others believed that it was right to ask Japan for a promise not to pursue a policy of remilitarization in future, in spite of the fact that it would be difficult for Japan to return to militarism (Zhang Tuosheng 2003: 25).

One of the most critical articles is probably that by Lin Zhibo (2004), a commentator of *Renmin ribao*, who believed that the 'new thinking' in China's Japan policy as advocated by Ma and Shi was unhelpful and even 'harmful'. He argued that it was misguided to suggest that China should be responsible for poor Sino-Japanese relations, and that the country that needed 'new thinking' was Japan rather than China. In Lin's view, Japan was responsible for causing concerns in China and tensions in Sino-Japanese relations. He cited Japan's changing defence policy, enhanced alliance relations with America, participation in the TMD system, proposals to amend its pacifist constitution, and the dispatch of the SDF to Iraq as indications of Japan's non-peaceful intentions. He contended that extreme nationalism as suggested by Ma and Shi did not exist in China.

Although the majority of scholars are in favour of responding to the security challenges of America and Japan in a measured way, some analysts seem to have advocated the adoption of a tougher stance. They are critical of the liberal view that economic development and globalization would assist China to become a powerful nation in the world. Professor Zhang Wenmu (2004) of CICIR argues that all the defeated powers in history were once rich countries. In his view, China's prosperity cannot guarantee its survival. It is important to have strong military capabilities to protect China's sovereignty and security interests. He warns that the Chinese should be under no illusion that the West would not be able to destroy China. He believes that the PRC is facing a hostile security environment in which America does not wish to see a powerful China. Zhang rejects the liberal argument that economic interdependence would lead to peace. He also criticizes other Chinese scholars for being too obsessed with Western theories in their analysis of security issues, rejecting such concepts of 'security dilemma', 'global governance' and so on.

A similar argument is put forward by Yang Fan (2004), who maintains that the bottom line of China's national security is the preservation of its national sovereignty and territorial integrity. He is particularly sceptical of the liberal argument that we are living in a global village where countries are more interested in trading than fighting with each other. China must not, in his view, try to integrate into the 'international community' at the expense of its national interest. He rejects the view that China has two decades of opportunity for peaceful development due to America's preoccupation with its anti-terrorist campaign. To Professor Yang, China must not assume that other countries do not have aggressive intent. It would be far more prudent to base its defence policy on 'imagined enemies'. More specifically, he asserts, China must not compromise on the Taiwan issue. It should take a tougher stance against Japan and, if necessary, be prepared to confront America. This type of uncompromising policy, according to Yang, would discourage China's neighbouring countries from following America, which would in turn make it difficult for Washington to contain China. He emphasizes the need to strengthen China's military power and to increase its defence spending in particular.

These critical comments may well be a reflection of the growing concern within the Chinese policy circles about the adoption of the slogan of 'peaceful rise' in expounding China's foreign policy strategy. Some critics argue that the word 'rise' (*jueqi*) has negative connotations and appears to be too threatening to China's neigbours. Others assert that China's emergence as a great power may actually be constrained by the word 'peaceful' (*heping*), and that the notion of 'peaceful' rise has failed to deter the independence forces in Taiwan. More importantly, some elites, especially MFA officials and PLA officers, worry that the cause of Chinese military modernization could be jeopardized by the emphasis on China's 'peaceful' path to ascendancy (Glaser and Medeiros 2007: 302–306). Indeed, PRC leaders began to replace the phrase 'peaceful rise' with 'peaceful development' (*heping fazhan*) in their official speeches and statements from April 2004.

Nevertheless, Chinese leaders have not banned academic research and public discussion on 'peaceful rise', and there is no sign of any significant change in China's foreign policy direction (Glaser and Medeiros 2007: 300, 301). Despite fewer references to the term in Chinese publications, scholars and think-tank specialists continue to engage in the peaceful rise discourse. They see no difference between peaceful rise and peaceful development in terms of their substance. Some scholars have openly defended the concept of peaceful rise, arguing that it should be considered China's strategic choice. Professor Liu Jianfei (2006), for example, asserts that China's path to ascendancy is constrained by forces of globalization, and that 'non-peaceful rise' is simply not a viable option.

Meanwhile, a growing number of Chinese scholars have suggested that China should focus more on 'soft power' in developing its strategy of 'peaceful rise'. They argue that Chinese philosophical and cultural heritage offers rich resources for the development of China's soft power. Specifically, the Chinese culture of 'harmony' (*hexie*) and the Confucius concept of 'benevolence' (*renyi*) are believed to be directly relevant to the cause of promoting a more stable and peaceful world (Ruan Zongze 2004: 32; Liu Aming 2005: 61–63; Li Jie 2005).

Indeed, Men Honghua (2007a, 2007b), a professor at the CCP's Central Party School, maintains that China's culture should be regarded as the first core element of its soft power. He points out that China has already had extensive cultural influence in Asia and other parts of the world through educational and cultural exchanges and other activities, and that it should therefore continue to strengthen its cultural attraction. The second core element is said to be related to conceptual innovation. As a rising power, Men argues, China needs to have idealistic aspirations and the ability to produce innovative ideas and achieve conceptual breakthrough. Another major element is China's development model which has emerged from its unique experience but has positive features for other countries to replicate. The fourth element, says Men, should be linked to the level of China's participation in international regimes. Finally, China's international image is considered a reflection of its soft power. He notes that external perceptions of China have improved substantially, but more can be done to improve the country's image.

Guo Shuyong (2007) concurs that China's soft power should be developed in relation to its international activity. Specifically, Guo argues that China should practise what he calls 'new internationalism' (*xin guoji zhuyi*) in foreign policy in order to strengthen its soft power. China can only rise to a great power status in a more favourable international environment, says Professor Guo, if its soft power is internationalized and acknowledged by the international community. By this, he means that China must fully integrate itself into multilateral institutions and international regimes. Moreover, Guo believes that China needs to make a serious effort to internalize world political culture as a way of developing its soft power. He shares the view expressed by Men Honghua and other Chinese scholars that China should strive to construct a positive great power image through different channels and at different levels.

Men Honghua (2007a) refers to the idea of building a 'harmonious world' (*hexie shijie*) as an example of conceptual innovation. This concept was first mentioned by Hu Jintao in Jakarta in April 2005 and elaborated upon at a UN speech in September of the same year. The concept of 'harmonious world' has effectively become a guiding principle of China's foreign policy since August 2006 (Wang Yi and Zhang Linhong 2007). It has appeared regularly in official speeches and statements, as well as the state media. This can be seen as an extension of the idea, advocated by the Chinese leadership over the past few years, of building a 'harmonious society' (*hexie shehui*) in China.

Essentially, the concept of a 'harmonious world' is based on the Confucius philosophy of *he er bu tong* (harmonious but dissimilar), which is believed to be deeply rooted in Chinese culture. This concept has been presented by PRC elites as a Chinese perspective on international relations. The Chinese believe that while there are dissimilarities between different countries and regions, it is possible to develop harmonious relationships among them. At the conceptual level, this emphasizes equality and justice, respect for independence, diversity and legality and promotion of confidence, trust and tolerance. At the operational level, each country's sovereignty, territorial integrity, domestic system and development path should be respected so that a 'harmonious world' can be constructed. Any difference or disagreement among states or other actors should be resolved via dialogue and peaceful negotiation. The concept of a 'harmonious world', Chinese scholars argue, represents a sophisticated combination of idealism and realism in international relations (Xu Jian 2007; Yu Xintian 2007).

Despite its philosophical origins and cultural underpinnings, the idea of constructing a 'harmonious world' appears to be a reformulation of China's 'Five Principles of Peaceful Co-existence' and its 'New Security Concept'. Many Chinese scholars have referred to the term 'harmonious world' in their writings, but so far little substantive work has been produced. If the concept of 'harmonious world' were to have a lasting impact as an intellectual discourse on international relations, more rigorous research would have to be conducted. Professor Wang Yizhou (2007), an eminent Chinese international relations specialist, admits that, with the exception of a small number of China scholars, few people are aware of the concept outside China. He notes that 'harmonious world' is probably seen by many as a utopian idea in a world driven by power politics. However, he cautions that whether the idea is embraced by the wider world would ultimately depend on China's international behaviour and diplomatic practice.

Theoretical analysis

The prime argument of this book is that China's perceptions of the major powers in East Asia should be analyzed in relation to its endeavour to construct a great power identity. Similarly, the response of Chinese scholars and analysts to the security challenge of the East Asian powers is linked to a process of identity formation. Thus, the Chinese response to the security strategies of the US, Japan and Russia must be understood in the broader context of China's assessment of the international environment, the wider implications of other great powers' global and regional strategy and China's role within the changing structure of the international system.

The analysis by Chinese scholars of the changing international structure clearly reflects the perspective of structural realism (Waltz 1979). The complexity of the post-Cold War world is perceived in the context of the rivalry among a number of great powers. This appears to be the lens through which some Chinese analysts view the radical change of a new era. Their rejection of unipolarity and obsession with multipolarity are directly related to China's position in the structure of the international system. From the neorealist standpoint, international relations are largely driven by the balance of power among the major powers. How they relate to each other will thus have a direct impact on the stability and security of the world. There is little doubt that Chinese specialists are influenced by this perspective in their analysis of the global security environment.

In the view of most PRC scholars, a prolonged period of unipolarity would strengthen America's superiority over other major powers and make it more difficult for China to achieve an equal relationship with the US in the international hierarchy. This is considered an undesirable situation, where China could be permanently condemned to the status of a second-ranking power. From the perspective of offensive realists, all countries will maximize their power at the expense of others (Mearsheimer 2001). This is precisely what worries many Chinese scholars. Even for those Chinese scholars who subscribe to defensive realism (Jervis 1978), America's unbalanced power would pose a potential threat to Chinese security interests, especially in the Asia-Pacific. As Stephen Walt (2005: 61) puts it: 'In a world of independent states, the strongest one is always a potential threat to the rest, if only because they cannot be entirely sure what it is going to do with the power at its command.' This concern is echoed by the work of Professor Yan Xuetong (2000), a realist scholar at Qinghua University.

But China's preference of multipolarity could also be explained by constructivist theory, in that China feels that its desire to shake off the shadow of the 'century of shame and humiliation' and to construct a great power identity is threatened by America's desire to perpetuate the 'unipolar moment'. In a world of multipolarity, PRC leaders and policy elites hope that China may occupy a space by which a distinct identity for their country could be constructed. This is reflective of the Chinese perception that China is a country with a history of 5,000 years of civilization and that it is entitled to establish a unique position in the contemporary world. In this sense, the Chinese conception of multipolarity is a product of social construction (Wendt 1992, 1995). Nevertheless, most Chinese scholars accept the current structure of what they call *yichao duoqiang* (one superpower and several great powers) and acknowledge that multipolarity is not within reach.

It can be argued that China's pursuit of great power diplomacy reflects the realist thinking of PRC leaders and analysts. The emphasis on developing cooperative relationships with other great powers in China's 'partnership strategy' is evidently linked to its promotion of multipolarity. Although Chinese leaders claim that its partnership diplomacy is not designed to target at any specific countries, it is clearly a response to the challenge of unipolarity. It may be seen as a 'soft balancing' measure, aiming to 'delay, frustrate, and undermine aggressive unilateral U.S. military policies' (Pape 2005: 10), as confronting America's preponderance directly is simply too costly for China. Indeed, some realist scholars argue that second-tier major powers such as China, Russia, France and Germany, have all engaged in soft balancing against the United States in the past few years (Pape 2005; Paul 2005).

But China's partnership strategy could also be explained by neoliberalism, in that Beijing is willing to extend its 'partnerships' beyond the major powers to include many other states in both the developed and developing countries. More interestingly, China has established partnerships with regional actors, such as the EU and ASEAN, with a strong emphasis on economic and trade interaction. This may reflect their appreciation that cooperation is possible under anarchy (Grieco 1995; Jervis 1978).

In addition, the motives behind the establishment of various partnerships are reflective of China's desire to construct a great power identity. As Professor Ye Zicheng (2000) argues, it is important for China to abandon its 'victim mentality' and interact with the outside world with confidence and a positive attitude. From the constructivist perspective, Chinese scholars' great power mentality is historically rooted and socially constructed (Kaplowitz 1990: 51–52; Mercer 1995: 241). Indeed, the influence of both realism and constructivism in the grand strategy suggested by some PRC scholars is apparent. As advocated by Tang Shiping (2000), Chinese leaders should adopt a realpolitik approach (Morgenthau 1978) to create an ideal security environment for China. The suggestions that China needs to retain its position as a continental power, maintain pragmatic relations with America and Japan, ensure its interests are not adversely affected by a united Korea and hostile South East Asian policies and to secure energy supplies from Central Asia and the Middle East are indicative of his theoretical position. In the meantime, Professor Tang's analysis of the status of Taiwan seems consistent with the social construction embedded in Chinese society that Taiwan is an integral and inseparable part of mainland China. 'A China without Taiwan', as Tang Shiping (2000: 43) puts it, 'would no longer be a China'. This illustrates the constructivist view that a state's national security interests are shaped by its identity (Jepperson, Wendt and Katzenstein 1996: 60).

It seems that many Chinese scholars are attracted to a broader interpretation of the concept of security and that they are familiar with Western debates on the (re) conceptualization of security since the end of the Cold War (Buzan, Weaver and De Wilde 1998). However, China's 'new security concept' is essentially state-centric, as the primary unit of analysis within the concept remains the nation-state. Little reference is made to concepts such as societal security and human security (Burgess and Taylor 2004) in Chinese security discourse. In this sense, the 'new security concept' is a neorealist concept of security rather than a new departure from existing paradigms.

Similarly, China's changing attitudes towards multilateral security cooperation in East Asia could be explained by realist considerations. Many PRC scholars believe that it would only be possible for China to play a prominent role in multilateral security forums if it was closely involved in the process. In their view, China's participation in multilateral security mechanisms would make it more difficult for America to isolate China. The PRC's active involvement in the six-party talks is a reflection of its concerns over the strategic implications of the North Korean nuclear crisis for China (see the analysis in Li 2003b). The leading role played by China in the creation and development of the SCO could also be seen as an attempt to counterbalance the growing influence of America in Central Asia. This is why China's increasing activities in multilateral security forums is supported by most Chinese realist scholars. All this provides concrete evidence for soft balancing through diplomatic channels against the United States (Layne 2006b: Ch. 3), although it may be dismissed by some scholars as normal diplomatic bargaining or response to regional security challenge (Brooks and Wohlforth 2005; Lieber and Alexander 2005).

From the liberal perspective, however, China's active participation in multilateral security forums is a positive development in that it helps create a political climate conducive to dialogue and cooperation in East Asia. This would contribute to the regularization and institutionalization of multilateral cooperation that is already being pursued with enthusiasm and rigour in the area of economic and trade interactions. Whether, and to what extent, China will be committed to multilateral security cooperation would require further empirical studies. Alastair Iain Johnston and Paul Evans (1999), Gerald Chan (2004a, 2004b, 2005), Marc Lanteigne (2005) and Guogang Wu (2007), among others, have produced some significant work in this area but more research remains to be done.

The liberal analysis is certainly accepted by constructivists, who believe that through constant and regular interactions between China and other East Asian countries a culture of cooperation can be developed. Over time, a collective identity that emphasizes harmony and cooperation, rather than rivalry and conflict, could be constructed in Asia. Collective identity is a key concept in constructivist theory, which draws on social identity theory (Abrams and Hogg 1990). The formation of a collective identity goes beyond the construction of role identities to amalgamate self and other. Alexander Wendt (1999: 225–28) distinguishes 'type' identity, which refers to an identity based on shared characteristics, from 'role' identity that has to be enacted within the context of a social structure. In his view, collective identity is 'a distinct combination of role and type identities', which is capable of inducing actors 'to define the welfare of the Other as part of that of the Self' (Wendt: 1999: 227). Wendt calls these actors 'altruistic actors'. If an actor is able to internalize group culture through imitation and social learning, he argues, it would give the actor an interest in preserving the culture. Thus, collective identity formation requires a redefinition of the boundary of self and other to constitute a 'common in-group identity' (Wendt 1999: 337–38).

An increasing number of PRC scholars are engaged in research on and discussion of ideas relating to formation of some sort of collective identity in East Asia. If their ideas were to be accepted by the Chinese government, they could have a significant impact on China's relations with other states in the region, including the major powers. It could even transform the entire East Asian security environment. This is by no means an easy task, given the mutual suspicion between China and some of its neighbours and the diversity of political systems in the region.

Wendt acknowledges that there will always be resistance to formation of collective identity, as individuals and groups fear that they may lose their distinctive identities and the fulfillment of their needs may be threatened. But he argues that '[T]he fact that states will resist collective identity formation does not mean that it can never be created' (Wendt 1999: 364). Perhaps the experience of ASEAN shows that it is not impossible for countries with differing types of political systems and levels of economic development to develop intersubjective knowledge and forge a common identity. Wendt (1999: 364) maintains that the formation of collective identity is compatible with the notion of anarchy in that states may still retain their individuality, but they can make 'the *terms* of their individuality more collective'.

China may be able to form a common identity with other East Asian countries in future. However, can it forge a collective identity with other members of the international community? Jonathan Mercer (1995) has questioned the possibility of creating what he calls an 'other-help' international system. To him, 'self-help' is 'a consequence of intergroup relations in anarchy'. Strong identification with an in-group, Mercer (1995: 251) contends, will only generate more discrimination against out-groups. Based on social identity theory, he argues that self-interested states cannot escape from the self-help system, because categorization and differentiation will inexorably lead to competition. However, Wendt (1999: 241–43) believes that Mercer has drawn the wrong conclusion from social identity theory, arguing that human beings are perfectly capable of overcoming their biological inclination to become social animals, which is essential to the formation of societies. In his view, states can also learn to identify themselves with each other. This identification may be driven initially by self-interested motives, he argues, but over time states can be internalized into accepting others as part of the self. Thus, the likelihood of forming a collective identity and establishing an 'other-help' system under anarchy should not be ruled out.

The discourse on collective identity formation among Chinese scholars will undoubtedly stimulate intellectual thinking on what sort of great power identity China should enact. If multilateralism is internalized as a constitutive part of Chinese identity, China would have a stronger interest in supporting it. Indeed, it has been argued that the success of Germany in reconstructing a new national identity since World War II is due to its '"self-entanglement" in regional and world institutions' (Jepperson, Wendt and Katzenstein 1996: 61). Similarly, if the idea of 'other-help' is incorporated into China's identity construction, it would be more likely for China to take into account the collective interest of international society when defining its national interest. As constructivists argue, change in a state's identity can cause considerable changes in its interests which shapes national security policy. On the other hand, states may develop interests during the process of forging or maintaining a specific identity (Jepperson, Wendt and Katzenstein 1996: 60–61). Therefore, if China were to be committed to the enactment of the identity of a responsible great power that is willing to engage in multilateral cooperation, its interests would change accordingly.

The discourse of China's 'peaceful rise' mirrors a long-standing and on-going debate among Chinese scholars on what path China should follow in its pursuit of a great power status, and how it should relate itself to the external world. The liberal scholars in China are active participants in this debate, arguing that China's future lies in its full integration into the international community. They have zealously advanced the argument that China should shake off its 'victim mentality' and demonstrate a willingness to play a constructive role in the international society. Liberal Chinese scholars argue that as an emerging power, China should not shy away from assuming responsibilities that are associated with its rising status. In many ways, the views of these scholars are influenced by the theory of neoliberal institutionalism, which postulates that international relations should not be seen as a zero-sum game, and that states should be more concerned about their 'absolute gains' rather than 'relative gains' (Keohane 1989, 1993).

From the constructivist perspective, the discourse of China's 'peaceful rise' can be seen as part of a process of identity construction. At the heart of the debate is what kind of great power status China seeks to achieve. The attempts of Chinese scholars to categorize China as a responsible power are significant in the sense that they identify their country not only as a rising power, but also as a responsible member of the international community. According to social identity theory, self-categorization 'brings self-perception and behaviour into line with the contextually relevant in-group prototype' (Hogg, Terry and White 1995: 260). 'Prototype' refers to the defining attributes of a specific social category or group, such as behaviours and attitudes. If China were to behave in a way that was consistent with the behaviour of other members of the 'in-group' (i.e. the international community), it would involve what the social identity theorists call 'depersonalization' (Turner *et al.*, 1987: 50; Stets and Burke, 2000: 231–32), which is a process whereby the identity of a unique individual is changed to that of a group member. This does not mean a loss of identity of the self. Rather, it is a way of integrating self-identity with group identity (Hogg, Terry and White 1995: 261).

A similar cognitive process in identity theory is known as 'self-verification', through which the self acts in a certain way in order to ensure that its behaviour corresponds with the 'identity standard' (Burke 1991). If China intends to construct an identity of a responsible power, it has to behave in accordance with the rules and norms of the international community. Recent research has indicated some positive signs in China's international behaviour. Whether this will continue depends on how serious China is in enacting its international role as a responsible great power.

For identity theorists, a role is 'a set of expectations prescribing behavior that is considered appropriate by others' (Hogg, Terry and White 1995: 257). When the meanings and expectations of such a role are incorporated into the self, its performance becomes relevant to identity. A person's status as a role member needs to be confirmed and validated through satisfactory role enactment. If one applies this theory to China's construction of its aspiring role, Chinese behaviour would have to fulfil the expectations of other members of the international community. Meanwhile, China would look at the responses of others, especially the great powers, to confirm its role identity. The 'reflected appraisals', or perceptions of how other actors evaluate China's performance, would influence its self-verification.

Self-verification of a role identity is important. Failure to achieve this may cause negative emotional responses such as depression and distress (Burke and Stets 1999: 349). In the context of international relations, lack of self-verification could result in low self-esteem, and possibly non-cooperative behaviour. On the other hand, positive evaluation of a person's performance would boost his or her self-esteem (Stryker 2002). It would also create a sense of self-efficacy in that the person feels that he or she has some sort of control over the environment (Gecas and Schwalbe 1983). In this sense, self-esteem and self-efficacy are important motivational processes in identity formation, as they help increase the confidence of the self and the feeling of its acceptance by significant others (Burke and Stets 1999). It can be argued that China has been involved in a process of self-verification since the late 1990s, looking for signs and signals of acceptance from the international community for its role identity as a responsible power. Certainly, the discourse of liberal and constructivist scholars in the PRC has contributed to this process.

In any society, including international society, 'commitment' by its members is essential to the preservation of order and stability. To some scholars, 'trust' is considered a crucial mechanism through which 'self-verification brings about commitment' (Burke and Stets 1999: 347).

What is trust? Trust refers to a belief that specific others hold both 'good will' and 'benign intent' towards the self. This can be developed through frequent interactions with specific others. Once trust is established, commitment will arise and the identity of the self is verified. This is arguably what China has been trying to achieve over the past decade. The PRC has been involved in a wide variety of international organizations and regimes, and interacted actively and regularly with many state and non-state actors in the world. However, it is premature to say that trust has been fully established between China and other countries, especially the major powers in East Asia.

According to identity theory, there is a direct link between the importance of a person's social relationships and the degree of his or her commitment to a particular role identity. Generally speaking, the level of identity salience is high if a person's social network is based heavily on the occupancy of a particular role, and if the network consists of a large number of persons (Stryker and Serpe: 1982). If one utilizes this theory to analyze China, it is not difficult to see a high level of identity salience, given that a constructive and beneficial relationship with the international community is predicated on China's occupancy of an identity of a responsible power. The fact that the majority of countries in the world are members of this 'social network' has also made China's identity more salient.

Similarly, there are strong incentives for China to show a high commitment to the role identity of a responsible rising power due to the significance of its 'social relationships' with the international community. Here, commitment is understood to be the 'degree to which the individual's relationships to particular others are dependent on being a given kind of person' (Stryker and Statham 1985: 345). In other words, China's relationships with the international community are dependent on assuming a specific kind of 'social identity' (Brewer 2001; Huddy 2001). If China is able to develop more 'trust' in significant others, particularly the major powers, through constant and sustained interactions, its 'commitment' should increase, leading to successful 'self-verification' of its identity as a responsible great power. It is evident that Chinese liberal and constructivist scholars are involved in this process of identity formation through their discourse and debate on the direction China should take in its rise to a great power status.

Many liberal scholars in the PRC seem to believe that China should become a great power that is able to play a prominent role in global and regional affairs, but at the same time command respect from other countries, particularly its neighbours. Such views are shaped by the perception that China was once powerful, yet admired and revered by its peripheral countries, which seems to be rooted in China's political thoughts on 'benevolent rule' (*wangdao*). This is not to say that China wishes to regain its past glory by conquering other countries in Asia. But the desire among PRC scholars and intellectuals to revive the Chinese nation is not in doubt. Their discussion on China's peaceful rise is often related to previous eras of power and prosperity, as well as 'shame and humiliation'. In this sense, the Chinese discourse on 'peaceful rise' is historically and socially constructed.

The idea that China should rise peacefully to a great power status is also supported by Chinese realist scholars. This is partly because they are well aware that China is not in a position to adopt a confrontational approach in response to the security challenge of other great powers. China cannot afford to have an unstable relationship with the US and Japan or face suspicion or hostility from its neighbouring countries. To Chinese realist scholars, the notion of 'peaceful rise' serves Chinese national interests, as it helps abate the possibility that other major powers and China's neighbouring countries would work together to forestall China's endeavours to pursue its great power aspirations. Thus, their views are a reflection of a realist assessment of the PRC's current security environment. This is consistent with the arguments of defensive realists who argue that cooperation among states is possible in a self-help system, albeit with some limitations (Glaser 1994/95; Krasner 1991).

To Chinese realists, 'peaceful rise' does not mean that China should not strengthen its military capabilities. On the contrary, they assert that China should accelerate its defence modernization during the current period of 'strategic opportunity'. Only with strong military power, they contend, can China's ascendancy be guaranteed (Yan Xuetong 2004a; Hu Angang and Liu Taoxiong 2004: 44–45).

This may be interpreted as a call for 'internal balancing' (Waltz 1979: 118; Mearsheimer 2001: 157) in the sense that China's sustained military development will deter any external powers from disrupting its 'peaceful rise' to a great power status. Similarly, realist scholars in the PRC support their leaders' efforts to enhance China's economic power, which could provide a solid foundation for 'hard balancing' against potentially hostile powers such as the US and Japan, should this become necessary in the future. This realist strategy of 'economic pre-balancing' could be seen as a response to the challenge of a unipolar era (Brawley 2004; Layne 2006b: Ch. 7).

Indeed, the appeal for China's closer integration with the international community is not without resistance. Liberal scholars have been criticized for being naïve in placing too much trust in the West, and compromising with America and Japan in particular. Their theories, approaches and findings have come under severe criticism. Specifically, liberal analysis of China's interdependent relationship with the outside world, and of the significance of globalization in Chinese economic development, is regarded as unrealistic at best. Critics of liberal scholars fervently argue that China should defend its national sovereignty and security interests more assertively, increase its military budget, and adopt a tougher policy towards America and Japan (Lin Zhibo 2004; Yang Fan 2004; Zhang Wenmu 2004). They are convinced that China can only rise peacefully if it is determined to augment its military power and stand up against other great powers. Under certain circumstances, it is argued, non-peaceful 'reunification' with Taiwan is necessary, and even desirable (Yan Xuetong 2004b). Many of their arguments seem to resonate with the views of offensive realists, who believe that all great powers are discontented with the status quo and that mutual security cannot be achieved in an anarchic world (Mearsheimer 2001).

Conclusion

This chapter has considered how Chinese scholars and analysts perceive the security challenge of the East Asian powers to China. The findings indicate that Chinese scholars tend to view the security strategies of the three major powers within a broader regional and global context. Clearly, the US, Japan and Russia are East Asian powers, but they all have global aspirations and interests. They are also apprehensive of the security implications of the rise of China. From the Chinese perspective, the three great powers are capable of frustrating China's desire to achieve a great power status through political, economic and military means. Their global influence and links with China's trade partners and neighbouring countries mean that they can potentially obstruct China's efforts to achieve its great power status. As such, the Chinese feel that they need to adopt a broader approach to face the challenges presented by the great powers.

The debate among Chinese scholars and international relations specialists on the nature of external security challenges has been examined in this chapter, including structural change in the international system and China's changing security environment. The Chinese do not expect to see a global war or an external invasion of

China in the near future. However, they are concerned about US 'hegemony' and a more assertive Japan, especially since 9/11 and the Iraq war. PRC security analysts are particularly worried about the possibility of regional conflict over Taiwan, North Korea and other issues. Nevertheless, they are reluctant to engage in a confrontation with other major powers. Many Chinese scholars believe that the best way of responding to the challenge of the US and Japan in a world of 'one power and several great powers' (*yichao duoqiang*) is to pursue 'great power diplomacy' and establish 'partnerships' with a variety of countries and regional actors.

At a regional level, most PRC scholars are in favour of the pursuit of what they call 'good neighbourly policy' and 'greater peripheral policy'. The majority of Chinese scholars and security experts believe that China's participation in multilateral security forums would help the PRC improve relations with its neighbouring countries. In their view, both official and unofficial security dialogue between China and other Asian countries would enhance their mutual confidence, thus making it easier for China to resist pressure from the great powers. It would also raise China's regional profile and its status as an ascendant power.

Another Chinese strategy of countering the challenge of the US and Japan is to promote the theory of 'peaceful rise' as a response to the 'China threat theory' allegedly created by America and Japan. The 'peaceful rise' discourse has generated lively debate among PRC scholars and policy analysts. As analyzed in this chapter, this should be seen as part of a process of identity formation, by which China's great power identity is constructed through debates among intellectuals and academics. Interestingly, this debate has been extended to Chinese society through the media and the Internet. A significant phenomenon of the rising China debate is the inclusion of the notion of 'soft power' (Nye 1990, 2004), with an emphasis on Chinese culture in China's foreign policy and the promotion of a harmonious world (*hexie shijie*) in international relations.

In the final section, China's responses to the security challenges of the three major powers are examined from the perspectives of various international relations theories. Structural realism appears to have an immense influence on Chinese discourse of unipolarity/multipolarity. However, the debate on the PRC's involvement in multilateral security cooperation and China's 'peaceful rise' does not seem to be dominated by any one single theoretical perspective. Chinese scholars of the realist, liberal and constructivist schools of thought have all actively contributed to the debate. These theoretical positions have been identified and analyzed in this chapter.

7 Conclusion

Chinese security discourse and its implications for the debate on the rise of China

In Chapter One, an extensive and critical review of the scholarly literature on the Western debate over the rise of China and on China's security perceptions of other great powers was provided. While the current literature offers some interesting insights into the security thinking of Chinese elites, there are few systematic studies of Chinese security perceptions on the United States, Japan and Russia within a broader analytical framework. Most of the extant literature is descriptive, policy-oriented and atheoretical. Little attempt has been made to apply the relevant International Relations theories to the analysis of Chinese security perceptions.

Drawing on the theoretical insights of realism, liberalism, constructivism and postmodernism, this book seeks to provide an in-depth analysis of China's security discourse on the US, Japan and Russia. The main objective of the study is to analyze the perceptions of Chinese policy elites on the global and Asia-Pacific security strategies of the three major powers in relation to the process of China's identity construction. Specifically, I raised a number of key questions that would be addressed by this book. First, how do PRC scholars and analysts perceive the three powers' global strategy and Asia-Pacific strategy in particular? Second, what is the changing political and intellectual environment within which they articulate their perceptions on the great powers? Third, how are the security perceptions of Chinese elites related to their conception of China's great power identity? Fourth, to what extent do they perceive the power, aspirations and security strategies of other East Asian powers as a threat to their desire to achieve a great power status for their country? Fifth, how do they respond to the security challenges emanating from the security strategies of the great powers?

In previous chapters, a vast amount of data which has not been systematically analyzed previously was examined. Specifically, I have looked at a wide range of articles from over a dozen Chinese-language journals relating to China's security perceptions and its perceptions of the US, Japan and Russia in particular. These articles were written by Chinese scholars and security experts whose views are likely to attract the attention of PRC leaders and government officials. Given their status and influence, their views are also taken seriously by the Chinese media. As such, these articles represent valuable data that is indispensable for Western scholars to gain a better insight into Chinese security discourse and China's perceptions of the strategic intentions and security strategies of the US, Japan and Russia.

While a small number of the articles consulted have been cited by other academics, they have not been analyzed, compared and contrasted with other relevant articles. In any case, the data collected for this study has not been utilized systematically by other scholars to analyze China's security perceptions of the three East Asian powers in relation to its global aspirations and efforts to construct a great power identity. In addition to documentary research, private conversations and formal and informal discussions over the past 15 years with Chinese scholars and international relations specialists from a range of research institutes, think-tanks and universities in China have been drawn upon. While specific arguments have not been attributed to them directly, I have benefited considerably from their knowledge and insights. It is hoped that this study has made a useful contribution to the existent literature on China's international relations and security studies.

In addition, this study seeks to make an original contribution to knowledge in the field in terms of providing analytical insights into Chinese security discourse. As discussed in Chapter One, the study of Chinese security perceptions is, by and large, lacking in theoretical analysis. This book has applied various IR theories, including realism, liberalism, constructivism and postmodernism, to the analysis of Chinese scholars and specialists' security perceptions of the US, Japan and Russia. Moreover, the way Chinese scholars employ various IR theories to examine the security strategies of the three major East Asian powers has been analyzed, wherever possible.

I have found that no one single theory can adequately explain Chinese security perceptions. While the realist emphasis on materialist interests is important, as the study has shown, institutional and ideational factors are equally, if not more, important in shaping the security perceptions of Chinese scholars. The book rejects the parsimonious approach that claims to be able to uncover the 'social reality' through the perspective of one single theory. Instead, it has adopted the approach of analytical eclecticism, combining the insights of various IR theories in examining Chinese security discourse. This has enabled us to provide a fuller explanation for Chinese scholars' perceptions of the three major powers.

Analytically, this study has gone beyond a mere description of the views of Chinese security specialists. It has analyzed Chinese perceptions of the East Asian powers in relation to China's efforts to construct a great power identity. The book has thus offered a unique perspective on Chinese perceptions of the global and Asia-Pacific security strategies of the US, Japan and Russia.

This book focuses on the analysis of Chinese security perceptions, and its findings are directly relevant to the scholarly and policy debate on the security implications of the growth of Chinese power. As mentioned previously, a profound understanding of the security perceptions of Chinese policy elites is essential to the assessment of the nature and repercussions of China's emergence as a great power in the international system. The study has examined China's security discourse of the East Asian powers in relation to its self-perception as an ascending power and its attempts to achieve a great power status. In this regard, the book can be seen as a contribution to the on-going debate on the rise of China.

In Chapter One, I put forward a hypothesis that China's perceptions of the major powers in East Asia are closely linked to its desire and efforts to construct a great power identity. As such, Chinese international relations specialists view the aspirations, power and security strategies of these countries primarily in terms of their implications for China's pursuit of a great power status in the 21st century. The principal findings of this study will now be summarized and confirmation on the validity of the hypothesis provided. The implications of these findings on Chinese security perceptions for the wider debate on the rise of China will also be considered with some policy recommendations.

Principal findings

The principal research findings of this book are presented in three main sections below.

China's security perceptions and its great power aspirations

In this section, findings are presented on Chinese scholars and security analysts' discourse of the US, Japan and Russia within the context of their perceptions of the changing international security environment since the end of the Cold War and China's role in the international system. This is followed by the presentation of the findings on the discussion and debate among Chinese policy elites on how to respond to their perceptions of the security challenges from the three major powers in East Asia.

The changing international security environment

The first key finding of this study is that the views of Chinese scholars and analysts on the post-Cold War international environment are ambivalent. On the one hand, they welcome the end of the Cold War which, for many years, was a major source of conflict and instability for China. On the other, they were apprehensive about the collapse of the bipolar system that led to the advent of a unipolar era. Most Chinese analysts agree that China's security environment has improved substantially, in that the PRC is not facing any immediate external threat to its national security and territorial integrity. There is no possibility of a global war, nor is there any prospect of a foreign invasion of China. This assessment is important for Chinese leaders because of their need to have a stable and peaceful environment to complete their modernization programme, which began in the late 1970s. To Chinese elites, successful modernization of China is essential in their aim of building a strong and powerful nation. In this sense, the post-Cold War international security environment is considered as favourable for China to fulfil its great power aspirations.

However, Chinese scholars have reassessed its security environment in the light of the events of 9/11 and the war on terrorism, and their evaluation is mixed. The research data indicates a change in their perceptions of China's overall environment. While there is no expectation of a dramatic rise in external threat to China, PRC analysts are concerned about the uncertainties engendered by the US-led war on terrorism. For example, they are worried about growing terrorist activities around the world and America's military reactions to this challenge, which may have negative repercussions on global political and economic stability. The US invasion of Iraq and the nuclear crisis on the Korean Peninsula are cases in point.

Nevertheless, Chinese scholars are aware of the opportunities arising from the post-9/11 situation for China to play a more prominent role as a great power. The PRC's active involvement in the six-party talks shows that this opportunity has not been missed. In short, the Chinese see both challenges and opportunities in the changing international security environment within which it seeks to construct a great power identity.

China's role in the post-Cold War international system

The data reveals a consensus among Chinese analysts that China is seeking to be a key player in the international system. This is linked to their self-perception as a rising power in the post-Cold War world. Indeed, Chinese scholars are reluctant to accept US unipolarity as it means that China is somewhat inferior to America in the hierarchy of the international structure. This explains why many PRC security experts wish to promote a multipolar system, within which China would occupy a significant position. What Chinese analysts aim to do is to ensure that China is seen to be an important strategic and economic player on the international stage. It is part of the process of the formation of a great power identity for China.

Since the late 1990s, however, most Chinese scholars have acknowledged that the process of multipolarization is a lengthy one, and that America will remain the most powerful country in the world for the foreseeable future. Given their unwillingness to accept the unipolar reality, Chinese specialists describe the current international structure as one of 'one superpower and several great powers'. This implies that America's dominance in the international system is not complete, despite its military and economic pre-eminence. Such a characterization of the international system would allow China to claim a major role in it. Chinese scholars have written extensively on the desirability of multipolarity which, according to them, is different from the unstable multipolar system in European history. To the Chinese, one way of promoting multipolarity is to establish what they call 'strategic partnerships' with other great powers, such as Russia and France. In this way, China could be seen as interacting with its counterparts on an equal footing. This is consistent with China's long-standing aspirations to become a great power in the international system.

US global and Asia-Pacific security strategy

The third major finding of the book is that Chinese security analysts perceive the United States as a major hindrance to their efforts of achieving a great power status for their country. The research data clearly indicates that America is thought to have a 'hegemonic' ambition, and that it is determined to preserve and prolong the 'unipolar moment' that it has enjoyed since the early 1990s. The Chinese see little difference between the Bill Clinton and George W. Bush administrations in terms of US external strategy, in that they both seek to extend American power and influence throughout the world in the name of democracy and freedom. Indeed, it is clear from the evidence that Chinese analysts perceive a strong continuation in the two administrations in terms of their emphasis on protecting America's economic interests, expanding its military power and promoting worldwide democratization. Chinese writings reveal a strong suspicion of US attempts to dominate both Europe and the Asia-Pacific through NATO and the US-Japan security alliance and other bilateral security arrangements.

The articles published in a wide range of Chinese academic and policy journals reveal Chinese concerns regarding a more assertive American global strategy since 9/11. There is a consensus among PRC scholars that Washington has exploited the 'war on terrorism' and its unrivalled military capabilities to perpetuate US global dominance. Some Chinese writers have referred to Bush's foreign policy as an 'imperial foreign policy'. Most Chinese scholars take the view that the Bush Doctrine reflects America's reluctance to be constrained by international law and international organizations in its pursuit of absolute security and its unipolar aspirations. The Iraq war is widely cited as an example illustrating this argument.

The findings also demonstrate that the Bush administration is believed to have become more proactive and assertive in shaping the Asia-Pacific security environment to serve US interests. The expansion of the geographical focus of US strategy in the Asia-Pacific to include Central and South Asia is of particular concern to Chinese security specialists. Washington's plan to develop and deploy a TMD system in Asia has also caused much trepidation among PRC elites. The data clearly points to a conclusion by the Chinese that America has been developing a security network in Asia designed to prevent China from emerging as a powerful force that could contest US interests. Nevertheless, the Chinese are aware of America's need and willingness to cooperate with China, both on global and regional levels.

The perception of a US 'strategic encirclement' of China since 9/11 is evident in the Chinese sources examined in this study. This concern is based on the Chinese observation of Washington's enhanced security relations with its Asian allies and closer security ties with a range of countries surrounding China. The Chinese fear that US security strategy would weaken China's power position and undermine its security. In this sense, America is perceived as a significant threat to the Chinese efforts of constructing a great power identity.

Japan's global and Asia-Pacific security strategy

Another major finding of this study is that PRC scholars and analysts regard Japan's security intentions with great suspicion. Chinese writings reveal deep concern towards Japan's attempts to become a 'political power' and even a military power. It is clear from the research data that Japan's 'UN diplomacy', participation in UN peacekeeping activities and involvement in multilateral security and economic organizations are interpreted as calculated moves to raise Japan's international profile. An examination of the Chinese academic and policy journals reveals China's apprehensions of the enhanced security relations between Japan and America. The evidence becomes stronger in the articles published after 9/11. Indeed, there are many Chinese publications that indicate Chinese misgivings regarding the passage of anti-terrorist legislation in Japan, Tokyo's support for US operations in Afghanistan and Iraq and the deployment of the SDF relating to anti-terrorist missions.

The findings also demonstrate a deep suspicion of Japan's Asia-Pacific strategy among Chinese scholars. In particular, the expansion of Japan's security alliance with America is seen by many Chinese specialists as the basis for US-Japan collaboration to contain China. PRC scholars have written extensively on how Japan may support US actions in the event of a Taiwan conflict. Chinese comments on Japan's participation in the TMD system are indicative of their fear of closer military relations between Tokyo, Washington and Taipei. It is within this context that Japan is perceived by the Chinese as an obstacle to the completion of their national mission of reunification with Taiwan. From the Chinese perspective, a failure to reunify with Taiwan would make it difficult for China to achieve a great power status.

Japan's relations with other Asian countries and its participation in multilateral security forums have also attracted much attention from Chinese analysts, but they tend to view Japan's regional activities as an integral component of its strategy of achieving the aim of a 'political power' and reducing China's influence in Asia. Chinese distrust of Japan's future intentions due to historical reasons, such as its wartime behaviour and the controversies over textbook revision, are also evident in most Chinese writings. It is clear from the evidence that Japan's security strategies are perceived by Chinese scholars and analysts as an impediment to China's pursuit of the status of a major power in the world.

Russia's global and Asia-Pacific security strategy

The fourth major finding of the study is that Russia is viewed by Chinese scholars as a strategic partner which is particularly valued by China in its quest for a great power status. China's Russia specialists have followed Russia's global strategy closely ever since the collapse of the Soviet Union. PRC analysts have exhibited an understanding of Moscow's frustrating experience of retaining a great power position during a period of national decline. However, they are critical of Russia's 'excessive dependence' on the West in its attempts to revive the Russian economy.

Chinese writings also reveal PRC scholars' disapproval of Russia's decision to tolerate NATO's continuing eastward expansion. Specifically, many Chinese articles show considerable reservation over Moscow's compromising stance in dealing with America. In particular, strong sentiment can be detected from some Chinese publications on Russia's consent of US entry into Central Asia, which is considered to be a threat to Chinese security interests. Criticisms of Russia's 'strategic contraction' are also evident in many articles. In the view of some PRC scholars, Putin's policy of 'strategic retreat' and 'contributions' to America's war on terrorism have failed to bring much tangible benefit for Russia. Nevertheless, there is widespread approval of Moscow's support for the idea of multipolarity. This is clearly linked to China's preference for a multipolar world, which is thought to provide a more favourable environment for China to fulfil its great power aspirations.

There is considerable interest among Chinese analysts in Russia's Asia-Pacific security strategy, but most articles indicate a strong economic focus on Russian policy in the region. Some concern has been raised in Chinese writings about a 'China threat' debate in Russia, and the Russian Far East in particular. Despite criticisms of certain Russian policies, Chinese scholars' analysis of Russia is on the whole positive. This is reflective of Chinese perception of Russia as a 'strategic partner' rather than a threat in China's attempts to construct a great power identity.

China's response to the security challenge of the major powers in East Asia

This section summarizes the findings on the discourse of Chinese scholars on how China should respond to the challenges emanating from the security strategies of the US, Japan and Russia. The evidence suggests that Chinese analysts perceive the security challenges of the three East Asian powers in a wider regional and global context. The majority of articles examined in this study show that PRC scholars tend to consider the security strategies of other great powers within the context of the post-Cold War global security environment and the changing structure of the international system.

While Chinese scholars are apprehensive of the nature and implications of the security strategies of the US and Japan, most of them are in favour of maintaining a stable and non-confrontational relationship with the two major powers. Many articles argue that it is not in China's interest to adopt a confrontational approach to the management of great power relations. Instead, they propose a strategy that emphasizes dialogue and diplomatic interactions. Realistically, China does not have the military capabilities to confront either America or Japan. The research data also indicates that most Chinese analysts argue against the use of force in dealing with unresolved territorial disputes with China's neighbours. Taiwan is, of course, an exception.

The general feeling among PRC policy elites is that engaging in an antagonistic relationship with other great powers does not help China fulfil its great power ambitions. The desire to become a great power that commands admiration, respect and recognition by the international community is evident in a majority of Chinese publications. Thus, this study has found that the pursuit of 'great power diplomacy' is advocated by many PRC scholars who believe that the establishment of a wide range of 'strategic partnerships' will help China enhance its status as a great power, but also ease the pressure from hostile countries.

Another suggestion for responding to the security challenge of other great powers in Chinese writings is to strengthen China's relations with a variety of countries through a 'good neighbourly policy' and a 'greater peripheral policy'.

In recent years, there has been a proliferation of articles in Chinese journals advocating China's participation in multilateral security forums. PRC scholars of different schools of thought are supportive of regional security cooperation, as this will contribute to the enhancement of China's status in the region, and in the world more generally. Since the late 1990s, Chinese scholars have engaged in rigorous debate on what path China should follow in pursuing its great power status. This can be seen as a response to the security challenge of America and Japan, who have allegedly promoted a 'China threat' theory. To the Chinese, this theory is designed to undermine China's friendly relations with other Asian and Western countries, thus creating widespread suspicion of the implications of a rising China.

A significant finding of this study is that the debate on China's 'peaceful rise' in the PRC has raised some fundamental questions about the nature and direction of China's rise and how it should relate to the outside world. It has also revealed a division between the Chinese scholars who believe that China should be fully integrated into the Western world and play a constructive and responsible role in the international community, and those who are profoundly sceptical of the potential encroachment of Western countries and global forces into Chinese national sovereignty on the other. This study has also found that a considerable number of PRC analysts are in favour of adopting a tougher stance towards the US and Japan as a response to their security challenge. In this sense, the debate on China's 'peaceful rise' within the Chinese academic and policy communities should be seen as part of an on-going process, through which China's identity as a great power is defined and constructed.

In response to the perceived security challenges from the US, Japan and Russia, Chinese scholars and analysts have put forward the following policy recommendations.

- To expand China's economic and political relations with neighbouring countries through bilateral and multilateral channels in order to offset the alleged attempts of the US and Japan to encircle China or reduce Chinese influence in East Asia.
- To develop bilateral military relations with neighbouring countries (e.g. military exchanges, joint/combined military exercises) to abate regional suspicion of China's military development.
- To promote 'partnership' relations with other great powers and major actors in Asia and other parts of the world, which would give China more room for diplomatic manoeuvres in a world of unipolarity.
- To find common grounds with the US and Japan and to identify areas for bilateral or trilateral cooperation with them; to maintain stable and mutually beneficial relations with the two major powers. This would hopefully minimize possibilities of tension and confrontation.
- To promote a positive image of China to the people of America and Japan, so that they would be less likely to support any anti-Chinese forces or official policies.

- To continue to develop and fortify China's 'strategic partnership' with Russia, including military cooperation, to dilute the effects of unipolarity without making the partnership an explicitly anti-US security alliance.
- To cooperate or coordinate with Russia in dealing with various regional and global security issues.
- To play a leading role in the SCO to ensure that China's military and energy security interests in Central Asia are safeguarded. SCO activities can also be used to counterbalance growing US influence in the region.
- To utilize multilateral institutions and forums to constrain any unilateral US actions and undesirable Japanese behaviour, and to enhance China's regional and global influence (e.g. via the UN, ASEAN-plus-three, EAS, etc.).
- To encourage ASEAN to play a significant, or even a leading role, in establishing an East Asian community or some sort of regional mechanism. This would make it more difficult for the US or Japan to dictate East Asian affairs, especially in the security sphere.
- To encourage East Asian countries to construct a 'collective identity' (*jiti rentong*) as the basis for regional cooperation in order to impede any great powers (such as the US and Japan) from dominating East Asia.
- To play a positive and proactive role in resolving regional security issues through bilateral and multilateral avenues (e.g. the six-party talks on the North Korean nuclear issue) to demonstrate China's credentials as a responsible power.
- To seek to settle unresolved territorial and border disputes with other Asian countries through diplomatic dialogue and negotiation.
- To seek to 'reunify' with Taiwan, through peaceful channels if possible, and by military means if necessary; to discourage the US and Japan from supporting Taiwanese independence by offering both incentives (economic and market opportunities, political and diplomatic cooperation) and disincentives (threat of the use of force).
- To engage in activities that tackle non-conventional security issues (e.g. global terrorism, transnational organized crime, piracy, environmental problems) as a way of promoting regional security cooperation and showing China's commitments to its 'new security concept'.
- To develop China's 'soft power' using its historical and cultural attraction to augment Chinese influence in Asia and beyond. The emphasis on the cultural underpinning of China's foreign policy, such as the notion of a 'harmonious world' (*hexie shijie*), is a prime example of this.
- To exploit China's rapidly expanding trade and investment opportunities to create a more propitious environment for its 'peaceful rise'. In other words, to make China's neighbours 'stakeholders' in its economic success, thus providing disincentives for other East Asian countries to support the US and Japan in the event of a regional conflict (e.g. over Taiwan or the Diaoyu/Senkaku islands).
- To strengthen China's military capability and develop China as a continental or maritime power, or both. PRC scholars generally agree that military power

is essential to the defence of Chinese security interests and China's endeavour to achieve its national goals and a great power status.

Chinese security perceptions in international relations theoretical perspectives

This section highlights the findings of Chinese security discourse from various international relations perspectives and how these IR theories have influenced the security thinking of PRC scholars and analysts.

Realism/neorealism

The traditional assumption in the literature is that there is a strong realist tendency in Chinese security thinking. This is particularly the case in existing studies of China's security perceptions of other great powers. As discussed in the literature review, however, few serious attempts have been made to analyze how Chinese perceptions are shaped by realist thinking. This study has found that there is indeed a strong influence of realist thought on Chinese scholars in their analysis of international affairs and security issues in particular. But it goes beyond this simple assumption to explore how Chinese security discourse is influenced by various variants of realism, including offensive realism and defensive/structural realism.

The evidence in this book shows that many Chinese scholars are heavily influenced by structural realism in their consideration of the structure of the international system and the interactions between China and the other three major powers. There is also strong evidence that some Chinese scholars subscribe to the theory of defensive realism, which emphasizes security rather than expansion in great power behaviour. They have applied this theory to the examination of Russia and, to a lesser extent, to Japan's security strategies. The realist theory that has attracted most attention from Chinese scholars is offensive realism. Specifically, they have utilized it to analyze America's global and regional strategy, using concepts such as 'off-shore balance' to describe America's strategy towards China. Nevertheless, many PRC scholars are critical of offensive realism, as it stresses power maximization in great power behaviour, which in their view may lead to aggressive foreign policy and international conflict. Their recommendations for responding to the challenge of unipolarity may be explained by the realist concepts of 'internal balancing', 'soft balancing' and 'economic prebalancing'.

Liberalism/neoliberalism

In recent years, liberalism has become rather popular among Chinese international relations scholars. The articles examined in this study have certainly indicated a growing influence of liberal thinking on Chinese discourse. Many of them are familiar with various liberal theories, such as economic interdependence theory and the theory of democratic peace. They have also used neoliberal institutionalism to analyze international cooperation. Some of them are able to compare this theory with defensive realism in their analysis of the utility of international organizations and regimes in promoting cooperation under anarchy.

Nevertheless, many Chinese scholars have little faith in the ability of international organizations to constrain the behaviour of great powers, as argued by the neoliberal institutionalists. They tend to use the United States as an example to illustrate their arguments. While Chinese scholars are not oblivious to the role of economic forces in the foreign policies of the three East Asian powers, their analysis is influenced more by mercantilism or economic nationalism than neoliberalism. This is not to say that they are unfamiliar with the theory of economic interdependence, which has indeed been utilized to analyze China's economic relations with the outside world. By and large, Chinese scholars are critical of democratic peace theory which is often referred to as a justification for Western criticism of non-liberal democratic regimes, such as that of China.

On their debate on how China should respond to the security challenge of other great powers, many Chinese scholars appear to subscribe to the views of neoliberal institutionalism, in that China's rising status should be built on the rules and norms of existing international institutions and regimes. In their view, China's integration into the international society is best achieved through multilateral institutions. There is also evidence indicating liberal influence on Chinese conception of the nature of power. The most prominent example of this is the growing debate among PRC scholars and analysts over the definition and utility of the concept of 'soft power' in relation to China's rise.

Constructivism

Until recently, constructivism was unknown to most Chinese scholars. However, it has fast become a popular theory among researchers in the PRC. An increasing number of Chinese analysts have used constructivist theory to analyze international issues, and great power relations in particular. Often these scholars begin their discussion of a particular problem with a critique of how realist thinking can lead to dangerous policy outcomes, and then proceed to use constructivist theory as an alternative avenue of analysis. The best example is their analysis of the 'security dilemma' in East Asia, especially the 'security dilemma' between China and America and the one between China and Japan.

Chinese scholars have also applied constructivism to their consideration of how regional security cooperation may contribute to the promotion of peace and security in the Asia-Pacific. They are especially interested in the idea of building a collective identity through the development of intersubjective knowledge among Asian countries. The constructivist idea of how an actor's interests are shaped by its identity has also been explored by Chinese scholars in their analysis of various countries. Moreover, the argument that ideational factors should be taken into account in considering a country's security policy has considerable appeal to PRC scholars in their debate on China's 'peaceful rise'. In addition, Japan's relations with China and Russia's changing identity have been analyzed from the constructivist perspective in that ideational factors are considered along with material forces.

Postmodernism

Despite its growing influence on the discipline of international relations in the West, postmodernism has had little influence on international relations studies in China. Very few, if any, Chinese scholars have drawn on the insights of postmodernism in analyzing security issues. While there is a conspicuous absence of postmodernist thought in Chinese analysis of great power relations, one can certainly utilize postmodernist concepts to unpack Chinese discourse of the major powers in East Asia. From a postmodernist perspective, the discursive constructions of America and Japan as 'other' would help reinforce the identity and cohesion of the 'self'. This is particularly apparent in Chinese writings on the 'threat' of the US and Japan to China. This type of 'discourse of danger' is widespread in Chinese publications on American and Japanese security strategies. The linkage between such a 'danger' and the formation of China's great power identity is clear. The perceived threat from the US and Japan is often discussed in relation to China's past 'humiliation' in order to illustrate the 'danger' of not recognizing and responding to external threat. The thinking behind this type of discourse is that the US and Japan are determined to prevent China from rising to a great power status, thus threatening China's efforts to construct a great power identity.

The political and intellectual context of Chinese security analysis

This section provides findings on the political and intellectual environment within which Chinese scholars and analysts analyze and debate the security issues relating to the three major powers in East Asia.

China's changing political environment

Prior to the late 1980s, international relations and security studies in China were tightly controlled by the government, and Chinese scholars faced serious constraints on what they could publish and what types of arguments they would be allowed to present. This began to change in the mid-1990s, when Chinese scholars were given relatively more freedom to express their views in academic work. By the end of the decade, one could discern a fairly lively discussion among academics of different schools of thought in international relations journals. This explains the academic debate in Chinese publications, which are quite similar to those in the West. Obviously, there are limits to this sort of debate and the bottom line appears to be clear to most scholars. Within certain political parameters, however, academics are allowed to challenge the views of each other. Examples of this include the Chinese debates on whether and in what ways China should adopt great power diplomacy, how to respond to the perceived challenges of America and Japan, what is the nature of US hegemony, whether China needs 'new thinking' in its policy towards Japan and, most importantly, how should China relate itself to the international community and what is the most appropriate path for China to rise to great power status.

As this study has shown, one can identify debates on major security issues in China due to the changing political climate in the country. This is extremely significant in that for the first time in the history of the PRC, outside scholars are able to follow academic debates on foreign policy issues that are taking place within China. The problem with this is that one cannot be confident in identifying individual scholars with specific bureaucracies or factions within the central leadership. Nevertheless, the changing political climate is encouraging for both Chinese scholars and Western academics studying China's international relations at a time when China is rising and changing rapidly.

Academic interactions with the outside world

As a result of the changing political environment in the PRC over the past two decades, Chinese scholars have been able to establish and maintain regular contacts with their counterparts in Asian and Western countries. Many scholars who study international security issues and great power relations have had opportunities to visit foreign countries and take part in overseas exchange programmes. As a result, they are able to exchange views directly with Western scholars in their field. In addition, many Chinese scholars and policy analysts are regularly invited to attend international conferences, both within China and abroad, and to participate in various types of Track-II meetings where they can discuss sensitive issues with foreign officials and academics on a non-attributable basis. All these activities have contributed to Chinese scholars' understanding of the complexity of the foreign and security policy of other countries and the latest academic and policy debates in the West. The publications examined in this study in some ways reflect the impact of Chinese scholars' interactions with Western analysts on their thinking.

The growth of China's international relations community

Another important factor contributing to the diversity of academic views and the rigour of some of the analyses produced by Chinese scholars is the rapid growth of the international relations community in China, and the increasing maturity of the discipline in the country. Over the past decade, the disciplines of international relations and security studies have developed at a pace that was unimaginable before the 1990s. This is, of course, related to the changing political climate previously mentioned. The academic work cited in this study is testimony to this progress.

Since the mid-1990s, the study of international relations has been introduced in many universities in China, and institutes or centres of international studies have been established in Peking, Qinghua, Renmin, Fudan, Nanjing, Nankai, Wuhan, Shandong, Liaoning, Zhongshan, Jinan, Sichuan and other universities. The expansion of the international relations community in China has led to a wide-ranging research agenda and greater emphasis on academic rigour in research and publications. PhD students are encouraged to pursue topics relating to a broad range of theories. As a result, Chinese studies of international relations and security affairs have become much more sophisticated than before. However, given that IR is still a relatively young academic discipline in China, it will be some time before the discipline matures.

Access to Western sources

Related to the previous point is Chinese scholars' growing familiarity with Western debates, theories and academic literature. The expansion of the international relations discipline in China, combined with increasing opportunities for researchers to interact with foreign scholars, has enabled Chinese scholars to gain unprecedented access to Western studies on international affairs and security issues relating to China in particular. The examination in this study of a wide range of PRC publications shows the breadth and depth of Chinese scholars' knowledge of Western theories and literature in the field. It is interesting to note that PRC scholars are able to cite some of the latest research in their work. The level of their understanding of Western theories is impressive, given that English is not their first language. They have regularly cited and critiqued articles published in Western journals such as *International Security*, *The Washington Quarterly* and *Foreign Affairs*. They are also able to refer to the original work of Western academics without relying on Chinese translations. It is worth pointing out that the majority of important Western studies in international relations, Asian security and Chinese foreign policy have been translated into Chinese and published in the PRC.

It is not unusual to see Chinese scholars citing Western theoretical work, including the books written by realist, liberal and constructivist scholars. The theoretical work that has been cited regularly includes that of Hans Morgenthau, Kenneth Waltz, John Mearsheimer, Robert Jervis, Robert Keohane, Joseph Nye and Alexander Wendt. Many Western IR scholars have been invited to visit China and discuss their theories and arguments with Chinese academics. For example, John Mearsheimer was invited to visit CASS's Institute of American Studies and met with PRC scholars in Beijing and Shanghai. Alexander Wendt was also invited to visit China, and his debate with the Chinese constructivist scholar Qin Yaqing has been published in China. The constructivist security specialists Peter Katzenstein and Alastair Iain Johnston are on the editorial board of the top IR journal *Shijie jingji yu zhengzhi* (World Economy and Politics).

Conclusion

The principal findings of this study clearly demonstrate that China's perceptions of the major powers in East Asia – the US, Japan and Russia – are closely linked to its desire and endeavour to construct a great power identity. The findings confirm that Chinese scholars and policy elites perceive the power, aspirations and security strategies of the three major East Asian powers primarily in terms of their implications for China's pursuit of a great power status in the 21st century. Thus, the hypothesis of this book set out in Chapter One is validated.

Implications for the debate on the rise of China

In the first chapter, I argue that a better understanding of Chinese security discourse is essential to the assessment of the nature of China's rise and its implications for global and regional security. This section will show how the book has contributed to its broader aim of advancing the debate on the security implications of the ascendancy of China.

One of the key issues in the debate on the rise of China is how China will interact with other great powers. To answer this question, one needs to have a thorough understanding of how China perceives the intentions and security strategies of other powers. This is precisely what the book has explored. The findings demonstrate that the Chinese remain deeply wary of the strategic intentions of the US and Japan, and that Chinese suspicion of Russia is minimal, at least for the time being. Nevertheless, the findings do not indicate that China is about to adopt an antagonistic stance towards the major powers or actively engage in hard balancing against them. Instead, it has responded to the security policies of the US and Japan by pursuing a strategy of hedging, as well as soft-balancing and internal balancing. This explains why China has been pursuing a 'great power diplomacy' and seeks to improve relations with other countries, especially its neighbours, through the 'good neighbourly policy' and 'greater peripheral diplomacy', while building up its economic strength and military power.

The existing evidence does not suggest that China will assertively challenge US pre-eminence or confront Japan in the near future. This is because Chinese elites are well aware of the fact that China's military capabilities are not as strong as those of America and Japan. They also understand that a confrontation with the two East Asian powers would be detrimental to Chinese economic interests, making it more difficult for China to fulfil its great power aspirations. However, should PRC leaders fail to attain their national goals through existing strategies, there is no guarantee that they will not pursue a belligerent policy towards the US and Japan. After all, the Chinese publications examined in this book clearly reveal a discursive construction of the two countries as threatening 'others' who seek to undermine China's efforts to achieve a great power status.

Another question in the rise of China debate is whether, and to what extent, China will respect the rules and norms of international society. The findings of this book show that the majority of Chinese policy elites are in favour of promoting China's integration into the international community. They also suggest that China should be closely involved in all major international organizations and regimes, playing a constructive and responsible role in the international community. As many PRC scholars admit, China has benefited immensely from participating in international organizations. It is therefore not in China's interest to stay outside of the international community.

Our findings indicate that China has adopted a strategy of integrating itself into the existing system, while seeking to exert influence on the agenda, rules and operation of various international institutions and regimes wherever possible. In the short term, China hopes to use its involvement in a wide range of international bodies to enhance its great power status. The evidence seems to suggest that the long-term goal of Chinese elites is to gradually reshape the norms and rules of the international society to reflect China's growing power and its expanding global interests. Some Chinese scholars believe that the traditional boundary between China and the outside world is no longer clear due to the challenge of globalization. To fully integrate into international society, Professor Pang Zhongying (2006a) argues that China should pay more attention to global values, such as global governance, and be more active in contributing to its development.

An important question that is often raised in the debate is whether China is a status quo power. For the moment, China can be regarded as a status quo power or quasi status quo power in the sense that it does not appear to have the intention of challenging the existing international system and overturning the rules and regulations accepted by the majority of the states. Indeed, some Chinese scholars counsel their government that China should remain an active member of existing international institutions, seeking to improve them only through incremental reform. On the other hand, China may be seen as a non-status quo power, as it is dissatisfied with the present structure of the international system. The resentment towards unipolarity and its constraining effects on China's quest for a great power status is prevalent among Chinese writings examined in this study. In addition, China is unhappy with the status quo in the Taiwan Strait where Taiwan is able to maintain its *de facto* independence while benefiting from trade and economic interactions with the PRC. As one prominent Chinese scholar puts it, China would be willing to become a status quo power only after Taiwan is 'reunified' with the mainland. In fact, some Chinese analysts have advocated the use of force to resolve the Taiwan issue, should peaceful means fail to achieve China's reunification goal. The passage of an anti-secession law by the NPC, China's parliament, in 2005, may be seen as confirmation of the potency of this sort of thinking. It would be interesting to see how China handles its relations with Taiwan during the Ma Ying-jeou presidency.

There is no question that China is determined to achieve a great power status, and this book has demonstrated that Chinese elites are actively engaged in the process of constructing China's great power identity. Many Chinese analysts support the notion of China's 'peaceful rise', but they also believe in the utility of military force in achieving Chinese national goals. The debate in the PRC on China's 'peaceful rise' does not provide conclusive evidence as to whether it is a reflection of short-term considerations aiming to minimize potential obstruction to China's ascendancy, or a long-term strategy that would renounce the use of force in fulfilling its great power aspirations.

Another uncertain factor is whether China can indeed rise peacefully, even if that is its chosen path to ascendancy. While most observers expect China to grow continuously, one must not forget that there are numerous domestic problems that may derail China's economic progress and cause instability in Chinese society.

This could have significant repercussions on China's external relations. For example, China might opt for an assertive or adventurous foreign policy as a result of internal factors such as serious economic crises, social and political turmoil, rising nationalistic sentiments and pressure from some quarters of the military. Thus, the West must prepare for various scenarios of a rising China, including the security implications of a strong but chaotic China.

The long-term peace and stability of East Asia depends heavily on whether China will rise peacefully, and this is closely linked to the ways Chinese leaders will handle their relations with other East Asian powers in the coming years. For the moment, Chinese elites and analysts are deeply apprehensive of US and Japanese security strategy. Their perceptions are based on both China's past encounters with the two major powers and its assessment of their future intentions. If perception is socially constructed, it may be altered via the development of intersubjective knowledge, ideas, norms and institutions. Indeed, as demonstrated in this study, Chinese elites' security discourse has undergone considerable changes over the past two decades due partly to China's increasing interactions with Western countries and its Asian neighbours.

Chinese security discourse of other East Asian powers is shaped by their security strategy, the broader regional and international security environment, China's self-perception as an ascending power, and external responses to its rise to a great power status. The departure of Prime Minister Fukuda, Presidents Bush and Putin and the arrival of President Dmitry Medvedev, Prime Minister Aso Taro and a new US president (John McCain or Barack Obama) will no doubt bring new dynamics to East Asian security relations. It is important for Western analysts and policy-makers to monitor any significant change in Chinese security perceptions and to seek to instil positive influence into Chinese thinking through all the available channels. The aim is to persuade China that the success of its emergence as a great power will rest on its willingness and ability to establish a stable and cooperative relationship with the major powers in East Asia, and indeed with other countries around the world.

The findings of this study suggest that PRC scholars and analysts have taken Western security discourse and policy debate very seriously, and have tried to engage with Asian and Western academics and security analysts. We should also take the discourse of and debate among Chinese scholars seriously and try to engage them at both intellectual and policy levels. We should not underestimate the impact of their discourse on China's foreign and security policy.

To be sure, many Chinese publications tend to repeat or elaborate what has been said by PRC leaders, or to provide academic justifications for official policies. Nevertheless, there is some genuine discussion in Chinese academic and policy circles on a whole range of significant security issues. Within certain, possibly strictly defined, political parameters, Chinese scholars and analysts are able to engage in internal debates. Some writers are trying to 'test the water' or push the boundary to see how far they can go in advocating new ideas and policy recommendations. What often happens is that they use officially acceptable jargon to challenge conventional wisdom in foreign policy thinking.

Since the late 1990s, leading international relations and security specialists at Chinese think-tanks and universities have been regularly consulted by government officials dealing with foreign affairs and security matters. For example, various types of seminars and meetings are frequently organized by the MFA to seek expert advice on specific issues. Scholars with particular expertise are usually consulted when China faces major diplomatic crises and international challenges, or just before Chinese leaders visit significant countries and attend international conferences. The results of foreign policy consultation are presented in different forms, such as briefings, summary of discussions and specially commissioned reports. They are distributed to and consulted by officials at different levels including high-level policy-makers (Wang Yizhou 2007).

Indeed, recent research has indicated a growing influence of Chinese scholars and think-tank specialists on China's foreign policy-making. The study of Bonnie Glaser and Evan Medeiros (2007) on the role of China's policy intellectuals in persuading the leadership to adopt the notion of 'peaceful rise' as its foreign policy strategy shows the relevance and significance of elite discourse in China. Similarly, PRC leaders have eschewed the phrase 'peaceful rise' precisely because of the concerns and objections raised by some security analysts and policy elites in their debate. Despite the change of the official terminology to 'peace and development', the theory of 'peaceful rise' continues to underpin China's diplomatic practice.

The activities of many Chinese scholars and intellectuals are arguably comparable to those of what Robert Herman (1996: 284) calls the 'specialist networks' in the former Soviet Union in the late 1970s and early 1980s. According to Herman, this group of reform-minded specialists played an instrumental role in reconceptualizing state interests and forging a new Soviet identity. The social construction of their new ideas can be seen as part of the process of identity formation in the Gorbachev era. This, argues Herman, led to the emergence of 'new thinking' in Soviet foreign policy and the end of the Cold War. Although it is too soon to judge the long-term impact of PRC scholars and policy elites' activities on the construction of Chinese national identity, their security discourse will certainly have significant influence on how Chinese leaders pursue their great power aspirations in the coming years.

Managing the rise of China is unquestionably a major challenge for the international community, but the world may face a greater challenge in the future. In an article published over a decade ago, I posed the question: 'Will China become a stabilizing or destabilizing force in the Asia-Pacific region, if and when it succeeds in achieving the "Four Modernizations"?'. In other words, how would China exercise its power after it has reached a great power status? I argued that 'this will depend on the political and economic situation in China as well as the security environment in the Asia-Pacific' (Li 1995: 341). Since then China's domestic situation and the Asian security environment have changed substantially, yet it remains as difficult as ever to answer that question. There are simply too many variables shaping the future direction of China and its domestic and foreign policy. Even the Chinese themselves do not have the answer.

What is clear, however, is that China has become much more powerful in both economic and military terms since the mid 1990s. Moreover, China's political influence on many regional and global issues has increased considerably. Meanwhile, the scale and intensity of its interactions with the wider world have been dramatically augmented. China is already an active participant in a variety of international organizations and regimes. 'Today's Western order', as John Ikenberry (2008: 24) observes, 'is hard to overturn and easy to join'. I would argue that the world has a vested interest in socializing China into adhering to and committing to the rules and norms of the international community, and playing the role of a constructive power.

There is no doubt that Chinese leaders and elites have ambitions of achieving a great power status for their country. The outside world cannot alter that. What it can do is try to persuade and encourage them to internalize multilateralism as a constitutive part of Chinese identity. The international community can also assist China to complete its 'self-verification' in constructing an identity of a responsible great power and maintain a strong 'commitment' to its role identity.[1] As China's identity changes, its interests will change accordingly.

The internalization of international norms in Chinese identity formation, and cultivation of intersubjective ideas of 'other-help' and collective identity between China and its Asian neighbours, will help curtail the tendency of belligerent behaviour, if and when China eventually joins the rank of the great powers. This is by no means easy but the outside world has an opportunity to do it now. It may be too late to shape Chinese security perceptions and behaviour in 15 or 20 years' time. A useful starting point is to gain a deeper and more sophisticated understanding of what Chinese policy elites are deliberating and debating with each other on prime security issues that impact not only on China but on East Asia and the rest of the world. It is for this purpose that this book seeks to make a contribution.

Appendix

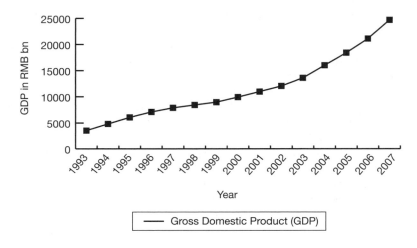

Sources: World Bank, http://siteresources.worldbank.org/CHINAEXTN/Resources/chinaei.pdf;
The US-China Business Council, http://www.uschina.org/statistics/economy.html

Figure 1.1 China's Gross Domestic Product (GDP) in RMB 1993–2007.

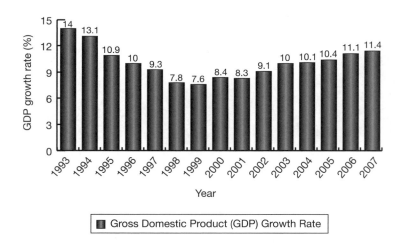

Sources: World Bank, http://siteresources.worldbank.org/CHINAEXTN/Resources/chinaei.pdf;
The US-China Business Council, http://www.uschina.org/statistics/economy.html

Figure 1.2 China's Gross Domestic Product Growth Rate 1993–2007.

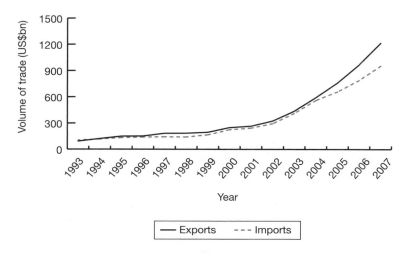

Sources: World Bank, http://siteresources.worldbank.org/CHINAEXTN/Resources/chinaei.pdf;
The US-China Business Council, http://www.uschina.org/statistics/tradetable.html

Figure 1.3 China's World Trade (US$bn) 1993–2007.

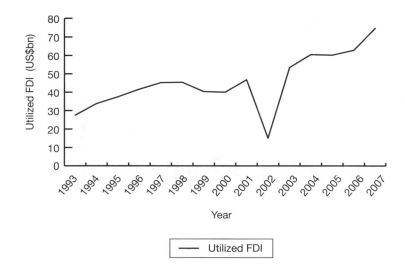

Sources: World Bank, http://siteresources.worldbank.org/CHINAEXTN/Resources/chinaei.pdf;
The US-China Business Council, http://uschina.org/public/documents/2008/02/2008-foreign-
investment.pdf

Figure 1.4 China's Utilized FDI Inflows.

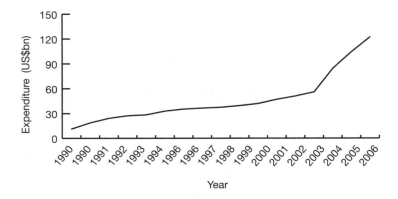

Sources: National Bureau of Asian Research (2008); IISS (2007)

Figure 1.5 China's Defence Expenditure (US$bn) 1990–2006.

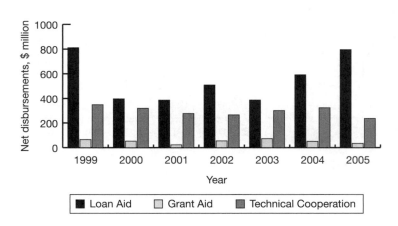

Source: The Ministry of Foreign Affairs of Japan,
http://www.mofa.go.jp/policy/oda/data/2004/01ap_ea01.html#CHINA

Figure 4.1 Japan's ODA Disbursements to China 1999–2005.

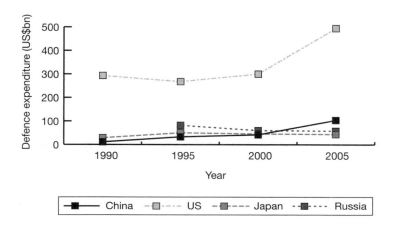

Source: National Bureau of Asian Research, Strategic Asia Programme,
http://strategicasia.nbr.org/
Note: The figure for Russia's defence expenditure in 1990 is not available.

Figure 6.1 Comparative Defence Spending of the Great Powers in East Asia.

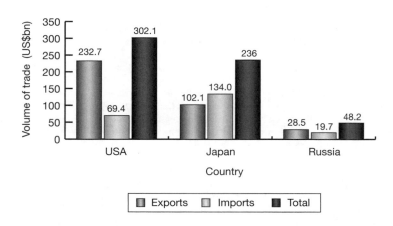

Source: The US-China Business Council, http://www.uschina.org/statistics/tradetable.html

Figure 6.2 China's Trade with Other East Asian Powers 2007.

Notes

1 A rising China, international relations theories and Chinese security discourse of East Asian powers

1 In this book I will use 'great powers' and 'major powers' interchangeably. The Chinese equivalent of the two terms is exactly the same, that is, *daguo*.
2 In terms of their disciplinary origins, social identity theory is developed from social psychology while identity theory from sociology.
3 According to some Chinese scholars, Marxism-Leninism, although a Western product, was the most radical anti-Western capitalist and imperialist thought, and could therefore be seen as a 'Western anti-Westernism'. See the book written by a Hong Kong scholar Jin Yaoji (1984: 87).
4 See, for example, Song Qiang, Zhang Cangcang and Qiao Bian *et al.* (1996); Song Qiang, Zhang Cangcang, Qiao Bian, Tang Zhengyu and Gu Qingsheng (1996).
5 Alternative views of the United States, Japan and Russia appear primarily in the military and strategic journals. Despite the importance of these publications in articulating military perspectives on major security issues, a systematic analysis of them is obviously beyond the scope of this project.

2 Hegemonic aspirations in a unipolar world

1 Du Gong (1992: 2–3), a leading scholar at the CIIS, estimated in 1992 that the transitional period between the end of the bipolar system and the emergence of a new world structure could last until the early 21st century. For further debates among Chinese scholars and analysts on the changing structure of the international system, see Chapter Six.
2 A detailed and in-depth analysis of the Gulf War, including the background to the conflict, the process of diplomatic negotiations, the military balance between the US and Iraq, the UN military operation, the weapons used in the war and other relevant information, can be found in an 881-page volume contributed by over 100 Chinese generals, military specialists and international relations analysts. See Zhang Xiangyuan, Wang Yong and Hu Donghua (1992).
3 However, some Chinese scholars argue that Bush, like his predecessors, paid more attention to Europe than to Asia. It was not until Clinton became the US president, they maintain, that America shifted its strategic focus significantly towards the Asia-Pacific region. See, for example, Li Dongyan (1996: 68).
4 This view of US policy towards China is shared by most Chinese scholars and analysts.
5 It is difficult to translate the exact meaning of 'engagement' into Chinese. The terms most commonly used by Chinese elites and specialists to describe the Western policy of engagement are *jiechu* (contact), *jiaowang* (interaction), and *canyu* (involvement).

6 'Constrainment' is sometimes translated as *qianzhi* by Chinese analysts. A different translation of the term 'containment' is *ezhi* which is also widely used in Chinese publications.

7 The original 'Guidelines for US-Japan Defense Co-operation' was signed in November 1978, which was designed primarily to strengthen US-Japan security ties against the perceived threat from the Soviet Union.

8 A comprehensive review of various dimensions of US-Taiwan relations in the Cold War years can be found in an edited volume contributed by some of China's leading American specialists. See Zi Zhongyun and He Di (1991).

3 September 11, pre-emption and the Bush Doctrine

1 Led by Hu Jintao, the Chairman of the CCP and Chinese President, this secretive group is responsible for co-ordinating China's foreign and defence policies.

2 See the last part of this section for more detailed discussion on Chinese discourse of US policy towards Taiwan.

3 The SCO was first established in April 1996 as a regional grouping called the Shanghai Five. It was joined by Uzbekistan in 2001 and transformed into a regional security organization.

4 Security, identity and strategic choice

1 The first set of National Defense Program Guidelines was published in 1976 and the second one in 1995.

2 See Chapter Six for an examination of the debate among Chinese scholars and analysts on 'new thinking' in Sino-Japanese relations.

3 This would involve the foreign and defence ministers of the two countries similar to the arrangements between Japan and the United States.

4 This is why Chinese scholars tend to use the term *banMei ruYa* (entering Asia with America) rather than *tuoMei ruYa* (leaving America to join Asia) to describe Japan's strategy of 'returning to Asia'.

5 The renewal of the US-Japan security alliance can be traced to the early 1990s when the United States suspected that North Korea was developing a nuclear programme. In response to the situation, Washington and Tokyo began to review the 1978 Guidelines for US-Japan Defense Cooperation. This intention was to be stated in a Joint Declaration during a scheduled visit of the then US President Bill Clinton to Japan in 1995. However, due to the cancellation of the visit the announcement of the Declaration had to be postponed until April 1996, a month after the Taiwan Strait crisis. I am indebted to Dr. Harumi Yoshino for drawing my attention to these important events.

6 For discussion of America's force realignment, see the section 'Japan and US Security Strategy' in Chapter Three.

7 For further details, see the section 'Russia and Japan' in Chapter Five.

8 The public protests were initially directed at Japan's efforts to gain a permanent seat on the UNSC and the history issue was brought in to support the argument against Japanese membership.

5 A key player in an emerging multipolar world

1 This was due mainly to Russia's unwillingness and inability to continue to provide financial aid, loans and other forms of economic support for its former allies in Asia, which seriously affected their economic development. For a Chinese analysis of this issue, see, for example, Yu Zhixian (1993: 54–57).

2 A more detailed examination of Chinese analysis of the shift in Russia's foreign policy towards the East in late 1992 will be provided in the next section.

3   Some Chinese scholars use the term 'multidirectional diplomacy' (*duofangwei waijiao*) to describe the new Russian foreign policy. See, for example, Yu Sui (1998).

4   'Colour revolutions' or 'flower revolutions' refer to the non-violent movements against authoritarian regimes in Central and Eastern Europe and Central Asia, where a particular colour or flower was adopted as the symbol of each movement. The 'colour revolutions' that led to the removal of unpopular governments took place in Serbia in 2000, Georgia in 2003, the Ukraine in 2004 and Kyrgyzstan in 2005.

6   China's response to the security challenge of the major powers in East Asia

1   Joseph S. Nye, Jr. has used the concepts of 'hard power resources' and 'soft power resources' to analyze America's changing position in world politics. Nye's concepts have attracted much attention from Chinese scholars, and many of them have applied the concepts to the analysis of US capabilities.

2   These are well-known slogans drawn from Deng Xiaoping's speeches.

3   *Zhanlue yu guanli* ceased publication soon after the heated debate on 'new thinking' towards Japan initiated by the journal. There are some speculations that the controversial debate may have been one of the main factors contributing to the demise of this well-respected policy journal.

7   Conclusion

1   See Chapter Six for discussion on the concepts of 'self-verification' and 'commitment' in relation to China's identity construction.

Bibliography

Chinese-language journals with English translation

Dangdai Yatai (Contemporary Asia-Pacific)
Dongbeiya luntan (Northeast Asia Forum)
Dongnanya (South East Asia)
Dongnanya zongheng (South East Asia Review)
Dongou Zongya yanjiu (East European and Central Asian Studies)
Eluosi Zhongya Dongou yanjiu (Journal of Russian, Central Asian and East European Studies)
Guoji guancha (International Observation)
Guoji guanxi xueyuan xuebao (Journal of the Institute of International Relations)
Guoji jingji pinglun (International Economic Review)
Guoji luntan (International Forum)
Guoji wenti yanjiu (Journal of International Studies)
Heping yu fazhan (Peace and Development)
Jinri qianSulian Dongou (The Former Soviet Union and Eastern Europe Today)
Meiguo yanjiu (American Studies)
Nanya yanjiu (South Asian Studies)
Nanya yanjiu jikan (South Asian Studies Quarterly)
Ouzhou (Europe)
Ouzhou yanjiu (European Studies)
Riben xuekan (Journal of Japanese Studies)
Shijie jingji yu zhengzhi (World Economy and Politics)
Shijie jingji yu zhengzhi luntan (Forum on World Economics and Politics)
Taipingyang xuebao (Pacific Journal)
Taiwan yanjiu (Taiwan Studies)
Taiwan yanjiu jikan (Taiwan Research Quarterly)
Waiguo wenti yanjiu (Research on Foreign Issues)
Xiandai guoji guanxi (Contemporary International Relations)
YaFei zongheng (Asia and Africa Review)
Yatai yanjiu (Asia-Pacific Studies)
Zhanlue yu guanli (Strategy and Management)

Chinese-Language Sources

An Huihou (2004) 'Yilake zhanzheng de yanzhong houguo he qishi' ('The Serious Consequences of and Lessons from the Iraq War'), *Guoji wenti yanjiu*, September 5: 11–16, 10.
Bai Ruchun (2004) 'Riben diqu waijiao zhanlue tiaozheng de ruogan wenti' ('Issues

Relating to the Adjustments in Japan's Regional Diplomatic Strategy'), *Riben xuekan*, November 6: 83–95.

Cao Xiaoyang (2006) 'Jiuyiyi shijian hou Meiguo zai Dongnanya de junshi cunzai ji qi yingxiang' ('America's Military Presence in South East Asia after the Events of September 11 and Its Impact'), *Dangdai Yatai*, March 3: 23–30.

Cao Yunhua (2001) 'Dongnanya diyuan zhengzhi geju de xinbianhua' ('The New Changes in the Geopolitical Structure of South East Asia'), *Dongnanya zongheng*, 12: 14–16.

—— (2003) 'Jiuyiyi shijian yilai Meiguo yu Dongmeng de guanxi' ('US-ASEAN Relations since the Events of September 11'), *Dangdai Yatai*, December 12: 36–41.

Cao Zhizhou (1996) 'Luelun Li Denghui dalu zhengce de "taidu" benzhi' ('On the Essence of "Taiwanese Independence" in Lee Teng-hui's Mainland Policy'), *Taiwan yanjiu*, September 3: 13–18.

Chen Baosen (1992) 'Ping Bushi de Yatai zhixing' ('On Bush's Visit to the Asia-Pacific'), *Yatai yanjiu*, 1: 46–50.

Chen Benshan (1997) 'Riben zhengzhi youqinghua he Diaoyutai wenti' ('The Right-wing Tendency in Japanese Politics and the Issue of the Diaoyu Islands'), *Dongbeiya luntan*, February 1: 92–97.

Chen Demin (1999) 'Duojihua rengshi dangjin shijie de fazhan qushi' ('Multipolarity Remains the Development Trend in Today's World'), *Xiandai guoji guanxi*, November 11: 4–8.

Chen Dezhao (1998) 'Jiushi niandai Meiguo jingji de bianhua yu zhanwang' ('The Changes in and Prospects for the US Economy in the 1990s'), *Guoji wenti yanjiu*, January 1: 21–23.

Chen Dongxiao (2006) '"Fuzaxing" yu ZhongMei guanxi jiegou de xinbianhua' ('"Complexity" and New Changes in the Structure of Sino-American Relations'), *Meiguo yanjiu*, June 2: 34–59.

Chen Luzhi (1992) 'Xinjiu geju zhuanhuan shiqi de Yatai diqu' ('The Asia-Pacific Region in the Transitional Period from the Old Structure to a New One'), in Du Gong and Ni Liyu, eds, *Zhuanhuanzhong de shijie geju* (The World Structure in Transition), Beijing: Shijie zhishi chubanshe, pp. 136–62.

Chen Qimao (1990) 'Shilun shijie cong liangji geju xiang douji geju de guodu' ('On the Transition from Bipolarity to Multipolarity in World Politics'), *Guoji wenti yanjiu*, 4: 1–7.

Chen Shixiang and Yan Ling (1995) 'Lengzhan qianhou Meiguo Yatai zhengce de yanbian' ('The Evolution of America's Asia-Pacific Policy Before and After the End of the Cold War'), *Waiguo wenti yanjiu*, 2: 20–23.

Chen Xiangyang (2005) 'Yatai diyuan zhanlue xintaishi yu Zhongguo anquan' ('The New Geostrategic Situation in the Asia-Pacific and China's Security'), *Taipingyang xuebao*, January 1: 83–88.

Cheng Chaoze (1997) *Shiji zhizheng – Zhongguo: yige jingji daguo de jueqi* (Rivalry in the New Century – China: The Rise of an Economic Power), Hong Kong: Zhonghua shuju.

Chu Shulong (2001) 'Jiuyiyi shijian yu Bushi zhengfu duiwai zhengce' ('The Events of 9/11 and the Bush Administration's Foreign Policy'), *Heping yu fazhan*, 4: 5–8.

Dai Chaowu and Li Chunling (2002) '9/11 shijian hou Meiguo dui Zhongya diqu de zhengce ji qi yingxiang' ('America's Policy Towards Central Asia After the Events of 9/11 and Its Impact'), *Shijie jingji yu zhengzhi luntan*, 1: 60–64.

Dai Dezheng and Zhang Yuhua (1998) 'Eluosi "quanfangwei waijiao" de jiben dingwei yu kuaisu tuijin' ('The Adoption and Rapid Development of Russia's Policy of "Omnidirectional Diplomacy"'), *Dongbeiya luntan*, February, 1: 13–18.

Dai Fan and Zhou Yue (2005) 'Zouxiang tongyi de Dongya zhixu?' ('Towards an Integrated East Asian Order?'), *Taipingyang xuebao*, 12: 20–27.

Deng Hao (2002) 'Zhongguo yu Zhongya guojia guanxi: huimou yu qianzhan' ('China's Relations with Central Asian Countries: Retrospects and Prospects'), *Guoji wenti yanjiu*, May 3: 8–9.

Deng Xiaoping (1983) *Deng Xiaoping wenxuan* (Selected Works of Deng Xiaoping), Beijing: Renmin chubanshe.

Ding Yingshun (1996) 'Zhanhou Riben dui Chao zhengce de yanbian ji qi qianzhan' ('The Evolution of Japan's Post-war Policy towards North Korea and Its Future Prospects'), *Riben xuekan*, March 2: 68–74.

—— (1998) 'RiChao guanxi zhengchanghua jincheng ji qi zhanwang' ('The Processes of and Prospects for the Normalisation of Japanese-North Korean Relations'), *Riben xuekan*, July 4: 93–98.

Ding Yuejin (1997) 'Lengzhan hou MeiRi guanxi de xinzouxiang' ('The New Trend of Post-Cold War US-Japan Relations'), *Dongbeiya luntan*, May 2: 19–22, 47.

Ding Zemin (1998) 'ZhongMei guanxi zhong zhide zhuyi de wenti' ('The Issues in Sino-US Relations that Deserve Attention'), *Dongbeiya luntan*, February, 1: 4–5.

Du Gong (1992) 'Shije jinruliao geju zhuanhuan de xinshiqi' ('The World Has Entered a New Era of Structural Change'), in Du Gong and Ni Liyu, eds, *Zhuanhuanzhong de shijie geju* (The World Structure in Transition), Beijing: Shijie zhishi chubanshe, pp. 1–11.

Du Gong and Ni Liyu (1992) eds, *Zhuanhuanzhong de shijie geju* (The World Structure in Transition), Beijing: Shijie zhishi chubanshe.

Duan Hong (1998) 'Shixi Yazhou jingji weiji dui Dongya anquan de yingxiang' ('A Preliminary Analysis of the Impact of the Asian Economic Crisis on East Asian Security'), *Guoji wenti yanjiu*, October 4: 43–44.

Fan Yuejiang (1997) 'Meiguo "yi Tai zhi Hua" zhengce de zhiyue yinsu ji qianjing' ('The Constraining Factors in and Prospects for America's policy of "Using Taiwan to Contain China"'), *Taiwan yanjiu*, September 3: 36–41.

—— (1999) 'Shixi yingxiang Riben dui Hua zhengce de "Taiwan qingjie"' ('A Preliminary Analysis of the Impact of the "Taiwan Complex" on Japan's Policy Towards China'), *Riben xuekan*, March 2: 24–36.

Fang Baihua (1998) 'Lengzhan hou Riben de guoji guonei huanjing he duiwai zhanlue de jiben zouxiang' ('Japan's Post-Cold War International and Domestic Environment and the Basic Trend of Its External Strategy'), *Riben xuekan*, January 1: 50–66.

Feng Shaolei (2002) 'Xianshizhuyi qiangjing taitou' ('The Re-emergence of Realism'), *Wenhuibao* (The Literary Daily), 9 January, p. 4.

Feng Tejun, ed., (1993) *Dangdai shijie zhengzhi jingji yu guoji guanxi, di er ban* (Contemporary World Politics, Economy and International Relations), 2nd edition, Beijing: Zhongguo renmin daxue chubanshe.

Feng Yongping (2005) 'Daguo jueqi beijingxia de ZhongRi anquan kunjing toushi' ('An Analysis of Sino-Japanese Security Dilemma in the Context of Great Power Emergence'), *Taipingyang xuebao*, 12: 46–54.

Feng Yujun (2004) 'Guoji shiyou zhanlue geju yu ZhongE nengyuan hezuo qianjing' ('The Structure of International Oil Strategy and Prospects for Sino-Russian Energy Cooperation'), *Xiandai guoji guanxi*, May 5: 23–28.

—— (2007) 'ZhongE guanxi zhong de Zhongguo guojia liyi' ('China's National Interest in Sino-Russian Relations'), *Eluosi yanjiu* (Russian Studies), 2: 41–48.

Feng Zhaokui (2003a) 'Gongyehua yu ZhongRi guanxi' ('Industrialization and Sino-Japanese Relations'), *Shijie jingji yu zhengzhi* (World Economy and Politics), 9: 11–14.

—— (2003b) 'Lun ZhongRi guanxi xinsiwei' ('On New Thinking in Sino-Japanese Relations'), *Zhanlue yu guanli*, 4: 1–17.

—— (2003c) 'Zailun duiRi guanxi xinsiwei' ('Further Considerations on New Thinking in Relations with Japan'), *Zhanlue yu guanli*, 5: 78–84.

—— (2003d) 'Sanlun duiRi guanxi xinsiwei' ('A Third Essay on New Thinking in Relations with Japan'), *Zhanlue yu guanli*, 6: 26–33.

—— (2004) 'Silun duiRi guanxi xinsiwei' ('The Fourth Essay on New Thinking in Relations with Japan'), *Zhanlue yu guanli*, 1: 49–54.

Fu Mengzi (2002) 'Meiguo waijiao de xin tiaozheng' ('New Adjustments in American Foreign Policy'), *Xiandai guoji guanxi*, 1: 22–26.

Fu Mengzi and Yang Wenjing (2004) 'Shixi Bushi zhengfu de Yazhou zhengce ji qi zouxiang' ('An Analysis of the Bush Administration's Asia Policy and Its Future Direction'), *YaFei zongheng*, 4: 1–6, 77.

Gao Haikuan (2006) 'Jingguo shenshe yu hesi jiaji zhanfan' ('The Yasukuni Shrine and the Enshrined Class A War Criminals at Yasukuni'), *Riben xuekan*, May 3: 20–31.

Gao Hui (2005) 'Chaohe wenti de zhengjie yu jiejue qianjing' ('The North Korean Nuclear Issue: Problems and Prospects'), *Shehui guancha*, 4: 25–28.

Gao Zichuan (2004) 'Zhongguo zhoubian anquan huanjing jiben taishi jiexi' ('An Analysis of China's Peripheral Security Environment'), *Dangdai Yatai*, 1: 9–10.

Gao Zugui (2004) 'Meiguo "xindiguo" zhanlue fenxi' ('An Analysis of America's "New Empire" Strategy'), *Guoji wenti yanjiu*, 6: 44–49.

Ge Lide (2002) 'Meiguo tuichu "Fandao Tiaoyue" ji zhanlue fandao xitong de fanzhan qianjing' ('America's Withdrawal from the "ABM Treaty" and the Prospects for the Development of the Strategic Anti-Missile System'), *Shijie jingji yu zhengzhi*, April 4: 37–42.

Geng Lihua (2000) 'Pujing shidai de Eluosi duiwai zhengce' ('Russia's External Policy in the Putin Era'), *Dongou Zhongya yanjiu*, 5: 61–66.

Gu Guanfu (1996) 'Eluosi dui Dongbeiya anquan de kaolu yu duice' ('Russia's Consideration of Northeast Asian Security and Its Response'), *Xiandai guoji guanxi*, June 6: 13–15.

Gu Guanfu and Tian Runfeng (1993) 'MeiE shounao huiwu ji MeiE guanxi qianjing' ('The US-Russian Summit and the Prospect for US-Russian Relations'), *Xiandai guoji guanxi*, 4: 1–5.

Gu Wenyan (1998) 'Meiguo jingji zai Xifang he yi yizhiduxiu' ('Why Does the US Economy Overshadow Other Economies in the West'), *Xiandai guoji guanxi*, June 6: 7–10.

Guan Xi (2006) 'Paitaxing de "haiquan lun" keyi xiuyi – xi Riben liuxing de "haiyang guojia zhanlue"' ('It is Time to End the Exclusive "Sea Power Theory" – An Analysis of Japan's Popular "Maritime State Strategy"'), *Riben xuekan*, July 4: 5–14.

Guo Shuyong (1999) 'Beiyue zai Nan baoxing dui guoji guanxi fazhan de si da tiaozhan' ('Four Challenges to the Development of International Relations Arising from NATO's Atrocity in Yugoslavia'), *Xiandai guoji guanxi*, August 8: 15–18.

—— (2007) 'Xin guoji zhuyi yu Zhongguo ruanshili waijiao' ('New Internationalism and China's Soft Power Diplomacy'), *Guoji guancha*, 2: 43–52.

Guo Xiangang (1992) 'Meiguo dui Yatai zhanlue de tiaozheng' ('The Adjustment in America's Asia-Pacific Strategy'), *Guoji wenti yanjiu*, 2: 41–45.

—— (2002) 'Bushi zhizheng yinianlai duiwai zhengce bianhua ji qi yingxiang' ('The Changes in the Bush Administration's Foreign Policy over the Past Year and Their Implications'), *Guoji wenti yanjiu*, March 2: 32–42.

—— (2003) 'Meiguo quanqiu zhanlue de zhongxin zhuanyi' ('The Shifting of US Global Strategic Priority'), *Guoji wenti yanjiu*, March 2: 17–22.

Guo Zhenyuan (2007) 'ZhongMei guanxi zhong de Taiwan wenti: bianhua yu yingxiang' ('The Taiwan Issue in Sino-US Relations: Changes and Implications'), *Guoji wenti yanjiu*, March 2: 20–25.

Ha Mei (1991) 'Lengzhan hou shiqi Meiguo duiwai zhanlue de tiaozheng' ('The Adjustment in US External Strategy in the Post-Cold War Era'), *Xiandai guoji guanxi*, 2: 13–17.

Han Shanbi (1988) *Deng Xiaoping pingzhuan* (A Critical Biography of Deng Xiaoping), Hong Kong: Dongxi wenhua shiye gongsi.

Hao Yufan (2005) '"Bushi Zhuyi" de zuoxiang yu ZhongMei guanxi' ('The Future of "The Bush Doctrine" and Sino-US Relations'), *Meiguo yanjiu*, 19 (4): 7–24.

He Fang (1996) 'Chuzai lishi zhuanzhe shiqi de Riben' ('Japan in a Period of Historical Transformation'), *Riben xuekan*, May 3: 1–23.

—— (1998) 'Gouzhu ZhongRi guanxi de disange qiannian' ('Developing Sino-Japanese Relations in the Third Millennium'), *Riben xuekan*, July 4: 10–18.

Hou Baoquan (1999) 'Eluosi wuqi chukou de xianzhuang ji qianjing fenxi' ('An Analysis of the Current Situation of and Prospects for Russia's Arms Export'), *Dongou Zongya yanjiu*, April 2: 69–74, 80.

Hu Angang and Liu Taoxiong (2004) 'ZhongMeiRiYin guofang shili bijiao' ('Comparison of the Defence Capabilities of China, America, Japan and India'), *Zhanlue yu guanli*, 6: 40–45.

Hu Jian (2006) 'Eluosi yingdui Zhongguo heping jueqi de zhanlue fenxi' ('An Analysis of Russia's Strategy of Responding to China's Peaceful Rise'), *Dangdai shijie yu shehuizhuyi* (The Contemporary World and Socialism), 2: 132–36.

Hu Jie (1990) 'Suzao Ouzhou weilai geju de jiaozhu' ('A Competition to Shape the Future European Structure'), *Guoji wenti yanjiu*, 4: 15–17.

Hu Jiping (2005) 'Cong xin fangwei dagang kan Riben anquan zhanlue de tiaozheng fangxiang' ('The New Defence Outline and the Direction of Adjustments in Japan's Security Strategy'), *Xiandai guoji guanxi*, January 1: 48–49, 52.

Hu Jiulong (2000) 'Shilun lengzhanhou Dongmeng yu Meiguo zai Yatai anquan shiwu zhong de xinguanxi' ('Comments on the New Relationships Between ASEAN and America in Asia-Pacific Affairs After the Cold War'), *Dongnanya*, 3/4: 28–34.

Hu Ning (2004) 'AoMei guanxi yu Yatai diqu anquan' ('Australia-America Relations and Asia-Pacific Security'), *Dangdai Yatai*, 1: 11–15.

Hu Rongzhong (2004) 'Riben junshi daguohua de xindongxiang' ('New Trends in Japan's Move Towards a Military Power'), *Riben xuekan*, September 5: 24–38.

Hu Zhiyong (2006) 'Cong YinMei hexieyi toushi Meiguo Nanya zhanlue' ('India-US Nuclear Agreement and America's South Asia Strategy'), *Zhongguo waijiao*, 8: 97–99.

Huang Dahui (2005), 'Yingxiang ZhongRi guanxi fazhan de shenceng yuanyin jiexi' ('Explanations for the Deep-rooted Causes That Affect the Development of Sino-Japanese Relations'), *Ribenxue luntan* (Japanese Studies Forum), 4: 35–39.

Huang Hong (1993), 'Meiguo quanqiu zhanlue tiaozhengzhong de neizai maodun ji zhiyue yinsu' ('The Inherent Contradictions and Constraining Factors in the Adjustment of America's Global Strategy'), *Xiandai guoji guanxi*, 3: 31–35.

Huang Suan (1992) 'Shijie jingji geju de xinbianhua' ('The Changes in the World Economic Structure'), in Du Gong and Ni Liyu, eds, *Zhuanhuanzhong de shijie geju* (The World Structure in Transition), Beijing: Shijie zhishi chubanshe, pp. 164–170.

Huang Yuerong (2007) '2006 nian Taiwan junshi qingkuang shuping' ('Comments on Taiwan's Military Situation in 2006'), *Taiwan yanjiu*, February 21: 17–21.

Ji Yin (1992) 'Shiqu gongtong diren hou de OuMei guangxi' ('Europe-America Relations in the Absence of a Common Enemy'), *Shijie zhishi*, May, p. 4.

Jia Chaowei (1997) 'Riben yu Dongmeng guanxi de xinjieduan' ('A New Stage in Japan-ASEAN Relations'), *Xiandai guoji guanxi*, April 4: 8–12.

Jia Qingguo (1995) 'Chongxin renshi ZhongMei guanxi' ('Reconceptualising Sino-American Relations'), *Meiguo yanjiu*, March 9 (1): 29–49.

Jiang Benliang (1997) 'Beiyue dongkuo de zhengfan xiaoying he yingxiang' ('The Positive and Negative Effects and Impact of NATO's Eastward Expansion'), *Guoji wenti yanjiu*, October 4: 35–38, 50.

Jiang Jianqing (1999) 'Cong Kesuowo zhanzheng kan Beiyue xinzhanlue' ('The Kosovo War and NATO's New Strategy'), *Guoji wenti yanjiu*, October 4: 4–5, 23.

Jiang Lifeng (2006) 'Wuwei de bianjie' ('Meaningless Justications'), *Riben xuekan*, September 5: 1–2.

Jiang Weiqing (1995) 'Cong Jiawu Zhanzheng dao "Maguan Tiaoyue" Riben qiangzhan Taiwan shimo' ('From the Sino-Japanese War of 1894–95 to the "Treaty of Shimonoseki" – the Full Story of Japan's Occupation of Taiwan'), *Taiwan yanjiu*, September 3: 5–9, 68.

Jiang Xiyuan (2005) 'Guoji tixi jiegou bianhua qushi ji qi dui xinxing daguo de rongna' ('The Trends in the Structural Changes in the International System and the Accommodation of Rising Powers'), *Taipingyang xuebao*, 57 (12): 3–11.

Jin Canrong (1995) 'Zhuixin bianhua de guiji – "lengzhanhou Meiguo guoji diwei xueshu taolunhui" zongshu' ('Tracing the Track of Change – Summary of the "Workshop on America's International Standing in the Post-Cold War Era"'), *Meiguo yanjiu*, September 3: 145–47.

Jin Junhui (1994) 'Kelindun zhengfu de waijiao zhengce sixiang chuxi' ('A Preliminary Analysis of the Clinton Administration's Foreign Policy Thinking'), *Guoji wenti yanjiu*, April 2: 1–5.
—— (1996) 'Yijiujiuwunian MeiE guanxi de tedian he jinhou qushi' ('The Main Features of US-Russian Relations in 1995 and Its Future Trend'), *Guoji wenti yanjiu*, January 1: 20–27.
Jin Linbo (1999) 'MeiRi tongmeng zaidingyi de beijing, guocheng ji qi yingxiang' ('The Background, Process and Impact of the Redefinition of the US-Japan Alliance'), *Guoji wenti yanjiu*, 1: 35–39. 29.
—— (2003) 'ChaoRi guanxi yu Dongbeiya xingshi' ('DPRK-Japan Relations and the Situation in North East Asia'), *Guoji wenti yanjiu*, January 1: 30–35.
Jin Xide (1998) 'RiE (Su) guanxi de dingwei ji qi yanbian qushi' ('The Evolution and Future Trend of the Relationship Between Japan and Russia/the Soviet Union'), *Riben xuekan*, May 3: 15–32.
—— (2002) 'Riben anquan zhanlue mianlin shizi lukou' ('Japan's Security Strategy at the Crossroads'), *Riben xuekan*, March 2: 1–15.
—— (2006) 'Riben dui Zhongdong zhengce de yanbian guiji' ('The Evolution of Japan's Policy Towards the Middle East'), *Riben xuekan*, July 4: 25–36.
Jin Yaoji (1984) *Zhongguo minzhu zhi kunju yu fazhan* (The Dilemma and Development of Chinese Democracy), Taipei: Shibao chuban gongsi.
Jin Zhengkun (2000) 'Zhongguo "huoban" waijiao zhanlue chutan' ('A Preliminary Analysis of China's "Partnership" Diplomatic Strategy'), *Zhongguo waijiao*, 4: 20–25.
Ke Juhan, Tao Jian and Gu Wenyan (1993a) 'Kelindun chongzhen Meiguo de yitao jihua' ('Clinton's Plans for Revitalising the American Economy'), *Xiandai guoji guanxi*, 3: 1–4, 25.
—— (1993b) 'Kelindun zhengfu weihe gaodu zhongshi duiwai maoyi' ('Why Does the Clinton Administration Pay Particular Attention to Foreign Trade'), *Xiandai guoji guanxi*, 7: 9–12.
Kong Fanhe and Ma Qian (2005) 'Feichuantong anquan shijiaoxia de anquan linian' ('Security Conceptions from the Non-traditional Security Perspectives'), *Taipingyang xuebao*, 57 (12): 72–79.
Li Bing (2006) 'Riben haishang zhanlue tongdao sixiang yu zhengce tanxi' (An Analysis of the Thinking and Policy of Japan's Strategic Sea Lanes'), *Riben xuekan*, January 1: 94–104.
Li Chuanxun (2004) 'Eluosi duiHua yulun xiaoji fangmian de lishi wenhua fenxi' ('A Historical and Cultural Analysis of the Negative Aspects of Russia's Media and Elite Opinion on China'), *Eluosi Zhongya Dongou yanjiu*, December 6: 7–15.
Li Dongyan (1996) 'Mengxiang gouzhu danji shijie geju de Meiguo' ('America That Dreams of Creating a Unipolar World Structure'), in Xi Runchang and Gao Heng, eds, *Shijie zhengzhi xingeju yu guoji anquan* (The New Global Political Structure and International Security), Beijing: Junshikexue chubanshe, pp. 54–79.
Li Fuxing (1995) 'RiE weirao "beifang lingtu" wenti de douzheng ji fazhan qianjing qiangtan' ('A Preliminary Analysis of the Struggle Between Japan and Russia over the Issue of the "Northern Territories" and Its Future Development'), *Dongbeiya luntan*, August 3: 30–33.
Li Genan (1996) 'RiMei anbao tizhi zai dingwei' ('The Renewal of the Japanese-US Security Treaty'), *Waiguo wenti yanjiu*, 2: 1–3.
Li Haidong (2006) 'Bushi shouci Nanya zhixing: quanmian tisheng MeiYin guanxi' ('Bush's First Visit to South Asia: Comprehensive Upgrading of US-India Relations'), *Dangdai shijie* (Contemporary World), 4: 18–20.
Li Jie (2005) 'Tisheng ruanquanli dui shixian woguo heping jueqi zhanlue de zuoyong' ('The Function of Promoting Soft Power for the Realization of China's Peaceful Rise Strategy'), *Taipingyang xuebao*, 57 (12): 64–71.
Li Jingjie (1997) 'Shilun ZhongE zhanlue shezuo huoban guanxi' ('On Sino-Russian Strategic Coordinative Partnership'), *Dongou Zongya yanjiu*, April 2: 3–5.

—— (2000) 'ZhongE zhanlue xiezuo huoban guanxi ji qi Meiguo yinsu' ('Sino-Russian Strategic Coordinative Partnership and the American Factor'), *Dongou Zhongya yanjiu*, 3: 3–14.

—— (2006) 'Xinshiji de ZhongE guanxi' ('Sino-Russian Relations in the New Century'), *Xiboliya yanjiu* (Siberia Studies), 4: 8–10. Reprinted in *Zhongguo waijiao* (China's Diplomacy), 12: 36–39.

Li Jingzhi (2003a) 'Shijie geju he daguo guanxi de xinbianhua: Yilake zhanzheng ji qi yingxiang xiping' ('The Changes in the World Pattern and Great Power Relations: an Analysis of the Iraq War and Its Impact'), *Guoji luntan*, 3: 1–8.

—— (2003b) 'Zhanlue jiyuqi he woguo de guoji zhanlue' ('Strategic Opportunity and China's International Strategy'), *Xinshiye* (New Horizon), 4: 10–13. Reprinted in *Zhongguo waijiao* (China's Diplomacy), 11: 2–7.

—— (2006) 'ZhongMeiRi guanxi yu Dongya anquan' ('China-US-Japan Relations and East Asian Security'), *Jiaoxue yu yanjiu* (Teaching and Research), 3: 20–26.

Li Quanyi (2004) '"Pujing zhizheng yilai Eluosi xingshi yu ZhongE guanxi" yantaohui zongshu' ('Summary of the Symposium on "the Situation in Russia and Sino-Russian Relations since Putin Came into Office"'), *Eluosi Zhongya Dongou yanjiu*, February 1: 72–76.

Li Wei (2007) 'Zhongguo guoji guanxi yanjiu zhong de "lilun jinbu" yu "wenti queshi"' ('The "Theoretical Advances" and "Problems and Weaknesses" in China's International Relations Research'), *Shijie jingji yu zhengzhi*, September 9: 23–30.

Li Xiao (2001) 'The Bush Administration's Strategy of "Using Japan to Constrain China" and its Impact', *Shijie jingji yu zhengzhi*, 6: 22–27.

Li Ye (1998) 'Diaoyudao wenti yu ZhongRi guanxi' ('The Issue of the Diaoyu Islands and Sino-Japanese Relations'), *Waiguo wenti yanjiu*, 2: 30–34.

Li Yongcheng and Zhang Yan (2004) 'Jingongxing xianshizhuyi shijiaoxia de daguo quanli-anquan jingzheng' ('Power-Security Competition Among the Great Powers – the Offensive Realism Perspective'), *Taipingyang xuebao*, 3: 23–32.

Li Yonghui (2004) 'Pujing zhizheng yilai de ERi guanxi' ('Russo-Japanese Since Putin Came into Office'), *Eluosi Zhongya dongou yanjiu*, June 3: 58–64.

—— (2005) '"shuyuan" de linju – ERi zhijian de xinren wenti' ('"Distant Neighbour" – the Issue of Trust between Russia and Japan'), *Eluosi Zhongya Dongou yanjiu*, April 2: 66–72.

Li Yonghui and Ping Zhanguo (2000) 'Xinshidai de ERi guanxi' ('Russo-Japanese Relations in a New Era'), *Dongou Zhongya yanjiu*, 4: 68–74.

Li Zhihong (1996) 'Qianxi BoHei zhanzheng yu heping de zhuanhua' ('A Preliminary Analysis of the War in Bosnia-Herzegovina and Its Transition to Peace'), *Guoji wenti yanjiu*, 2: 18–20.

Li Zhongcheng (1996) 'Eluosi jianghua "xin Dongfang zhengce"' ('The Strengthening of Russia's "New Oriental Policy"'), *Xiandai guoji guanxi*, April 4: 13–17, 38.

Li Zhongjie (2002) 'Renshi he tuidong shijie duojihua jincheng' ('Understanding and Promoting the Process of Multipolarization'), *Liaowang* (Outlook), 23: 3–9.

Lian Degui (2007a) '"Weizhi yishi" yu Riben zhanlue wenhua de tedian' ('"Consciousness of Position" and the Characteristics of Japan's Strategic Culture'), *Riben xuekan*, May 3: 92–104.

—— (2007b) 'Xin Futian zhuyi yu ZhongRi guanxi' ('NeoFukudaism and Sino-Japanese Relations'), *Xiandai guoji guanxi*, December 12: 58–62.

Lian Wen (1998) 'Dui jinnianlai RiTai guanxi fazhan de jidian sikao' ('Reflections on the Development in Japan-Taiwan Relations in Recent Years'), *Waiguo wenti yanjiu*, 4: 28–30.

Liang Gencheng (1996) 'Bian jiechu, bian ezhi – Kelindun zhenfu de dui Hua zhengce pouxi' ('Engaging While Containing – an In-depth Analysis of the Clinton Administration's China Policy'), *Meiguo yanjiu*, June 10 (2): 7–20.

Liang Tao and Ding Liang (2005) 'Minzhu heping lilun de fumian yingxiang' ('The Negative Impact of the Democratic Peace Theory'), *Guoji guanxi xueyuan xuebao*, 2: 1–4.

Liang Yunxiang (1997) 'Lengzhan hou Riben waijiao zhengce juece tizhi de bianhua ji qi tedian he yuanyin' ('The Characteristics and Causes of the Change in Japan's Post-Cold War Foreign Policy-making Structure'), *Riben xuekan*, March 2: 67–81.

Lin Hongyu (1997) 'Lengzhan hou Meiguo de Yatai zhanlue he duihua zhengce' ('America's Asia-Pacific Strategy and China Policy in the Post-Cold War Era'), *Guoji guanxi xueyuan xuebao*, March 1: 1–6.

Lin Limin (2000) 'Guanyu Zhongguo 21 shijichu duiwai zhanlue de jidian sikao' ('Some Thoughts on China's External Strategy in the Early 21st Century'), *Xiandai guoji guanxi*, 3: 11–16.

Lin Xiaoguang (1998a) 'Lengzhan hou RiMei anbao tizhi de bianhua he tiaozheng' ('The Change and Adjustment in the Japanese-US Security Treaty in the Post-Cold War Era'), *Waiguo wenti yanjiu*, 2: 6–10, 5.

—— (1998b) 'RiE guanxi: jiushi niandai yilai de fazhan yu bianhua' ('Japan-Russia Relations: Developments and Changes in the 1990s'), *Waiguo wenti yanjiu*, 4: 31–37.

Lin Zhibo (2004) 'Dui dangqian ZhongRi guanxi ruogan wenti de kanfa' ('Perspectives on Current Issues in Sino-Japanese Relations'), *Zhanlue yu guanli*, 63 (2): 89–93.

Ling Xingguang (2003) 'Zhanlue duitou zhanshu qiantuo' ('A Correct Strategy but Inappropriate Tactics'), *Shijie jingji yu zhengzhi*, 9: 17–21.

Liu Aming (2005) 'Ruanquanli lilun yu Zhongguo heping jueqi' ('The Theory of Soft Power and China's Peaceful Rise'), *Taipingyang xuebao*, 57 (12): 55–63.

Liu Aming and Wang Lianhe (2005) 'Xianfazhiiren yu yufangxing zhanzheng bianxi: yi Bushi zhengfu guojia anquan zhanlue weili' ('An Analysis of Pre-emption and Preventive War: a Case Study of Bush's National Security Strategy'), *Guoji zhengzhi* (International Politics) 2: 75–81.

Liu Dexi (1997) 'Eluosi waijiao zhanlue de tiaozheng yu ZhongE guanxi' ('The Adjustments in Russia's Diplomatic Strategy and Sino-Russian Relations'), *Waiguo wenti yanjiu*, 3: 33–37; 50.

Liu Guiling (1998a) 'Eluosi de Yatai waijiao zhanlue' ('Russia's Diplomatic Strategy in the Asia-Pacific'), *Xiandai guoji guanxi*, January 1: 29–33.

—— (1998b) 'ZhongE zai anquan lingyu hezuo de qianjing ji wenti' ('Sino-Russian Security Co-operation: Prospects and Problems'), *Xiandai guoji guanxi*, December 12: 18–21.

—— (1999) 'Eluosi yingdui Beiyue dongkuo jucuo ji EMei guanxi qianjing' ('Russia's Countermeasures against NATO's Eastward Expansion and Prospects for Russian-US Relations'), *Xiandai guoji guanxi*, June 6: 31–33.

—— (2005) 'Lengzhan jieshu yilai ERi guanxi de xinbianhua' ('Changes in Russo-Japanese Relations Since the End of the Cold War'), *Xiandai guoji guanxi*, November 12: 40–44.

Liu Jianfei (2003) 'Yilake zhanzheng dui guoji jushi de yingxiang yu Zhongguo de guoji zhanlue xuanze' ('The Impact of the Iraq War on the International Situation and China's International Strategic Choice') *Dangdai shijie yu shehuizhuyi*, 4: 24–28.

—— (2006) 'Heping jueqi shi Zhongguo de zhanlue xuanze' ('Peaceful Rise is China's Strategic Choice'), *Shijie jingji yu zhengzhi*, 2: 36–40.

—— (2007) 'ZhongMei jianshexing hezuo guanxi de xinfazhan' ('New Developments in Sino-US Constructive and Cooperative Relations'), *Guoji wenti yanjiu*, September 5: 1–6.

Liu Jiangyong (1993) 'Jiushi niandai Yatai duobian anquan jizhi de jianli' ('The Establishment of Multilateral Security Mechanisms in the Asia-Pacific in the 1990s'), *Yatai yanjiu*, 5: 6–7.

—— (1996a) 'Riben meihua qinlue lishi de dongxiang ji qi genyuan' ('The Roots of Japan's Attempts to Adorn Its History of Aggression'), *Xiandai guoji guanxi*, September 9: 2–8, 32.

—— (1996b) 'Lun Diaoyudao de zhuquan guishu wenti' ('On the Issue of Sovereignty over the Diaoyu Islands'), *Riben xuekan*, November 6: 13–28.

—— (1997) 'Xin "RiMei fangwei hezuo zhizhen" heyi lingren youlu' ('Why Have the New "Guidelines for Japanese-US Defense Co-operation" Caused Concerns'), *Xiandai guoji guanxi*, November 11: 7–12.

—— (2007) 'Lun Riben de "jiazhiguan waijiao"' ('On Japan's "Value-oriented Diplomacy"'), *Riben xuekan*, November 6: 46–59.

Liu Jinghua, Niu Jun and Jiang Yi (1997) 'Lun Beiyue dongkuo' ('On NATO's Eastward Expansion'), *Meiguo yanjiu*, September 3: 39–81.

Liu Jinzhi (2004) 'Shiping xiao Bushi de diguo waijiao' ('On Bush's Imperial Foreign Policy'), *Guoji zhengzhi yanjiu* (International Political Studies), 4: 83–92.

Liu Jun (2004a) 'Quanqiuhua yu Eluosi waijiao zhengce de xingcheng – cong Gebaerqiaofu dao Pujing' ('Globalization and the Formation of Russian Foreign Policy – From Gorbachev to Putin'), *Eluosi Zhongya Dongou yanjiu*, August 4: 53–56.

—— (2004b) 'Quanli, weixie yu Daxiyang Tongmeng de weilai' ('Power, Threat and the Future of the Transatlantic Alliance'), *Ouzhou yanjiu*, August 22 (4): 14–24.

Liu Qingcai (1995) 'ZhongE guanxi: jincheng, xianzhuang yu qianjing' ('Sino-Russian Relations: Progress, Current Situation and Prospect'), *Dongbeiya luntan*, August 3: 24–29.

Liu Shan (2001) 'The Change in World Structure', *Guoji wenti yanjiu*, 5: 1–6.

Liu Shaohua (2007) 'Dongya quyu hezuo de lujing xuanze' ('The Choice of Paths for East Asian Regional Cooperation'), *Guoji wenti yanjiu*, September 5: 53–58.

Liu Shilong (1998) 'Lengzhan hou Riben dui Mei zhengce zouxiang' ('The General Trend of Japan's Policy Towards the United States Since the End of the Cold War'), *Riben xuekan*, September 5: 1–13.

—— (2003) 'Lengzhanhou Riben de waijiao zhanlue' ('Japan's Foreign Strategy After the Cold War'), *Riben xuekan*, September 5: 23–38.

—— (2006) 'Riben zai Chaoxian Zhanzheng zhong de zuoyong' ('The Role of Japan in the Korean War'), *Riben xuekan*, September 5: 53–62.

Liu Xuecheng (2004a) 'Feichuantong anquan de jiben texing ji qi yingdui' ('Non-traditional Security: Main Characteristics and Responses'), *Guoji wenti yanjiu*, 1: 32–35.

—— (2004b) 'Xin guojia anquan zhanlue xia de Meiguo quanqiu junli tiaozheng' ('US Global Military Adjustments under the New National Security Strategy'), *Taipingyang xuebao*, December 4: 40–43.

Liu Zhongmin (2007) 'Guanyu haiquan yu daguo jueqi wenti de ruogan xikao' ('Reflections on Sea Power and the Issue of the Rise of Great Powers'), *Shijie jingji yu zhengzhi*, December 12: 6–14.

Lu Chuan (2006) 'Lengzhanhou Riben junshi zhanlue siwei de jiben guilu tanxi' ('An Analysis of the Basic Pattern of Japan's Post-Cold War Military Strategic Thinking'), *Riben xuekan*, May 3: 41–64.

Lu Guozhong (1997) 'Xin xingshi xia Riben de diwei, zuoyong yu zouxiang' ('Japan's Position, Its Role and Future Directions in a New Environment'), *Guoji wenti yanjiu*, 1: 41–47.

—— (1999) 'Xiaoyuan shangtai yilai Riben jingji he waijiao de zoushi' ('The General Trend of Japan's Economic and Foreign Policies Since Obuchi Keizo Came into Power'), *Guoji wenti yanjiu*, 1: 30–34.

Lu Junyuan (1995) 'Cong diyuan zhengzhi kan Riben de anquan zhanlue' ('Japan's Security Strategy in Geopolitical Perspective'), *Riben xuekan*, May 3: 16–24.

—— (1996) 'Diyuan zhanlue zhong de Taiwan ji qi dui daguo de zuoyong' ('Taiwan's Geostrategic Position and Its Significance for the Security of the Great Powers'), *Taiwan yanjiu*, March 1: 33–37.

Lu Ning (2005) '"ZhongMei changqi duihua" zongshu' ('A Summary of "Sino-US Long-term Dialogue"'), *Meiguo yanjiu*, 19 (4): 152–155.

Lu Qichang (1999) 'Cong Beiyue baoxing kan Meiguo de quanqiu zhanlue' ('NATO's Babaric Acts and America's Global Strategy'), *Xiandai guoji guanxi*, June 6: 7–10.

Lu Yaodong (2006) 'Shixi Riben de minzu baoshou zhuyi ji qi texing' ('A Preliminary

Analysis of Japan's Nationalistic Conservatism and Its Characteristics'), *Riben xuekan*, September 5: 5–15.

Lu Yi (1997) 'Anlihui changren lishiguo – Riben de mubiao yu dongxiang' ('Permanent Membership of the UN Security Council – Japan's Aims and Activities'), *Waiguo wenti yanjiu*, 4: 1–6.

Lu Zhongwei (2002) 'Bawo shijie jushi de maibo' ('Grasping the Overall Trend of the World Scene'), *Xiandai guoji guanxi*, January 1: 2–3.

Ma Jiali (2001a) '9/11 shijian hou Meiguo Nanya zhengce de bianhua' ('The Changes in America's South Asia Policy After 9/11'), *Nanya yanjiu*, 2: 3–7.

—— (2001b) 'Qianxi Mei, Yin, Ba sanjiao guanxi de bianhua' ('An Analysis of the Changes in the Triangular Relationships Among America, India and Pakistan'), *Xiandai guoji guanxi*, November 11: 32–35.

Ma Licheng (2002) 'DuiRi guanxi xinsiwei' ('New Thinking in China's Relations with Japan'), *Zhanlue yu guanli*, 6: 41–47.

Ma Yuan (1996) 'Junshi zai lengzhan hou guoji guanxi zhong de diwei he zuoyong' ('The Role and Function of the Balance of Power in Post-Cold War International Relations'), *Guoji guanxi xueyuan xuebao*, December 4: 14–19.

Ma Zhengang (1997) 'Riben jinqi tiaozheng dui Tai zhengce de yuanyin he yitu' ('The Reasons for and Intentions of Japan's Recent Adjustment in Its Taiwan Policy'), *Guoji guanxi xueyuan xuebao*, September 3: 18–22.

—— (2007) 'Zhongguo de zeren yu "Zhongguo zeren lun"' ('China's Responsibility and the "China Responsibility Theory"', *Guoji wenti yanjiu*, May 3: 1–3.

Man Bin (1997) 'Cong BoHei zhanzheng kan Beiyue canyu Lianhequo weihe xingdong' ('NATO's Participation in the United Nations' Peace-keeping Operations in the War in Bosnia-Herzegovina'), *Ouzhou*, June 15 (3): 76–80.

Mao Desong (1993) 'Wei jianli xin de guoji zhixu er douzheng' ('Struggling for the Establishment of a New International Order'), in Zhang Maiqiang and Zhu Chaolan, eds, *Xinbian shijie zhengzhi jingji yu guoji guanxi* (A New Text on World Politics, Economy and International Relations), Hefei: Zhongguo kexuejishudaxue chubanshe, pp. 411–43.

Men Honghua (2004) 'Zhongguo jueqi yu guoji zhixu' ('The Rise of China and International Order'), *Taipingyang xuebao*, 2: 4–13.

—— (2007a) 'Zhongguo ruanshili pinggu baogao (shang)' ('A Report on the Evaluation of China's Soft Power (First Part)'), *Guoji guancha*, 2: 15–26.

—— (2007b) 'Zhongguo ruanshili pinggu baogao (xia)' ('A Report on the Evaluation of China's Soft Power (Second Part)'), *Guoji guancha*, 3: 37–46, 28.

Ni Feng (2004) 'Guanyu duojihua de yixie sikao' ('Some Thoughts on Multipolarization'), *Taipingyang xuebao*, 12: 3–17.

Ni Lexiong (2007) 'Cong luquan dao haiquan de lishi biran' ('The Historical Inevitability of the Transition from Continental Power to Sea Power'), *Shijie jingji yu zhengzhi*, November 11: 22–32.

Ni Shixiong and Guo Xuetang (1997) '"Minzhu heping lun" yu lengzhan hou Meiguo waijiao zhanlue' ('The "Theory of Democratic Peace" and Post-Cold War American External Strategy'), *Ouzhou*, October 5: 13–20.

Ni Shixiong and Wang Yiwei (2002) 'Shilun guoji guanxi minzhuhua' ('On Democratization of International Relations'), *Guoji wenti yanjiu*, May 3: 22–26.

Ni Xiaoquan (1993) 'Xifang yuanzhu he Eluosi duiwai zhengce zouxiang' ('Western Assistance and the General Direction of Russia's Foreign Policy'), *Dongou Zongya yanjiu*, June 3: 56–60, 84.

Ni Xiaoquan and Luobote Luosi, eds, (1993) *Meizhongsu sanjian guanxi* (The Triangular Relationship between the United States, China and the Soviet Union), Beijing: Renmin chubanshe.

Ning Sao (2000) 'Xuanze huoban zhanlue, yingzao huoban guanxi' ('Choosing Partnership Strategy, Shaping Partnership Relations'), *Xinshiye* (New Horizon), 4: 10–13. Reprinted in *Zhongguo waijiao* (China's Diplomacy), 6: 2–7.

Niu Hanzhang (2001) 'Terrorism and Anti-terrorism: Theoretical Considerations on a Different Type of War in the 21st Century', *Shijie jingji yu zhengzhi luntan*, 6: 41–44.

Niu Jun (1995) 'Duoshi zhiqiu – ZhongMei guanxi de xianzhuang ji qianjing' ('Troubled Times – the Current Situation and the Future of Sino-US Relations'), *Meiguo yanjiu*, December 4: 131–34.

—— (1996) '"Jiuliu Taiwan haixia weiji yu ZhongMei guanxi xueshu yantaohui" zongshu' ('Summary of the "Symposium on the 1996 Taiwan Strait Crisis and Sino-US Relations"'), *Meiguo yanjiu*, September 3: 152–54.

—— (1998) 'Lun Kelindun zhengfu dier renqi dui Hua zhengce de yanbian ji qi tedian' ('On the Evolution and Characteristics of the Clinton Administration's China Policy During its First Term'), *Meiguo yanjiu*, March 12 (1): 7–28.

Pan Guanghui (2003) 'Lengzhanhou de Eluosi yu Chaoxian bandao' ('Russia and the Korean Peninsula After the Cold War'), *Eluosi Zhongya Dongou yanjiu*, August 4: 63–68.

Pan Shiying (1993) *Xiandai zhanlue sikao – lengzhan hou de zhanlue lilun* (Contemporary Strategic Thinking – A Post-Cold War Strategic Theory), Beijing: Shijie zhishi chubanshe.

Pan Tongwen (1992) 'Bu Shen de shijie xinzhixu chutan' ('A Preliminary Analysis of Bush's New World Order'), in Zhu Tingxun, ed., *Bianqianzhong de shijie geju* (The Changing World Structure), Beijing: Changzheng chubanshe, pp. 382–92.

Pan Zhongqi (2007) 'Zhongguo zai shijie zhixu zhong de canyu, shouyi he yingxiang' ('China in the World Order: Participation, Benefits and Implications'), *Shijie jingji yu zhengzhi*, March 3: 48–54.

Pang Zhongying (2001) 'Peace for a New Century? – Reflections on the World Order', *Guoji jingji pinglun*, 6: 29–31.

—— (2003) 'Duili jiaju huanshi hezuo shenhua?' ('Increasing Confrontation or Intensifying Cooperation?'), *Shijie jingji yu zhengzhi*, 9: 14–17.

—— (2006a) 'Quanqiuhua, shehuibianhua yu Zhongguo waijiao' ('Globalization, Social Change and China's Diplomacy'), *Shijie jingji yu zhengzhi*, 2: 7–13.

—— (2006b) 'Lanyong fankong ji qi houguo' ('Abusing Anti-terrorism and Its Consequences'), *Xiandai guoji guanxi*, September 9: 22–23.

Pang Zhongying, Shi Yinhong, Li Jingzhi *et al.* (2001) 'Kongbu xiji hou de guoji geju' ('The International Structure after the Terrorist Attacks'), *Guoji zhengzhi* (International Politics), December 12: 150–53.

Piao Jianyi (2003a) 'Chaoxian hewenti ji qi weilai zouxiang' ('The North Korean Nuclear Issue and Its Future Developments'), *Dangdai Yatai*, March 3: 23–26.

—— (2003b) 'Beijing liufang huitan yu Chaoxian hewenti qianjing' ('The Six-Party Talks and Future Development of the North Korean Nuclear Issue'), *Dangdai Yatai*, October 10: 42–46.

Pu Guoliang (2004) 'Chaoxian bandao heweiji wenti de lishi youlai ji qi shizhi' ('The Historical Development and Nature of the Nuclear Crisis on the Korean Peninsula'), *Zhongguo teshi shehui zhuyi yanjiu*, 5: 70–73.

Pu Ning (1997) 'Shixi Taiwan wenti zai Zhongguo duiwai zhanlue zhong de Dingwei' ('A Preliminary Analysis of the Role of the Taiwan Issue in China's External Strategy'), *Taiwan yanjiu jikan*, December 4: 4–6.

Qian Chunyuan, Lu Qichang and Tao Jian (1993) 'Kelindun zhengfu de neiwai zhengce tiaozheng ji qi qianjing' ('The Adjustment in the Clinton Administration's Domestic and Foreign Policies and Its Prospects'), *Xiandai guoji guanxi*, 8: 20–22.

Qian Wenrong (1999) 'Lianheguo mianlin bei bianyuanhua de weixian' ('The UN is Facing the Danger of Being Marginalized'), *Guoji wenti yanjiu*, October 4: 9–10, 16.

—— (2002) 'Fankong yu guoji zhixu' ('Anti-terrorism and the International Order'), *Guoji wenti yanjiu*, May 3: 27–32.

Qiao Linsheng (2006) 'Shilun xinshiji Riben dui Dongmeng de waijiao zhengce' ('On Japan's Foreign Policy towards ASEAN in the New Century'), *Dongbeiya luntan*, 2: 100–04.

Qiao Mu (2002) 'Duojihua qushi buhui gaibian' ('The Trend in Multipolarization Will Not Change'), *Dangdai Yatai*, 6: 10–13.

Qin Yaqing and Wei Ling (2007) 'Jiegou, jincheng yu quanli de shehuihua – Zhongguo yu Dongya diqu hezuo' ('Structure, Process and the Socialization of Power – China and East Asian Regional Cooperation'), *Shijie jingji yu zhengzhi*, March 3: 7–15.

Ren Jingjing (2005) 'Zhanlue xiezuo huoban guanxi kuangjiaxia de ZhongE keji hezuo' ('Sino-Russian Scientific and Technical Cooperation Within the Framework of Strategic Coordinative Partnership'), *Zhongguo waijiao*, 7: 46–48.

Ren Junsheng (1995) 'Shilun ZhongMei jingmao guanxi de yingxiang yinsu he fazhan qiangjing' ('An Analysis of the Influencing Factors of and Future Prospects for Sino-US Economic and Trade Relations'), *Dongbeiya luntan*, August 3: 20–23.

Ren Xiao (2007) 'Lun Dongya Fenghui ji yu Meiguo de guanxi' ('On East Asian Summit and Its Relations with the United States'), *Guoji wenti yanjiu*, July 4: 49–54.

Ren Zhengde and Wu Jianxin (1993) 'Wei jianli guoji zhengzhi jingji xinzhixu er douzheng' ('Struggling for the Establishment of a New International Political and Economic Order'), in Ren Zhengde, Shao Hande and Wu Jianxin, eds., *Dangdai shijie zhengzhi jingji* (Contemporary World Politics and Economy), Beijing: Xinhua chubanshe, pp. 372–95.

Ruan Zongze (2001) 'Gouzhu xinshiji dazhoubian waijiao' ('Building a Greater Peripheral Diplomacy in a New Century'), *Liaowang* (Outlook) 38: 3–5.

—— (2002) 'Fankong lianmeng ji qi mianlin de tiaozhan' ('The Anti-Terrorist Coalition and the Challenge It Faces'), *Guoji wenti yanjiu*, May 3: 36–41.

—— (2004) 'Zhongguo heping jueqi fazhan daolu de lilun tantao' ('A Theoretical Analysis of the Path of China's Peaceful Rise'), *Guoji wenti yanjiu*, 4: 28–33.

Sa Benwang (2003) 'Lun "Bushi zhuyi" – Meiguo fadong Yilake zhanzheng de zhidao sixiang' ('On the "Bush Doctrine" – the Underpinning Theory of America's Launch of the Iraq War'), *Heping yu fazhan*, 2: 1–5, 10.

—— (2004) 'Tuijin Yatai duobian anquan hezuo de jiyu yu tiaozhan' ('The Opportunities and Challenges of Promoting Multilateral Security Cooperation in the Asia-Pacific'), *Heping yu fazhan*, 1: 6–12.

Sa Benwang and Shang Hong (2001) 'Meiguo Kelindun zhengfu waijiao zhengce pingxi' ('An Analysis of the Clinton Administration's Foreign Policy'), *Waijiao xueyuan xuebao* (Journal of Foreign Affairs College), 2: 39–46.

Shi Lan and Li Wenjing (2002) 'Afuhan chongjian shi yichang xinde jiaoliang' ('The Reconstruction of Afghanistan Is a New Contest'), *Dangdai Yatai*, April 4: 25–28.

Shi Yinhong (1997) 'Yu fuza jushi xiangwei de jiandanhua zhengce – lun lengzhan shiqi Meiguo zai Dongya de anquan zhengce' ('An Oversimplified Policy That Is Incompatible with Complex Circumstances – On US Security Policy in East Asia During the Cold War Era'), *Meiguo yanjiu*, 2: 7–26.

—— (2000) 'Anquan liangnan yu Dongya quyu anquan tizhi de biyao' ('The Security Dilemma and the Necessity for East Asian Security Mechanisms'), *Zhanlue yu guanli*, 41 (4): 86–92.

—— (2001) '9/11 shijian yu Meiguo duiwai Taishi' ('The Events of 9/11 and US External Posture'), *Meiguo yanjiu*, December 4: 21–28.

—— (2002) 'Reflections on Three Major Issues After 'September 11'', *Xiandai guoji guanxi*, January 1: 44–47.

—— (2003a) 'ZhongRi jiejin yu "waijiao geming"' ('Sino-Japanese *Rapprochement* and the "Diplomatic Revolution"'), *Zhanlue yu guanli*, 2: 71–75.

—— (2003b) 'Guanyu ZhongRi guanxi de zhanlue sikao' ('Strategic Thinking on Sino-Japanese Relations'), *Shijie jingji yu zhengzhi*, 9: 10–11.

Shi Yongming (1996) 'Yatai anquan huanjing yu diqu duobianzhuyi' ('The Security Environment in the Asia-Pacific and Regional Multilateralism'), *Guoji wenti yanjiu*, January 1: 41–47.

Shi Ze (1995) 'Eluosi zai Yatai zhanlue diwei de bianhua ji qi yingxiang' ('The Change in Russia's Strategic Position in the Asia-Pacific and Its Impact'), *Guoji wenti yanjiu*, April 2: 1–4.

——— (1996) 'Lun xinshiqi de ZhongE guanxi' ('On Sino-Russian Relations in the New Era'), *Guoji wenti yanjiu*, April 2: 1–4.

——— (2007) 'Eluosi jueqi yu EMei guanxi' ('The Rise of Russia and Russian-American Relations'), *Guoji wenti yanjiu*, September 5: 31–35.

Shu Xiangdi (1994) 'Eluosi de Yatai zhengce' ('Russia's Asia-Pacific Policy'), *Xiandai guoji guanxi*, December 12: 38–42.

Shu Xiangdi and Wang Lijiu (1995) 'ZhongE guanxi de fazhan yu qianjing' ('The Development of and Prospect for Sino-Russian Relations'), *Xiandai guoji guanxi*, October 10: 10–14.

Shun Jianshe (1993) 'Qianxi Eluosi waijiao dongyi de yuanyin' ('A Brief Analysis of the Reasons for the shift of Russia's Foreign Policy towards the East'), *Jinri qianSulian Dongou*, April 2: 17–19.

Song Kui (2007) 'Eluosi Yatai zhanlue ji dui ZhongE hezuo de yiyi' ('Russia's Asia-Pacific Strategy and Its Significance for Sino-Russian Cooperation'), *Dangdai Yatai*, January 1: 5–10.

Song Qiang, Zhang Cangcang and Qiao Bian *et al.* (1996) *Zhongguo keyi shuobu* (China Can Say No), Beijing: Zhongguo gongshang lianhe chubanshe.

Song Qiang, Zhang Cangcang, Qiao Bian, Tang Zhengyu and Gu Qingsheng (1996) *Zhongguo haishi neng shuobu* (China Can Still Say No), Beijing: Zhongguo wenlian chubanshe.

Song Yimin (1992) 'Sulian jubian he zhanhou shijie geju de jieti' ('The Upheaval in the Soviet Union and the Disintegration of the Post-war World Structure'), in Du Gong and Ni Liyu, eds, *Zhuanhuanzhong de shijie geju* (The World Structure in Transition), Beijing: Shijie zhishi chubanshe, pp. 12–59.

——— (1994) 'Eluosi neiwai zhengce xinzouxiang zhendong xifang shijie' ('New Directions in Russia's Domestic and Foreign Policy Have Shaken the Western World'), *Guoji wenti yanjiu*, April 2: 11–16.

——— (1997) 'ZhongE, MeiE, ZhongMei guanxi yiji sanzhejian de xianghu zuoyong' ('Sino-Russian, US-Russian and Sino-American Relations, and the Interactions Among Them'), *Guoji wenti yanjiu*, July 3: 12–18.

——— (1998) 'Meiguo yishi deshou bingwei gaibian duojihua jinyibu fazhan qushi' ('America's Temporary Attainment Has Not Altered the Trend of Further Development of Multipolarity'), *Guoji wenti yanjiu*, January 1: 7.

——— (2000) 'Jingji quangiuhua he Meiguo de zouxiang' ('Economic Globalization and America's Future Direction'), *Guoji wenti yanjiu*, November 6: 13–18.

——— (2001) 'Bushi zhengfu duiwai zhengce zhong de Yatai anquan wenti' ('Asia-Pacific Security Issues in Bush Administration's External Policy'), *Guoji wenti yanjiu*, May 3: 1–6.

Song Yuhua (2002) 'Dangqian Zhongguo mianlin de guoji jingji huanjing' ('China's Current International Economic Environment'), *Guoji wenti yanjiu*, May 3: 49–54.

Song Yuhua and Lu Huajun (1997) 'Guanyu Meiguo waimao nicha yu waimao diwei de sikao' ('On America's Trade Deficit and Its Foreign Trade Status'), *Meiguo yanjiu*, September 3: 82–103.

Su Chi (1992) *Lun Zhongsugong guanxi zhengchanghua, 1979–1989* (On the Normalisation of Sino-Soviet Communist Relations, 1979–1989), Taipei: Sanmin shuju.

Su Ge (2001) 'Meiguo quanqiu zhanlue yu Taiwan wenti' ('America's Global Strategy and the Taiwan Issue'), *Guoji wenti yanjiu*, July 4: 1–7.

——— (2003) 'Ping Meiguo guojia anquan zhanlue de tiaozheng' ('On the Adjustment in the US National Security Strategy'), *Guoji wenti yanjiu*, March 2: 5–10, 22.

Su Hao (1998) '"MeiRi anbao guanxi de tiaozheng yu Yatai anquan wenti" xueshu yantaohui zongshu' ('Summary of the Symposium on "the Adjustment in US-Japan Security Relations and Asia-Pacific Security"'), *Meiguo yanjiu*, March 12 (1): 143–47.

—— (2000) 'Zhongguo waijiao de "huoban guanxi" kuangjia' ('The Framework for China's Diplomatic "Partnerships"'), *Shijie zhishi* (World Knowledge), 5: 11–12.

Sun Changdong and Yang Xianghong (2000) 'Pujing zhizhenghou dui Eluosi waijiao zhengce de tiaozheng' ('The Adjustments in Russia's Foreign Policy After Putin Coming into Power'), *Dongou Zhongya yanjiu*, 5: 55–60.

Sun Cheng (2005) 'Meiguo tiaozheng quanqiu junshi bushu yu MeiRi tongmeng' ('America's Global Military Realignment and US-Japan Alliance'), *Guoji wenti yanjiu*, March 2: 42–46, 10.

Sun Jian (2001) 'YinE guanxi pingxi' ('On Indian-Russian Relations'), *Shijie jingji yu zhengzhi luntan*, 3: 32–33.

Sun Jinzhong (2005) 'Fankong hezuo yu ZhongMei guanxi' ('Anti-terrorist Cooperation and Sino-American Relations'), *Guoji wenti yanjiu*, February 2: 15–18.

Sun Ru (2005) 'Yatai duobian anquan hezuo yu ZhongMei guanxi: zhidu de shijiao' ('Multilateral Security Cooperation in the Asia-Pacific and Sino-US Relations: an Institutional Perspective'), *Meiguo yanjiu*, 19 (4): 100–13.

Sun Suyuan (2004) 'Rentong weiji yu MeiOu guanxi de Jiegouxing bianqian' ('Identity Crisis and the Structural Change in US-Europe Relations'), *Ouzhou yanjiu*, October 5: 52–63.

Tang Shiping (2000) 'Lixiang anquan huanjing yu xinshiji Zhongguo dazhanlue' ('China's Ideal Security Environment and Its Grand Strategy in the New Century'), *Zhanlue yu guanli*, 6: 42–49.

—— (2001) 'Zailun Zhongguo de dazhanlue' ('On China's Grand Strategy'), *Zhanlue yu guanli*, 4: 29–37.

Tang Zhichao (2002) 'Meiguo weihe zhao Alaboren hen' ('Why America is Hated by the Arabs'), *Huanqiu shibao* (Global Times), 10 January, p. 6.

Tao Wenzhao (2005) 'Guanyu Meiguo de quanqiu junshi datiaozheng' ('On America's Global Military Adjustments'), *Taipingyang xuebao*, 1: 51–55.

Tian Chunsheng (2005) 'Eluosi Dongbeiya diqu de nengyuan zhanlue yu Zhongguo de xuanze' ('Russia's Energy Strategy in North East Asia and China's Choice'), *Taipingyang xuebao*, 6: 46–57.

Wan Shirong (1996) 'Shiren zhumu de Beiyue zuzhi dongkuo wenti' ('NATO's Eastward Expansion: an Issue that Has Attracted Worldwide Attention'), *Guoji wenti yanjiu*, 1: 14.

Wang Anqi (1993) 'Eluosi Dongfang zhengce de chutai, shehui beijing ji qi shishi' ('The Formulation of Russia's Oriental Policy and Its Social Background and Implementation'), *Yatai yanjiu*, 3: 33–39.

Wang Bingyin (2003a) 'Eluosi yuanhe guanzhu Chaoxian bandao jushi' ('Why is Russia Concerned about the Situation on the Korean Peninsula'), *Dangdai Yatai*, 5: 11–15.

—— (2003b) 'ZhongE zai Chaoxian bandao de liyi yu liangguo zhanlue xiezuo huoban guanxi de fazhan' ('The Interest of China and Russia in the Korean Peninsula and the Development of their Strategic Coordinative Partnership'), *Eluosi Zhongya Dongou yanjiu*, August 4: 69–74.

Wang Bingyin and Zhou Yanli (2001) 'Eluosi tong Chaoxian bandao liangguo jiaqiang waijiao guanxi de jingji yitu' ('The Economic Motives of the Strengthening of Russia's Relations with the Two Countries on the Korean Peninsula'), *Dongou Zhongya yanjiu*, October 5: 24–28.

Wang Chiming (2005) 'Meijun quanqiu bushu tiaozheng yu Riben mianlin de jueze' ('The Global Realignment of US Forces and the Choice Facing Japan'), *Taipingyang xuebao*, 1: 56–63.

Wang Chuanjian (2005) 'MeiRi tongmeng yu lengzhanhou Riben de Chaoxian bandao zhengce' ('US-Japan Alliance and Japan's Policy Towards the Korean Peninsula'), *Dangdai Yatai*, 9: 28–34.

Wang Fengwu and Xing Aifen (1993) 'Meiguo baquan diwei de xiaoruo' ('America's Declining Hegemonic Position'), in Ren Zhengde, Shao Hande and Wu Jianxin, eds,

Dangdai shijie zhengzhi jingji (Contemporary World Politics and Economy), Beijing: Xinhua chubanshe, pp. 103–37.

Wang Gonglong (1997) 'Jiushi niandai Riben dui Dongmeng de waijiao zhengce' ('Japan's Foreign Policy towards ASEAN in the 1990s'), *Riben xuekan*, July 4: 55–68.

—— (2002) 'Dui RiMei tongmeng "zaidingyi" de zai renshi' ('Re-thinking the "Re-definition" of the Japan-US Alliance'), *Riben xuekan*, September 5: 18–31.

Wang Haihan (1995) 'Dui dangqian MeiOu guanxi de jidian kanfa' ('Perspectives on the Current US-Europe Relations'), *Guoji wenti yanjiu*, 2: 29–32.

—— (1996) 'Tiaozheng Daxiyang liangan guanxi rengran bulu weijian' ('The Adjustment in Trans-Atlantic Relations Remains Intractable'), *Guoji wenti yanjiu*, 2: 23–26, 29.

—— (1997) 'Lun Kelindun zhengfu de dui Hua zhengce ji qi qianjing' ('On the Clinton Administration's China Policy and its Future Trend'), *Guoji wenti yanjiu*, January 1: 3–9.

Wang Haiyun (2007) 'Eluosi congxin jueqi de qiangjing ji qi shijie yingxiang' ('The Prospects for Russia's Re-emergence and Their Impact on the World'), *Eluosi Zhongya Dongou yanjiu*, February 1: 1–7.

Wang Hongfang (2004) 'Dongya anquan hezuo ji qi mushi xuanze' ('East Asian Security Cooperation and the Choice of Models'), *Xiandai guoji guanxi*, 1: 39–44.

Wang Hongwei (2002) 'Guanyu "xiee zhouxin" lun de yidian sikao' ('Reflections on the "Axis of Evil"'), *Dangdai Yatai*, April 4: 22–24.

Wang Houkang and Jin Yingzhong, eds, (1992) *Guoji geju* (International Structure), Shanghai: Shanghai shehui kexueyuan chubanshe.

Wang Jian (2003) 'Yilake zhanzheng hou de Zhongdong jushi yu Meiguo quanqiu zhanlue zouxiang' ('The Situation in the Middle East after the Iraq War and the Future Directions of America's Global Strategy'), *Shijie jingji yanjiu* (World Economy Studies), 8: 47–50.

Wang Jie (2000) 'Meiguo de kuashiji quanqiu zhanlue yu lianheguo' ('US Global Strategy at the Turn of the Century and the United Nations'), *Guoji guancha*, 1: 1–6.

Wang Jisi (1992) 'Zhengzai tuotai de Meiguo quanqiu xinzhanlue' ('The Birth of America's New Global Strategy'), *Shijie zhishi* (World Knowledge), January 1: 9.

—— ed., (1995) *Wenming yu guoji zhengzhi – Zhongguo xuezhe ping Hengtingdun de wenming chongtulun* (Civilisations and International Politics – Chinese Scholars on Huntington's Thesis on the Clash of Civilisations), Shanghai: Shanghai renmin chubanshe.

—— (1996) '"Ezhi" haishi "jiaowang"? – ping lengzhan hou Meiguo dui Hua zhengce' ('"Containment" or "Engagement"? – on US China Policy in the Post-Cold War Era'), *Guoji wenti yanjiu*, January 1: 1–6.

—— (1997a) 'Shiji zhijiao de ZhongMei guanxi' ('Sino-US Relations at the Turn of the Century'), *Meiguo yanjiu*, June 2: 134–37.

—— (1997b) 'Gao chu bu sheng han – lengzhan hou Meiguo de shijie diwei chutan' ('Lonely at the Top – A Preliminary Consideration of America's World Status in the Post-Cold War Era'), *Meiguo yanjiu*, September 3: 7–38.

—— (2003) 'Meiguo baquan de luoji' ('The Logic of American Hegemony'), *Meiguo yanjiu*, 17 (3): 1–29.

—— (2004) 'Meiguo guoji diwei zoushi pinggu' ('Assessment on America's International Status'), *Xiandai guoji guanxi*, 3: 1–3.

Wang Mingming (1996) 'Zhengdang zhengzhi daguo de Riben' ('Japan That Strives to Become a Political Power'), in Xi Runchang and Gao Heng, eds, *Shijie zhengzhi xingeju yu guoji anquan*, pp. 102–22.

Wang Naicheng (1995) 'Weilai Ouzhou anquan geju de zhudaoquan' ('The Power of Dominating the Future European Security Structure'), *Ouzhou*, October 13 (5): 46–52.

Wang Qinghai and Zhou Zhenkun (1997) 'Ri dui E waijiao zhengce zuo zhongda tiaozheng' ('A Major Adjustment in Japan's Foreign Policy Towards Russia'), *Xiandai guoji guanxi*, October 10: 14–18.

Wang Shan (2001) '"Fankong" waijiao yu Riben de zhanlue' ("Anti-terrorism" Diplomacy and Japan's Strategy'), *Xiandai guoji guanxi*, December 12: 1–5, 22.

Wang Sheng (1999) 'Shiji zhijiao: ZhongRi guanxi de huigu yu zhanwang' ('Sino-Japanese Relations at the Turn of the Century: Retrospect and Prospect'), *Riben xuekan*, March 2: 5–14.

Wang Shi (1993) 'Qiantan Lianmeng jieti dui Eluosi de de yu shi' ('Brief Comments on the Positive and Negative Impact of the Disintegration of the Soviet Union on Russia'), *Jinri qianSulian Dongou*, February 1: 16–17, 21.

Wang Tingdong (2002) 'Jiuyiyi shijian yu quanqiu kongbu zhuyi zhili' ('The Events of 9/11 and the Strategies Against Global Terrorism'), *Shijie jingji yu zhengzhi*, 4: 50–54.

Wang Wenfeng (1997) 'Xin de Yatai junshi: Meiguo neng chengwei pinghengguo ma?' ('The New Balance of Power in the Asia-Pacific: Can the US Be a Balancer?'), *Guoji guanxi xueyuan xuebao*, June 2: 8–10.

Wang Xiaoquan (2005) 'Pujing zhengfu de Eluosi Dongbeiya zhengce tedian ji yingxiang' ('The Characteristics and Impact of the Putin Government's North East Asian Policy'), *Dangdai Yatai*, 4: 48–55.

Wang Yi and Zhang Linhong (2007), 'Hexie shijie de goujian' ('Constructing a Harmonious World'), *Heping yu fazhan*, 2: 27–30.

Wang Yide (1993) 'Meiguo de zhengzhi jingji ji quanqiu zhanlue' ('American Politics, Economy and Global Strategy'), in Zhang Maiqiang and Zhu Chaolan, eds., *Xinbian shijie zhengzhi jingji yu guoji guanxi* (A New Text on World Politics, Economy and International Relations), Hefei: Zhongguo kexuejishudaxue chubanshe, pp. 87–131.

Wang Yizhou (1999) 'Mianxiang ershiyi shiji de Zhongguo waijiao' ('China's Diplomacy in the 21st Century'), *Zhanlue yu guanli*, 42 (6): 18–27.

—— (2003) 'ZhongRi guanxi de shige wenti' ('Ten Issues in Sino-Japanese Relations'), *Shijie jingji yu zhengzhi*, 9: 8–9.

—— (2004) 'Zhongguo guoji guanxi xue: jianyao pinggu' ('International Relations Studies in China: A Brief Evaluation'), *Ouzhou yanjiu*, December 22 (6): 137–49.

—— ed., (2006) *Zhongguo guoji guanxi yanjiu (1995–2005)* (China's International Relations Research (1995–2005)), Beijing: Beijing daxue chubanshe.

—— (2007) 'Zhongguo waijiao sanshinian: dui jinbu yu buzu de ruogan sikao' ('Thirty Years of China's Diplomacy: Reflections on Its Progress and Deficiency'), *Waijiao pinglun* (Diplomacy Review), 5:10–22. Reprinted in *Zhongguo waijiao*, 12: 2–12.

Wang Yuan (1996) 'MeiRi maoyi moca ji qi fazhan qushi' ('US-Japan Trade Friction and Its Future Trend'), *Waiguo wenti yanjiu*, 2: 35–39.

Wang Zhenhua (1996) 'Daxiyang liangan guanxi de bianhua yu Ouzhou anquan jizhi de tiaozheng' ('The Changes in Trans-Atlantic Relationships and the Adjustment in the European Security Mechanism'), *Ouzhou*, February 14 (1): 60–61.

—— (2004) 'An Analysis of Russia's International Position and the future direction of Russian-US Relations', *Ouzhou yanjiu*, 3: 129–142.

Wang Zhenxi (1997) 'Huanhe yu duojihua shitou qiangjing, baquan yu lengzhan siwei yicun – yijiujiuqinian guoji xingshi zongshu' ('Hegemonism and the Cold War Mentality Coexist with the Potent Forces of Détente and Multipolarity – A Review of the International Situation in 1997'), *Guoji guanxi xueyuan xuebao*, December 4: 1–7.

Weng Jieming, Zhang Ximing, Zhang Tao and Qu Kemin, eds., (1997) *Baipibaogaoshu: Zhongguo fazhan zhuangkuang yu qushi, 1996–1997* (The White Paper: The Current Situation in China's Development and Its Future Trend, 1996–1997), Hong Kong: Tiandi tushu youxian gongsi.

Wu Dahui (2007) 'Cong zhanlue tuoxie dou zhanlue fanzhi: Pujing dui Mei zhengce de xin xuanze' ('From Strategic Compromise to Strategic Response: the New Choice of Putin's Policy Towards America'), *Eluosi Zhongya Dongou yanjiu*, October 5: 49–55.

Wu Guifu (1992) 'Meiguo Yatai zhanlue tiaozheng de zouxiang' ('The General Direction of the Adjustment in America's Asia-Pacific Strategy'), *Yatai yanjiu*, 5: 56–65.

Wu Huaizhong (2006a) 'Riben "Dongya Gongtongti" zhanlue jiexi' ('An Analysis of Japan's "East Asian Community" Strategy'), *Riben xuekan*, May 3: 65–74.

—— (2006b) 'RiMei "zaibian" xieshang yu Riben anquan zhanlue tiaozheng' ('The Japan-US "Realignment" Consultation and the Adjustments in Japan's Security Strategy'), *Riben xuekan*, July 4: 15–24.

—— (2007) 'Riben "jiti ziweiquan" wenti de yanbian he yingxiang' ('The Evolution and Implications of the Issue of Japan's "Rights of Collective Self-Defense"'), *Riben xuekan*, September 5: 42–55.

Wu Jinan (1996) 'Riben xinshengdai zhengzhijia de jueqi ji qi yingxiang' ('The Emergence of Japan's New Generation Politicians and Its Impact'), *Riben xuekan*, November 6: 54–66.

—— (2002) *Riben xinshengdai zhengzhijia* (Japan's New Generation Politicians) Beijing: Shishi chubanshe.

Wu Wanhong (2005) 'RiTai guanxi de xinzouxiang' ('New Trends in Japan-Taiwan Relations'), *Riben xuekan*, March 2: 24–31.

Wu Xianbin (2002) 'TMD yu Taiwan wenti' ('TMD and the Taiwan Issue'), *Dangdai Yatai*, April 4: 41–49.

—— (2004) 'Bushi zhengfu duiTai zhengce de tedian ji qi yuanyin' ('The Sources and Characteristics of the Bush Administration's Taiwan Policy'), *Dangdai Yatai*, 3: 16–23.

Wu Xinbo (2003) 'Riben yu Dongbeiya zhanqu daodan fangyu' ('Japan and TMD in North East Asia'), *Guoji wenti yanjiu*, September 5: 44–48.

—— (2007) 'Shixi Bushi zhengfu duiHua anquan zhengce de hexin gainian' ('An Analysis of the Core Concepts in the Bush Administration's Security Policy towards China'), *Meiguo yanjiu*, December 21 (4): 7–22.

Xi Runchang and Gao Heng (1996) eds., *Shijie zhengzhi xingeju yu guoji anquan* (The New Global Political Structure and International Security), Beijing: Junshikexue chubanshe.

Xia Liping (2002) 'Meiguo "chongfan Dongnanya" ji qi dui Yatai anquan de yingxiang' ('America's 'Return to South East Asia' and Its Impact on Asia-Pacific Security'), *Xiandai guoji guanxi*, August 8: 18–22.

—— (2004) 'Meiguo duiHua zhanlue ji qi neizai maodun' ('America's China Strategy and Its Internal Contradictions'), *Dangdai Yatai*, 2: 3–11.

Xia Yishan (1997a) 'Chongzhen daguo diwei de Eluosi waijiao' ('Russia's Foreign Policy: Regaining Its Great Power Status'), *Guoji wenti yanjiu*, January 1: 22–26.

—— (1997b) 'E he Xifang weirao Beiyue dongkuo de dajiaoliang' ('A Major Trial of Strength between Russia and the West over NATO's Eastward Expansion'), *Guoji wenti yanjiu*, July 3: 32–38.

—— (1999) 'Kesuowo zhanzheng dui guoji zhanlue geju de yingxiang' ('The Impact of the Kosovo War on the International Strategic Structure'), *Guoji wenti yanjiu*, October 4: 1–3.

Xiao Feng (1998) 'Hou lengzhan shiqi lengzhan siwei de chanwu – RiMei xin fangwei hezuo zhizhen pingxi' ('The Product of the Cold War Mentality in the Post-Cold War Era – Comments on the New Guidelines for US-Japan Defense Cooperation'), *Dongbeiya luntan*, 1: 8–12.

—— (1999) 'Dui guoji xingshi zhong jige redian de kanfa' ('Perspectives on Several Major Issues in the International Environment'), *Xiandai guoji guanxi*, December 12: 1–5.

Xiao Rong (1995) '"Meiguo yu Taiwan guanxi xueshu yantaohui" zongshu' ('Summary of the "Symposium on US-Taiwan Relations"'), *Meiguo yanjiu*, September 3: 147–50.

Xie Yixian (1993) *Waijiao zhihui yu moulue – xin Zhongguo waijiao lilun he yuanze* (Wisdom and Strategy in Diplomacy – New China's Diplomatic Theory and Principles), Zhengzhou: Henan renmin chubanshe.

Xing Guangcheng *et al.* (1993) 'QianSulian diqu yinian xingshi de huigu yu zhangwang' ('The Situation in the Former Soviet Union During the Past Year: Retrospects and Prospects'), *Dongou Zongya yanjiu*, February 1: 21–32.

Xu Heming (2007) 'Toushi Meiguo de "Dazhongya" zhanlue' ('On America's "Greater Central Asia" Strategy'), *Guoji wenti yanjiu*, October 4: 36–41, 24.

Xu Heming and Wang Haihan (1997) 'Shixi Kelindun zhengfu dierren waijiao zhengce quxiang' ('A Preliminary Analysis of the Clinton Administration's Foreign Policy Trend During Its Second Term'), *Guoji wenti yanjiu*, 3: 26–31.

Xu Jian (2007) 'Jianshe "hexie shijie" de lilun sikao' ('Theoretical Considerations of Building a "Harmonious World"'), *Guoji wenti yanjiu*, January 1: 1–6.

Xu Kaixin (1996) 'Shixi xinxing de ZhongE guanxi' ('A Preliminary Analysis of the New Pattern in Sino-Russian Relations'), *Dongbeiya luntan*, August 3: 57–60.

Xu Kaiyi (2004) '21 shijichu Zhongguo waijiao de zhanlue sikao' ('Strategic Thinking on China's Diplomacy in the Early 21st Century'), *Dangdai Yatai*, 6: 51–57.

Xu Kui (1996) 'ZhongE guanxi de xianzhuang he qiangjing' ('The Current Situation of and Prospects for Sino-Russian Relations'), *Dongou Zongya yanjiu*, December 6: 3–9, 20.

Xu Ping (2007) 'Zai bian yu bubian zhong bawo ZhongRi guanxi de daju' ('Grasping the Bigger Picture of Sino-Japanese Relations between Change and Continuity'), *Riben xuekan*, September 5: 15–27.

Xu Ping and Zhao Qinghai (2007) 'Zhongguo zhoubian anquan huanjing touxi' ('An Analysis of China's Peripheral Security Environment'), *Guoji wenti yanjiu*, March 2: 26–31.

Xu Shiquan (2003) 'Examining the Bush Administration's Taiwan Policy', *Guoji wenti yanjiu*, November, 6: 1–6.

Xu Zhixin (2004) 'Pujing shiqi Eluosi duiwai zhanlue jiexi' ('An Analysis of Russia's External Strategy in the Putin Era'), *Eluosi Zhongya Dongou yanjiu*, June 3: 50–57.

—— (2005) 'Eluosi de Yatai zhengce' ('Russia's Asia-Pacific Policy'), *Dangdai Yatai*, 2: 13–20.

Xue Li (2003) 'ZhongRi guanxi nengfou chaoyue lishi wenti' ('Can Sino-Japanese Relations Transcend Historical Issues'), *Zhanlue yu guanli*, 59 (4): 28–33.

Xue Mouhong (1992) 'Haiwan zhanzheng dui shijie geju de yingxiang' ('The Impact of the Gulf War on the World Structure'), in Du Gong and Ni Liyu, eds, *Zhuanhuanzhong de shijie geju*, pp. 210–39.

Ya Yan (2001) 'Mulin youhao, gonggu zhoubian' ('Friendly Neighbour, Secure Periphery'), *Liaowang* (Outlook), 27: 52–53.

Yan Xiangjun (1991) 'Beiyue de zhanlue tiaozheng yu zouxiang' ('The Strategic Adjustment and Future Development of NATO'), *Xiandai guoji guanxi*, 3: 21–25.

Yan Xiangjun and Huang Tingwei (1993) 'Yatai anquan xingshi ji gefang dui anquan jizhi de shexiang' ('Asia-Pacific Security Situation and Conceptions of Security Mechanism by the Parties Concerned'), *Xiandai guoji guanxi*, May 5: 1–5.

Yan Xuetong (1996) 'Xifangren kan Zhongguo de jueqi' ('Western Perspectives on the Rise of China'), *Xiandai guoji guanxi*, September 9: 36–45.

—— (2000) 'Dui Zhongguo anquan huanjing de fenxi yu sikao' ('The Analysis of and Some Thoughts on China's Security Environment'), *Shijie jingji yu zhengzhi*, 2: 5–10.

—— (2004a) 'Heping jueqi yu baozhang heping' ('Peaceful Rise and Peace Building'), *Guoji wenti yanjiu*, 3: 12–16.

—— (2004b) 'Wuli ezhi taidu fali duli de libi fenxi' ('An Analysis of the Benefits and Costs of Using Force Against Taiwanese Independence'), *Zhanlue yu guanli*, 3: 1–5.

Yang Dazhou (1995) 'Meiguo dui qianNansilagu weiji de lichang chuxi' ('A Preliminary Analysis of America's Position on the Crisis in the Former Yugoslavia'), *Meiguo yanjiu*, 4: 121–31.

Yang Fan (2004) 'Xinshiqi Zhongguo guojia anquan de jiban yuanze' ('The Fundamental Principles of China's National Security in a New Era'), *Zhanlue yu guanli*, 2: 85–93.

Yang Jiemian (2000) 'Kuashiji shijie geju zhong de Meiguo quanqiu zhanlue' ('US Global Strategy in the World Structure at the Turn of the Century'), *Guoji wenti yanjiu*, November 6: 23–30.

—— (2001) 'ZhongMei guanxi mianlin kaoyan: Bushi xinzhengfu duiHua zhengce' ('Sino-American Relations Facing a New Test: The Bush Administration's Policy Towards China'), *Meiguo yanjiu*, June 15 (2): 21–35.

—— (2003) 'Meiguo de quanqiu zhanlue he Zhongguo de zhanlue jiyuqi' ('America's Global Strategy and China's Strategic Opportunity'), *Guoji wenti yanjiu*, 2: 11–16.

Yang Jin (2001) 'An Analysis of the Events of September 11 and the Approaches to International Anti-terrorism', *Jiaoxue yu yanjiu* (Teaching and Research), 11: 55–57.

Yang Mingjie (2006) 'Tuijin fankong yao chaoyue lengzhan siwei' ('Advancing Anti-terrorism Needs to Go Beyond Cold-War Mentality'), *Xiandai guoji guanxi*, September 9: 18–21.

Yang Mingjie, He Xiquan, Li Wei *et al.* (2002) 'Kongbu zhuyi genyuan tanxi' ('Analyses of the Sources of Terrorism'), *Xiandai guoji guanxi*, January 1: 54–62.

Yang Wenjing (2004) 'Zhongguo rongru guoji jizhi yu Meiguo yinsu' ('China's Integration into International Institutions and the US Factor'), *Xiandai guoji guanxi*, October 10: 29–41, 5.

Yang Yanyi (2003) 'Dui gaishan he fazhan ZhongRi youhao hezuo huoban guanxi de jidian kanfa' ('Some Thoughts on Improving and Developing Sino-Japanese Friendly and Cooperative Partnership'), *Shijie jingji yu zhengzhi*, 9: 26–29.

Yang Yunzhong (1995) 'Jiushi niandai zhonghouqi Riben Yatai waijiao de jiben zoushi' ('The Basic Trend of Japan's Asia-Pacific Diplomacy in the Second Half of the 1990s'), *Riben xuekan*, May 3: 36–47.

—— (1996) 'RiTai guanxi jinru zhongshi zhengzhi jiaowang de xinjieduan' ('Japan-Taiwan Relations: A New Stage That Emphasises Political Interactions'), *Riben xuekan*, May 3: 24–38.

—— (1998) 'Riben de zhoubian junshi waijiao' ('Japan's Military Diplomacy Towards Its Neighbouring Countries'), *Riben xuekan*, September 5: 28–44.

—— (2002a) 'Jiuyiyi shijian dui guoji zhanlue taishi de shenke yingxiang' ('The Profound Impact of the Events of September 11 on the International Strategic Situation'), *Dangdai Yatai*, March 3: 3–13.

—— (2002b) 'Riben jiasu xiang shijie junshi daguo mubiao maijin' ('Japan: Speeding Up Its Progress in Achieving the Goal of a World Military Power'), *Dangdai Yatai*, May 5: 11–18.

—— (2003a) 'Lun ZhongMei guanxi pingwen fazhan de jichu yu tezheng' ('The Foundation and Characteristics of the Stable Development of Sino-American Relations'), *Dangdai Yatai*, 2: 3–13.

—— (2003b) 'Riben fangwei zhengce mianlin zhongda zhuanzhe' ('Japan's Defence Policy: Facing Significant Changes'), *Dangdai Yatai*, 5: 3–10.

—— (2004) 'RiTai guanxi de xinfazhan' ('New Developments in Japan-Taiwan Relations'), *Dangdai Yatai*, 1: 16–23.

Yao Chunling (1995) 'Meiguo yu Dongnanyatiaoyuezuzhi de jianli' ('The United States and the Establishment of the Southeast Asia Treaty Organisation'), *Riben xuekan*, 3: 110–126.

Yao Wang *et al.*, eds, (1992) *Kua shiji duihua* (A Dialogue Standing on the Century-dividing Point), Chengdu: Sichuan renmin chubanshe.

Yao Wenli (2003) '21 shiji chuqi Riben anquan zhanlue tiaozheng chuyi' ('Comments on the Adjustments in Japan's Security Strategy in the Early 21st Century'), *Riben xuekan*, November 6: 44–55.

Ye Jiang (2003) '"Anquan kunjing" xilun' ('An Analysis of the "Security Dilemma"'), *Meiguo yanjiu*, December 4: 7–21.

Ye Ruan (1992), 'Guoji xinzhixu de butong gouxiang' ('Different Conceptions of the New International Order'), in Du Gong and Ni Liyu, eds, *Zhuanhuanzhong de shijie geju*, pp. 299–338.

Ye Zicheng (2000) 'Zhongguo shixing daguo waijiao zhanlue shizai bixing' ('China Must Practice Great Power Diplomatic Strategy'), *Shijie jingji yu zhengzhi*, 1: 5–10.

—— (2007a) 'Zhongguo de heping fazhan: luquan de huigui yu fazhan' ('China's Peaceful Development: The Return and Development of Continental Power'), *Shijie jingji yu zhengzhi*, February 2: 23–31.

—— (2007b) 'Cong dalishi guankan diyuan zhengzhi' ('Geopolitics in Macro-historical Perspective'), *Xiandai guoji guanxi*, June 6: 1–6.

Yin Chunling (1992) 'Jianli guoji shehui xinzhixu' ('Establishing a New Order in the International Society'), in Wang Xingfang and He Ping, eds, *Dangdai shijie zhengzhi jingji yu guoji guanxi* (Contemporary World Politics, Economy and International Relations), Beijing: Shishi chubanshe, pp. 270–95.

Yin Jianping (1999) 'Eluosi Yuandong jingji fazhan qianzhan' ('Prospects for Economic Development in the Russian Far East'), *Dongbeiya luntan*, February 1: 52–56.

Ying Xiaoyan (1995) 'Cong ZhongMei guanxi de lishi fazhan kan Meiguo duiwai zhanlue de shizhi' ('Analysing the Essence of America's External Strategy within the Context of the Historical Development in Sino-US Relations'), *Waiguo wenti yanjiu*, 3/4: 119–121.

Yu Guozheng (1998) 'Eluosi "xin Dongfang zhengce" yu Dongbeiya diqu jingji hezuo' ('Russia's "New Oriental Policy" and Economic Cooperation in North East Asia'), *Dongou Zongya yanjiu*, June 3: 38–42.

—— (2002) 'Eluosi yuandong diqu yu Zhongguo guanxi de zhiyue yinsu fenxi' ('An Analysis of the Constraining Factors for the Russian Far East's Relations with China'), *Dongou Zhongya yanjiu*, August 4: 60–65.

Yu Sui (1996) 'Eluosi zai Dongbeiya de diwei he zuoyong' ('Russia's Position and Its Role in Northeast Asia'), *Dongou Zongya yanjiu*, October 5: 55–57.

—— (1998) 'Beiyue dongkuo yilai de Eluosi waijiao' ('Russian Foreign Policy Since NATO's Eastward Expansion'), *Guoji wenti yanjiu*, July 3: 1–5.

—— (2004) 'Shijie duojihua wenti' ('The Issue of Multipolarity in the World'), *Shijie jingji yu zhengzhi*, 3: 15–20.

—— (2007) 'Lun ZhongE zhanlue xiezuo huoban guanxi' ('On Sino-Russian Strategic Coordinative Partnership'), *Guoji wenti yanjiu*, May 3: 4–10, 69.

Yu Xintian (2007) '"Hexie shijie" yu Zhongguo de heping fazhan daolu' ('A "Harmonious World" and China's Path of Peaceful Development'), *Guoji wenti yanjiu*, January 1: 7–12, 18.

Yu Zhixian (1993) 'Sulian jieti dui Yazhou yixie guojia jingji de yingxiang' ('The Impact of the Disintegration of the Soviet Union on the Economies of Some Asian Countries'), *Dongou Zongya yanjiu*, August 4: 54–57.

Yuan Di (2001) 'Guoji fan kongbuzhuyi zhanlue: Meiguo, Bajisitan yu Yindu' ('International Anti-terrorist Strategy: America, Pakistan and India'), *Nanya yanjiu jikan*, 4: 32–36.

Yuan Jian (1997) 'Lengzhan hou lixiang zhuyi sichao de fazhan ji qi dui Meiguo waijiao zhengce de yingxiang' ('The Development of Idealist Thinking in the Post-Cold War Era and Its Impact on US Foreign Policy'), *Guoji wenti yanjiu*, April 2: 12–19.

—— (1998) 'Xinbaoshouzhuyi de waijiao sixiang ji qi zai Meiguo de yingxiang' ('The Foreign Policy Thinking of Neo-Conservatism and Its Influence in the United States'), *Guoji wenti yanjiu*, April 2: 19–28.

Yuan Ming (1996) 'Ershiyi shijichu Dongbeiya daguo guanxi' ('Great Power Relations in Northeast Asia in the Early 21st Century'), *Guoji wenti yanjiu*, October 4: 19–23.

Yuan Ming and Fan Shiming (1995) 'Lengzhan hou Meiguo dui Zhongguo anquan xingxiang de renshi' ('China's Security Role in Post-Cold War American Perceptions'), *Meiguo yanjiu*, December 9 (4): 7–29.

Zhan Shiliang (1992) 'Lengzhan hou de MeiRi guanxi' ('Post-Cold War US-Japan Relations'), *Guoji wenti yanjiu*, 2: 1–2.

—— (2003) 'Cong Yilake zhanzheng pouxi Meiguo quanqiu zhanlue' ('The Iraq War and an Analysis of America's Global Strategy'), *Guoji wenti yanjiu*, 4: 1–6.

Zhang Baoxiang (1991) 'Bianhuazhong de Ouzhou geju' ('The Changing European Structure'), *Xiandai guoji guanxi*, March 2: 26–31.

Zhang Dalin (1996a) 'RiMei tongmeng xiang hechu qu' ('Where Will US-Japan Alliance Go'), *Guoji wenti yanjiu*, January 1: 26–30.

—— (1996b) 'Ping "RiMei anquan baozhang lianhe xuanyan"' ('On "US-Japan Declaration on Security Alliance"'), *Guoji wenti yanjiu*, October 4: 24–28.

Zhang Jianxin (2003) 'Cong Bushi zhuyi dao xindiguozhiyi' ('From the Bush Doctrine to New Imperialism'), *Dangdai Yatai*, 6: 15–20.

Zhang Jing (2005) 'Qianxi Riben zhengdang Anlihui changren lishiquo' ('An Analysis of Japan's Bid for Permanent Membership of the UN Security Council'), *Taipingyang xuebao*, 5: 87–94.

Zhang Jinshan (2003) 'Qianxi Riben "youshi fazhi" de beijing qi yitu' ('An Analysis of the Background and Intentions of Japan's "War-contingency Plan"'), *Riben xuekan*, July 4: 77–89.

—— (2007) 'Dangdai Riben de minzu baoshou zhuyi: shengcheng, gainian he shiyi' ('Nationalistic Conservatism in Contemporary Japan: Formation, Concept and Explanations for the Puzzle'), *Riben xuekan*, May 3: 5–21.

Zhang Liangui (2004) 'Chaoxian hewenti de guoqu, xianzai he weilai' ('The North Korean Issue: Past, Present and Future'), *YaFei zongheng*, 1: 46–51.

Zhang Shuxiao (1998) 'Shijie jingji zengzhang zhongxin de zhuanyi yu Eluosi de duice' ('The Shift in the Centre of Economic Growth in the World and Russia's Response'), *Dongou Zongya yanjiu*, June 3: 33–35.

Zhang Shuxiao and Li Chunyan (1996) 'Eluosi dui wai zhengce de xinzhongdian yu ZhongE jingmao guanxi' ('The New Emphasis in Russia's Foreign Policy and Sino-Russian Economic and Trade Relations'), *Waiguo wenti yanjiu*, 1: 29–32.

Zhang Tiejun (2005) 'Zhongguo yu Dongya gongtongti' ('China and East Asian Community'), *Taipingyang xuebao*, 12: 12–19.

Zhang Tuosheng (2003) 'Dui ZhongRi guanxi de jidian sikao' ('Some Thoughts on Sino-Japanese Relations'), *Shijie jingji yu zhengzhi*, 9: 22–26.

Zhang Wang (2003) 'Riben shifou zhengzai congzou juguozhuyi laolu' ('Is Japan Returning to the Old Path of Militarism?'), *Zhanlue yu guanli*, 4: 23–27.

Zhang Weiwei (2007) 'Riben yu Yindu: gouzhu "quanqiu zhanlue huoban guanxi"' ('Japan and India: Constructing a "Global Strategic Partnership"'), *Guoji wenti yanjiu*, November 6: 33–38, 54.

Zhang Wenmu (2002) 'Afuhan zhanzheng yu buduicheng shijie geju' ('The War in Afghanistan and the Asymmetric World Structure'), *Zhanlue yu guanli*, 2: 42–43.

—— (2003) 'Jingji quanqiuhua yu Zhongguo haquan' ('Economic Globalization and China's Sea Power'), *Zhanlue yu guanli*, 1: 86–94.

—— (2004) 'Daguo jueqi de lishi jingyan yu Zhongguo de xuanze' ('The Historical Experience of Great Power Emergence and China's Choice'), *Zhanlue yu guanli*, 63 (2): 70–84.

Zhang Xiangyuan, Wang Yong and Hu Donghua, eds, (1992) *Haiwan zhanzheng zonglan* (A Comprehensive Survey of the Gulf War), Beijing: Haijun haichao chubanshe.

Zhang Xiaoming (2006) 'Zhongguo yu zhoubian guojia guanxi de lishi yanbian: mushi yu guocheng' ('The Historical Evolution of China's Relations with Its Peripheral Countries: Models and Processes'), *Guoji zhengzhi yanjiu*, 1: 57–71.

Zhang Youxia (2003) 'Yilake zhanzheng: dui guoji zhanlue geju ji woguo anquan huanjing de yingxiang' ('The Iraq War: The Impact on the International Strategic Pattern and China's Security Environment'), *Guoji zhanwang* (International Outlook), 14: 71–73.

Zhang Yueming (1993) 'Yijiujiuer nian de qian Sulian Dongou diqu' ('The Former Soviet Union and Eastern Europe in 1992'), *Jinri qianSulian Dongou*, April 2: 3.

Zhao Dawei (1999) 'Riben junshi anquan zhanlue ji qi qianjing' ('Japan's Military Security Strategy and Its Prospects'), *Guoji wenti yanjiu*, April 2: 49–54.

Zhao Guangrui (1996) 'Riben zhengzai "huigui" Yazhou' ('Japan Is "Returning" to Asia'), *Riben xuekan*, January 1: 30–37.

Zhao Guilin (1991) 'Guanyu shijie zhanlue geju de jige wenti' (Several Issues Concerning the Global Strategic Structure), *Xiandai guoji guanxi*, February 2: 8–12, 17.

Zhao Huasheng (2007) 'Zhongguo Zhongya waijiao de lilun he shijian' ('The Theory and Practice of China's Central Asian Diplomacy'), *Guoji wenti yanjiu*, July 4: 19–25, 54.

Zhao Huirong (2004) 'Eluosi de duoji shijie gouxiang yu waijiao' ('Russia's Conception of a Multipolar World and Its Foreign Policy'), *Eluosi Zhongya Dongou yanjiu*, October 5: 49–56.

Zhao Jieqi (1992) 'RiMei zai Yatai jingji geju zhong de diwei bianhua yu zhudaoquan zhi zheng' ('The Changing Status of Japan and America in the Asia-Pacific Economic Structure and Their Contention for a Dominant Role in the Region'), *Yatai yanjiu*, 5: 21–25.

—— (1993) 'Riben Yazhou waijiao de xin quxiang' ('New Trends of Japan's Asia Diplomacy'), *Yatai yanjiu*, 2: 29–34, 49.

Zhao Mingwen (2004) 'Eluosi zhanlue shousuo ji qi yingxiang' ('Russia's Srategic Contraction and Its Impact'), *Guoji wenti yanjiu*, January 1: 36–42, 35.

Zhao Qinghai (2007) '"Siguo tongmeng": gouxiang yu xianshi' ('"The Four-Nation Alliance": Conception and Reality'), *Guoji wenti yanjiu*, November 6: 28–32.

Zhen Bingxi (1998a) 'Xinxi geming yu Zibenzhuyi shijie jingji di wu ci changzhouqi' ('Information Revolution and the Fifth Long Cycle of the Capitalist World Economy'), *Guoji wenti yanjiu*, April 2: 9–12.

—— (1998b) 'Meiguo "xin jingji" ji qi dui shijie jingji de yingxiang' ('The "New Economy" in the United States and Its Impact on the World Economy'), *Guoji wenti yanjiu*, July 3: 42–44.

Zhongguo Guoji Wenti Yanjiu Suo (1997) 'Woguo duiwai guanxi dashiji' ('China's Foreign Relations: A Chronicle'), *Guoji wenti yanjiu*, April 2: 58–62.

Zhongguo shibao (1997) 10, 11 April. Cited in Xiao Feng (1998), p. 10.

Zhou Bolin (1999) 'Meiguo jinqi texian jingongxing zhanlue dongxiang' ('The Direction of America's Recent Offensive Strategy'), *Liaowang* (Outlook), 50: 50–51.

Zhou Guiyin (2003) 'Lijie duiRi "waijiao geming"' ('Understanding the "Diplomatic Revolution" Towards Japan'), *Zhanlue yu guanli*, 59 (4): 18–22.

Zhou Hong and Liu Jinghua (1997) 'Ping Hengtingdun de "Wenming de chongtu he shijie zhixu de chongjian"' ('Review of Huntington's "The Clash of Civilizations and the Remaking of World Order"'), *Ouzhou*, October 5: 77–82.

Zhou Jianming (2002) 'Meiguo fangqi "jiechu zhanlue"' ('America Has Abandoned Its "Engagement Strategy"'), *Huanqiu shibao* (Global Times), 14 March, p. 7.

Zhou Jirong (1991) 'Shijie geju bianhua de qushi' ('The Trend in the Changing World Structure'), *Xiandai guoji guanxi*, 2: 3–7.

Zhou Qi (1995) 'Lengzhan hou de ZhongMei guanxi xianzhuang – gongtong liyi yu zhengzhi' ('An Appraisal of Post-Cold War Sino-US Relations – Common Interests and Disputes'), *Meiguo yanjiu*, December 9 (4): 30–50.

—— (2007) '"Bushi Zhuyi" yu Meiguo xin baoshouzhuyi' ('The "Bush Doctrine" and America's Neoconservatism'), *Meiguo yanjiu*, Summer 21 (2): 7–27.

Zhou Rongyao (1995) 'Shei zhudao Ouzhou?' ('Who Leads Europe?'), *Ouzhou*, February 13 (1): 49–52.

Zhou Yongsheng (2006) 'Xiaoquan neige de waijiao zhengce qianxi' (An Analysis of the Koizumi Cabinet's Foreign Policy'), *Riben xuekan*, September 5: 28–39.

—— (2007) 'Riben Anbei neige waijiao kuangjia toushi' ('An Analysis of the Abe Government's Diplomatic Framework'), *Guoji wenti yanjiu*, September 5: 59–64.

Zhou Zhihuai (1998) 'Guanyu 1995–1996 nian Taihai weiji de sikao' ('Reflections on the 1995–1996 Taiwan Strait Crisis'), *Taiwan yanjiu jikan*, Summer 2: 1–7.

—— (2007) 'Lun fandui "Taidu" yu weihu Zhongguo guojia anquan' (On Opposing "Taiwanese Independence" and Safeguarding China's National Security'), *Taiwan yanjiu*, October 5: 3–8.

Zhou Zhongfei (1998) 'Cong Yatai anquan geju bianhua kan MeiTai quanxi' ('Analysing US-Taiwan Relations within the Context of the Change in the Asia-Pacific Security Structure'), *Taiwan yanjiu jikan*, June 2: 11–13.

Zhu Feng (2001) 'MeiE guanxi xinzouxiang' ('New Trends in US-Russian Relations'), *Xiandai guoji guanxi*, November 11: 24–31.

—— (2003) 'Bushi zhengfu de bandao zhengce yu Chaoxian heweiji' ('The Bush Administration's Policy towards the Korean Peninsula and the North Korean Nuclear Crisis'), *Xiandai guoji guanxi*, February 2: 1–7.

Zhu Fenglan (2005) 'ZhongRi Donghai zhengduan ji qi jiejue de qianjing' ('The Sino-Japanese Dispute in the East China Sea and the Prospects for Its Resolution'), *Dangdai Yatai*, July 7: 3–16.

—— (2006) 'Yatai guojia de haiyang zhengce ji qi yingxiang' ('The Maritime Policy of Asia-Pacific Countries and Its Impact'), *Dangdai Yatai*, May 5: 30–36.

Zhu Kun (2004) 'Cong baquanzhuyi dao xindiguozhuyi' ('From Hegemonism to New Imperialism'), *Taipingyang xuebao*, 1: 48–53.

Zhu Liqun (1997) 'Ouzhou anquan jiegou zhong de Xioulianmeng' ('The West European Union in the Security Structure of Europe'), *Ouzhou*, December, 15 (6): 56–61.

Zhu Weidong (2006) '1996–2005 nian haixia liangan guanxi zongping' ('General Comments on Cross-strait Relations in 1996–2005'), *Taiwan yanjiu*, August 4: 1–6.

Zhu Zinchang and Shi Xiaojie (1999) 'Jiushi niandai RiMei guanxi de tiaozheng ji qi yingxiang' ('The Adjustment in Japan-US Relations in the 1990s and Its Implications'), *Riben xuekan*, May 3: 1–16.

Zi Zhongyun (1996) 'Bainian sixiang de chongji yu zhuangji' ('A Hundred Years' Interactions and Clashes'), *Meiguo yanjiu*, December 4: 7–29.

—— ed., (1998) *Guoji zhengzhi lilun tansuo zai Zhongguo* (In Search of Theories of International Politics in China), Shanghai: Shanghai renmin chubanshe.

Zi Zhongyun and He Di, eds, (1991) *MeiTai guanxi sishinian, 1949–1989* (Forty Years of US-Taiwan Relations, 1949–1989), Beijing: Renmin chubanshe.

English-Language Sources

Abbott, Kenneth W. and Snidal, Duncan (1998) 'Why States Act Through Formal Organizations', *Journal of Conflict Resolution*, February 42 (1): 3–32.

Abe, Shinzo (2006) Policy Speech by Prime Minister Shinzo Abe to the 165th Session of the Diet, 29 September, http://www.kantei.go.jp/foreign/abespeech/2006/09/29speech_e.html.

—— (2007) 'Japan and NATO: Toward Further Collaboration', Speech by Prime Minister Shinzo Abe at the North Atlantic Council, 12 January, http://www.mofa.go.jp/region/europe/pmv0701/nato.html.

Abrams, Dominic and Hogg, Michael A., eds, (1990) *Social Identity Theory: Constructive and Critical Advances*, London: Harvester Wheatsheaf.

Acharya, Amitav (2003/04) 'Will Asia's Past Be Its Future?', *International Security*, Winter 28 (3): 149–64.

Alagappa, Muthiah, ed., (1998) *Asian Security Practice: Material and Ideational Influences*, Stanford: Stanford University Press.

Anderson, Benedict (2006) *Imagined Communities: Reflections on the Origin and Spread of Nationalism*, Revised edition, London: Verso Books.

Anderson, Jennifer (1997) *The Limits of Sino-Russian Strategic Partnership*, Adelphi Paper 315, London: International Institute for Strategic Studies.

Angell, Norman (1935) *The Great Illusion*, London: Heinemann.

Archibugi, Daniele and Held, David, eds, (1995) *Cosmopolitan Democracy*, Cambridge: Polity Press.

Armstrong, David (1994) 'Chinese Perspectives on the New World Order', *Journal of East Asian Affairs* 8 (2), Summer/Fall.

258   *Bibliography*

Asahi Shimbun (2004) 'SDF Mission in Iraq Extended', 10 December.

Ash, Robert, Howe, Christopher and Kueh, Y. Y. (2003) *China's Economic Reform: A Study with Documents*, London: RoutledgeCurzon.

Ash, Robert, Shambaugh, David and Takagi, Seiichiro, eds, (2006) *China Watching: Perspectives from Europe, Japan and the United States*, London: Routledge.

Associated Press (2007) 'Abe: Japan, China Moving toward Strategic Relationship', *International Herald Tribune*, 1 January.

Axelrod, Robert, ed., (1976) *Structure of Decision: The Cognitive Maps of Political Elites*, Princeton: Princeton University Press.

Bacani, Cesar (2003) *The China Investor: Getting Rich with the Next Superpower*, Indianapolis, IN: John Wiley.

Bachman, David (1994) 'Domestic Sources of Chinese Foreign Policy', in Samuel S. Kim, ed., *China and the World*, 3rd edn, Boulder, Colorado: Westview Press, pp. 42–59.

Baker III, James A. (1991/92) 'America in Asia: Emerging Architecture for a Pacific Community', *Foreign Affairs*, Winter 5: 1–18.

Barnett, A. Doak (1985) *The Making of Foreign policy in China: Structure and Process*, London: I. B. Tauris.

BBC (2001a) 'China Asks US to Look Beyond NATO', 13 September, http://news.bbc. co.uk/hi/english/world/americas/newsid_1541000/1541656.stm.

—— (2001b) 'China Demands US Attack Evidence', 18 September, http://news.bbc.co.uk/ hi/english/world/asia-pacific/newsid_1550000/1550495.stm.

—— (2001c) 'US Normalises Trade with China', 28 December, http://www.news.bbc. co.uk/hi/english/business/newsid_1731000/1731451.stm.

—— (2002a) 'US "Has Nuclear Hit List"', 9 March, http://news.bbc.co.uk/1/hi/world/ americas/1864173.stm.

—— (2002b) 'New Era Hailed in US-Russia Ties', 24 May, http://news.bbc.co.uk/hi/ english/world/europe/newsid_2007000/2007048.stm.

—— (2002c) 'Russia Reassures China Over NATO', 31 May, http://news.bbc.co.uk/hi/ english/world/asia-pacific/newsid_2016000/2016917.stm.

—— (2002d) 'ASEAN Makes Anti-terror Pact with US', http://news.bbc.co.uk/1/hi/world/ asia-pacific/2165552.stm.

—— (2004) 'US Questions Japan's Pacifism', 13 August, http://news.bbc.co.uk/1/hi/world/ asia-pacific/3561378.stm.

—— (2005) 'Thousands Join Anti-Japan Protest,' 16 April, http://news.bbc.co.uk/1/hi/ world/asia-pacific/4450975.stm.

—— (2007) 'China and Japan PMs Hail Progress', 28 December, http://news.bbc.co.uk/go/ pr/fr/-/2/hi/asia-pacific/7160993.stm.

Beeson, Mark, ed., (2006) *Bush and Asia: America's Evolving Relations with East Asia*, London: Routledge.

Berger, Thomas (1996) 'Norms, Identity, and National Security in Germany and Japan', in Peter J. Katzenstein, ed., *The Culture of National Security*, Columbia: Columbia University Press, pp. 317–56.

—— (2000) 'Set for Stability? Prospects for Conflict and Cooperation in East Asia', *Review of International Studies*, July 26 (3): 405–28.

—— (2003) 'Power and Purpose in Pacific East Asia: A Constructivist Interpretation', in G. John Ikenberry and Michael Mastanduno, eds, *International Relations Theory and the Asia-Pacific*, New York: Columbia University Press, pp. 387–419.

Berkofsky, Axel (2003) 'Koizumi: US Ties Beat Out Public Opinion', *Asia Times*, 20 March, http://www.atimes.com/atimes/Japan/EC20Dh01.html.

Bernstein, Richard and Munro, Ross H. (1997a) 'The Coming Conflict with America', *Foreign Affairs*, March/April 76 (2): 18–32.

—— (1997b) *The Coming Conflict with China*, New York: Alfred A. Knopf.

Bilveer, S. (1998) 'East Asia in Russia's Foreign Policy: a New Russo-Chinese Axis?', *The Pacific Review*, 11 (4): 485–503.

Blasko, Dennis J. (2005) *The Chinese Army Today: Tradition and Transformation for the 21st Century*, London: Routledge.

Blix, Hans (2004) *Disarming Iraq: The Search for Weapons of Mass Destruction*, London: Bloomsbury.

Bloom, William (1993) *Personal Identity, National Identity and International Relations*, paperback edition, Cambridge: Cambridge University Press.

Blum, Samantha (2003) 'Chinese Views of US Hegemony', *Journal of Contemporary China*, May 12 (35): 239–64.

Blumer, Herbert (1986) *Symbolic Interactionism: Perspective and Method*, Berkeley: University of California Press.

Booth, Ken and Trood, Russell, eds, (1999) *Strategic Cultures in the Asia-Pacific Region*, Basingstoke: Macmillan.

Booth, Ken and Wheeler, Nicholas, eds, (2007) *The Security Dilemma: Fear, Cooperation and Trust in World Politics*, Basingstoke: Palgrave Macmillan.

Brawley, Mark (2004) 'The Political Economy of Balance of Power Theory', in T.V. Paul, James J. Wirtz and Michel Fortmann, eds, *Balance of Power: Theory and Practice in the Twenty-first Century*, Stanford: Stanford University Press, Ch. 3.

Breslin, Shaun (1996) *China in the 1980s: Centre-Province Relations in a Reforming Socialist State*, Basingstoke: Palgrave Macmillan.

—— (2005) 'Power and Production: Rethinking China's Global Economic Role', *Review of International Studies*, 31: 735–53.

—— (2007) *China and the Global Political Economy*, Basingstoke: Palgrave Macmillan.

Brewer, Marilynn B. (2001) 'Many Faces of Social Identity: Implications for Political Psychology', *Political Psychology*, March 22 (1), pp. 115–25.

Brooks, Stephen G. and Wohlforth, William C. (2002) 'American Primacy in Perspective', *Foreign Affairs*, July/August 81 (4): 20–33.

—— (2005) 'Hard Times for Soft Balancing', *International Security*, Summer 30 (1): 72–108.

Burgess, J. Peter and Taylor, Owen, eds, (2004) Special Section: What is "Human Security"?, *Security Dialogue*, September 35 (3): 345–87.

Burke, Peter J. (1991) 'Identity Processes and Social Stress', *American Sociological Review*, 56: 836–49.

Burke, Peter J. and Stets, Jan E. (1999) 'Trust and Commitment through Self-Verification', *Social Psychology Quarterly*, December 62 (4): 347–60.

Bush, George W. (2001) 'Address to a Joint Session of Congress and the American People', 20 September.

—— (2002) 'President Bush Delivers Graduation Speech at West Point, United States Military Academy', June, http://www.whitehouse.gov/news/releases/2002/06/20020601-3.html.

Buszynski, Leszek, ed., (2004) *Asia Pacific Security: Values and Identity*, London: Routledge.

Buzan, Barry and Segal, Gerald (1994) 'Rethinking East Asian Security', *Survival*, Summer 36 (2): 3–21.

Buzan, Barry, Weaver, Ole and De Wilde, J. (1998) *Security: A New Framework for Analysis*, Boulder, Colorado: Lynne Reinner.

Cable, Vincent and Ferdinand, Peter (1994) 'China as an Economic Giant: Threat or Opportunity?', *International Affairs*, April 70 (2): 243–61.

Calder, Ken E. (1996) 'Asia's Empty Tank', *Foreign Affairs*, March/April 75 (2): 55–69.

Callahan, William A. (2004) 'National Insecurities: Humiliation, Salvation, and Chinese Nationalism', *Alternatives*, 29: 199–218.

—— (2005) 'How to Understand China: the Dangers and Opportunities of Being a Rising Power', *Review of International Studies*, 31: 701–14.

Campbell, David (1998) *Writing Security: United States Foreign Policy and the Politics of Identity*, Minnesota: University of Minnesota Press.

Carr, E.H. (1962) *The Twenty Years Crisis, 1919–1939*, London: Macmillan.

Chan, Gerald (1999) *Chinese Perspectives on International Relations: A Framework for Analysis*, Basingstoke: Macmillan.

—— (2004a) 'China and the WTO: the Theory and Practice of Compliance', *International Relations of the Asia-Pacific*, February 4 (1): 47–72.

—— (2004b) 'China's Compliance in Global Environmental Affairs', *Asia Pacific Viewpoint*, 45 (1): 69–86.

—— (2005) *China's Compliance in Global Affairs: Trade, Arms Control, Environmental Protection, Human Rights*, Singapore: World Scientific Publishing.

Chan, Stephen (2005) *Out of Evil: New International Politics and Old Doctrines of War*, London: I.B. Tauris.

Chan, Stephen, Mandaville, Peter and Bleiker, Roland, eds, (2001) *The Zen of International Relations: IR Theory from East to West*, Basingstoke: Palgrave.

Chan, Steve (2007) *China, the US and the Power-Transition Theory*, London: Routledge.

Chang, Gordon G. (2001) *The Coming Collapse of China*, London: Century.

Chen, Jian (1993) 'Will China's Development Threaten Asia-Pacific Security?', *Security Dialogue*, June 24 (2): 193–96.

Chen, Jie (1994) 'China's Spratly Policy', *Asian Survey*, October 33 (10): 893–903.

Chen, Qimao (1987) 'The Taiwan Issue and Sino-U.S. Relations', *Asian Survey*, November 27 (11): 1162–75.

—— (1993) 'New Approaches in China's Foreign Policy: The Post-Cold War Era', *Asian Survey*, March 33 (3): 237–51.

—— (1996) 'The Taiwan Strait Crisis: its Crux and Solutions', *Asian Survey*, November 36 (11): 1055–66.

—— (2004) 'The Taiwan Conundrum: Heading Towards a New War?', *Journal of Contemporary China*, November 13 (41): 705–15.

Chen, Rosalie (2003) 'China Perceives America: Perspectives of International Relations Experts', *Journal of Contemporary China*, May 12 (35): 285–97.

Cheng, Chu-yuan (1990) *Behind the Tiananmen Massacre: Social, Political, and Economic Ferment in China*, Boulder, Colorado: Westview Press.

Cheng, Joseph Y.S. (1996) 'China's Japan Policy in the Mid-1990s: Adjusting to the Evolving Multipolar World', *Pacifica Review*, November/December 8 (2): 1–30.

—— (2004) 'The ASEAN-China Free Trade Area: Genesis and Implications', *Australian Journal of International Affairs*, 58 (2): 257–77.

Cheng, Yu-shek and Ngok, K.L. (2004) 'The Potential for Civil Unrest in China', in Annelies Heijmans, Nicola Simmonds and Hans van de Veen, eds, *Searching For Peace in Asia-Pacific: An Overview of Conflict Prevention and Peacebuilding Activities*, Boulder, Colorado: Lynne Reinner, pp. 166–80.

Cheung, Tai Ming (1987) 'The Impact of Research Institutes in the Post-Mao Period on Peking's Foreign Policy-Making', *Issues and Studies*, July 23 (7): 86–101.

Christensen, Thomas J. (1996) 'Chinese Realpolitik', *Foreign Affairs*, September/October 75 (5): 37–52.

—— (1999) 'China, the U.S.-Japan Alliance, and the Security Dilemma in East Asia', *International Security*, Spring 23 (4): 49–80.

—— (2001) 'Posing Problems Without Catching Up: China's Rise and Challenges for U.S. Security Policy', *International Security*, Spring 25 (4).

—— (2002) 'The Contemporary Security Dilemma: Deterring a Taiwan Conflict', *The Washington Quarterly*, Autumn 25 (4): 7–21.

—— (2006). 'Fostering Stability or Creating a Monster? The Rise of China and US Policy Toward East Asia', *International Security*, Summer 31 (1): 81–126.

CIA (2002) *Foreign Missile Developments and the Ballistic Missile Threat Through 2015*, January, http://www.cia.gov/nic/pubs/other_products/Unclassifiedballisticmissile final.htm.

CNN (2002) 'China Cautious on Iraq Action', 14 September, http://edition.cnn.com/2002/WORLD/asiapcf/east/09/14/china.iraq/index.html.

—— (2003a) 'China Adds Voice to Iraq War Doubts', 23 January, http://edition.cnn.com/2003/WORLD/asiapc/east/01/23/sprj.irq.china/index.html.

—— (2003b) 'China Calls for Diplomatic Solution on Iraq', 27 January, http://edition.cnn.com/2003/WORLD/asiapc/east/01/26/china.iraq/index.html.

—— (2003c) 'More Inspections Enjoyed Broad U.N. Support', 14 February, http://edition.cnn.com/2003/WORLD/meast/02/14/sprj.irq.un.world.reax/index.html.

—— (2003d) 'China Says Peace Still Possible', 18 March, http://edition.cnn.com/2003/WORLD/asiapc/east/03/17/china.iraq/index.html.

—— (2003e) 'Japan to Send Troops to Iraq', 9 December, http://edition.cnn.com/2003/WORLD/asiapc/east/12/09/japan,troops/index.html.

Cobden, Richard (1903) *The Political Writings of Richard Cobden*, London: T. Fischer Unwin.

Conable, Jr, Barber B. and Lampton, David M. (1992/93) 'China: the Coming Power', *Foreign Affairs*, Winter 71 (5): 133–49.

Cook, Ian G. and Murray, Geoffrey (2001) *China's Third Revolution: Tensions in the Transition to Post-Communism*, Surrey: Curzon Press.

Copeland, Dale C. (1996) 'Economic Interdependence and War: a Theory of Trade Expectations', *International Security*, Spring 20 (4): 5–41.

—— (2003) 'Economic Interdependence and the Future of U.S.-Chinese Relations', in G. John Ikenberry and Michael Mastanduno, eds, *International Relations Theory and the Asia-Pacific*, New York: Columbia University Press, pp. 323–52.

Council on East Asian Community (2005) *The State of the Concept of East Asian Community and Japan's Strategic Response Thereto* (Tokyo: The Council on East Asian Community), http://www.ceac.jp/e/pdf/policy_report_e.pdf.

Council on Foreign Relations (2007) 'U.S.-China Relations: An Affirmative Agenda, A Responsible Course', Report of an Independent Task Force (New York: Council on Foreign Relations), http://www.cfr.org/content/publications/attachments/ChinaTaskForce.pdf.

Cox, Robert (1999) 'Civil Society at the Turn of the Millennium: Prospects for an Alternative', *Review of International Studies*, 25 (1).

Crotty, Michael J. (1998) *The Foundation of Social Research: Meaning and Perspectives in the Research Process*, London: Sage.

CSIS (1996) *Pacific Forum CSIS PacNet Newsletter*, Centre for Strategic and International Studies, 26 April, p. 17.

Daniel, Donald C.F., Dombrowski, Peter and Payne, Rodger A. (2005) 'The Bush Doctrine Is Dead; Long Live the Bush Doctrine?', *Orbis*, Spring 49 (2): 199–212.

de Burgh, Hugo, ed., (2005) *China and Britain: The Potential Impact of China's Development*, London: The Smith Institute.

Deans, Phil (2000) 'Contending Nationalisms and the Diaoyutai/Senkaku Dispute', *Security Dialogue*, March 31 (1): 119–31.

—— (2001) 'Taiwan in Japan's Foreign Relations: Informal Politics and Virtual Diplomacy', *The Journal of Strategic Studies*, December 24 (4): 151–76.

Deng, Yong (1998) 'The Chinese Conception of National Interests in International Relations', *The China Quarterly*, June 154: 88–109.

—— (2001) 'Hegemon on the Offensive: Chinese Perspectives on U.S. Global Strategy', *Political Science Quarterly*, Fall 116 (3): 343–65.

Deng, Yong and Wang, Fei-Ling, eds, (1999) *In the Eyes of the Dragon: China Views the World*, Lanham: Rowman & Littlefield.

—— eds, (2005) *China Rising: Power and Motivation in Chinese Foreign Policy*, Lanham: Rowman & Littlefield.

Denoon, David B.H. and Frieman, Wendy (1996) 'China's Security Strategy: The View from Beijing, ASEAN, and Washington', *Asian Survey*, April 36 (4): 422–39.

Dent, Christopher M. (2003) 'The Asia-Pacific's New Economic Bilateralism and Regional Political Economy', in Christopher M. Dent, ed., *Asia-Pacific Economic and Security Cooperation: New Regional Agendas*, Basingstoke: Palgrave Macmillan, pp. 72–94.

—— (2006) *New Free Trade Agreements in the Asia Pacific*, Basingstoke: Palgrave Macmillan.

—— (2008) *East Asian Regionalism*, London: Routledge.

Denzin, Norman K. (1989) *Sociological Methods*, New York: McGraw-Hill.

Der Derian, James (1987) *On Diplomacy: A Genealogy of Western Estrangement*, Oxford: Blackwell.

Der Derian, James and Shapiro, Michael J., eds, (1989) *International/Intertexual Relations: Postmodern Readings of World Politics*, Massachusetts: Lexington Books.

Derrida, Jacques (2001) *Writing and Difference*, London: Routledge.

Digital Chosunilbo (2002) 'China and ASEAN Agree to Create World's Biggest FTA' (English Edition), 5 November.

Dittmer, Lowell (1992) *Sino-Soviet Normalization and Its International Implications, 1945–1990*, Seattle: University of Washington Press.

—— (1994) 'China and Russia: New Beginnings', in Samuel S. Kim, ed., *China and the World: Chinese Foreign Relations in the Post-Cold War Era*, Boulder, Colorado: Westview Press, pp. 94–112.

—— (2004) 'Ghost of the Strategic Triangle: The Sino-Russian Partnership', in Suisheng Zhao, ed., *Chinese Foreign Policy: Pragmatism and Strategic Behaviour*, New York: M.E. Sharpe, pp. 207–23.

Dittmer, Lowell and Kim, Samuel S. (1993) 'In Search of a Theory of National Identity', in Lowell Dittmer and Samuel S. Kim, eds, *China's Quest for National Identity*, Ithaca, NY: Cornell University Press, pp. 1–31.

Downs, Erica Strecker and Saunders, Phillip C. (1998/99) 'Legitimacy and the Limit of Nationalism: China and the Diaoyu Islands', *International Security*, Winter 23 (3): 114–46.

Doyle, Michael (1983) 'Kant, Liberal Legacies, and Foreign Affairs, Part I', *Philosophy and Public Affairs*, Summer 12 (3): 205–35.

—— (1986) 'Liberalism and World Politics', *American Political Science Review*, December 80 (4): 1151–69.

Drifte, Reinhard (2003) *Japan's Security Relations with China Since 1989: From Balancing to Bandwagoning?*, London: RoutledgeCurzon.

—— (2006) 'The Ending of Japan's ODA Loan Programme to China – All's Well That Ends Well?', *Asia-Pacific Review*, 13 (1): 94–117.

—— (2008) *Japanese-Chinese Territorial Disputes in the East China Sea – Between Military Confrontation and Economic Cooperation*, Asia Research Centre Working Paper 24, London: London School of Economics and Political Science.

Durkheim, Emile (1997) *The Division of Labor in Society*, reprinted edition, New York: The Free Press.

Economy, Elizabeth (2001) 'The Impact of International Regimes on Chinese Foreign Policy-making: Broadening Perspectives and Policies ... but Only to a Point', in David M. Lampton, ed., *The Making of Chinese Foreign and Security Policy in the Era of Reform*, Stanford: Stanford University Press.

Ellison, Herbert J., ed., (1982) *The Sino-Soviet Conflict: A Global Perspective*, Seattle: University of Washington Press.

Erikson, Erik H. (1994) *Identity and the Life Cycle*, New York: W.W. Norton and Company.

—— (1998) *The Life Cycle Completed*, extended version with new chapters by Joan M. Erikson, New York: W.W. Norton and Company.

Fairbank, John, K., ed., (1968) *The Chinese World Order*, Cambridge: Harvard University.

—— (1969) 'China's Foreign Policy in Historical Perspective', *Foreign Affairs*, April 47 (3): 449–63.

Fan, Maureen (2006) 'Japan's Abe Greeted with Fanfare in China', *The Washington Post*, 9 October.

Farrell, Theo (2002) 'Constructivist Security Studies: Portrait of a Research Program', *International Studies Review*, Spring 4 (1): 49–72.

Feeney, William R. (1994) 'China and the Multilateral Economic Institutions', in Samuel S. Kim, ed., *China and the World: Chinese Foreign Relations in the Post-Cold War Era*, Boulder, Colorado: Westview Press, pp. 226–51.

Ferdinand, Peter (1992) 'Russian and Soviet Shadows over China's Future', *International Affairs*, April 68 (2): 279–92.

—— (2007a) 'Russia and China: Converging Responses to Globalization', *International Affairs*, 83 (4): 655–80.

—— (2007b) 'Sunset, Sunrise: China and Russia Construct a New Relationship', *International Affairs*, 83 (5): 841–67.

Fewsmith, Joseph and Rosen, Stanley (2001) 'The Domestic Context of Chinese Foreign Policy: Does "Public Opinion" Matter?', in David M. Lampton, ed., *The Making of Chinese Foreign and Security Policy in the Era of Reform*, Stanford: Stanford University Press, pp, 151–87.

Findlay, Christopher (1995) 'China and the Regional Economy', in Stuart Harris and Gary Klintworth, eds, *China as a Great Power: Myths, Realities and Challenges in the Asia-Pacific Region*, Melbourne: Longman, pp. 284–305.

Findlay, Christopher and Watson, Andrew (1997) 'Economic Growth and Trade Dependency in China', in David S.G. Goodman and Gerald Segal, eds, *China Rising: Nationalism and Interdependence*, London: Routledge, pp. 107–33.

Fitzgerald, C.P. (1964) *The Chinese View of Their Place in the World*, London: Oxford University Press.

Flick, Uwe (1998) *An Introduction to Qualitative Research*, London: Sage.

FlorCruz, Jaime (2001) 'China's Dilemma in the Fight Against Terrorism', 19 September, http://asia.cnn.com/2001/WORLD/asiapcf/east/09/19/ret.china.dilemma/

Foot, Rosemary (2006) 'Chinese Strategies in a US-hegemonic Global Order: Accommodating and Hedging', *International Affairs*, 82 (1): 77–94.

Foucault, Michel (1972) *Archaeology of Knowledge*, New York: Pantheon Books.

Friedberg, Aaron L. (1993/94) 'Ripe for Rivalry: Prospects for Peace in a Multipolar Asia', *International Security*, Winter 18 (3): 5–33.

—— (2005) 'The Future of U.S.-China Relations: Is Conflict Inevitable?' *International Security*, Fall 30 (2): 7–45.

Friedman, Edward (1997) 'Chinese Nationalism, Taiwan Autonomy and the Prospects of a Larger War', *Journal of Contemporary China*, March 6 (14): 5–32.

Fukuda, Yasuo (2007a) Policy Speech by Prime Minister Yasuo Fukuda to the 168th Session of the Diet, 1 October, http://www.kantei.go.jp/foreign/hukudaspeech/2007/10/01syosin_e.html.

—— (2007b) Press Conference by Prime Minister Yasuo Fukuda Following His Visits to the United States and Singapore, 21 November, http://www.mofa.go.jp/region/asia-paci/eas/press0711.html.

—— (2007c) 'Forging the Future Together', Speech by H.E. Mr. Yasuo Fukuda, Prime Minister of Japan at Peking University, Beijing, People's Republic of China, 28 December, http://www.mofa.go.jp/region/asia-paci/china/speech0712.html.

Fukuyama, Francis (1992) *The End of History and the Last Man*, London: Hamish Hamilton.

Funabashi, Yoichi, Oksenberg, Michel and Weiss, Heinrich (1994) *An Emerging China in a World of Interdependence*, New York: The Trilateral Commission.

Garnaut, Ross (2005) 'The Sustainability and Some Consequences of Chinese Economic Growth', *Australian Journal of International Affairs*, December 59 (4): 509–18.

Garnett, Sherman W., ed., (2000) *Rapprochement or Rivalry? Russia-China Relations in a Changing Asia*, Washington D.C.: Carnegie Endowment for International Peace.

—— (2001) 'Challenges of the Sino-Russian Strategic Partnership', *The Washington Quarterly*, Autumn 24 (4): 41–54.

Garrett, Banning (2003) '"Strategic Straightjacket": The United States and China in the

21st Century', http://www.acus.org/docs/0310-Strategic_Straightjacket_United_States_ China_21st_Century.pdf.

Garrett, Banning and Glaser, Bonnie (1989) 'Chinese Assessments of Global Trends and the Emerging Era in International Relations', *Asian Survey*, April 29 (4): 347–62.

—— (1994) 'Multilateral Security in the Asia-Pacific Region and its Impact on Chinese Interests: Views from Beijing', *Contemporary Southeast Asia*, June 16 (1): 14–34.

—— (1995) 'Looking Across the Yalu: Chinese Assessments of North Korea', *Asian Survey*, June 35 (6): 528–45.

—— (1995/96) 'Chinese Perspectives on Nuclear Arms Control', *International Security*, Winter 20 (3).

—— (1997a) 'Chinese Apprehensions About Revitalization of the U.S.-Japan Alliance', *Asian Survey*, April 37 (4): 383–402.

—— (1997b) 'China's Pragmatic Posture Toward the Korean Peninsula', *The Korean Journal of Defense Analysis*, Winter 9 (2): 63–91.

Garver, John (1980) 'Chinese Foreign Policy in 1970: The Tilt Toward the Soviet Union', *China Quarterly*, June 82: 214–49.

—— (1982) *China's Decision for Rapprochement with the United States*, Boulder: Westview.

—— (1992) 'China's Push Through the South China Sea: the Interaction of Bureaucratic and National Interests', *The China Quarterly*, December 132: 999–1028.

Gecas, Viktor and Schwalbe, Michael L. (1983) 'Beyond the Looking-Glass Self: Social Structure and Efficacy-Based Self-Esteem', *Social Psychology Quarterly*, June 46 (2): 77–88.

George, Alexander and Keohane, Robert (1980) 'The Concept of National Interests: Uses and Limitations', in Alexander George, *Presidential Decisionmaking in Foreign Policy*, Boulder, Colorado: Westview Press, pp. 217–37.

Gertz, Bill (2002) *China Threat: How the People's Republic Targets America*, Washington, DC: Regnery.

Gilboy, George and Heginbotham, Eric (2001) 'China's Coming Transformation', *Foreign Affairs*, July–August 80 (4): 26–39.

Gill, Bates (1999) 'Limited Engagement', *Foreign Affairs*, July/August 78 (4): 66.

—— (2001) 'Two Steps Forward, One Step Back: The Dynamics of Chinese Nonproliferation and Arms Control Policy-Making in an Era of Reform', in David M. Lampton, ed., *The Making of Chinese Foreign and Security Policy in the Era of Reform*, Stanford: Stanford University Press, pp. 257–88.

—— (2007) *Rising Star: China's New Security Diplomacy*, New York: Brookings Institution Press.

Gill, Steven (1995) 'Globalisation, Market Civilisation, and Disciplinary Neoliberalism', *Millennium*, 24 (3): 399–423.

Gilley, Bruce (2004) *China's Democratic Future: How It Will Happen and Where It Will Lead*, New York: Columbia University Press.

Gilpin, Robert (1981) *War and Change in International Politics*, New York: Cambridge University Press.

—— (1987) *The Political Economy of International Relations*, Princeton: Princeton University Press.

Ginsberg, Norton (1968) 'On the Chinese Perception of a World Order', in Tang Tsou, ed., *China in Crisis*, Volume 2, Chicago: University of Chicago Press, pp. 73–92.

Gittings, John (1968) *Survey of the Sino-Soviet Dispute: A Commentary and Extracts from the Recent Polemics, 1963–1967*, London: Oxford University Press.

—— (1974) *The World and China, 1922–1972*, New York: Harper & Row, 1974.

Glaser, Bonnie S. (1993) 'China's Security Perceptions: Interests and Ambitions', *Asian Survey*, March 33 (3): 252–71.

Glaser, Bonnie S. and Medeiros Evan S. (2007) 'The Changing Ecology of Foreign Policy-Making in China: The Ascension and Demise of the Theory of "Peaceful Rise"', *The China Quarterly*, June 190: 291–310.

Glaser, Bonnie S. and Saunders, Phillip C. (2002) 'Chinese Civilian Foreign Policy Research Institutes', *The China Quarterly*, 598–616.

Glaser, Charles L. (1994/95) 'Realists as Optimists: Cooperation as Self-help', *International Security*, Winter 19 (3): 50–90.

—— (1997) 'The Security Dilemma Revisited', *World Politics*, October 50 (1): 171–201.

Goldstein, Avery (1997/98) 'Great Expectations: Interpreting China's Arrival', *International Security*, Winter 23 (3): 36–73.

—— (2005) *Rising to the Challenge: China's Grand Strategy and International Security*, Stanford: Stanford University Press.

Goodman, David S. G. (1994) *Deng Xiaoping and the Chinese Revolution: A Political Biography*, London: Routledge.

Goodman, David S.G. and Segal, Gerald, eds, (1997) *China Rising: Nationalism and Interdependence*, London: Routledge.

Gorshkov, Nikolai (2002) 'Asian Security Bloc Boosted', 7 June, http://news.bbc.co.uk/hi/english/world/asia-pacific/newsid_2031000/2031906.stm.

Gottlieb, Thomas (1977) *Chinese Foreign Policy Factionalism and the Origins of the Strategic Triangle*, Santa Monica: The Rand Corporation, Report R-1902-NA.

Grieco, Joseph M. (1995) 'Anarchy and the Limits of Cooperation: a Realist Critique of the Newest Liberal Institutionalism', in Charles W. Kegley, Jr. ed., *Controversies in International Relations Theory: Realism and the Neoliberal Challenge*, New York: St. Martin's Press, pp. 151–71.

Gries, Peter Hays (2005a) 'Social Psychology and the Identity-Conflict Debate: Is a "China Threat" Inevitable?', *European Journal of International Relations*, 11 (2): 235–65.

—— (2005b) 'China Eyes the Hegemon', *Orbis*, Summer, 401–12.

—— (2005c) 'China's "New Thinking" on Japan', *The China Quarterly*, 831–50.

Griffith, William E. (1964) *The Sino-Soviet Rift*, Cambridge: Mass.: M.I.T. Press.

Guo, Sujian, ed., (2006) *China's 'Peaceful Rise' in the 21st Century: Domestic and International Conditions*, Aldershot: Ashgate.

Gurtov, Mel (2006) *Superpower on Crusade: The Bush Doctrine in US Foreign Policy*, Boulder, Colorado: Lynne Reinner.

Gurtov, Mel and Van Ness, Peter, eds, (2005) *Confronting the Bush Doctrine: Critical Views from the Asia-Pacific*, London: Routledge.

Halpern, Nina (1988) 'Social Scientists as Policy Advisers in Post-Mao China: Explaining the Pattern of Advice', *The Australian Journal of Chinese Affairs*, 19/20: 215–40.

Hamrin, Carol Lee and Zhao, Suisheng, eds., (1995) *Decision-Making in Deng's China: Perspectives from Insiders*, New York: M.E. Sharpe.

Harris, Stuart (1997) 'China's Role in the WTO and APEC', in David S.G. Goodman and Gerald Segal, eds, *China Rising: Nationalism and Interdependence*, London: Routledge, pp. 134–55.

—— (2005) 'China's Regional Policies: How Much Hegemony?', *Australian Journal of International Affairs*, December 59 (4): 481–92.

Harris, Stuart and Klintworth, Gary, eds., (1995) *China as a Great Power: Myths, Realities and Challenges in the Asia-Pacific Region*, Melbourne: Longman.

He, Baogang (1997) *The Democratic Implications of Civil Society in China*, Basingstoke: Macmillan.

Heidegger, Martin (2002) *Identity and Difference*, translated by Joan Stambaugh, Chicago: University of Chicago Press.

Heisbourg, Francois (2003) 'A Work in Progress: The Bush Doctrine and Its Consequences', *The Washington Quarterly*, Spring 26 (2): 75–88.

Henderson, Callum (1999) *China on the Brink*, New York: McGraw-Hill.

Herman, Robert G. (1996) 'Identity, Norms, and National Security: The Soviet Foreign Policy Revolution and the End of the Cold War', in Peter J. Katzenstein, ed., *The Culture of National Security*, Columbia: Columbia University Press, pp. 271–316.

Herz, John H. (1950) 'Idealist Internationalism and the Security Dilemma', *World Politics*, 2 (2): 157–81.

Hinton, Harold C. (1976) *The Sino-Soviet Confrontation: Implications for the Future*, New York: Crane, Russak & Company.

Hoffmann, Stanley, ed., (1960) *Contemporary Theory in International Relations*, Englewood Cliffs, NJ: Prentice-Hall.

Hogg, Michael A., Terry, Deborah J. and White, Katherine M. (1995) 'A Tale of Two Theories: A Critical Comparison of Identity Theory with Social Identity Theory', *Social Psychology Quarterly*, December 58 (4): 255–69.

Holsti, Kal J. (1970) 'National Role Conceptions in the Study of Foreign Policy', *International Studies Quarterly*, September 14: 233–309.

Holz, Carsten A. (2001) 'Economic Reforms and State Sector Bankruptcy in China', *The China Quarterly*, 166: 342–67.

Honneth, Axel (1996) *The Struggle for Recognition*, Cambridge, MA: MIT Press.

Hook, Glenn (1996) *Militarization and Demilitarization in Contemporary Japan*, London: Routledge.

Hook, Glenn D., Gilson, Julie, Hughes, Christopher W. and Dobson, Hugo (2001) *Japan's International Relations: Politics, Economic and Security*, London: Routledge.

Hu, Weixing (1993) 'Beijing's New Thinking on Security Strategy', *Journal of Contemporary China*, Summer 3: 50–65.

—— (1995) 'China's Security Agenda After the Cold War', *The Pacific Review*, 8 (1): 117–35.

—— (1999) 'Nuclear Nonproliferation', in Yong Deng and Fei-Ling Wang, eds., *In the Eyes of the Dragon: China Views the World*, Lanham: Rowman & Littlefield, pp. 119–40.

Huddy, Leonie (2001) 'From Social Identity to Political Identity: A Critical Examination of Social Identity Theory', *Political Psychology*, March 22 (1), pp. 127–56.

Hughes, Christopher R. (1997) *Taiwan and Chinese Nationalism: National Identity and Status in International Society*, London: Routledge.

—— (2005) 'Nationalism and Multilateralism in Chinese Foreign Policy: Implications for Southeast Asia', *The Pacific Review*, March 18 (1): 119–35.

—— (2006) *Chinese Nationalism in the Global Era*, London: Routledge.

Hughes, Christopher W. (2004a) *Japan's Re-emergence as a 'Normal' Military Power*, Oxford: Oxford University Press for IISS.

—— (2004b) 'Japan's Security Policy, the US-Japan Alliance, and the "War on Terror": Incrementalism Confirmed or Radical Leap?', *Australian Journal of International Affairs*, December 58 (4): 427–45.

Hughes, John A. and Sharrock, Wesley W. (1997) *The Philosophy of Social Research*, London: Addison Wesley Longman.

Hunt, Michael H. (1984) 'Chinese Foreign Relations in Historical Perspective', in Harry Harding, ed., *China's Foreign Relations in the 1980s*, New Haven: Yale University Press, pp. 1–42.

—— (1993) 'Chinese National Identity and the Strong State', in Lowell Dittmer and Samuel S. Kim, eds, *China's Quest for National Identity*, Ithaca, NY: Cornell University Press, pp. 62–79.

Huntington, Samuel P. (1991) 'America's Changing Strategic Interests', *Survival*, January/February 33 (1): 12.

—— (1993) 'The Clash of Civilizations?', *Foreign Affairs*, Summer 72 (3): 22–49.

—— (1996a) 'The West: Unique, Not Universal', *Foreign Affairs*, November/December 75 (6): 28–46.

—— (1996b) *The Clash of Civilizations and the Remaking of World Order*, New York: Simon and Schuster.

Huxley, Tim and Willett, Susan (1999) *Arming East Asia*, Adelphi Paper 329, Oxford: Oxford University Press for IISS.

IISS (1992) *The Military Balance 1992–1993*, London: Brassey's for IISS.

—— (1994) *The Military Balance 1994–1995*, London: Brassey's for IISS.

—— (2001/2002) *Strategic Survey*, Oxford: Oxford University Press for IISS.

—— (2002/2003) *Strategic Survey*, Oxford: Oxford University Press for IISS.

—— (2007) *The Military Balance*, London: Routledge.

Ikenberry, G. John (1998/99) 'Institutions, Strategic Restraint, and the Persistence of American Postwar Order', *International Security*, Winter 23 (3): 44–55.

—— (2008) 'The Rise of China and the Future of the West: Can the Liberal System Survive?', *Foreign Affairs*, January/February 87 (1): 23–37.

Issues & Studies (2002) Special Book Review Section, June 38 (2): 235–63.

Jackson, Richard (2005) *Writing the War on Terrorism: Language, Politics and Counter-Terrorism*, Manchester: Manchester University Press.

Jackson, Robert and Sorensen, Georg (2003) *Introduction to International Relations: Theories and Approaches*, Oxford: Oxford University Press.

Japanese Ministry of Foreign Affairs (2005a) *Joint Statement: U.S.-Japan Security Consultative Committee*, http://www.mofa.go.jp/region/n-america/us/security/scc/joint0502.html.

—— (2005b) *Joint Statement on North Korea*, http://www.mofa.go.jp/region/n-america/us/fmv0502/n_korea.html.

—— (2006) *The First Meeting of the Japan-China Joint History Research Committee (Summary)*, http://www.mofa.go.jp/region/asia-paci/china/meet0612.html.

Japanese Defense Agency (2004) *National Defense Program Guidelines for FY 2005 and After*, 10 December, http://www.jda.go.jp/e/index_.htm.

Jepperson, Ronald L., Wendt, Alexander and Katzenstein Peter J. (1996) 'Norms, Identity, and Culture in National Security', in Peter J. Katzenstein, ed., *The Culture of National Security*, Columbia: Columbia University Press, 33–75.

Jervis, Robert (1976) *Perception and Misperception in International Politics*, Princeton: Princeton University Press.

—— (1978) 'Cooperation under the Security Dilemma', *World Politics*, 30: 167–214.

—— (1999) 'Realism, Neoliberalism, and Cooperation: Understanding the Debate', *International Security*, Summer 24 (1): 42–63.

—— (2003) 'Understanding the Bush Doctrine,' *Political Science Quarterly*, Fall 118 (3): 365–88.

—— (2005) 'Why the Bush Doctrine Cannot Be Sustained', *Political Science Quarterly*, Fall 120 (3): 351–77.

Ji, Guoxing (1996) 'Energy Security Cooperation in the Asia Pacific', *The Korean Journal of Defense Analysis*, Winter 8 (2): 269–95.

—— (1998) 'China Versus South China Sea Security', *Security Dialogue*, March 29 (1): 101–12.

Jia, Qingguo (1996) 'Economic Development, Political Stability and International Respect', *Journal of International Affairs*, Winter 49 (2): 572–89.

—— (2001) 'Frustrations and Hopes: Chinese Perceptions of the Engagement Policy Debate in the United States', *Journal of Contemporary China*, 10 May (27): 321–30.

—— (2005) 'Learning to Live With the Hegemon: Evolution of China's Policy Toward the US Since the End of the Cold War', *Journal of Contemporary China*, August 14 (44): 395–407.

Jin, Canrong (2001) 'The US Global Strategy in the Post-Cold War Era and its Implications for China-United States Relations: A Chinese Perspective', *Journal of Contemporary China*, May 10 (27): 309–15.

Johnston, Alastair Iain (1995) *Cultural Realism: Strategic Culture and Grand Strategy in Chinese History*, Princeton: Princeton University Press.

—— (1996) 'Cultural Realism and Strategy in Maoist China', in Peter J. Katzenstein, ed., *The Culture of National Security*, Columbia: Columbia University Press, pp. 216–68.

—— (1999) 'Realism(s) and Chinese Security Policy in the Post-Cold War Period', in Ethan B. Kapstein and Michael Mastanduno, eds., *Unipolar Politics: Realism and State Strategies After the Cold War*, New York: Columbia University Press, pp. 261–318.

268 Bibliography

—— (2003) 'Is China a Status Quo Power?', *International Security*, Spring 27 (4): 5–56.

Johnston, Alastair Iain and Evans, Paul (1999) 'China's Engagement with Multilateral Security Institutions', in Alastair Iain Johnston and Robert S. Ross, eds, *Engaging China: The Management of an Emerging Power*, London: Routledge, pp. 235–72.

Johnston, Alastair Iain and Ross, Robert S., eds, (1999) *Engaging China: The Management of an Emerging Power*, London: Routledge.

Journal of East Asian Affairs (1998) 'Guidelines for Japanese-US Defense Co-operation' (Seoul) Winter/Spring 12 (1): 307–17.

Kahn, Joseph (2006) 'China and Japan Take Steps to Mend Fences', *The New York Times*, 9 October.

Kang, David C. (2003) 'Getting Asia Wrong: The Need for New Analytical Frameworks', *International Security*, Spring 27 (4): 57–85.

—— (2003/04) 'Hierarchy, Balancing and Empirical Puzzles in Asian International Relations', *International Security*, Winter 28 (3): 165–80.

—— (2007) *China Rising: Peace, Power and Order in East Asia*, Columbia: Columbia University Press.

Kaplowitz, Noel (1990) 'National Self-images, Perception of Enemies, and Conflict Strategies: Psychopolitical Dimensions of International Relations', *Political Psychology*, March 11 (1): 39–82.

Kapur, Harish, ed., (1987) *As China Sees the World: Perceptions of Chinese Scholars*, London: Pinter.

Katzenstein, Peter J. (1996) 'Introduction: Alternative Perspectives on National Security', in Peter J. Katzenstein, ed., *The Culture of National Security*, Columbia: Columbia University Press, pp. 1–32.

Katzenstein, Peter J. and Okawara, Nobuo (2001/02) 'Japan, Asian-Pacific Security, and the Case for Analytical Eclecticism', *International Security*, Winter 26 (3): 153–85.

Kaufman, Robert G. (2007) *In Defense of the Bush Doctrine*, Lexington: The University Press of Kentucky.

Kennedy, Paul (1988) *The Rise and Fall of the Great Powers: Economic Change and Military Conflict from 1500 to 2000*, London: Fontana.

Keohane, Robert O. (1984) *After Hegemony: Cooperation and Discord in the World Political Economy*, Princeton: Princeton University Press.

—— (1989) *International Institutions and State Power*, Boulder, Colorado: Westview Press.

—— (1993) 'Institutional Theory and the Realist Challenge After the Cold War', in David A. Baldwin, ed., *Neorealism and Neoliberalism: The Contemporary Debate*, New York: Columbia University Press, pp. 269–300.

Keohane, Robert and Nye, Joseph S. (1977) *Power and Interdependence: World Politics in Transition*, Boston: Little, Brown.

Kerr, David (2005) 'The Sino-Russian Partnership and US Policy Toward North Korea: From Hegemony to Concert in Northeast Asia', *International Studies Quarterly*, September 49 (3): 411–38.

Kim, Samuel S. (1991) *China In And Out of the Changing World Order*, World Order Studies Program Occasional Paper Number 21, Center of International Studies, Princeton: Princeton University.

—— (1994) 'China's International Organizational Behaviour', in Thomas W. Robinson and David Shambaugh, eds, *Chinese Foreign Policy: Theory and Practice*, Oxford: Clarendon Press, pp. 401–34.

—— (2004) 'Northeast Asia in the Local-Regional-Global Nexus: Multiple Challenges and Contending Explanations', in Samuel S. Kim, ed., *International Relations of Northeast Asia*, Lanham: Rowman & Littlefield, pp. 3–61.

Kim, Samuel S. and Dittmer, Lowell (1993) 'Wither China's Quest for National Identity?', in Lowell Dittmer and Samuel S. Kim, eds, *China's Quest for National Identity*, Ithaca, NY: Cornell University Press, pp. 237–90.

Klintworth, Gary and Ball, Des (1995) 'China's Arms Buildup and Regional Security', in Stuart Harris and Gary Klintworth, eds, *China as a Great Power: Myths, Realities and Challenges in the Asia-Pacific Region*, Melbourne: Longman, pp. 258–83.

Klintworth, Gary (1996) 'Greater China and Regional Security', in Gary Klintworth, ed., *Asia-Pacific Security: Less Uncertainty, New Opportunities?*, Melbourne: Longman, pp. 35–49.

Koo, Nicholas and Smith, Michael L.R. (2005) 'Correspondence: China Engages Asia? Caveat Lector', *International Security*, Summer 30 (1): 196–205.

Krasner, Stephen D., ed., (1983) *International Regimes*, Ithaca, NY: Cornell University Press.

—— (1991) 'Global Communication and National Power: Life on the Pareto Frontier', *World Politics*, April 43 (3): 336–66.

—— (1994) 'International Political Economy: Abiding Discord', *Review of International Political Economy*, Spring 1 (1): 13–19.

Krause, Jill and Renwick, Neil, eds, (1996) *Identities in International Relations*, Basingstoke: Palgrave Macmillan.

Krauthammer, Charles (1990/91) 'The Unipolar Moment', *Foreign Affairs*, Winter 70 (1): 23–33.

—— (1995) 'Why We Must Contain China', *Time*, 31 July, p. 72.

—— (2002/03) 'The Unipolar Moment Revisited', *The National Interest*, Winter 70: 5–17.

—— (2004) *Democratic Realism: An American Foreign Policy for a Unipolar World*, Washington, D.C.: The AEI Press.

Kristof, Nicholas D. (1993) 'The Rise of China', *Foreign Affairs*, November/December 72 (5): 59–74.

Kubalkova, Vendulka, ed., (2001) *Foreign Policy in a Constructed World*, New York: M.E. Sharpe.

Kurlantzick, Joshua (2007) *Charm Offensive: How China's Soft Power is Transforming the World*, New Haven: Yale University Press.

Kyodo News (2005) 'Japan, U.S. Set Security Goals, Eye Taiwan, N. Korea', 20 February.

Labs, Eric J. (1997) 'Beyond Victory: Offensive Realism and the Expansion of War Aims', *Security Studies*, Summer 6 (4): 1–49.

Lam, Willy Wo-Lap (2001) 'China Sends Condolences to U.S.', 12 September, http://asia.cnn.com/2001/WORLD/asiapcf/east/09/11/china.us.reax/index.html.

—— (2003a) 'China Calls for End to War', 24 March, http://edition.cnn.com/2003/WORLD/asiapc/east/03/24/sprj.irq china/index.html.

—— (2003b) 'China Readies for Future U.S. Fight', 25 March, http://edition.cnn.com/2003/WORLD/asiapc/east/03/24/willy.column/index.html.

Lampton, David M. (1992/93) 'China: The Coming Power', *Foreign Affairs*, Winter 71 (5): 146–56.

—— ed., (2001a) *The Making of Chinese Foreign and Security Policy in the Era of Reform*, Stanford: Stanford University Press.

—— (2001b) 'China's Foreign and National Security Policy-Making Process: Is It Changing and Does It Matter?', in David M. Lampton, ed., *The Making of Chinese Foreign and Security Policy in the Era of Reform*, Stanford: Stanford University Press, pp. 1–36.

—— (2007) 'The Faces of Chinese Power', *Foreign Affairs*, January/February 86 (1): 115–127.

Lanteigne, Marc (2005) *China and International Institutions: Alternative Paths to Global Power*, London: Routledge.

Lardy, Nicholas R. (1994) *China in the World Economy*, Washington, DC: Institute for International Economics.

—— (2006) 'China: Rebalancing Economic Growth', *China: The Balance Sheet*, Peterson Institute for International Economics/Center for Strategic and International Studies, http://www.chinabalancesheet.org/Documents/01RebalancingEconGrowth.pdf.

Layne, Christopher (1993) 'The Unipolar Illusion: Why New Great Powers Will Rise', *International Security*, Spring 17 (4): 5–51.

—— (2006a) 'The Unipolar Illusion Revisited: The Coming End of the United States' Unipolar Moment', *International Security*, Fall 31 (2): 7–41.

—— (2006b) *The Peace of Illusions: American Grand Strategy from 1940 to the Present*, Ithaca, N.Y: Cornell University Press.

Lee, Pak K. (2005) 'China's Quest for Oil Security: Oil (Wars) in the Pipeline?' *The Pacific Review*, 18 (2): 265–301.

Leifer, Michael (1995) 'Chinese Economic Reform and Security Policy: the South China Sea Connection', *Survival*, Summer 37 (2): 44–59.

Levine, Steven I. (1994) 'Perception and Ideology in Chinese Foreign Policy', in Thomas W. Robinson and David Shambaugh, eds., *Chinese Foreign Policy: Theory and Practice*, Oxford: Oxford University Press, pp. 34–46.

Li, Chenghong (2007) 'Limited Defensive Strategic Partnership: Sino-Russian Rapprochement and the Driving Forces', *Journal of Contemporary China*, August 16 (52): 477–97.

Li, Hongshan and Hong, Zhaohui, eds, (1998) *Image, Perception, and the Making of U.S.-China Relations*, Lanham, MD: University Press of America.

Li, Jingjie (2000) 'Pillars of the Sino-Russian Partnership', *Orbis*, Fall: 527–39.

Li, Rex (1995) 'China and Asia-Pacific Security in the Post-Cold War Era', *Security Dialogue*, September 26 (3): 331–44.

—— (1996) 'The Taiwan Strait Crisis and the Future of China-Taiwan Relations', *Security Dialogue*, December 27 (4): 449–58.

—— (1997) 'China in Transition: Nationalism, Regionalism and Transnationalism', *Contemporary Politics*, December 3 (4): 365–80.

—— (1999a) 'Unipolar Aspirations in a Multipolar Reality: China's Perceptions of US Ambitions and Capabilities in the Post-Cold War World', *Pacifica Review*, June 11 (2): 115–49.

—— (1999b) 'The China Challenge: Theoretical Perspectives and Policy Implications', *Journal of Contemporary China*, November 8 (22): 443–76.

—— (1999c) 'Partners or Rivals? Chinese Perceptions of Japan's Security Strategy in the Asia-Pacific Region', *The Journal of Strategic Studies*, December 22 (4): 1–25.

—— (2000) 'US-China Relations: Accidents Can Happen', *The World Today*, May 56 (5): 17–20.

—— (2002) 'War or Peace? Potential Conflict Across the Taiwan Strait', *World Defence System*, August 2: 157–60.

—— (2003a) 'A Rising Power with Global Aspirations: China', in Mary Buckley and Rick Fawn, eds, *Global Responses to Terrorism: 9/11, Afghanistan and Beyond*, London: Routledge, pp, 210–20.

—— (2003b) 'The North Korean Nuclear Crisis and China's Strategic Calculus', *Chinese Military Update*, London: Royal United Institute for Defence and Security Studies, July 2: 8–10.

—— (2003c) 'Changing China-Taiwan Relations and Asia-Pacific Regionalism: Economic Co-operation and Security Challenge', in Christopher M. Dent, ed., *Asia-Pacific Economic and Security Co-operation: New Regional Agendas*, Basingstoke: Palgrave Macmillan, pp. 185–96.

—— (2004a) 'Security Challenge of an Ascendant China: Great Power Emergence and International Stability', in Suisheng Zhao, ed., *Chinese Foreign Policy: Pragmatism and Strategic Behavior*, New York: M.E. Sharpe, pp. 23–57.

—— (2004b) 'China and Regional Security: External Perceptions and Responses', in Annelies Heijmans, Nicola Simmonds and Hans van de Veen, eds, *Searching For Peace in Asia-Pacific: An Overview of Conflict Prevention and Peacebuilding Activities*, Boulder, Colorado: Lynne Reinner, pp. 181–201.

—— (2006) 'North-East Asia', in Mary Buckley and Robert Singh, eds, *The Bush Doctrine and the War on Terrorism: Global Responses, Global Consequences*, London: Routledge, pp. 75–88.

—— (2008) 'A Regional Partner or a Threatening Other? Chinese Discourse of Japan's Changing Security Role in East Asia', in Christopher M. Dent, ed., *China, Japan and Regional Leadership in East Asia*, Cheltenham: Edward Elgar, pp. 101–28.

Lieber, Keir A. and Alexander, Gerard (2005) 'Waiting for Balancing: Why the World Is Not Pushing Back?', *International Security*, Summer 30 (1): 109–39.

Lieberthal, Kenneth (1977) 'The Foreign Policy Debate in Peking as Seen Through Allegorical Articles, 1973–76', *The China Quarterly*, September 71: 528–54.

—— (1995) 'A New China Strategy', *Foreign Affairs*, November/December 74 (6): 35–49.

—— (2005) 'Preventing a War over Taiwan', *Foreign Affairs*, March/April 84 (2): 53–63.

Little, Richard and Smith, Steve, eds, (1988) *Belief Systems and International Relations*, Oxford: Basil Blackwell.

Lo, Bobo (2004) 'The Long Sunset of Strategic Partnership: Russia's Evolving China Policy', *International Affairs*, March 80 (2): 295–309.

Lukin, Alexander (2002a) 'Russian Perceptions of the China Threat', in Herbert Yee and Ian Storey, eds, *The China Threat: Perceptions, Myths and Reality*, London: RoutledgeCurzon, pp. 86–114.

—— ed., (2002b) *The Bear Watches the Dragon: Russia's Perceptions of China and the Evolution of Russian-Chinese Relations Since the Eighteenth Century*, New York: M.E. Sharpe.

Lu, Ning (1997) *The Dynamics of Foreign-Policy Decisionmaking in China*, Boulder, Colorado: Westview Press.

Mainichi Daily News (2004) http://mdn.mainichi.co.jp/news/20041229p2a00m0fp006000c. html.

Malik, J. Mohan (1993) 'Conflict Patterns and Security Environment in the Asia Pacific Region – the Post-Cold War Era', in Kevin Clements, ed., *Peace and Security in the Asia Pacific Region: Post-Cold War Problems and Prospects*, Tokyo: United Nations University Press, pp. 31–57.

—— (2002) 'Dragon on Terrorism: Assessing China's Tactical Gains and Strategic Losses After 11 September,' *Contemporary Southeast Asia*, August 24 (2): 252–93.

Mancall, Mark (1984) *China at the Center: 300 Years of Foreign Policy*, New York: The Free Press.

Mansfield, Edward D. and Snyder, Jack (1995) 'Democratization and the Danger of War', *International Security*, Summer 20 (1): 5–38.

Marquand, Robert (2005) 'As China Rises, US Taps Japan as Key Asia Ally', *The Christian Science Monitor*, 21 March.

Mastanduno, Michael (1997) 'Preserving the Unipolar Moment: Realist Theories and U.S. Grand Strategy After the Cold War', *International Security*, Spring 21 (4): 49–88.

McGregor, Charles (1993) 'Southeast Asia's New Security Challenges', *The Pacific Review*, 6 (3): 267–76.

Mearsheimer, John J. (1990) 'Back to the Future: Instability in Europe After the Cold War', *International Security*, Summer 15 (1): 5–56.

—— (1994/95) 'The False Promise of International Institutions', *International Security*, Winter 19 (3): 5–49.

—— (2001) *The Tragedy of Great Power Politics*, New York: W.W. Norton.

Mearsheimer, John J. *et al.* (2002) 'War in Iraq is Not in America's National Interest' (Paid advertisement), *The New York Times*, 26 September.

Mearsheimer, John J. and Walt, Stephen M. (2003) 'An Unnecessary War', *Foreign Policy*, January/February 134: 51–60.

Medeiros, Evan S. and Fravel, M. Taylor (2003) 'China's New Diplomacy', *Foreign Affairs*, November/December 82 (6): 22–35.

Menges, Constantine C. (2005) *China: The Gathering Threat*, Nashville, TN: Thomas Nelson.

Mercer, Jonathan (1995) 'Anarchy and Identity', *International Organization*, Spring 49 (2): 229–52.

Minzner, Carl (2007) 'Social Instability in China: Causes, Consequences and Implications', *The China Balance Sheet in 2007 and Beyond (Phase II Papers)*, Peterson Institute for International Economics/Center for Strategic and International Studies, http://www.chinabalancesheet.org/Documents/03SocialInstability.pdf.

Monten, Jonathan (2005) 'The Roots of the Bush Doctrine: Power, Nationalism, and Democracy Promotion in U.S. Strategy', *International Security*, Spring 29 (4): 112–56.

Moore, Thomas G. and Yang, Dixia (2001) 'Empowered and Restrained: Chinese Foreign Policy in the Age of Economic Interdependence', in David M. Lampton, ed., *The Making of Chinese Foreign and Security Policy in the Era of Reform, 1978–2000*, Stanford: Stanford University Press, pp. 191–229.

Morgenthau, Hans J. (1978) *Politics Among Nations: The Struggle for Power and Peace*, revised 5th edn, New York: Alfred A. Knopf.

Morita, Akio and Ishihara, Shintaro (1991) *The Japan That Can Say 'No': The New US-Japan Relations Card*, New York: Simon and Schuster.

Mosher, Steven W. (2000) *Hegemon: China's Plan to Dominate Asia and the World*, New York: Encounter Books.

Murray, Geoffrey and Cook, Ian G. (2002) *Green China: Seeking Ecological Alternatives*, London: RoutledgeCurzon.

Nathan, Andrew (2006) 'Present at the Stagnation: Is China's Development Stalled?', *Foreign Affairs*, July/August 85 (4): 177–82.

Nathan, Andrew J. and Link, Perry, eds, (2002) *The Tiananmen Papers*, London: Abacus.

Nathan, Andrew J. and Ross, Robert S. (1997) *The Great Wall and the Empty Fortress: China's Search for Security*, New York: W.W. Norton.

National Bureau of Asian Research (2008) Strategic Asia Programme, http://strategicasia.nbr.org/Data/Cview/.

Naughton, Barry (2006) *The Chinese Economy: Growth and Transitions*, Cambridge, Mass: MIT Press.

Nelson, Harvey W. (1989) *Power and Insecurity: Beijing, Moscow, and Washington, 1949–1988*, Boulder, Colorado: Lynne Rienner Publishers.

Neumann, Iver B. (1992) 'Identity and Security', *Journal of Peace Research*, May 29 (2), pp. 221–26.

Ng-Quinn, Michael (1983) 'The Analytic Study of Chinese Foreign Policy', *International Studies Quarterly*, June 27: 203–24.

—— (1984) 'International Systemic Constraints on Chinese Foreign Policy', in Samuel S. Kim, ed., *China and the World*, Boulder, Colorado: Westview Press, pp. 82–109.

Nye Jr., Joseph S. (1990) *Bound to Lead: The Changing Nature of American Power*, New York: Basic Books.

—— (2004) *Soft Power: The Means to Success in World Politics*, New York: Public Affairs.

Ohn, Daewon (2000) *The Resurgent Great Power in the World System: China's Grand Strategy and Military Modernisation, 1978–1998*, PhD Thesis, London School of Economics and Political Science, University of London.

Ong, Russell (2002) *China's Security Interests in the Post-Cold War Era*, Surrey: Curzon Press.

—— (2007) *China's Security Interests in the 21st Century*, London: Routledge.

Onishi, Norimitsu (2007) 'China Leader Pledges Amity, But Warns Japan', *The New York Times*, 13 April.

Onuf, Nicholas G. (1989) *World of Our Making: Rules and Rule in Social Theory and International Relations*, Columbia: University of South Carolina Press.

Organski, A.F.K. (1958) *World Politics*, New York: Knopf.

Organski, A.F.K. and Kugler, Jacek (1980) *The War Ledger*, Chicago: University of Chicago Press.

Overholt, William H. (1996) 'China After Deng', *Foreign Affairs*, May/June 75 (3): 63–78.

Pan, Chengxin (2004) 'The "China Threat" in American Self-Imagination: The Discursive Construction of Other as Power Politics', *Alternatives*, 29: 305–31.

Pape, Robert A. (2005) 'Soft Balancing Against the United States', *International Security*, Summer 30 (1): 7–45.

Paul, T.V. (2005) 'Soft Balancing in the Age of U.S. Primacy', *International Security*, Summer 30 (1): 46–71.

Payne, Anthony and Gamble, Andrew (1996) 'Introduction: The Political Economy of Regionalism and World Order', in Andrew Gamble and Anthony Payne, eds, *Regionalism and World Order*, Basingstoke: Macmillan, pp. 1–20.

PBS (2004) 'Richard Armitage's Interview with Charlie Rose on PBS', 20 December, http://www.state.gov/s/d/rm/39973.htm.

Pei, Minxin, 'Is China Democratizing?' (1998), *Foreign Affairs*, January/February 77 (1): 68–82.

People's Daily Online (2006) 'China, Japan Launch First-ever Joint Historical Research', 27 December, http://english.people.com.cn/200612/27/eng20061227_336036.html.

—— (2007) 'Japanese, Chinese Scholars Begin Joint History Study Talks', *People's Daily Online*, 20 March, http://english.people.com.cn/200703/20/eng20070320_359129.html.

Pilling, David (2007) 'Abe Puts Relations with China as Priority', *Financial Times*, 1 January.

Pillsbury, Michael (2000) *China Debates the Future Security Environment*, Washington, DC: National Defense University Press.

Pye, Lucian W. (1971) 'Identity and the Political Culture', in Leonard Binder *et al.*, eds, *Crises and Sequences in Political Development*, Princeton: Princeton University Press, pp. 101–34.

Ra'anan, Uri (1968) 'Peking's Foreign Policy "Debate", 1965–1966', in Tang Tsou, ed., *China in Crisis*, Volume 2, Chicago: University of Chicago Press, pp. 23–72.

Rachman, Gideon (1995) 'Containing China', *The Washington Quarterly*, Winter 19 (1): 129–39.

Rice, Condoleezza (2000) 'Promoting the National Interest', *Foreign Affairs*, January/February 79 (1): 45–62.

—— (2005) Remarks at Sophia University, Tokyo, 19 March, http://www.state.gov/secretary/rm/2005/43655.htm.

Rimmer, Peter J. (1995) 'Integrating China into East Asia: Cross-border Regions and Infrastructure Networks', in Harris and Klintworth, eds, *China as a Great Power*, pp. 306–27.

Robinson, Thomas W. (1994) 'Interdependence in China's Foreign Relations', in Samuel S. Kim, ed., *China and the World: Chinese Foreign Relations in the Post-Cold War Era*, Boulder, Colorado: Westview Press, pp. 187–201.

Robinson, Thomas W. and Shambaugh, David, eds, (1994) *Chinese Foreign Policy: Theory and Practice*, Oxford: Clarendon Press.

Rose, Caroline (1998) *Interpreting History in Sino-Japanese Relations: A Case Study in Political Decision-making*, London: Routledge.

—— (2005) *Sino-Japanese Relations: Facing the Past, Looking to the Future?*, London: Routledge.

Rosecrance, Richard (1986) *The Rise of the Trading State: Commerce and Conquest in the Modern World*, New York: Basic Books.

Rosenau, James (1967) 'Foreign Policy as an Issue Area', in James Rosenau, ed., *Domestic Sources of Foreign Policy*, New York: The Free Press, pp. 11–50.

Ross, Robert S. (1988) *The Indochina Tangle: China's Vietnam Policy, 1975–1979*, New York: Columbia University Press.

—— ed., (1993) *China, the United States, and the Soviet Union: Tripolarity and Policy Making in the Cold War*, New York: M.E. Sharpe.

—— (1997) 'Beijing as Conservative Power', *Foreign Affairs*, March/April 76 (2): 33–45.

—— (1999) 'The Geography of the Peace: East Asia in the Twenty-first Century', *International Security*, Spring 23 (4): 81–118.

Roy, Denny (1993) 'Consequences of China's Economic Growth for Asia-Pacific Security', *Security Dialogue*, June 24 (2): 181–91.

—— (1994) 'Hegemon on the Horizon? China's Threat to East Asian Security', *International Security*, Summer 19 (1): 149–68.

—— (1995) 'Assessing the Asia-Pacific "Power Vacuum"', *Survival*, Autumn 37 (3): 45–60.

—— (1996a) 'The "China Threat" Issue: Major Arguments', *Asian Survey*, August 36 (8): 754–71.

—— (1996b) 'China's Threat Environment', *Security Dialogue*, December 27 (4): 437–48.

—— (2002) 'China and the War on Terrorism', *Orbis*, Summer 46 (3): 511–21.

—— (2003) 'China's Reaction to American Predominance', *Survival*, 45 (3): 57–78.

Rozman, Gilbert (1985) 'China's Soviet Watchers in the 1980s: A New Era in Scholarship', *World Politics*, July 37 (4): 435–74.

—— (1987) *The Chinese Debate About Soviet Socialism, 1978–1985*, Princeton: Princeton University Press.

—— (1999) 'China's Quest for Great Power Identity', *Orbis*, Summer 43 (3): 383–402.

—— (2000) 'Sino-Russian Relations: Mutual Assessments and Predications', in Sherman W. Garnett, ed., *Rapprochement or Rivalry? Russia-China Relations in a Changing Asia*, Washington D.C.: Carnegie Endowment for International Peace, pp. 147–74.

Rummel, R.J. (1995) 'Democracies ARE Less Warlike than Other Regimes', *European Journal of International Relations*, December 1 (4): 457–79.

Russett, Bruce (1993) *Grasping the Democratic Peace: Principles for a Post-Cold War World*, Princeton: Princeton University Press.

Salameh, Mamdouh G. (1995–96) 'China, Oil and the Risk of Regional Conflict', *Survival*, Winter 37 (4): 133–46.

Sanger, David E. (2001) 'U.S. Would Defend Taiwan, Bush Says', *New York Times*, 26 April, p. A1.

Sartre, Jean-Paul (2003) *Being and Nothingness: An Essay on Phenomenological Ontology*, 2nd edition, London: Routledge.

Saunders, Phillip C. (2000) 'China's America Watchers: Changing Attitudes Towards the United States', *The China Quarterly*, March 161: 41–65.

Schwartz, Benjamin (1968a) 'The Chinese Perception of the World Order', in John K. Fairbank, *The Chinese World Order*, Cambridge: Harvard University, pp. 288–97.

—— (1968b) 'China and the West in the "Thought of Mao Tse-tung"', in Tang Tsou, ed., *China in Crisis*, Volume 1, Chicago: University of Chicago Press, pp. 365–79.

Scott, David (2007) *China Stands Up: The PRC and the International System*, London: Routledge.

Segal, Gerald (1982) *The Great Power Triangle*, Basingstoke: Macmillan.

—— (1985) *Sino-Soviet Relations After Mao*, Adelphi Paper 202, London: The International Institute for Strategic Studies.

—— (1994) *China Changes Shape: Regionalism and Foreign Policy*, Adelphi Paper 287, London: Brassey's for IISS.

—— (1995) 'Tying China into the International System', *Survival*, Summer 37 (2): 60–73.

—— (1996) 'East Asia and the "Constrainment of China"', *International Security*, Spring 20 (4): 107–35.

—— (1999) 'Does China Matter?', *Foreign Affairs*, September/October.

Shambaugh, David (1987) 'China's National Security Research Bureaucracy', *The China Quarterly*, June 110: 276–304.

—— (1991) *Beautiful Imperialist: China Perceives America, 1972–1990*, Princeton: Princeton University Press.

—— (1992) 'China's Security Policy in the Post-Cold War Era', *Survival*, Summer 34 (2): 88–106.

—— (1994a) 'The Insecurity of Security: The PLA's Evolving Doctrines and Threat Perceptions Towards 2000', *Journal of Northeast Asian Studies*, Spring.

—— (1994b) 'Growing Strong: China's Challenge to Asian Security', *Survival*, Summer 36 (2): 43–59.

—— (1996) 'Containment or Engagement of China? Calculating Beijing's Responses', *International Security*, Fall 21 (2): 180–209.

—— (1997) 'Chinese Hegemony Over East Asia by 2015?', *The Korean Journal of Defense Analysis*, Summer 9 (1): 7–28.

—— (1999) 'China's Military Views the World', *International Security*, December 24 (3): 52–79.

—— (2002a) *Modernizing China's Military: Progress, Problems and Prospects*, Berkeley: University of California Press.

—— (2002b) 'China's International Relations Think Tanks', *The China Quarterly*, 575–96.

—— (2004/2005) 'China Engages Asia: Reshaping the Regional Order', *International Security*, Winter 29 (3): 64–99.

—— ed., (2005) *Power Shift: China and Asia's New Dynamics*, Berkeley: University of California Press.

Shapiro, Michael J. (1989) 'Textualizing Global Politics', in James Der Derian and Michael J. Shapiro, eds, *International/Intertexual Relations: Postmodern Readings of World Politics*, Massachusetts: Lexington Books, pp. 11–22.

Shi, Guangsheng (2002) Chinese Minister of Foreign Trade and Economic Cooperation, 'Five Positive Changes for China's Opening to Outside World', 14 November, http://english.moftec.gov.cn/article/200211/20021100050256_1xml.

Shi, Tianjian (1999) 'Economic Development and Village Elections in Rural China', *Journal of Contemporary China*, November 8 (22): 425–42.

Shih, Chih-yu (1990) *The Spirit of Chinese Foreign Policy: A Psychocultural View*, Basingstoke: Macmillan.

—— (1993) *China's Just World: The Morality of Chinese Foreign Policy*, Boulder, Colorado: Lynne Reinner.

—— (2005) 'Breeding a Reluctant Dragon: Can China Rise into Partnership and away from Antagonism?', *Review of International Studies*, 31: 755–74.

Shinn, James, ed., (1996) *Weaving the Net: Conditional Engagement with China*, New York: Council on Foreign Relations Press.

Shirk, Susan (2007) *China: Fragile Superpower*, New York: Oxford University Press.

Singer, J. David (1961) 'The Level-of-Analysis Problem in International Relations', in Klaus Knorr and Sydney Verba, eds., *The International System: Theoretical Essays*, Princeton: Princeton University Press, pp. 77–92.

Singh, Robert (2006) 'The Bush Doctrine', in Mary Buckley and Robert Singh, eds, *The Bush Doctrine and the War on Terrorism*, London: Routledge, pp. 12–31.

Smith, Anthony D. (1991) *National Identity*, Harmondsworth, Middlesex: Penguin Books.

Smith, Steve (1997) 'New Approaches to International Theory', in John Baylis and Steve Smith, eds, *The Globalization of World Politics*, Oxford: Oxford University Press, pp. 165–90.

Smith, Steve, Booth, Ken and Zalewski, Marysia, eds, (1996) *International Theory: Positivism and Beyond*, Cambridge: Cambridge University Press.

Snyder, Richard, Bruck, H.W. and Sapin, Burton, eds, (1962) *Foreign Policy Decision-*

making: An Approach to the Study of International Politics, New York: The Free Press.

Sorensen, Georg (1992) 'Kant and Process of Democratization: Consequences for Neorealist Thought', *Journal of Peace Research*, 29 (4): 398–99.

Spence, Jonathan D. (1990) *The Search for Modern China*, London: Hutchinson.

Sprout, Harold and Sprout, Margaret (1956) *Man-Milieu Relationship Hypotheses in the Context of International Politics*, Princeton: Princeton University Centre for International Studies.

Stein, Arthur, A. (1982) 'Coordination and Collaboration Regimes in an Anarchic World', *International Organization*, Spring 36: 294–324.

Stets, Jan. E. and Burke, Peter J. (2000) 'Identity Theory and Social Identity Theory', *Social Psychology Quarterly*, September 63 (3): 224–37.

Stryker, Sheldon (2002) *Symbolic Interactionism: A Social Structural Version*, originally published in 1980 and reprinted with a new forward from the author, New Jersey: Blackburn Press.

Stryker, Sheldon and Serpe, Richard T. (1982) 'Commitment, Identity Salience, and Role Behavior', in W. Ickes and E.S. Knowles, eds, *Personality, Roles, and Social Behavior*, New York: Springer-Verlag, pp. 199–218.

Stryker, Sheldon and Statham, Anne (1985) 'Symbolic Interaction and Role Theory', in Gardner Lindzey and Elliot Aronson, eds, *The Handbook of Social Psychology*, 3rd edition, New York: Random House, pp. 311–78.

Sutter Robert (2005a) 'China's Regional Strategy and Why It May Not Be Good for America', in David Shambaugh, ed., *Power Shift: China and Asia's New Dynamics*, Berkeley: University of California Press, pp. 289–305.

—— (2005b) *China's Rise in Asia: Promises and Perils*, Lanham: Rowman & Littlefield.

Suzuki, Shogo (2007) 'The Importance of "Othering" in China's National Identity: Sino-Japanese Relations as a Stage of Identity Conflicts', *The Pacific Review*, 20 (1): 23–47.

Swaine, Michael and Tellis, Ashley (2000) *Interpreting China's Grand Strategy: Past, Present, and Future*, Santa Monica, CA: RAND.

Swaine, Michael D. (2001) 'Chinese Decision-Making Regarding Taiwan, 1979–2000', in David M. Lampton, ed., *The Making of Chinese Foreign and Security Policy in the Era of Reform*, Stanford: Stanford University Press, pp. 289–336.

Taliaferro, Jeffrey W. (2000/01) 'Security Seeking under Anarchy: Defensive Realism Revisited', *International Security*, Winter 25 (3): 128–61.

Taylor, Robert (1996) *Greater China and Japan: Prospects for an Economic Partnership in East Asia*, London: Routledge.

The Times (2003), 3 May, p. 22.

Timperlake, Edward and Triplett II, William C. (2002) *Red Dragon Rising: Communist China's Military Threat to America*, Washington DC: Regnery.

Tonnesson, Stein (2000) 'China and the South China Sea: a Peace Proposal', *Security Dialogue*, September 31 (3): 307–26.

—— (2004) 'The Imperial Temptation', *Security Dialogue*, September 35 (3): 329–43.

Tow, William T. (1991) 'Post-Cold War Security in East Asia', *The Pacific Review*, 4 (2): 97–108.

—— (1994) 'China and the International Strategic System', in Thomas W. Robinson and David Shambaugh, eds, *Chinese Foreign Policy: Theory and Practice*, Oxford: Oxford University Press, pp. 115–57.

Tsang, Steve, ed., (2004) *Peace and Security Across the Taiwan Strait*, Palgrave: Basingstoke.

—— ed., (2005) *If China Attacks Taiwan: Military Strategy, Politics and Economic*, London: Routledge.

Tsou, Tang and Halperin, Morton (1965) 'Mao Tse-tung's Revolutionary Strategy and Peking's International Behaviour', *American Political Science Review*, March 69 (1): 80–99.

Turner, John C., Hogg, Michael A., Oakes, Penelope J., Reicher, Stephen D. and Wetherell, Margaret S. (1987) *Rediscovering the Social Group: A Self-Catergorization Theory*, Oxford: Blackwell.

US-China Business Council (2008) US-China Trade Statistics and China's World Trade Statistics, http://www.uschina.org/statistics/tradetable.html.

US Department of Defense (1997) The Report of the Quadrennial Defense Review.

—— (2001) Quadrennial Defense Review Report, 30 September.

—— (2005) *Annual Report on the Military Power of the People's Republic of China*, Department of Defense, July, http://www.defenselink.mil/news/Jul2005/d20050719china. pdf.

—— (2006a) Quadrennial Defense Review Report, 6 February, http://www.defenselink. mil/pubs/pdfs/QDR20060203.pdf.

—— (2006b) *Annual Report on the Military Power of the People's Republic of China*, Department of Defense.

—— (2007) *Annual Report on the Military Power of the People's Republic of China*, Department of Defense, http://www.defenselink.mil/pubs/pdfs/070523-China-Military-Power-final.pdf.

US Department of State (1990) *A Strategic Framework for the Asian Pacific Rim: Looking Toward the 21st Century*.

—— (1997) *A National Security Strategy for a New Century*.

—— (2001) US Department of State International Information Programs, 'Transcript: President Bush, China's Jiang Zemin Meet in Shanghai', 19 October, http://www.usinfo. state.gov/regional/ea/uschina/bshjiang.htm.

—— (2002a) US Department of State International Information Programs, 'Transcript: Admiral Blair Discusses Military Cooperation in Southeast Asia', 29 January, http:// www.usinfo.state.gov/regional/ea/easec/blair9.htm.

—— (2002b) *The National Security Strategy of the United States of America*, September, http://www.whitehouse.gov/nsc/nss.pdf.

—— (2004) 'Making America More Secure by Transforming Our Military', 16 August, http://www.whitehouse.gov/news/release/2004/08/20040816-5.html.

—— (2006) *The National Security Strategy of the United States of America*, March, http:// www.whitehouse.gov/nsc/nss/2006/nss2006.pdf.

Valencia, M.J. (2007) 'The East China Dispute: Context, Claims, Issues, and Possible Solutions', *Asian Perspectives*, 31 (1): 127–67.

Van Evera, Stephen (1999) *Causes of War: The Structure of Power and the Roots of War*, Ithaca, NY: Cornell University Press.

Van Ness, Peter (1970) *Revolution and Chinese Foreign Policy: Peking's Support for Wars of National Liberation*, Berkeley: University of California Press.

—— (1993) 'China as a Third World State: Foreign Policy and Official National Identity', in Lowell Dittmer and Samuel S. Kim, eds, *China's Quest for National Identity*, Ithaca, NY: Cornell University Press, pp. 194–214.

—— (2006) 'China's Responses to the Bush Doctrine: Four More Years', in Mark Beeson, ed., *Bush and Asia: America's Evolving Relations with East Asia*, London, Routledge.

Vasquez, John A. (1983) *The Power of Power Politics: A Critique*, New Brunswick: Rutgers University Press.

Verba, Sidney (1971) 'Sequences and Development', in Leonard Binder *et al.*, eds, *Crises and Sequences in Political Development*, Princeton: Princeton University Press, pp. 283–316.

Vogel, Ezra F., ed., (1997) *Living with China: U.S./China Relations in the 21st Century*, New York: W.W. Norton.

Waldron, Arthur (1995) 'Deterring China', *Commentary*, October 100 (4): 18.

Walker, R.B.J. (1993) *Inside/Outside: International Relations as Political Theory*, Cambridge: Cambridge University Press.

Walker, Stephen, ed., (1987) *Role Theory and Foreign Policy Analysis*, Durham: Duke University Press.

Walt, Stephen M. (1987) *The Origins of Alliances*, Ithaca, NY: Cornell University Press.
—— (2002) 'Keeping the World "Off Balance"', in G. John Ikenberry, ed., *America Unrivaled: The Future of the Balance of Power*, Ithaca, NY: Cornell University Press.
—— (2005) *Taming American Power: The Global Response to US Primacy*, New York: Norton.
Waltz, Kenneth N. (1959) *Men, the State, and War: A Theoretical Analysis*, New York: Columbia University Press.
—— (1979) *Theory of International Politics*, Reading, MA: Addison-Wesley.
—— (1993) 'The Emerging Structure of International Politics', *International Security*, Fall 18 (2): 44–79.
—— (2000) 'Structural Realism after the Cold War', *International Security*, Summer 25 (1): 5–41.
Wan, Ming (2006) *Sino-Japanese Relations: Interaction, Logic, and Transformation*, Stanford: Stanford University Press.
Wang, Gungwu (2004) 'The Fourth Rise of China: Cultural Implications', *China: An International Journal*, September 2 (2): 311–22.
Wang, Jianwei (2000) *Limited Adversaries: Post-Cold War Sino-American Mutual Image*, New York: Oxford University Press.
Wang, Jianwei and Lin, Zhimin (1992) 'Chinese Perceptions in the Post-Cold War Era: Three Images of the United States', *Asian Survey*, October 32 (10): 902–17.
Wang, Jisi (1994) 'International Relations Theory and the Study of Chinese Foreign Policy: A Chinese Perspective', in Thomas W. Robinson and David Shambaugh, eds., *Chinese Foreign Policy: Theory and Practice*, Oxford: Clarendon Press, pp. 481–505.
—— (1997) 'The Role of the United States as a Global and Pacific Power: a View from China', *The Pacific Review*, 10 (1): 1–18.
—— (2004) *China's Changing Role in Asia*, The Atlantic Council of the United States, Asia Programs Occasional Paper, http://www.acus.org/docs/0401-China_Changing_Role_Asia.pdf.
—— (2005) 'China's Search for Stability with America', *Foreign Affairs*, September/October 84 (5). Electronic version is available from http://www.foreignaffairs.org.
Weart, Spencer (1994) 'Peace Among Democratic and Oligarchic Republics', *Journal of Peace Research*, 32 (3): 299–316.
Weigert, Andrew, Teitge, J. Smith and Teitge, Dennis W. (1986) *Society and Identity: Toward a Sociological Psychology*, Cambridge: Cambridge University Press.
Wendt, Alexander (1992) 'Anarchy is What States make of It: The Social Construction of Power Politics', *International Organization*, Spring 46 (2): 391–425.
—— (1995) 'Constructing International Politics', *International Security*, Summer 20 (1): 71–81.
—— (1999) *Social Theory of International Politics*, Cambridge: Cambridge University Press.
White, Gordon, Howell, Jude and Shang, Xiaoyuan (1996) *In Search of Civil Society: Market Reform and Social Change in Contemporary China*, Oxford: Clarendon Press.
Whiting, Allen (1960) *China Crosses the Yalu: The Decision to Enter the Korean War*, New York: Macmillan.
—— (1989) *China Eyes Japan*, Berkeley: University of California Press.
—— (1995) 'Chinese Nationalism and Foreign Policy after Deng', *The China Quarterly*, June 142: 295–316.
Wilson, Jeanne (2004) *Strategic Partners: Russian-Chinese Relations in the Post-Soviet Era*, New York: M.E. Sharpe.
Wohlforth, William C. (1999) 'The Stability of a Unipolar World', *International Security*, Summer 24 (1): 5–41.
Wu, Anne (2005) 'What China Whispers to North Korea', *The Washington Quarterly*, Spring 28 (2): 35–48.

Wu, Baiyi (2001) 'The Chinese Security Concept and its Historical Evolution', *Journal of Contemporary China*, May 10 (27): 275–83.
Wu, Guoguang, ed. (2007) *China Turns to Multilateralism: Foreign Policy and Regional Security*, London: Routledge.
Wu, Xinbo (1998) 'China: Security Practice of as Modernizing and Ascending Power', in Muthiah Alagappa, ed., *Asian Security Practice: Material and Ideational Influences*, Stanford: Stanford University Press, pp. 115–56.
—— (2000) 'The Security Dimension of Sino-Japanese Relations', *Asian Survey*, February 40 (2).
—— (2001) 'Four Contradictions Constraining China's Policy Behaviour', *Journal of Contemporary China*, May 10 (27): 293–301.
—— (2004) 'The Promise and Limitations of a Sino-U.S. Partnership', *The Washington Quarterly*, Autumn 27 (4): 115–26.
—— (2005) 'The End of the Silver Lining: A Chinese View of the US-Japanese Alliance', *The Washington Quarterly*, Winter 29 (1): 119–30.
Xia, Liping (2001) 'China: A Responsible Great Power', *Journal of Contemporary China*, February 10 (26): 17–25.
Xinhua (2004) *China's National Defense in 2004*, 27 December.
Xu, Xin (1993) *Changing Chinese Security Perceptions*, North Pacific Co-operative Security Dialogue, Working Paper Number 27, Ontario: York University.
Yahuda, Michael (1972) 'Kremlinology and the Chinese Strategic Debate, 1965–66', *China Quarterly*, January 49: 32–75.
—— (1983) *China's Foreign Policy After Mao: Towards the End of Isolationism*, London: Macmillan.
—— (1997) 'How Much Has China Learned About Interdependence?', in David S.G. Goodman and Gerald Segal, eds., *China Rising: Nationalism and Interdependence*, London: Routledge, pp. 6–26.
Yang, Bojiang (2006) 'Redefining Sino-Japanese Relations After Koizumi', *Washington Quarterly*, Autumn 29 (4): 129–37.
Yang, Jian (2001) *China's Security Strategy Towards Japan: Perceptions, Policies and Prospects*, Centre for Strategic Studies Working Paper 17/01, Wellington: Victoria University of Wellington.
Yang, Jiemian (2001) 'The Quadrilateral Relationship Between China, the United States, Russia and Japan at the Turn of the Century – A View from Beijing', *Pacifica Review*, February 13 (1): 107–15.
—— (2002) 'Sino-US and Cross-Strait Relations under the Post-"11 September" Strategic Settings', *Journal of Contemporary China*, November 11 (33): 657–72.
Yee, Herbert and Storey, Ian, eds, (2002) *The China Threat: Perceptions, Myths and Reality*, London: RoutledgeCurzon.
Yuan, Jing-dong (2005) 'Chinese Perspectives and Responses to the Bush Doctrine', in Mel Gurtov and Peter Van Ness, eds, *Confronting the Bush Doctrine: Critical Views from the Asia-Pacific*, London: Routledge, pp. 108–29.
Yu, Bin (1994) 'The Study of Chinese Foreign Policy: Problems and Prospect', *World Politics*, January 46 (2): 235–61.
—— (1999) *Containment by Stealth: Chinese Views of and Policies Toward America's Alliances with Japan and Korea After the Cold War*, Discussion Paper, Stanford University, September.
—— (2005) 'China and Russia: Normalizing Their Strategic Partnership', in *Power Shift: China and Asia's New Dynamics*, Berkeley: University of California Press, pp. 228–44.
—— (2007) 'China-Russia Relations: Between Cooperation and Competition', *Comparative Connections*, 15 October, http://www.csis.org/media/csis/pubs/0703qchina_russia.pdf.
Zabriskie, Phil (2001) 'Many Voices', *Asia Time*, 4 October, http://www.time.com/time/asia/news/printout/0,9788,176993,00.html.

Zagoria, Donald (1962) *The Sino-Soviet Conflict, 1956–1961*, Princeton: Princeton University Press.

—— (1968) 'The Strategic Debate in Peking', in Tang Tsou, ed., *China in Crisis*, Volume 2, Chicago: University of Chicago Press, pp. 237–68.

—— (1993) 'Clinton's Asia Policy', *Current History*, December 92 (578): 404.

Zakaria, Fareed (2007/2008) 'The Rise of a Fierce Yet Fragile Superpower', *Newsweek*, 31 December–7 January, 1: 20–21.

Zhang, Biwu (2005) 'Chinese Perceptions of American Power, 1991–2004', *Asian Survey*, September/October XLV (5): 667–86.

Zhang, Yunling and Tang, Shiping (2005) 'China's Regional Strategy', in *Power Shift: China and Asia's New Dynamics*, Berkeley: University of California Press, pp. 48–68.

Zhao, Quansheng (1992) 'Domestic Factors of Chinese Foreign Policy: From Vertical to Horizontal Authoritarianism', *The Annals of the American Academy of Political and Social Science*, January 519: 158–75.

—— (2005) 'Impact of Intellectuals and Think Tanks on Chinese Foreign Policy', in Yufan Hao and Lin Su, eds, *China's Foreign Policy Making: Societal Force and Chinese American Policy*, Aldershot: Ashgate, pp. 123–38.

Zhao, Suisheng (1997) 'Chinese Intellectuals' Quest for National Greatness and Nationalistic Writing in the 1990s', *The China Quarterly*, December 152: 725–45.

—— ed., (2004a) *Chinese Foreign Policy: Pragmatism and Strategic Behavior*, New York: M.E. Sharpe.

—— (2004b) 'China's Perception of External Threats to its Security and Stability', in Annelies Heijmans, Nicola Simmonds and Hans van de Veen, eds, *Searching For Peace in Asia-Pacific: An Overview of Conflict Prevention and Peacebuilding Activities*, Boulder, Colorado: Lynne Reinner, pp. 203–19.

—— (2004c) *A Nation-State by Construction: Dynamics of Modern Chinese Nationalism*, Stanford: Stanford University Press.

—— (2005–6) 'China's Pragmatic Nationalism: Is It Manageable?', *The Washington Quarterly*, Winter 29 (1): 131–44.

Zheng, Bijian (2003) 'A New Path for China's Peaceful Rise and the Future of Asia', 3 November, http://history.boaoforum.org/English/E2003nh/dhwj/t20031103_184101. btk.

Zheng, Yongnian (1999) *Discovering Chinese Nationalism in China: Modernization, Identity, and International Relations*, Cambridge: Cambridge University Press.

Zhu, Zhiqun (2006) *US-China Relations in the 21st Century: Power Transition and Peace*, London: Routledge.

Zoellick, Robert (2005) 'Whither China: From Membership to Responsibilities?', Remarks to National Committee on U.S.-China Relations, New York, 21 September, http://www. ncuscr.org/articlesandspeeches/Zoellick.htm.

Name Index

Subject Index